STUDIES IN
IMPERIALISM

general editor John M. MacKenzie

When the 'Studies in Imperialism' series was founded more than twenty-five years ago, emphasis was laid upon the conviction that 'imperialism as a cultural phenomenon had as significant an effect on the dominant as on the subordinate societies'. With more than eighty books published, this remains the prime concern of the series. Cross-disciplinary work has indeed appeared covering the full spectrum of cultural phenomena, as well as examining aspects of gender and sex, frontiers and law, science and the environment, language and literature, migration and patriotic societies, and much else. Moreover, the series has always wished to present comparative work on European and American imperialism, and particularly welcomes the submission of books in these areas. The fascination with imperialism, in all its aspects, shows no sign of abating, and this series will continue to lead the way in encouraging the widest possible range of studies in the field. 'Studies in Imperialism' is fully organic in its development, always seeking to be at the cutting edge, responding to the latest interests of scholars and the needs of this ever-expanding area of scholarship.

Labour and the politics of Empire

D1594482

MANCHESTER
1824

Manchester University Press

Labour and the politics of Empire

BRITAIN AND AUSTRALIA 1900 TO THE PRESENT

Neville Kirk

MANCHESTER
UNIVERSITY PRESS
Manchester and New York
distributed in the United States exclusively by
PALGRAVE MACMILLAN

Published by Manchester University Press
Oxford Road, Manchester M13 9NR, UK
and Room 400, 175 Fifth Avenue, New York, NY 10010, USA
www.manchesteruniversitypress.co.uk

Distributed exclusively in the USA by
Palgrave, 175 Fifth Avenue, New York NY 10010, USA

Distributed exclusively in Canada by
UBC Press, University of British Columbia, 2029 West Mall,
Vancouver, BC, Canada V6T 1Z2

British Library Cataloguing-in-Publication Data
A catalogue record for this book is available from the British Library

Library of Congress Cataloging-in-Publication Data
A catalog record for this book is available from the Library of Congress

ISBN 978 0 7190 8079 1 *hardback*
ISBN 978 0 7190 9131 5 *paperback*

First published by Manchester University Press 2011

First digital paperback edition published 2014

Printed by Lightning Source

I would like to dedicate this book to Kate, Bob and Ella Kirk and the memory of Charlie Brown. They will be glad to know that it is no longer 'almost finished'.

CONTENTS

CONTENTS

LIST OF FIGURES

GENERAL EDITOR'S INTRODUCTION

It is one of the enlivening characteristics of recent historical writing that historians are beginning to abandon the old, and very tired, framework of the individual nation-state. We are increasingly appreciating that history in and of one country is a great deal less illuminating than approaches that adopt a trans-national focus. This book constitutes a significant contribution to this new and exciting trend. Here Neville Kirk convincingly demonstrates that the history of the Labour/Labor parties in Britain and Australia, together with their search for and exercise of governmental power, can be considerably illuminated by being studied in parallel. Their origins were not dissimilar. The ideologies which inspired them and which they proceeded to adapt, sometimes severely, within a global context were closely related. Socialism, in all its variants, was by its nature an international political philosophy which socialist or labourist parties had to embrace in some national shape or form. The objectives of both parties, at least as defined in their political rhetoric, were in each case to create fairer societies in which workers (theoretically) exerted as much influence as the capitalist and other elites which imagined that they had a natural right to govern. Yet both had to adopt pragmatic approaches to specific circumstances, circumstances which embraced a mix of international and local dimensions. These necessitated adaptations which forced (it may be argued) significant elements of divergence as the twentieth century progressed. Moreover, both political systems seemed for some time to be inseparably connected through the imperial and Commonwealth networks of a British world system, one which progressively lost its European epicentre.

Kirk's purpose is also to demonstrate that conventional interpretations, based upon elements of class struggle and essentially domestic and national conditions, can be modified in the light of these comparative perspectives. Labour discourses were just as likely to run along the lines of issues of race, nation, patriotism and empire, as well as those of class, working conditions and standard-of-living issues. In all of these, Labour/Labor politicians were forced to respond to the issues of the day, not least to the manner in which they were framed by the other parties and politicians with whom they contested the search for electoral power within a democratic system. Moreover, there was always an international dimension. Such parties had to respond to issues of war and aggression, as in the First and Second World Wars, and to international ideological clashes, notably that between the supposedly free market and capitalist United States and communist Russia or China – with related local wars – and later to clashes involving militant, radical elements in Islam. Increasingly, as the twentieth century wore on and the possibility of nationalised means of production and related command economies in Anglophone countries progressively retreated, such parties also had to find ways of responding to the pressures and dilemmas of running capitalist economies within international financial systems while still remaining true to some vestiges of their commitment to social justice.

The contexts in which these political, rhetorical and ideological battles were conducted changed over time. The conditions of the period before the First World War were very different from those of the so-called interwar years, and were again transformed in the era after the Second World War. Further change came in the developing circumstances of the later twentieth and early twenty-first centuries. Moreover, the capacity of these parties – at opposite sides of the world – to respond to their problems and opportunities were also very different. Their successes came and went in a political cycle that was seldom in tandem. Yet they did set about learning from each other, particularly in the modern era. Each kept a close watch on the other's fortunes, not least on the manner in which they manipulated their respective electorates. Press 'barons' were held in common, raising the same issues of placating international power centres connected to the marketing of newspapers. It is indeed intriguing that in 2010 the political systems of both countries have produced coalitions, one without the Labour party, the other with.

Kirk has made an admirable start to the analysis of the fortunes of these two parties in settings that demonstrate both similarities and differences. This book is a major contribution to trans-national studies and the examination of Labour politics (or indeed any politics) across the British world. But the author would be the first to acknowledge that this is not the last word. More can yet be written about (for example) the responses of these two parties to developing decolonisation after the Second World War, to changing diplomatic relationships within a global system of nation-states, with the United Nations, with the new Asian 'tiger' economies, with the complexities of multi-cultural societies, with aspects of world-wide religious fundamentalism, and with the ever-changing, and often difficult to comprehend, politics of the United States, of the Middle East, of Africa and Latin America. Some of these are woven in and out of Kirk's assessments in fascinating and illuminating ways, but more can yet be written about all of them. But his book will be a starting point for all such future studies.

John M. MacKenzie

ACKNOWLEDGEMENTS

Generous financial assistance made it possible for me to carry out the research and writing of this book in Britain, Australia and Canada during the past decade. I am extremely grateful to the following funding bodies: the Lever-hulme Trust (Study Abroad Fellowship), the Australian National University (the award of Visiting Fellowships in the Humanities Research Centre, the National Europe Centre, the History Program, Research School of the Social Sciences and the Australian Dictionary of Biography), the University of Sydney (Work and Organisational Studies, Faculty of Economics and Business) and Manchester Metropolitan University (Manchester and European Research Institute). The University of Toronto, the Australian National University and the University of Sydney also kindly provided me with office space, computing and other facilities. Academic and administrative staff in these universities were invariably welcoming and helpful. I am grateful for their support.

I also owe a massive debt of gratitude to the many librarians and archivists who guided me to and through the relevant material in the Labour History Archive and Study Centre, the People's History Museum, Manchester, the John Rylands Library, University of Manchester, the Modern Records Centre, University of Warwick, the National Library of Scotland, the National Library of Australia, the Noel Butlin Archives Centre at the Australian National University and the Mitchell Library, State Library of New South Wales. I am especially grateful to Darren Treadwell of the Labour History Archive and Study Centre, and Pennie Pemberton of the Noel Butlin Archives for their unstinting efforts on my behalf.

My past and present comparative and trans-national research has derived great benefit from the encouragement, support and critical engagement of a truly international group of colleagues and friends. In terms of the research for this particular book, I would like to thank the following: Rick Halpern and his colleagues at the University of Toronto; Paul Pickering and Melanie Nolan, the Australian National University; Chris Lloyd, University of New England; Sean Scalmer and Stuart Macintyre, the University of Melbourne; Greg Patmore and John Shields, the University of Sydney; Chris Wrigley, University of Nottingham; Kevin Morgan, University of Manchester. Kevin, Chris Wrigley, Stuart, Sean, Melanie and Paul very kindly read and offered extremely valuable comments on the text, as did two anonymous readers and one reviewer for Manchester University Press. I would like to thank them deeply for their hard work, constructive criticisms and generosity. I am grateful to Teny Wyke for compiling the index.

ACKNOWLEDGEMENTS

Aspects of the research were presented at seminars and conferences at the University of Toronto, University of Reading, the Newberry Library, Chicago, the People's History Museum, Manchester, University of Melbourne, the Australian National University and the University of Central Lancashire. I am grateful to participants for their valuable comments.

Neville Kirk, New Mills, August 2010

ABBREVIATIONS

ACTU   Australian Council of Trade Unions
ALP   Australian Labor Party
ASIO   Australian Security and Intelligence Organisation
ASU   Anti-Socialist Union
AWNL   Australian Women's National League
AWU   Australian Workers' Union
BLP   British Labour Party
BNP   British National Party
CPA   Communist Party of Australia
CPGB   Communist Party of Great Britain
DLP   Democratic Labor Party
EEC   European Economic Community
GLC   Greater London Council
GST   Goods and Services Tax
ILP   Independent Labour Party
IWW   Industrial Workers of the World
LRC   Labour Representation Committee
NEC   National Executive Committee (of the Labour Party)
NHS   National Health Service
NUM   National Union of Mineworkers
NUX   National Union of Ex-Servicemen
RSSILA   Returned Soldiers' and Sailors' Imperial League of Australia
SDF   Social Democratic Federation
SDP   Social Democratic Party
TNT   Thomas National Transport
TUC   Trades Union Congress
UAP   United Australia Party
UN   United Nations

PART I

Setting the scene

CHAPTER ONE

Subject matter, debates and issues

The main focus of this book rests upon the ways in which questions of empire and commonwealth, nation, race and their interplay with class have influenced the character and fortunes of the Australian Labor Party (ALP) and the British Labour Party (BLP) from their formation at the beginning of the twentieth century to the present day. Primary, but by no means exclusive, focus rests upon Labour's electoral fortunes in the two countries. While there have been many individual studies of these parties within their respective national contexts and some interest in their 'third way' politics,[1] there has not appeared a comparative book-length study of the kind undertaken here.[2] Concern also rests with the neglected trans-national dimension. The latter has manifested itself in important, but variable, personal, institutional and ideological connections, exchanges and mutual influences between the Australian and British labour movements during the chosen period.

The aims of my study are to fill gaps in the literature and, more ambitiously, to make a new and original contribution to the further development of imperial, comparative cross-national and trans-national history. It is based upon extensive secondary- and primary-based research in Britain and Australia over several years. The primary sources consulted have unearthed much undiscovered and neglected material in personal papers, newspapers and journals, the records of political parties and accounts of visits, exchanges and encounters among members, observers and critics of the Australian and British labour movements.[3]

The book offers new explanations and points of emphasis in relation to Labour and other forms of working-class politics. Explanations of these politics in Australia and Britain have traditionally been heavily rooted in domestic 'bread and butter', socio-economic factors, including the much-debated issue of social class. In turn these factors have been located predominantly in the structures, conditions and subjective, nationally based experiences of industrialisation, urbanisation, demography, living standards, working conditions, economic trends, policies and management and workers' relations with employers and other groups. 'Traditionalists' have not neglected other factors, including domestic patterns of working-class culture, sources of commonality, difference and conflict in communities (for example, class versus status) and the nature of local and national political cultures (the nature and extent of democracy, the coercive or liberal nature of the state, the attitudes and actions of ruling classes and so on). However, these 'other factors' have often been seen as largely secondary to, or derived from, the 'hard' underpinnings of domestic material life, while the cross-national comparative and trans-national aspects of workers' politics have been largely absent from traditional accounts.[4]

Since the 1970s and 1980s there have been two main challenges to traditionalism. First, the structures, representations and feelings of gender – of historical constructions of femininity and masculinity – have been fruitfully incorporated into the framework of political analysis. This has sometimes been to the detriment, but at other times to the enrichment, of class analysis. In any event it has acted as a very useful corrective to the traditional common sense that workers were white, male and production based and that labour politics largely had little or nothing to do with women and questions of gender.[5]

Second, there has taken place a very strong academic reaction, especially in Britain, against the predominantly class-based materialism of the traditional orthodoxy in favour of the importance, and in some cases overriding importance, of political factors – the languages and representations of political actors and institutions and the influence of political institutions themselves – in the determination of political outcomes, including Labour politics. This reaction has been underpinned by the notion that socio-economic factors, such as industrialisation and urbanisation, do not necessarily or sufficiently produce or 'give' political outcomes and that these outcomes involve far more than class consciousness. For example, rather than expressing a simple causal link between class and left politics, industrial workers have historically displayed a wide range of political preferences and allegiances. These range, in the cases of Britain and Australia, from Conservatism, to Liberalism, to Labour, to communism and to various forms of 'populism'.

Some historians, especially in Britain, have argued that what mattered most in the construction of these political allegiances and identities were political rather than material or 'social' factors. Others, more so in Australia than in Britain, have adopted a more eclectic and less dualistic approach. While they have welcomed the new or perhaps a renewed emphasis upon the 'political', they have also maintained that the latter, especially in its 'primacy of politics' form, has underplayed and even ignored the 'social' to the detriment of accurate and balanced historical scholarship. This 'other' group often see themselves as further developing E.P. Thompson's practice of *engaging*, rather than separating and isolating, the cultural, political and socio-economic aspects of being and consciousness, the 'cultural' and the 'social', in flexible, non-reductionist ways.[6] This 'Thompsonian' practice of flexible engagement centrally informs the present study.

'Traditional' and 'revisionist' accounts have greatly advanced our knowledge and understanding of labour movements in general and labour politics in particular. This book could not have been conceived and written without them and accordingly engages at appropriate moments with their key concerns. In this context it is important to inform the reader that while my primary concern rests with the ways in which nation, empire and race have engaged with class, I also attempt to pay due attention to their interplay with those aspects of gender and politics relevant to my subject matter. For example, as we will see at various points in this study, gender influenced the key issue of Labour and anti-Labour loyalty to nation and empire.

Whether consciously or not, the neglected factors of empire, nation and race have been widely assumed to have exerted far less influence upon working-class politics than the socio-economic and/or politico-cultural factors outlined above. In the eyes of many historians, workers' undoubtedly important 'bread and butter' concerns with jobs, housing, living standards and social-welfare provision – with 'making ends meet' – have constituted the staple diet of popular politics. The factors of nation, empire, citizenship, patriotism and race have, on balance, appeared to be less immediate and relevant, and, apart from periods of war and crisis, often been seen far more as the preserve of mainly rich and powerful males than of working-class men and women.[7] My study seeks to make a contribution towards redressing the balance. It concludes that, on balance, nation, empire and race exerted far more, albeit variable, influence upon Labour and anti-Labour politics in the two countries in question than so far suggested in the relevant literature.

At the same time, however, it must be recorded that scholarly neglect of these factors has been much more evident in relation to the history of Britain than that of Australia. An important reason for this is to be sought in the different locations, combined with the different, conflicting, similar and shared experiences, of the two countries within the British imperial and commonwealth systems.

Before moving to a consideration of the supporting empirical evidence, it is first of all necessary briefly to highlight three aspects of imperial historiography which shed important light on the question of British neglect and the complex and at times contradictory nature of British and Australian imperial experience.

First, many historians of Britain traditionally assumed that up to the post-World War Two period of decolonisation and increasing black and Asian immigration, the country largely formed its own national, class-based and homogeneous, 'white', 'island' history, rather than having been shaped, albeit to varying degrees over time, by influences imported from the countries and subjects of its worldwide empire.[8] This inward-looking, racialised assumption was, and continues to be, frequently accompanied by the notion that influences passed, mainly in 'top down' fashion, far more from the British imperial 'core' to the 'colonial periphery' than vice versa. These influences, moreover, were perceived, on balance, to be far more 'enlightened' and beneficent than 'coercive' and harmful in character and effect.[9]

Second, there has recently emerged the increasingly influential viewpoint, articulated most strongly by Australian scholars, but also by some British scholars working within the paradigm of 'the British World', that during the first half of the twentieth century most Britons and Australians willingly shared mainly beneficent notions of 'Britishness' and the British Empire. These notions are perceived to have developed far more out of common, similar, mutual and reciprocal experiences than the 'core–periphery' model would suggest. Moreover, in opposition to the radical-nationalist and mainly anti-British school of Australian thought, proponents of the view of 'the British World' strongly maintain that Australian nationalism and empire patriotism were compatible elements. The ALP, for example, expressed its nationalism within a framework of loyalty to the 'enlightened' empire and to a 'pure' form of 'white', British 'race patriotism'. Lastly, it is claimed by Stuart Ward and others that this sense of a shared British identity collapsed in the wake of decolonisation and imperial decline during the third quarter of the twentieth century.[10]

It will be observed that this second school of historiography highlights not only the fundamentally shared, consensual and 'organic' nature of British-ness, but also its wide purchase upon relatively equal 'white' imperial subjects in Britain and Australia. In contrast, the first school emphasises not only the largely 'top down' export of British-ness from the metropolitan heartland, but also, whether explicitly or not, notions of imperial domination and colonial subordination, of superiority and inferiority, of colonial childhood or 'immaturity' developing, at least in the 'white' Australian case, into the 'maturity' of 'adulthood'. On balance, however, both schools, at least with reference to imperial and commonwealth relationships between Britain and

Australia, favour the 'enlightened', as opposed to 'coercive', view of British imperialism.

Third, a bundle of discrete, but related, issues revolve around the extent and depth of imperial and imperialist consciousness among the British population, the nature and influence of support for and criticisms of the Empire at home and abroad and whether cultural studies of the British and other empires have suffered from insufficient attention to politics and materiality.[11]

While I attend to this bundle of issues at relevant points in the book, my immediate concerns are twofold in character. First, with reference to the first school of thought, I maintain that not only radical, but also largely conservative 'top down' and 'core–periphery' modes of thinking influenced, at various points in time, the 'bottom up' perspectives on empire, race and nation of the British labour movement. Second, in terms of 'the British World' paradigm, I suggest that alongside its early and mid twentieth-century support for British-ness, 'white' race patriotism and the enlightened British Empire, the ALP also expressed criticisms of aspects of the imperial tie.

The empirical evidence in support of my first proposition may be summarised in the following way. Despite its historically subordinate position within British society, a capacity to challenge conservative definitions of the nation, to criticise 'coercive' imperialism and a tradition of class-based interest in and support for labour movements and subaltern groups throughout the Empire and beyond, the British labour movement has also been a part of the ruling imperial nation, a very part of the motive force of the British Empire. Members of that movement and the wider working class routinely encountered in their daily lives 'top down' imperial ideas, practices and symbols – in comic books, in the press, in public ceremonies and monuments, in architecture, in the music hall, the cinema and radio and in their personal and domestic memorabilia – which highlighted, above all else, notions of British superiority and Britain's global and imperial 'civilising' 'duties' and 'mission' towards 'colonials', the 'coloured races' and others.

These 'top down' ideas, practices and symbols also expressed the viewpoint that there was mainly a *one-way* flow of influences from the metropolitan 'core' to the colonial 'periphery'. Reciprocal influences from Australia and other parts of the imperial 'periphery', especially the 'coloured' parts, upon Britain were perceived, on balance, to carry far less weight. They often appeared to be remote and indirect, of 'Little Englander' or 'Little Britisher' concern only in so far as they impinged upon 'prevailing domestic issues and concerns'. The latter, in the eyes of the British labour movement, revolved around 'bread and butter' living and working conditions, relations with employers, governments and the state and the condition of their *own* labour movement.[12]

As we will observe throughout this study, British labour movement leaders who focused upon Australian experience between 1900 and the present day often expressed viewpoints reflecting the complex, changing, ambiguous and contradictory nature of their movement's and their own experiences within the British Empire and Commonwealth. On the one hand, there is no doubt that at various points in time some leaders, albeit in all probability a minority over the period as a whole, took a keen interest in, expressed genuine admiration for and even sought to draw domestic inspiration and lessons from the impressive achievements of their Australian labour movement 'comrades and cousins'. On the other hand, many placed their abiding faith in the deeply ingrained elitist and imperialist view that metropolitan labour had far more to teach and far less to learn from its 'colonial' counterparts on the 'periphery'. In some cases labour leaders and their institutions expressed a combination of these views.

Genuine admiration, cooperation, mutuality and reciprocity characterised the following three cases. First, the socialists Margaret and Ramsay MacDonald, Keir Hardie, Tom Mann and Dora Montefiore formed part of what Andrew Scott has termed that 'remarkable procession' of late nineteenth and early twentieth-century British labour movement activists who visited Australia and New Zealand and who were largely united in their praise for these countries as being more 'advanced' than Britain.[13]

This was reflected in the Australian case in, for example, the early achievement, by international standards, of votes for both men and women (the latter were enfranchised at both federal and state level by 1909), and in the remarkable and rapid gains made by the infant ALP and Australian trade unionism. Formed nationally in 1901, the ALP gained federal office in 1910 with 50 per cent of the vote and stayed in power for most of the period up to 1916. This was at a time when the young BLP remained largely in the shadow of the Liberal Party and entertained no prospect of national office in its own right. By 1918 the Australian trade union movement had surpassed the nineteenth-century British pioneer to top the world's league table of union density.

The movement in 'old' Britain needed to understand and take on board relevant lessons from 'new world' Australia, the latter a country in which the labour movement was effectively exerting its 'domination' or 'rule', according to Hardie and many other like-minded British, Irish and European labour movement commentators upon and visitors to Australia. 'Some day', concluded Hardie, something 'similar' would happen in Britain.[14]

Second, on the death of Hardie's 'old friend and colleague' from Ayrshire, Andrew Fisher, in 1928, Arthur Henderson, as secretary, sent a letter of 'deep regret' on behalf of the National Executive Committee of the BLP to Mrs Fisher. In the letter Henderson not only extolled the contribution of Fisher to the Australian movement – having emigrated from Scotland in 1885 the latter had become Prime Minister of the first majority Labor government in Australia's history (1910–13) and Prime Minister again in 1914 and 1915 – but also highlighted the fact that Fisher's successes in Australia 'had their place in assisting the growth and development of our own Party in this country'. Fisher's period as 'Premier' [sic] of the Commonwealth had given British labour, 'a standing throughout the world that it had not previously attained and its influence upon our struggles here at home was altogether beneficial and helpful', according to Henderson.[15]

Third, during the 1980s and 1990s Tony Blair and some of his colleagues visited Australia not only to win the approval and backing of Rupert Murdoch and his *Sun* newspaper for their 'modernising' political 'project', but also to discover the secrets and learn lessons from the unprecedented and continuous federal election victories achieved by the ALP, under 'modernisers' Bob Hawke and Paul Keating, between 1983 and 1996. The aim was to apply these lessons, where appropriate, to British politics in order to overturn the long period of Conservative rule dating from Margaret Thatcher's victory in 1979.[16]

It is also important to note that Blair's thinking and practice were influenced significantly by the Australian Peter Thomson, a community-minded Anglican cleric who was keen to build links between 'social entrepreneurs and the business sector' and end the 'dependency' culture, and the future ALP leaders Kim Beazley and Geoff Gallop (they became the party leader and premier of Western Australia respectively), whom he met as an undergraduate student at Oxford University and with whom he has stayed in contact. Thomson, who died in early 2010, declared that 'What people in Britain don't understand about Tony Blair is that basically he's an Australian.'[17] In turn Blair's 'apparent success' in 'reforming' the BLP and New Labour's victory in 1997 awakened a 'keen interest' among 'a number of Australian Labor Party members' who wished to heed the 'possible lessons for the ALP' in the wake of Paul Keating's federal defeat in 1996 at the hands of the Liberal veteran John Howard.[18]

On the other hand, for much of the period covered in this book British labour leaders continued to see their movement and their country as not only the pioneer but also the 'true' home of imperial and worldwide organised labour, the 'essential' source of the ideas, practices and personnel which had inspired, and continued greatly to influence, the birth and development of labour movements on an international and global scale. To be sure, in opposition to a crude 'core–periphery' model, and as seen above, they realised that there indeed was far more than a one-way flow of ideas and influences at work. But the crucial point to note is that the dominant British labour movement perception was that, for the most part, it was not an *equal* reciprocal process. The balance was seen to rest far more in favour of the outward movement from Britain rather than the inward flow from Australia.

Let me give two brief examples. First, in his capacity as a member of the Empire Parliamentary Delegation to Australia, Arthur Henderson, while genuinely well intentioned in his praise for the achievements of the Australian movement and observing that workers' living standards were higher in Australia than Britain, could still reach the somewhat ambiguous and possibly patronising conclusion in 1927 that 'Australia may yet become the Greater Britain of the Southern Seas'. This could be interpreted as suggesting that, despite their 'promise' and shared British-ness, Australia and Australian labour still had some way to go before reaching the more 'advanced' and 'mature' state of the 'mother country'.[19]

Second, Australian-born Marion Phillips, who won a scholarship to the London School of Economics in her early twenties and who became the British Labour Party's Chief Women's Officer in the post-1918 period, rejected her privileged Australian background (Phillips had been born into an eminent Jewish family in the St Kilda district of Melbourne and graduated from Melbourne University) as 'crude and uncivilized' in comparison with the 'intellectual, artistic and cultural life' of her adopted Britain and Europe.[20] We will see throughout this book that British labour historiography has taken much of its character and direction from this mainly insular and at times elitist metropolitan labour movement tradition.[21]

In contrast, as a 'settler' colony within the British Empire, albeit of an increasingly 'mature' and 'independent kind' within the 'Commonwealth family', Australia's very modern existence and character were fundamentally shaped by an 'outside' force: British imperial 'rule'. This inescapable 'fact of life' took concrete form in what Manning Clark aptly termed the facts and symbols of 'dual loyalty' to their own country and Britain. These were seen in defence ties and naval requirements, the design of the flag, the currency and postage stamps, the presence and continuing power of British-born Governors-General and state governors, the widespread celebration of Empire Day and the massive and continuing popularity of the monarchy. In sum, Australians' position vis-à-vis the 'mother country' and questions of dependence, autonomy and nationhood – of radicalism, nationalism and patriotism towards Britain and the British 'race' – were at the very core of their experience and consciousness.[22]

To be sure, we will observe in the course of this book that, as argued by Ward and other leading proponents of 'the British World' viewpoint, the very strong British imprint upon Australia's and the ALP's consciousness declined, with some qualifications, considerably from the 1960s onwards. Britain henceforth turned more to Europe and Australia looked less to the 'mother country' and the British Commonwealth and increasingly more to the USA for 'protection' and the Asia-Pacific region for trade. In terms of my period as a whole, however, I endorse Michael Davie's view that Britain and her Empire figured much larger in Australia and Australian consciousness than Australia did in Britain and British consciousness.[23]

In terms of the period between 1900 and the late 1930s, this study, as noted above, also endorses the thesis of 'British world' scholars that the Australian movement reconciled its local patriotism with loyalty to British-ness and the Empire. Yet I also wish to highlight the point that this process of reconciliation was by no means devoid of criticism and conflict.

At times criticisms of both these phenomena were sharp. For example, as I have demonstrated elsewhere, the Australian labour movement in this period, along with its British counterpart, consistently condemned those aspects of British-ness and the British Empire associated with class-based and national oppression and exploitation (their records on racial oppression were far more mixed), hereditary 'aristocratic' privilege, coercion and opposition to democracy and equality of opportunity. These aspects constituted the antithesis of the attempt to construct a 'Workers' Paradise' in Australia rooted in democracy, social justice, openness and, despite its gendered and racialised limitations, the egalitarianism of 'mateship'. The mainstream Australian movement also sought greater independence and autonomy for its country within the desired framework of a generally more 'enlightened' and egalitarian empire, while a minority of its constituent parts offered an outright rejection of imperialism in general and British imperialism in particular. Lastly, there were strong criticisms of the 'mixed race' character of the British Empire. Organised workers in Australia saw themselves as being 'more British than the British' in their racial 'purity' and their 'whiteness'.[24]

I will elaborate upon these criticisms at relevant points in the text. At this juncture I wish to make three general observations. First, nations and empires are constructed and reconstructed over time rather than simply 'given' or 'fixed' once and for all time. Second, they may be seen to contain varying elements and combinations of consensus and conflict, voluntarism and coercion, contestation, agreement and accommodation, domination and subordination. Third, I suggest that in their eagerness to distance themselves from the radical-nationalist school of Australian history, complete with its key tenet of hostility and conflict with Britain, advocates of 'the British world paradigm' run the risk of exaggerating the consensual and harmonious aspects of early to mid twentieth-century British-ness and the British Empire and underestimating both the criticisms made by Australian labour and the points of difference and conflict between Australia and Britain.

Although part of the British Empire, the majority of early and mid twentieth-century Australians, as noted above, rejected its 'mixed race' character in favour of 'whiteness'. 'Race' and racial conflict, of course, were already well established features of Australian life, in part as a result of the 'encounters' between the indigenous Aboriginal people and 'white' 'settlers' and the presence and animosity towards Asian and other immigrants during the nineteenth century. The formal seal was placed on the racialised character of the country when the policy of 'White Australia' was adopted as a key plank of Federation and the New Commonwealth in 1901.

Given this context it is not surprising that the issue of race, in addition to those of nation and empire, has strongly informed Australian historiography in general. At the same time, however, all three issues have traditionally exerted far less influence upon the study of labour politics. Notwithstanding recent signs of change, the majority of Australian labour historians have traditionally taken their cue from British 'traditionalists', such as Eric Hobsbawm, in seeking explanations for labour politics first and foremost in 'underlying' socio-economic factors, such as trends in the economy, workplace relations and developments in trade unionism.[25]

Cross-national comparisons

The explanations and emphases presented in this book are set within a cross-national comparative approach to the study of the Labour and other kinds of 'popular' politics in Australia and Britain. As noted above, this approach has been either neglected by or absent from most of the relevant and predominantly nationally focused literature.

I maintain that the strengths of the comparative approach greatly outweigh its weaknesses. Above all, it provides us with a wider and potentially more fruitful way of studying my subject matter than the nationally based approach. Even though traditionalists and revisionists alike have employed general explanatory categories, such as industri-alisation, urbanisation, class and political languages to explain politics, they have mainly applied these to the specific national contexts of the two countries in question. The dominant assumptions, whether made implicitly or explicitly, have been that the nation-state constitutes the natural object of historical investigation and that the particular manifestations of the general phenomena in question – industrialisation, class structure, the languages of class, populism, liberalism and so on – were unique or 'peculiar' to the particular nation-state under review. Resort to the comparative method, whereby we compare two or more case studies and tease out and explain commonalities, similarities and differences between or among them, allows us more accurately to decide whether these assumptions are indeed correct.[26]

In its examination of nationally based comparisons and contrasts, the cross-national mode of comparative analysis operates at a high level of generalisation. As such it runs the risk of paying insufficient attention to developments at other levels, such as the local, the regional and the global. A further potential pitfall is the presentation of somewhat superficial generalisations and insufficiently complex, contextualised, new and original arguments. This often results from a sole or undue reliance upon secondary sources and the conclusions derived from them, the failure sufficiently to quarry and question the relevant primary material and rigorously to engage the evidence against existing theo-ries and arguments in an attempt to produce fresh conclusions and hypotheses. It is also important to gain a thorough knowledge and understanding of the individual case studies under review in order to avoid errors of fact and judgement concerning different national and related histories. Lastly, we must be careful to ensure that we are comparing 'like with like' case studies across national boundaries, and that we are sufficiently alive to their differences as well as their similarities of character and context.

For example, we may usefully compare the languages of politics, patterns of voting and electoral outcomes in Britain and Australia, while being at the same time fully aware that Australia had achieved political democracy earlier than Britain and that, unlike the latter, it had a federal system of government, from 1924 onwards compulsory and preferential voting for federal elections and more extensive state intervention, regulation and protection in its general system of political economy.[27]

The nub of my argument is that we should both be alive to the potential methodological and substantive strengths and weaknesses outlined above and engage with the historical evidence at a variety of appropriate geographical, spatial and societal levels. This exercise must be conducted in a 'scientifically' open-minded and critical rather than a closed and predetermined 'ideological' way. If we adhere to these principles, then we can employ the comparative method in new and productive ways. This is a key methodological thread running throughout this study.[28]

Trans-nationalism

My comparative approach is accompanied by an interest in relevant trans-national matters. I concern myself not only with comparative commonalities, similarities and differences, but also what John French has termed the trans-national phenomena of 'super-national processes' and 'extra-national connections', and their effects upon the ALP's and the BLP's attitudes and practices towards questions of nation, empire, race and class.[29] While imperialism, capitalism, urbanisation and industrialisation are examples of these 'super-national' processes, 'extra-national connections' link people, ideas, cultures, institutions, goods, services and so on, and their movements, encounters, exchanges and mutual influences, across national boundaries.[30]

There were considerable migratory flows between Britain and Australia and important labour movement visits, encounters, exchanges, influences and connections between the two countries during the period under review (Figures 1 and 2). Brief attention has already been drawn above to these processes and connections, and they will be considered in more detail at relevant points throughout this study. For the moment reference to the important biographical case study of Andrew Fisher and his relations with British labour leaders serves to underline the full importance of trans-national connections.

Fisher was born in the coalmining village of Crosshouse, near Kilmarnock, in Ayrshire in 1862. Upon the retirement of his coalminer father on grounds of ill health, Andrew ended his formal schooling and began work in the local pit at around the age of ten in order to supplement the family income. In 1879, aged only seventeen but already noted locally for his integrity and leadership qualities, he was elected secretary of the Crosshouse district branch of the Ayrshire Miners' Union. Two years later he was to be found alongside 'the already legendary' Keir Hardie 'in the forefront of a prolonged miners' strike that convulsed the Ayrshire coalfield', according to Fisher's biographer, David Day.[31]

The strike was lost, but it marked the beginning of an enduring but necessarily 'intermittent' association between 'the two rising political reformers'. Both shared commitments not only to the political and industrial struggles of the labour movement, including the fight for

Figure 1 Keir Hardie in the company of fellow British socialists
Tom Mann, H.H. Champion and Ben Tillett, and the Victorian labour
activist J.P. Jones, in Melbourne, 1908

socialism, but also to education and teetotalism. Hardie, of course, went on to become Britain's first Labour MP in 1892, the leader of the socialist Independent Labour Party, founded in 1893, and a key figure in the Labour Party.

Fisher was sacked from his job as a result of his prominence in the strike of 1881 and a further dispute in 1885. 'Blacklisted' locally, he emigrated to Queensland. Working first as a coalminer and subsequently as a gold miner and engine driver, he endured further unemployment and 'blacklisting' for his labour movement activities. Fisher soon gained prominence in the Gympie labour movement as a candidate of the local Labor Party, formed in 1891, and as one of the founders of the *Gympie Truth* in 1896. Liverpool-born Henry Boote became the editor of this newspaper and a close friend of Fisher. Boote subsequently became 'the most outstanding Labour journalist in Australia' as editor of the Brisbane-based *Worker* and the Sydney-based *Australian Worker*.[32]

It was during the period from his election as a federal Labor candidate in 1899 to his death in 1928 that Fisher became most widely

Figure 2 Arthur Henderson and other Labour MPs in the Empire
Parliamentary Association Delegation to Australia, 1926

known and admired nationally and internationally. Instrumental in
the formation of the Commonwealth Labor Party in 1901, he was a
minister in the first federal Labor government formed by John Christian
Watson in 1904. In 1908–9 Fisher served as both treasurer and prime
minister in the second minority Labor government. In 1910 he successfully led Labor to victory as a majority government and, as noted
above, the ALP remained in office for most of the period up to 1916.
In 1915 Fisher retired as prime minister on health grounds and became
the Australian High Commissioner in London until his period of office
ended at the beginning of 1921. He then returned to Australia, but
resisted attempts to restore him as leader of the ALP. Between 1922
and his death Fisher lived in London. However, his deteriorating health
meant that it became impossible for him to fulfil his hope of obtaining
a seat in the House of Commons.[33] Fisher had been 'one of the most
successful Australian politicians' and left an enduring legacy of 'reforms
and national development', according to D.J. Murphy.[34]

Throughout his career Fisher retained strong, if not completely harmonious, links with his comrades in Britain. He was probably closest to Hardie. The latter was a conspicuous companion during Fisher's trips to Britain in 1902 and 1911. During the latter Fisher not only attended the royal coronation and the Imperial Conference, but paid two trips to Ayrshire, where he was feted by the Miners' Union at a banquet in Kilmarnock presided over by Hardie and at a celebration organised by the villagers of Crosshouse.

At the banquet Hardie spoke warmly of Fisher's continuing comradeship and his achievements in Australia. Fisher and the Australian movement represented the 'future', the 'rule of the common people'. Yet at the same time he took issue with the Fisher government's moves 'to establish naval and military forces and to introduce conscription', albeit 'for home defence, and not for the exploitation of other peoples'. In response Fisher offered a vigorous defence of his policies. He saw them as being a vital response to Australia's exposed position in the Asia-Pacific region and the possibility of invasion, especially from 'non-white' 'inferior' and 'degraded' Asiatic and South Sea islander peoples.[35]

Before leaving Britain in 1911 Fisher accompanied Hardie on a visit to the coalfields of South Wales and Hardie's constituency of Merthyr Tydfil. At Tonypandy, the scene of bitter industrial conflict and the death of a miner in the previous year, 'thousands of miners gathered to hear Fisher give them encouragement in their fight'. In such ways did labour solidarity and racism appear as perfectly 'natural' bedfellows to Fisher and Australian labour.[36]

Four years earlier, on his 'world tour', Hardie had visited Fisher in Australia and signed a fundraising postcard expressing 'Fraternal Greetings from the workers in the Old Home Land to their comrades in the new'. The aim of both groups was the same: 'The Economic Emancipation of earth's toiling millions' (Figure 3). While in Australia Hardie also received beautifully illustrated 'Addresses of Welcome' from the Sydney Labor Council and the Political Labor League of New South Wales (see cover illustration) and from the Women's Political Labor League of New South Wales in December 1907. The former declared that 'Your Australian Comrades and friends share your conviction of the solidarity of Labor throughout the world', while the latter thanked Hardie for his 'earnest and consistent advocacy of Womanhood Suffrage'.[37]

In February 1930 Ramsay MacDonald unveiled a stone memorial above Fisher's grave at Hampstead cemetery. As Day observes, 'Nearly overcome with emotion, and describing Fisher as "my old friend"', MacDonald declared him to have been '"a great servant of the British

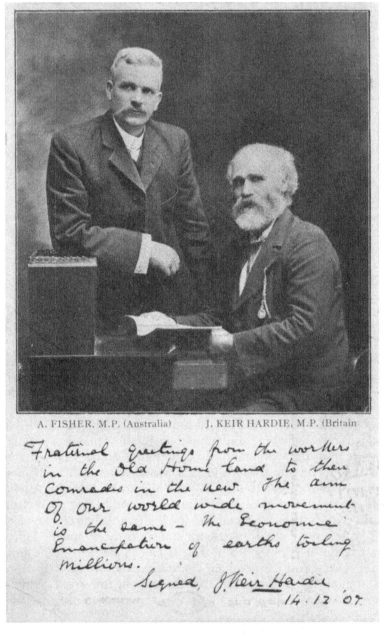

A. FISHER, M.P. (Australia)   J. KEIR HARDIE, M.P. (Britain

Fraternal greetings from the workers in the Old Home land to their Comrades in the new. The aim of our world wide movement is the same – the Economic Emancipation of earths toiling millions.

Signed, J Keir Hardie

14 . 12 . '07

Figure 3 Andrew Fisher and Keir Hardie, December 1907

SUBJECT MATTER, DEBATES AND ISSUES

Empire"', and '"more than a Prime Minister"'.[38] It was not only labour solidarity and 'whiteness' that could, and at times did, coexist 'naturally', but also the causes of organised labour, the nation and the British Empire.

The wider comparative context

The case for the comparison of Labour politics must be seen as part of an argument in favour and set within the context of the wider comparative study of labour, society and politics in Australia and Britain. The latter is also mainly a new subject area for historians.[39]

The case for a wider comparative picture is based to a great extent upon the deep and enduring connections between the two countries.[40] From the point of view of political economy these have revolved around British 'settlement' in 1788, the traditionally very close economic ties and the shifting interplay of continuity and change, conflict and consensus between the two countries.

For example, notwithstanding the growth of a strong spirit of independence and nationalism in Australia in the nineteenth and twentieth centuries, including nationalism of an anti-British republican kind, and the undeniably serious decline of the 'British connection' and British influence, albeit unevenly, from the mid-twentieth century onwards, the British monarch remains to the present day the head of state of Australia. Furthermore, between 1996 and 2007 Prime Minister John Howard and his ruling Liberal-National coalition were strongly committed to the 'western' alliance, with the USA and Britain at its core, and the 'celebration' and staunch defence of 'our Anglo-Celtic past'. Despite its stated commitment to the withdrawal of troops from Iraq, its celebration of diversity and its wish to represent not only Anglo-Celts but 'All Australians', including those born in Australia and those 'who have come from afar', Kevin Rudd's Labor government, which succeeded the Coalition in office as a result of the November 2007 federal election, also reaffirmed Australia's strong attachment to the West, especially the USA.[41]

In terms of demographic connections, the development of the Australian labour movement from the mid nineteenth century onwards owed much to the organisational skills and ideologies of radical migrants from Britain, both 'unfree' and 'free'. As Paul Pickering and others have shown, British trade unionists, Chartists and other radical 'pioneers' exported their 'trade of agitation' to Australia, New Zealand and other 'settler' and colonial societies, while two of the New Commonwealth's early Labor Prime Ministers, Fisher, as noted above, and William Morris, 'Billy', Hughes, were born in Britain.

Yet by the time of World War One the Australian movement had outgrown its 'apprenticeship' to its British 'master'. As noted above, it demonstrated remarkable advancement both politically and industrially. Moreover, it saw itself as a 'new world' beacon to workers and labour movements in the rest of the world, including those suffering from lower living standards and poorer working conditions in 'old world' Britain. Australia now stood at the cutting edge of modernity.[42]

In far less enlightened fashion some British migrants also carried the seeds of 'White Australia' to their new country. This was reflected in their adherence to notions of British and Caucasian superiority and the British Empire's Christian and 'civilising' 'mission'. There were also to be found in their ranks holders of anti-'coloured', anti-Asian, anti-Irish Catholic, anti-Protestant and anti-Jewish prejudices. At the same time it is important to remember that these prejudices were contested by a minority of domestic and emigrant/immigrant British and Australian radicals, Liberals and socialists on humanitarian and class-based grounds.[43]

The 'colonising project' and the differences of workers' 'settler' experiences in Australia, as compared with their former lives in Britain and Ireland, also go a long way towards explaining both the depth and longevity of Australian workers' and their labour movement's 'whiteness', and the much greater obstacles facing the formation and development of an anti-racist movement in Australia. As 'settlers' they now felt themselves to be superior to Aboriginals and other 'coloureds', whereas 'at home' they had often been treated as class-based and sometimes, as in the case of the Irish, racial 'inferiors' by their 'betters'.[44]

Many Australians, moreover, saw their adopted country as a remote, fragile and beleaguered outpost of 'whiteness' and 'western-ness' in the southern hemisphere. The creation of a 'Workers' Paradise' in the antipodes was seen to be threatened by waves of 'low capacity', 'cheap' and 'degraded' Asian immigrants. There was also perceived to be a growing possibility of invasion by an 'aggressively imperialistic' and self-confident Japan, especially after its military victories over China in 1894 and Russia in 1905. The British view that the Japanese were allies rather than potential enemies of the countries within the British Empire, including Australia, was treated with great scepticism in the latter country.

While nineteenth- and early twentieth-century Britain experienced continual immigration and generally maintained its 'open door' policy towards all subjects of its empire, it did not possess an indigenous 'black' population with anything like the long-standing presence (at least in many rural as opposed to large urban areas), history and traditions of the Aborigines in Australia. Furthermore, it did not experience the waves and volume of Asian immigration affecting Australia. And it stood at the head of a vast empire and was relatively free from the threat of invasion. In sum, British Labourites and socialists lived in a far more established, secure and confident 'white' country than their defensive, insecure, fearful and sometimes violent 'settler' counterparts in Australia.[45]

These demographic features pertaining to labour and race must be set within the wider picture of a society dominated by people of Anglo Saxon and Celtic descent. As a result of the formation of the New Commonwealth in 1901 approximately 100,000 Aborigines were excluded from the census and most of the rights of citizenship.[46] At the same time some 98 per cent of the enumerated Australian population of 3,825,000 were emigrants from Britain and Ireland. Following the introduction of the 1901 'White Australia' policy, which made provision for intending immigrants to pass a Dictation Test of fifty words in a language chosen by an immigration official (usually a European language), that population became progressively 'whiter' between 1901 and 1940. In 1933, 97 per cent of Australia's population was 'still of British stock'. Between 1945 and 1950 a further influx of some 250,000 British and European immigrants took place. This was designed to preserve a largely 'British Australia' committed to 'Christian ideals' and the 'traditions of its inherited culture'.[47]

The fact that Irish Catholics constituted a much greater presence within, and exerted a much stronger influence upon Australia, the ALP and Australian trade unionism than upon Britain, the BLP and British trade unionism, is of considerable importance to this study. In contrast to the ALP, the rise and development of the BLP nationally owed far more to the influence of Protestant nonconformity than Catholicism.

In Australia the religious factor – including not only Catholicism, but also Protestantism, religious sectarianism and conflict – manifested itself with particular force and with devastating effects at key points in the ALP's history. For example, as we will see in Part II, while by no means uniformly anti-British and anti-empire, Irish Catholics were prominent among the ALP's nationalist 'critics of empire', including conscription for overseas military service, during the early part of the twentieth century. In contrast Irish Protestant Australians were frequently staunch defenders of conscription and Australia's overriding loyalties to the throne and the imperial connection. As such, the Irish were key players in the 'politics of loyalism' which, as we will observe in Part III, did so much to benefit the Right and harm the ALP between the period of World War One and the 1930s. We will also observe, in Part IV, that during the Cold War years Irish Catholic opposition to communism and its 'fellow travellers' was a crucial factor in bringing about the ALP's disastrous Split in 1955. This split helped to keep the ALP out of federal office until 1973 and contributed significantly to the 'long' mid-century political hegemony of the conservative Robert Menzies. In contrast, while Catholic influence, sectarian conflict and Catholic anti-socialism and anti-communism were by no means absent in Britain, as seen for example in the history of the west of Scotland and Liverpool, they did not generally operate with the same force and debilitating influence, especially at the national level.[48]

Up to the mid 1960s only a 'trickle' of Asians and other non-Europeans were allowed into Australia under the 'distinguished and highly qualified' category. However, the increasing failure of Britain and north-west Europe to meet Australia's immigration needs, Britain's turn towards Europe during the 1960s, domestic and external opposition and embarrassment in the face of the continuation of 'White Australia' and Australia's closer trading, defence and diplomatic links with Asia and the USA, led to the marked liberalisation of immigration policy from the mid 1960s onwards. 'White Australia' was formally ended by Gough Whitlam's Labor government of 1972–75.

Since the 1970s Australia has opened up its formerly sheltered and protected society and economy to Asian and wider global forces. At least one quarter and generally one third or more of annual settler arrivals have been from Asia since 1980. Yet, as Gavin Jones observes, the ending of 'White Australia' 'came too late for a fully multicultural society to develop'. The 'British majority, and more generally the European-descended population' still constitute 'above 60 per cent of the total population' in the early years of the new millennium. In these circumstances it is not surprising that ties among family and friends 'back home' in Britain and 'down under' in Australia remain extremely strong.[49]

Long-standing ties are also evident in the areas of leisure and tourism. For example, many Australians and English people share a traditional love of cricket. This also often arouses intense national passion and rivalry. The 1932 'bodyline' tour demonstrated to many Australians that the Poms 'did not always play fair'.[50] More recently the 2005 Ashes series in England, in which the English team was victorious, was accompanied by an unprecedented level of domestic interest and enthusiasm, often among people who are not regular cricket followers. This did much to develop English national pride in the midst of the increasingly unpopular war in Iraq.[51] It has also become the recent custom for Australian touring sides to England to visit the sites of fallen 'Diggers', at Gallipoli in Turkey and in northern France, before their arrival in Britain. This ritual has been undertaken in order to boost their pride and humility in being Australian, to remind them of their duty towards their country and, with great irony, to fortify their minds in preparation for the physical battles against the English, the 'traditional enemy'.[52]

Sydney, the most popular tourist city in the world, Melbourne, Brisbane and Perth continue to attract large numbers of Britons, while Byron Bay and other surfing and leisure centres have become fixed points on the popular British student backpacker trail of Australia, New Zealand and the Far East. West London is 'home' to many Australians resident in Britain.

Finally, in addition to the British labour activists referred to above, there has also been considerable interest among advanced Liberals, Fabian collectivists and European radicals and socialists in Australia and New Zealand as 'social laboratories'. This was seen most prominently in the late nineteenth and early twentieth centuries, with reference to Australia not only as a 'Workers' Paradise', but also as a progressive, socially just, harmonious and collectivist alternative to 'old world' competitive capitalism, unbridled individualism and class conflict. The New Commonwealth was committed to advanced social welfare provision in the form of government pensions, maternity allowances and the living wage for male heads of households and their dependent families. It also supported women's suffrage, 'new protection' – in the form of tariff protection for those employers who paid 'fair and reasonable' wages – and compulsory arbitration. In practice the latter amounted to institutionalised collective bargaining between unionised workers and employers.

In Britain, notwithstanding the revival of socialism and the growth of New Liberalism, state intervention in economic and social life was more limited than in Australia and New Zealand, and voluntarism and self-help more pronounced. The key question, at least from the perspectives of 'new' Liberals and Fabians, was whether the 'social experiments' in the antipodes would successfully resolve capitalism's key problem of how to combine strong economic growth with social harmony between the classes.[53]

These deep-seated connections, however, have resulted in few comparative and trans-national historical studies of either the rich and powerful or 'ordinary' people in Australia and Britain.[54] This study contributes to the correction of this neglect.

Notes

1 For recent examples see John Faulkner and Stuart Macintyre (eds), *True Believers: The Story of the Federal Labor Party* (Crows Nest, New South Wales: Allen and Unwin, 2001); Jim Hagan and Ken Turner, *A History of the Labor Party in New South Wales 1891–1991* (Melbourne: Longman Cheshire, 1991); R. Neil Massey, 'A

Century of Labourism, 1891–1993: An Historical Interpretation', *Labour History*, 66 (May 1994), 33–45; Keith Laybourn, *A Century of Labour: A History of the Labour Party 1900–2000* (Stroud: Sutton Publishing, 2000); Pat Thane, Nick Tiratsoo and Duncan Tanner (eds), *Labour's First Century* (Cambridge: Cambridge University Press, 2000); Duncan Tanner, Chris Williams and Deian Hopkins (eds), *The Labour Party in Wales 1900–2000* (Cardiff: Cardiff University Press, 2000); Gary Hassan, *The Scottish Labour Party: History, Institutions and Ideas* (Edinburgh: Edinburgh University Press, 2004); David Coates (ed.), *Paving the Third Way* (London: Merlin Press, 2003); David O'Reilly, *The New Progressive Dilemma: Australia and Tony Blair's Legacy* (Basingstoke: Palgrave Macmillan, 2007); Chris Pierson and Francis G. Castles, 'Australian Antecedents of the Third Way', *Political Studies*, 50:4 (September 2002), 683–702.

2 Stefan Berger and Greg Patmore, 'Comparative Labour History in Britain and Australia', *Labour History*, 88 (May 2005), 9–24. For a recent article which provides a most welcome overview of Labour politics see Leighton James and Ray Markey, 'Class and Labour: The British Labour Party and the Australian Labor Party Compared', *Labour History*, 90 (May 2006), 23–41.

3 Special attention should be drawn to the wealth of newspaper, biographical and autobiographical material, political party records and personal papers available to the student of Labour politics at the Labour History Archive and Study Centre, the People's History Museum, Manchester, the Modern Record Centre, University of Warwick (even though the Centre's primary focus is upon trade unionism and industrial relations), the National Library of Scotland, Edinburgh, the Mitchell Library, State Library of New South Wales, Sydney, the National Library of Australia, Canberra and the Noel Butlin Archives Centre at the Australian National University, Canberra.

4 For a good overview of 'traditionalism' in general and British traditionalism in particular see Mary Hilson, *Political Change and the Rise of Labour in Comparative Perspective: Britain and Sweden 1890–1920* (Lund: Nordic Academic Press, 2006), Introduction, pp. 29–41, Conclusion; Neville Kirk, *Change, Continuity and Class: Labour in British Society 1850–1920* (Manchester: Manchester University Press, 1998), pp. 5–11. For examples of the various emphases of the Australian literature see James and Markey, 'Class and Labour'; Greg Patmore, *Australian Labour History* (Melbourne: Longman Cheshire, 1991); Ray Markey, *The Making of the Labor Party in New South Wales* (Kensington: New South Wales University Press, 1988); Bruce Scates, *A New Australia: Citizenship Radicalism and the First Republic* (Melbourne: Cambridge University Press, 1997); Frank Bongiorno, *The People's Party: Victorian Labor and the Radical Tradition 1875–1914* (Carlton, Melbourne University Press, 1996). For a partial exception to comparative neglect see Don W. Rawson's *Labor in Vain? A Survey of the Australian Labor Party* (Croydon, Victoria: Longmans, 1966), especially pp. 3–13.

5 Lucy Taksa, 'What's in a Name? Labouring Antipodean History in Oceania', in Jan Lucassen (ed.), *Global Labour History: A State of the Art* (Bern: Peter Lang, 2006), pp. 339, 359–61, 365; Eileen Yeo, 'Gender in Labour and Working-Class History', in Lex Heerma van Voss and Marcel van der Linden (eds), *Class and Other Identities: Gender, Religion and Ethnicity in the Writing of European Labour History* (New York: Berghahn Books, 2002), pp. 73–87; Karen Hunt, 'Gender and Labour History in the 1990s', *Mitteilungsblatt des Instituts fur soziale Bewegungen*, 27 (2002), 185–200; special issue of *Labour History Review*, *Working Class Masculinities in Britain 1850 to the Present*, 69:2 (August 2004); Raelene Frances, *The Politics of Work: Gender and Labour in Victoria 1880–1939* (Cambridge: Cambridge University Press, 1993); Patmore, *Australian Labour*, ch. 7.

6 For the turns to politics and language in Britain see Hilson, *Political Change*, Introduction, pp. 41–57, ch. 3; Kirk, *Change, Continuity and Class*, pp. 9–11, 79–83, ch. 8; Steven Fielding and John W. Young (eds), *The Labour Governments 1964–70*, vol. 1, Steven Fielding, *Labour and Cultural Change* (Manchester: Manchester University Press, 2003), pp. 20–7; Lawrence Black, '"What Kind of People are You?":

Labour the People and the "New Political History", in John Callaghan, Steven Fielding and Steve Ludlam (eds), *Interpreting The Labour Party: Approaches to Labour Politics and History* (Manchester: Manchester University Press, 2003). For relevant developments in Australia see Scates, *New Australia*; Bongiorno, *People's Party*; Nick Dyrenfurth, 'Rethinking Labor Tradition: Synthesising Discourse and Experience', *Labour History*, 90 (May 2006), 177–99. For an interesting attempt to reconcile the 'political' and the 'social' see Jon Lawrence, *Speaking for the People: Party, Language and Popular Politics in England 1867–1914* (Cambridge: Cambridge University Press, 1998). For debates concerning Thompson's notion of 'experience' see Geoff Eley and Keith Nield, *The Future of Class in History: What's Left of the Social?* (Ann Arbor: University of Michigan Press, 2007), pp. 34–5, 104–19, 153–6. For a stimulating discussion of the relationship between 'culture' and 'structure' see Frederick Cooper, *Colonialism in Question: Theory, Knowledge, History* (London: University of California Press, 2005), pp. 5, 7, ch. 3.

7 For a sample of the relevant literature, including important attempts to develop the study of gender and empire, see Antoinette Burton, *Burdens of History: British Feminists Indian Women and Imperial Culture 1865–1915* (Chapel Hill: University of North Carolina Press, 1994); Clare Midgley (ed.), *Gender and Imperialism* (Manchester: Manchester University Press, 1998); Julia Bush, *Edwardian Ladies and Imperial Power* (Leicester: Leicester University Press, 2000); John MacKenzie (ed.), *Imperialism and Popular Culture* (Manchester: Manchester University Press, 1986), Introduction; Miles Taylor, 'Patriotism, History and the Left in Twentieth-Century Britain', *Historical Journal*, XXXIII (1990), 971–87; Berger and Patmore, 'Comparative Labour History'; Raphael Samuel, 'Introduction: Exciting to be English', in Raphael Samuel (ed.), *Patriotism: The Making and Unmaking of British National Identity*, vol. 1, *History and Politics* (London: Routledge, 1989).

For full and partial British exceptions to the general labour history rule see Henry Pelling, 'British Labour and British Imperialism', in his *Popular Politics and Society in Late Victorian Britain* (London: Macmillan, 1968), pp. 82–100; Richard Price, *An Imperial War and the British Working Class* (London: Routledge and Kegan Paul, 1972); Partha Sarathi Gupta, *Imperialism and the British Labour Movement 1914–1964* (New Delhi: Sage, 2002); Hugh Cunningham, 'The Language of Patriotism', in Samuel, *Patriotism*; Stephen Howe, *Anticolonialism in British Politics: The Left and the End of Empire 1918–1964* (Oxford: Oxford University Press, 1993); Paul Ward, *Red Flag and Union Jack: Englishness Patriotism and the British Left 1881–1924* (Woodbridge: Boydell Press, 1998); Paul Ward, *Unionism in the United Kingdom 1918–1974* (Basingstoke: Palgrave, 2005); Neville Kirk, *Comrades and Cousins: Globalization Workers and Labour Movements in Britain, the USA and Australia from the 1880s to 1914* (London: Merlin Press, 2003); Paul Corthorn and Jonathan Davis, *The British Labour Party and the Wider World* (London: I. B. Tauris, 2008); Rhiannon Vickers, *The Labour Party and the World*, vol. 1, *The Evolution of Labour's Foreign Policy 1900–51* (Manchester: Manchester University Press, 2003); John Callaghan, *The Labour Party and Foreign Policy: A History* (Abingdon: Routledge, 2007); Billy Frank, Craig Horner and David Stewart (eds), *The British Labour Movement and Imperialism* (Newcastle upon Tyne: Cambridge Scholars Publishing, 2010).

For the more general neglect of the influence of empire upon British and 'British-ness' see Catherine Hall, *Civilising Subjects: Metropole and Colony in the English Imagination 1830–1867* (Cambridge: Polity Press, 2002); Shula Marks, 'History, the Nation and Empire: Sniping at the Periphery', *History Workshop Journal*, 29 (1999), 111–19.

8 As Wendy Webster has observed, 'One symptom of the neglect of questions of race and ethnicity in British history until recently was the separation of the domestic from an imperial context. The idea that racial difference was also about differences of place – a racial separation between empire and metropolis, where non-white people belonged in an empire under British colonial rule – was current in Britain up to the mid-twentieth century and beyond. It was replicated in much of the litera-ture on British history which maintained a separation between the imperial and

the domestic . . . there was practically no work that considered whether, or how far, empire shaped British society'. See Wendy Webster, 'Transnational Journeys and Domestic Histories', *Journal of Social History*, 39:3 (Spring 2006), 653; Richard Price, 'One Big Thing: Britain, Its Empire and Their Imperial Culture', *Journal of British Studies*, 45:3 (July 2006), 602–27; Bernard Porter, 'Further Thoughts on Imperial Absent-Mindedness', *Journal of Imperial and Commonwealth History*, 36:1 (March 2008), 110–11; Antoinette Burton, 'Who Needs the Nation: Interrogating "British" History', in Catherine Hall (ed.), *Cultures of Empire: A Reader* (Manchester: Manchester University Press, 2000).

  9 See, for example, David Cannadine, *Ornamentalism: How the British Saw Their Empire* (London: Penguin, 2001); Niall Ferguson, *Empire: How Britain Made the Modern World* (London: Penguin, 2003). For good critiques of this metropolitan-centred and 'official' approach see Price, 'One Big Thing', and Fredrick Cooper, 'Empire Multiplied: A Review Essay', *Comparative Studies in Society and History*, 46:2 (April 2004), 247–72. For a useful overview of competing approaches to the study of the British Empire see Simon J. Potter, 'The British Empire', *Historian*, 81 (Spring 2004), 32–7.

10 Stuart Ward, *Australia and the British Embrace: The Demise of the Imperial Ideal* (Melbourne: Melbourne University Press, 2001); Neville Meaney, 'Britishness and Australian Identity: The Problem of Nationalism in Australian History and Historiography', *Australian Historical Studies*, 32:116 (April 2001), 76–90; Neville Meaney, 'Britishness and Australia: Some Reflections', *Journal of Imperial and Commonwealth History*, 31:2 (May 2003), 121–35; Alan Sykes, 'Their Island Story', in Carl Bridge (ed.), *New Perspectives in Australian History* (London: Sir Robert Menzies Centre for Australian Studies, Institute of Commonwealth Studies Occasional Seminar Papers, no. 5, 1990); Carl Bridge and Kent Fedorowich (eds), *The British World: Diaspora Culture and Identity*, a special issue of the *Journal of Imperial and Commonwealth History*, XXXI:2 (May 2003); Kirk, *Comrades and Cousins*, pp. 61, 126–9; Frank Bongiorno, 'British to Their Bootheels too; Britishness and Australian Radicalism', the Trevor Rees Memorial Lecture, 2006, Menzies Centre for Australian Studies, King's College, London. I am grateful to Frank Bongiorno for a copy of his lecture.

11 MacKenzie, *Imperialism and Popular Culture*, Introduction; John MacKenzie, *Propaganda and Empire: the Manipulation of British Public Opinion 1880–1960* (Manchester: Manchester University Press, 1984); Bernard Porter, *The Absent-Minded Imperialists: How the British Really Saw Their Empire* (Oxford: Oxford University Press, 2004); Porter, 'Further Thoughts', 102, 106–10; Price, 'One Big Thing'; Wendy Webster, *Englishness and Empire 1939–1965* (Oxford: Oxford University Press, 2005); Stuart Ward, 'Echoes of Empire', *History Workshop Journal*, 62 (2006), 264–78; John Newsinger, *The Blood Never Dried: A People's History of the British Empire* (London: Bookmarks, 2006); Andrew Thompson, *The Empire Strikes Back: The Impact of Imperialism on Britain from the Mid-nineteenth Century* (Harlow: Pearson Education, 2005).

12 See MacKenzie and the other contributors to *Imperialism and Popular Culture*; Stephen Howe, 'Labour Patriotism, 1939–83', in Samuel, *Patriotism*, pp. 127–39; Kirk, *Comrades and Cousins*, p. 149.

13 Andrew Scott, *Running on Empty: 'Modernising' the British and Australian Labour Parties* (Annandale: Pluto Press, 2000), pp. 19–23; Karen Hunt, 'Transnationalism in Practice: The Effect of Dora Montefiore's International Travel on Women's Politics in Britain before World War I', in P. Jonsson, S. Neusinger and J. Sangster (eds), *Crossing Boundaries: Women's Organizing in Europe and the Americas 1880s–1940s* (Uppsala: Uppsala Studies in Economic History, 80, 2007), pp. 73–94.

14 *Manchester Guardian*, 18 April 1910; Kirk, *Comrades and Cousins*, pp. 71–3, 77–8, 101–11; Papers of Andrew Fisher, National Library of Australia (hereafter NLA), MS 2919, Series 1, General Correspondence, correspondence from Ramsay MacDonald on Fisher becoming 'Premier of the Commonwealth', 2919/1/42 and from Keir Hardie asking Fisher and the ALP for support on the issue of women's suffrage, 2919/1/41.

15 Fisher Papers, Series 1, 2919/1/617.
16 O'Reilly, *New Progressive Dilemma*, pp. 13–14, 66–86, 153–61; 'The Rt. Hon. Tony Blair MP, Leader of the British Labour Party Speaking at News Corp Leadership Conference, Hayman Island, Australia, on Monday, 17 July 1995', ms copy of Blair's speech held in the Labour History Archive and Study Centre, People's History Museum, Manchester, UK; Scott, *Running on Empty*, Introduction; John Rentoul, *Tony Blair: Prime Minister* (London: Time Warner, 2003).
17 See Andrew Mawson's obituary of Thomson, who died, aged 73, of emphysema, in the *Guardian*, 26 January 2010.
18 John Pandazopoulos and Steve Booth, Discussion Paper, 'The Blair Project – Labour Win 97', n.d., courtesy of Paul Pickering, the Australian National University.
19 Rt. Hon. Arthur Henderson MP, 'Life and Labour in Australia', *Labour Magazine*, V:10 (February 1927), 435–8; *Worker*, 30 March 1927.
20 Beverley Kingston, 'Phillips Marion (1881–1932)', *Australian Dictionary of Biography*, vol. 11 (Carlton: Melbourne University Press, 1988), pp. 216–17.
21 As two labour historians of Britain have written recently, 'On the whole, the history of twentieth-century labour has remained "our island story"'. Alan Campbell and John McIlroy, 'Britain: The Twentieth Century', in Joan Allen, Alan Campbell and John McIlroy (eds), *Histories of Labour: National and International Perspectives* (Pontypool: Merlin Press, 2010), p. 114.
22 Charles Manning H. Clark, *A History of Australia*, vol. V, *The People Make Laws 1888–1915* (Carlton: Melbourne University Press, 1999), pp. 1–4, 32–3, 177–82, 331; Charles Manning H. Clark, *A History of Australia*, vol. VI, *'The Old Dead Tree and the Young Tree Green' 1916–1935* (Carlton: Melbourne University Press, 1999), pp. 136, 150–2, 171; Russel Ward, 'Two Kinds of Australian Patriotism', *Victorian History Magazine: Journal and Proceedings of the Royal Historical Society of Victoria*, 41:1 (February 1970), 225–43; Meaney, 'Britishness and Australia'; Sykes, 'Island Story'; Bridge and Fedorowich, *British World*; Kosmas Tsokhas, *Making a Nation State: Cultural Identity Economic Nationalism and Sexuality in Australian History* (Carlton: Melbourne University Press, 2001); Kirk, *Comrades and Cousins*, pp. 128–9.
23 Michael Davie, *Anglo-Australian Attitudes* (London: Secker and Warburg, 2000).
24 Kirk, *Comrades and Cousins*, pp. 61, 126–9; Neville Kirk, '"Australians for Australia": The Right, the Labor Party and Contested Loyalties to Nation and Empire in Australia, 1917 to the early 1930s', *Labour History*, 91 (November 2006), 95–111.
25 See the references to Australia in note 4 above. For the importance of nation, race and empire to the Australian labour movement see, for example, Sarah Gregson, 'Footsoldiers for Capital: The Influence of RSL Racism on Interwar Industrial Relations in Kalgoorlie and Broken Hill' (PhD dissertation, University of New South Wales, 2003); Humphrey McQueen, *A New Britannia: An Argument Concerning the Social Origins of Australian Radicalism and Nationalism* (Ringwood, Victoria: Penguin, 1970); Kirk, '"Australians for Australia"'; Bongiorno, 'British to Their Bootheels Too'.
26 Burton, 'Who Needs the Nation?'; Kirk, *Comrades and Cousins*, Introduction.
27 For example, in contrast to Britain's system of voluntary collective bargaining and dominant commitment to free trade, the Australian Commonwealth was characterised by a compulsory system of arbitration, centralised (industry-wide) wage fixation and economic protectionism. For similarities and differences in the political economy of the two countries see Greg Patmore and David Coates, 'Labour Parties and the State in Australia and the UK', *Labour History*, 88 (May 2005), 123–9; Stuart Macintyre, *The Oxford History of Australia*, vol. 4, *The Succeeding Age 1901–1942* (Melbourne: Oxford University Press, 1997), pp. 236–7; Neville Kirk, 'Why Compare Labour in Australia and Britain?', *Labour History*, 88 (May 2005), 4; Judith Brett, *Australian Liberals and the Moral Middle Class: From Alfred Deakin to John Howard* (Cambridge: Cambridge University Press, 2003), pp. 167–72; James and Markey, 'Class and Labour', 24.
28 Hilson, *Political Change*, Conclusion; Kirk, *Comrades and Cousins*, Introduction, Conclusion; Neville Kirk, 'Global Labour History: A State of the Art', *Labor: Studies*

in *Working-Class History of the Americas*, 4:3 (Fall 2007), 134–6; Neville Kirk, *Labour and Society in Britain and the USA*, 2 vols (Aldershot: Scolar Press, 1994); Marcel van der Linden, 'Doing Comparative Labour History: Some Preliminaries', in his *Transnational Labour History: Explorations* (Aldershot: Ashgate, 2003); Sabyasachi Bhattacharya, 'Paradigms in the Historical Approach to Labour Studies on South Asia', in Jan Lucassen (ed.), *Global Labour History*, pp. 157–9.

29 John French used these terms in his address to the opening plenary session of the 'Workers, the Nation-State and Beyond: The Newberry Conference on Labor History across the Americas', Newberry Library, Chicago, 18–20 September 2008. I am grateful to John for permission to quote.

30 Ann Curthoys, 'Does Australian History Have a Future?', *Australian Historical Studies*, 33:118 (2002), 140–52; Kirk, 'Why Compare Labour?', 1–2. See the special issues of *Labour History Review*, 74:3 (December 2009) and 75:1 (April 2010). Edited by Don MacRaild, Melanie Nolan and Neville Kirk, these are devoted to the theme of trans-national labour history.

31 David Day, *Andrew Fisher: Prime Minister of Australia* (Sydney: Fourth Estate, 2008), p. 23. See also D.J. Murphy, 'Fisher, Andrew (1862–1928)', *Australian Dictionary of Biography*, vol. 8 (Carlton: Melbourne University Press, 1981), pp. 502–7.

32 Frank Farrell, 'Boote, Henry Ernest (1865–1949)', *Australian Dictionary of Biography*, vol. 7 (Carlton: Melbourne University Press, 1979), pp. 342–3; Ian Syson, 'Henry Ernest Boote: Putting the Boote into the Australian Literary Archive', *Labour History*, 70 (1996), 77–9.

33 Day, *Fisher*, ch. 14.

34 Murphy, 'Fisher', p. 507.

35 Day, *Fisher*, pp. 222–40, 83–7; Fisher Papers, Series 10, Newsclippings, 2919/10/108, *Shropshire Weekly*, 3 June 1911.

36 Day, *Fisher*, pp. 241, 83–7, 9–101.

37 Kenneth O. Morgan, *Keir Hardie: Radical and Socialist* (London: Weidenfeld and Nicolson, 1975), p. 196. The 'Addresses of Welcome' are to be found in the Keir Hardie and Emrys Hughes Papers in the National Library of Scotland, MS 176, Volumes and Other Items, 7(i) and 7(ii).

38 Day, *Fisher*, p. 411; Fisher Papers, Series 10, News Clippings, 2919/10/109a, *Daily Sketch*, 8 February 1930; Emrys Hughes, *Keir Hardie* (London: George Allen and Unwin, 1956), p. 222.

39 The work of the UK–Australian Labour History Project is a useful start. For details see the thematic section, 'Australia/UK Comparative Labour History', *Labour History*, 88 (May 2005), v–145. For more general comparisons between Britain and Australia see, for example, J.D. Miller (ed.), *Australians and British Social and Political Connections* (North Ryde, NSW: Methuen, 1987); Mary Kooyman and Peter Beckingham (eds), *Australia and Britain: The Evolving Relationship* (Monash: McPherson's Publishing Group, 1993); Ward, *Australia and the British Embrace.*

40 Kirk, 'Why Compare Labour?', 1–7.

41 Mark McKenna, *The Captive Republic: A History of Republicanism in Australia 1788–1996* (Cambridge: Cambridge University Press, 1996); Ward, *Australia and the British Embrace*; Stuart Macintyre, 'Australia and Britain', in Robin Winks (ed.), *The Oxford History of the British Empire*, vol. V, *Historiography* (Oxford: Oxford University Press, 1999); Kirk, 'Why Compare Labour?', 4–5; *Sydney Morning Herald*, 26, 27 November 2007; *Sun-Herald*, 18 November 2007 (Paul Keating); *Herald Sun*, 27 November 2007 (Geoffrey Blainey).

42 Paul Pickering, 'Chartism and the "Trade of Agitation" in Early Victorian Britain', *History*, 76 (1991), 221–37; Paul Pickering, ' "The Finger of God", Gold and Political Culture in Colonial New South Wales', in Ian D. McCalman (ed.), *Gold: Forgotten Histories and Lost Artefacts of Australia* (Cambridge: Cambridge University Press, 2001); Antony Taylor and Luke Trainor, 'Monarchism and Anti-Monarchism: Anglo-Australian Comparisons c. 1870–1901', *Social History*, 24:2 (May 1999), 158–73; Kirk, *Comrades and Cousins*, ch. 1, pp. 112–33; Kirk, 'Why Compare Labour?', 3.

43 For these prejudices and their contestations see, for example, Neville Kirk, 'Class Ethnicity and Popular Toryism', in his *The Growth of Working Class Reformism in Mid-Victorian England* (Beckenham: Croom Helm, 1985); Kirk, *Comrades and Cousins*, ch. 3; Dorothy Thompson, 'Ireland and the Irish in English Radicalism before 1850', in James Epstein and Dorothy Thompson (eds), *The Chartist Experience: Studies in Working Class Radicalism and Culture 1830–1860* (London: Macmillan, 1982); Kenneth Lunn, 'A Racialized Hierarchy of Labour? Race, Immigration and the British Labour Movement, 1880–1950', in Peter Alexander and Rick Halpern (eds), *Racializing Class Classifying Race: Labour and Difference in Britain the USA and Africa* (Basingstoke: Macmillan, 2000); Panikos Panayi, *Immigration Ethnicity and Racism in Britain 1815–1945* (Manchester: Manchester University Press, 1994); Colin Holmes, *John Bull's Island: Immigration and British Society 1871–1971* (Basingstoke: Macmillan, 1988); David Feldman, *Englishmen and Jews: Social Relations and Political Culture 1840–1914* (New Haven: Yale University Press, 1994); Ann Curthoys, 'Liberalism and Exclusionism: A Pre-History of the White Australia Policy', in Laksiri Jayasuriya, David Walker and Jan Gothard (eds), *Legacies of White Australia: Race Culture and Nation* (Crawley: University of Western Australia Press, 2003); Julia Martinez, 'Questioning "White Australia": Unionism and "Coloured" Labour, 1911–37', *Labour History*, 76 (May 1999), 1–19; Gregson, 'Footsoldiers for Capital'; James Jupp, *From White Australia to Woomera: The Story of Australian Immigration* (Cambridge: Cambridge University Press, 2002).

44 For the much-debated notion of 'whiteness' see Laura Tabili, 'Race Is a Relationship not a Thing', *Journal of Social History*, 37:1 (Fall 2003), 125–30; Laura Tabili, *"We Ask for British Justice": Workers and Racial Difference in Late Imperial Britain* (Ithaca: Cornell University Press, 1994); Kirk, *Comrades and Cousins*, ch. 3; Jeremy Krikler, *White Rising: The 1922 Insurrection and Racial Killing in South Africa* (Manchester: Manchester University Press, 2005); Jonathan Hyslop, 'The Imperial Working Class makes itself "White": White Labourism in Britain, Australia and South Africa before the First World War', *Journal of Historical Sociology*, 12:4 (December 1999), 398–421; Dagmar Engelken, 'The Labour Movement and the Chinese Labour Question in Britain and South Africa, 1900–1914' (PhD dissertation, University of Essex, 2010); William Kenefick, 'Confronting White Labourism: Socialism, Syndicalism and the Role of the Scottish Radical Left in South Africa before 1914', *International Review of Social History*, 55:1 (April 2010), 29–62; Jonathan Hyslop, 'Scottish Labour, Race and Southern African Empire c. 1880–1922: A reply to Kenefick', *IRSH*, 55:1 (April 2010), 63–81; Marilyn Lake and Henry Reynolds, *Drawing the Global Colour Line: White Men's Countries and the Question of Racial Equality* (Carlton: Melbourne University Press, 2008); Alastair Bonnett, *White Identities: Historical and International Perspectives* (Harlow: Pearson Education, 2000).

45 Neville Kirk, 'Capacities, Co-operation and Conflict: Labour and the Issues of Class, Race and Nation in Australia and Britain from the later nineteenth century to the 1970s', unpublished paper, 2007.

46 John Chesterman, *Civil Rights: How Indigenous Australians Won Formal Equality* (St Lucia: University of Queensland Press, 2005); Macintyre, *Succeeding Age*, p. 34.

47 Gavin W. Jones, 'White Australia, National Identity and Population Change', in Jayasuriya, Walker and Gothard, *Legacies of White Australia*, pp. 8–32; Michael Roe, *Australia, Britain and Migration: A Study of Desperate Hopes 1915–1940* (Cambridge: Cambridge University Press, 1995); Stephen Constantine, 'British Emigration to the Empire and Commonwealth since 1880: From Overseas Settlement to Diaspora?', *Journal of Imperial and Commonwealth History*, 31:2 (May 2003), 16–35; Papers of Arthur Calwell, MS 4738, National Library of Australia, Canberra, series 15, 'Immigration', box 56, 'Newspaper Cuttings, White Australia Policy, 1950–1964'. Calwell, a fierce defender of 'White Australia', was Minister for Immigration in Chifley's post-war Labor administration (1945–1949). He went on to become Deputy Leader and Leader of the ALP. He resigned in 1967 and was succeeded by Whitlam.

48 Malcolm Campbell, *Ireland's New Worlds: Immigrants Politics and Society in the United States and Australia 1815–1922* (Madison: University of Wisconsin Press, 2007), pp. 156, 168–70, 175–6, 180–2; Macintyre, *Oxford History of Australia*, pp. 187–91; Scott, *Running on Empty*, pp. 37, 136. For the mixed picture of Irish Catholic involvement in the British labour movement and the debilitating effects of religious sectarianism see, for example, William Kenefick, *Red Scotland! The Rise and Fall of the Radical Left c. 1872 to 1932* (Edinburgh: Edinburgh University Press, 2007), pp. 2, 13–18; Sam Davies, *Liverpool Labour: Social and Political Influences on the Development of the Labour Party in Liverpool 1900–1939* (Keele: Keele University Press, 1996).

49 Jones, 'White Australia', pp. 118–27.

50 Humphrey McQueen, *Social Sketches of Australia 1888–2001* (St Lucia: University of Queensland Press, 2004), p. 136.

51 Famous footballer David Beckham's remark, 'I have never been a cricket fan, but I think that everyone was gripped by the Ashes', captured the public mood. See Andrew Culf's article in the *Guardian*, 12 December 2005. In this context see also *Observer*, 18 September 2005 (Jamie Jackson, Vic Marks), 25 September 2005 (Vic Marks).

52 Steve Waugh, *Out of My Comfort Zone* (London: Penguin, 2006), pp. 597–8; Clare Connor, 'Why Australia lead way in the Art of Captaincy' [sic], *Observer*, 12 June 2005.

53 Kirk, *Comrades and Cousins*, pp. 62–6.

54 Kirk, 'Why Compare Labour?', 5.

CHAPTER TWO

Labour and elections

Introduction

I have organised this study around a central concern with elections and the performances of the ALP and the BLP in these elections. This has enabled me to meet three key objectives. First, to impose order and coherence upon a vast and sometimes unwieldy mass of primary and secondary material. Second, to compare and contrast continuities, changes, similarities and differences in Labour and anti-Labour attitudes and policies towards the factors of empire, nation, race and class at particular electoral points in time over the past century. Third, to evaluate the individual and combined influences of these factors and others upon the nature and outcomes of elections.

It should also be observed that my study of elections is qualitative rather than quantitative in character. As such, and while I pay due attention to voting patterns, I concentrate far more upon the languages, representations and analyses of electoral politics offered by more culturally inclined contemporary and historical observers, rather than the quantitative methods and findings of opinion pollsters and some political scientists.

The focus on elections, moreover, has constituted a necessary rather than a sufficient basis upon which to construct more general arguments about the character, aims, similarities and differences and shifting fortunes of the ALP and BLP and their relations with other political parties, the state and different social groups. In order to attain, or at least strive towards, a sufficient measure of explanation, a wider focus upon a combination of political, economic, social and cultural factors is adopted.

The electoral record

Labour's record of electoral performance between 1900 and the present day may usefully be broken down into four chronological periods:

from 1900 to the time of World War One; from 1917 in Australia and 1918 in Britain to 1939; from the era of World War Two to the late 1970s; and from the latter to the present.

Between 1901 and 2006 the BLP enjoyed national office for thirty-three years (including the wartime coalition of the 1940s), while the ALP held federal power for thirty-four years. As such, they spent more time in federal and national opposition than in office. At the same time, however, the BLP established a very strong urban base, especially in the north of England, Scotland and Wales, while the ALP was the dominant electoral power in the leading states of New South Wales, Queensland and, albeit more recently, Victoria. The ALP was also far more successful than the BLP in building up support among workers and small producers in rural areas.

Early in 2007 the ALP controlled 'all the states and Territories', and Labour held office nationally and in Scotland (before its historic defeat by the Scottish Nationalists by one seat in the May elections for the Scottish parliament), Wales and London. In Australia the federal election of November 2007 resulted in defeat for John Howard after more than eleven years in office. Seemingly 'dead and buried' in 2005, the ALP rallied under its new leader, Kevin Rudd, to show up well in the opinion polls of 2006 and early 2007 and subsequently to achieve a landslide victory in the federal contest of November 2007.[1]

In May and June 2010 the ALP's support at the polls declined precipitously as a result of its retreat on a carbon emissions tax and its failure to win the battle with the mining companies over their 'super-profits'. Rudd was effectively forced to step down in favour of his erstwhile deputy, Julia Gillard. Yet Gillard failed to secure an outright majority in the federal election of August 2010. The election resulted in a hung parliament. At the time of writing the nature of the next government has still to be decided. In Britain Tony Blair's successor as Prime Minister, Gordon Brown, was defeated at the May 2010 general election. A Conservative-Liberal Democrat coalition is now in power.[2]

The first period covers the years from 1901 to 1916 in the Australian case and 1900 to 1918 in terms of Britain. As noted above, it was during these years that the infant ALP, formed in 1901, experienced a remarkable rise. The 'oldest of all labour parties internationally', the ALP as a national body developed out of the colonial Labour parties formed during the 1890s. The results were most impressive. Labor formed a minority colonial government in Queensland in 1899, and a minority national government in 1904. Although short-lived, these were 'the first examples of labour or social democratic rule in the world'. By 1910 the ALP held majority governments nationally, in

New South Wales and in South Australia. Between 1910 and 1916 the ALP held federal office for an impressive five years and four months.[3]

In Britain the Labour Party's electoral record was far less impressive. The TUC- (Trades Union Congress) inspired Labour Representation Committee (LRC) of 1900 officially became the Labour Party in 1906. Yet up to 1918 the Labour Party's electoral 'rise' was slow and uneven. Gains made at the municipal level could not conceal the fact that the Progressive Alliance, formed in 1903 between Labour and the Liberals, and in which Labour was very much the junior partner at Westminster, 'was generally maintained up to 1914'. Labour did not attain national office during this phase. There is now a general consensus among historians that it was the experiences of World War One that under-pinned the Labour Party's 'true', post-war 'rise', especially in the major urban areas. These comprised the advantages of 'collectivism' over 'individualism' during wartime, the attendant crisis of Liberalism, the positive and negative results for the labour movement of the massive increase in state intervention and labour leaders' active involvement in the war effort.[4]

The second period, from 1917 to 1939 in Australia and 1918 to 1939 in Britain, witnessed very mixed results for both parties. In Australia there was a sharp reversal and persistent downturn in the electoral fortunes of the ALP at the federal level. This was triggered in 1916 and 1917 by the disastrous split within the ALP over the issue of conscription for overseas military service, the expulsion of the more moderate, pro-conscription and pro-British leaders, most prominently 'Billy' Hughes, growing anti-war sentiment within the labour move-ment's ranks and the involvement of Hughes and other prominent ex-Labor leaders with the Liberals in the 'Win-the-War' Nationalist Party, formed in 1917. Between the federal elections of 1917 and 1929 the conservative Nationalists and their successors, the Nationalist-Country Party coalition, formed in the aftermath of the 1922 election, ruled the federal roost.

In 1929 Labor was elected under James Scullin. However, this was to prove a short-lived and isolated federal victory. Scullin's govern-ment was unable to find effective solutions to the Depression, while the labour movement as a whole split around the formulation and implementation of an economic policy best suited to meet the needs of itself, the working class, the nation and Britain. In December 1931 the ALP was heavily defeated by the recently formed United Australia Party (UAP). The latter was headed by the prominent Labor 'rat', Joseph Lyons. The UAP ruled the federal electoral scene for the remain-der of the 1930s on the basis of 'policies of "sound finance", economic salvation, and conservative loyalty to nation and empire'.[5]

Results in the states were more mixed. Queensland was Labor's flagship, with the ALP holding continuous office there from 1915 to 1929 and from 1932 to 1957. The ALP performed well in Western Australia and Tasmania from the mid 1920s onwards. In New South Wales, regarded as the ALP's 'natural' constituency from the 1940s to the 1960s, there was a marked contrast between, on the one hand, Labor's almost complete electoral domination between 1910 and 1916 and, on the other hand, its chequered performance between 1917 and 1930. Moreover, for most of the 1930s the ALP in New South Wales was split and out of office. In South Australia and Victoria the ALP was also out of power for most of the interwar years. In overall terms the ALP's interwar performance in the states was better than at the federal level, but inferior to both that of the Right during the same period of time and its own pre-1916 record.[6]

In sum, the ALP, complete with its beliefs in the 'onward march of labour' and the inevitable advent of a socialistic 'Workers' Paradise', experienced serious setbacks from 1917 onwards. Although the trade union movement retained much of its strength and militancy during the 1920s, it suffered during the Depression and the ALP lost its pre-war electoral hegemony to the Right. In 1920 the astute Victorian socialist Bob Ross maintained that 'Labor dominance' had 'penetrated into the whole of Australian thought . . . the spirit of Australianism', and that it had 'permeated opponents to an extent that would have made their fathers shudder'. It is 'in and about all our national bases and outlook', concluded Ross.[7] By the 1930s no one would realistically offer the same conclusion.

Whereas the ALP 'fell' from its pre-war ascendancy during the inter-war years, the post-war British Labour Party appeared to have begun its 'rise' in earnest.[8] The party had received under 8 per cent of the vote in the two general elections of 1910. In contrast, it commanded 22 per cent in the general election of 1918. By the early 1920s the BLP had come to replace the Liberals as the main opposition to the Conservative Party. The Labour Party benefited from the fact that its trade union majority had supported the war, that no irrevocable split took place with anti-war socialists (including the future Prime Minister, Ramsay MacDonald), that millions of working-class men and women, the party's 'natural' constituency, were enfranchised in 1918 and 1928, that it increasingly managed to put down firm roots in urban working-class localities and that party organisation, finances and publicity were greatly improved. In 1924 Labour formed its first, minority, government with 30 per cent of the vote and 191 seats, overtaking the Liberals in both votes and seats. Between 1924 and the general election of 1929 Labour's confidence, strength and advancement grew apace, while those of the Liberals continued to decline. As a result of the general election of 1929 Labour gained office, once again on a minority basis, with a very impressive 40 per cent of the total vote and 287 seats.

However, as in Australia, the BLP failed effectively to tackle, and became irreparably divided over, policies to tackle the Depression. Like its Australian counterpart, it paid a very heavy price for failure and lack of unity. In August 1931 the Labour cabinet split over expenditure cuts and MacDonald formed a National Government. The 6.5 million votes cast in favour of Labour in the ensuing general election returned only 52 Labour MPs (including those of the Independent Labour Party), while the National Government enjoyed a landslide victory. The most prominent British Labour 'rat' or 'traitor', Ramsay MacDonald, became leader of the Conservative-dominated National Government. Claiming to put the 'national' above the 'sectional' interest, the National Government ruled supreme throughout the remainder of the 1930s. In the general election of 1935 Labour slightly exceeded its vote of 1929, but won only 154 seats. As Andrew Thorpe observes, notwithstanding gains at the municipal level, in 1935 Labour 'seemed to be condemned to Opposition for the foreseeable future'.[9] In sum, Labour's 'rise' in interwar Britain was real but limited. As in Australia, the outstanding political developments of this second period were the hegemony of the Right and the subordination of Labour.

Initially at least, Labour's fortunes improved markedly in the third period, from the 1940s to the late 1970s. As we will see in Part IV, during World War Two and beyond Labour in both countries successfully resorted to the discourses and practices of radical patriotism. These manifested themselves in the protection of freedom and democracy against the twin threats of fascism and communism, the defence and further advancement of 'the people's' material and other 'needs and interests', including those of the 'workers', and close identification with the reconstructed, progressive and modern nation and 'enlightened' Commonwealth.

In Britain the Labour Party took part in the wartime coalition, assumed office under Clement Attlee in 1945, for the first time in a majority capacity, and remained in power until 1951. In Australia the ALP regained federal office in 1941 and, under the wartime and immediate post-war leadership of John Curtin and Ben Chifley respectively, stayed there until the election of 1949.[10]

In both countries, but more so in Australia, there followed long periods of anti-Labour rule.[11] In Australia the Liberal-Country Party coalition, the main beneficiary of the 1950s and 1960s boom years, enjoyed twenty-three years of unbroken federal rule. The coalition was led, up to his retirement in 1966, by the Anglophile Sir Robert

Menzies, an unbending Cold War critic not only of the Australian Communist Party and the 'global designs' of international communism, but also of the 'fellow-travelling', 'extreme' and 'disloyal' ALP. The coalition also benefited immensely from the disastrous split in the ALP's ranks in the mid 1950s around the influences of anti-communist Catholics and communists in the party.

Cast into the federal political wilderness and facing a new rival in the form of the anti-left and Catholic-inspired Democratic Labor Party (DLP), the ALP, nevertheless, fared better in some of the states where its socio-economic policies and appeal were vital to its successes. From the 1940s to the late 1970s it was the dominant force in Tasmania and New South Wales (albeit with a ten-year gap in the latter, from 1966 to 1976). It governed uninterruptedly from 1932 to 1957 in Queensland, but was then out of office for thirty-two years, patchily in Western Australia throughout, very badly in South Australia from the 1940s to the mid 1960s, but enjoying continuous power there from 1970 to 1979, and very badly in Victoria almost continuously.

As we will see in Parts III and IV, although anti-communism, anti-socialism and the tarring of the mainstream labour movement with the brushes of 'red' extremism and disloyalty to the nation constituted important factors in British electoral politics during the 1920s, in 1945 and during the 1970s, both their presence and influence in that country were, on the whole, more variable and often far less pronounced than in Australia.[12] Of key importance during the 1950s was the fact that the Conservatives came to terms with the post-war settlement of the Welfare State, 'full' employment and the mixed economy, largely abandoned Winston Churchill's failed 1945 tactic of tarring the mainstream labour movement as totalitarian and 'un-British', and played the 'you've never had it so good' card very effectively. They kept Labour out of national office for 'thirteen wasted years' between 1951 and 1964.

Yet Labour's revival began earlier in Britain than in Australia, and the national hegemony of the Right was less complete in the former than in the latter country. Between 1964 and 1970 Labour Prime Minister Harold Wilson sought to create a 'New Britain' rooted in technological change, professional expertise and a more democratic, open and just society. Wilson's commitment to the 'progressive modernization' of the nation was presented as an effective antidote to outmoded British 'traditionalism' and economic 'decline'.[13]

Although Wilson lost in 1970, he regained electoral power in 1974 in the face of 'Ted' Heath's fierce campaign against Labour and trade union 'extremism' and 'sectionalism'. Labour was in office until Margaret Thatcher's watershed victory of 1979. Thatcher's victory owed much to her successful campaign against labour movement 'extremism', 'disloyalty' to the nation and the 'free world' and her pledges to reverse economic 'decline' and restore Britain's 'greatness'.[14]

In Australia Labor's commitments to progressivism and modernisation brought long-awaited federal success under the leadership of Gough Whitlam in 1972. Yet Whitlam was defeated by Malcolm Fraser in 1975 and the ALP did not return to federal office until 1983.

Notwithstanding their mixed and in some ways contrasting post-war electoral fortunes, both the BLP and the ALP reached membership peaks during the 1950s (75,000 in 1954 in the Australian case, 1 million in Britain in 1951–52). This was an expression of the fact that during the first half of the twentieth century Australia and Britain were dominated numerically by urban and rural manual workers. Characterised by their male-dominated, workplace, betting and pub-based cultures, increasing numbers of these workers, along with rural and urban petty producers, others of the 'middling sort' and progressive professionals, gave their support to Labour.[15]

The fourth period, from 1980 to the present day, has been the era of neo-liberal 'globalisation'. Up to the financial crisis of 2008–9 deregulation was the era's ruling common sense as opposed to the post-war international hegemony of Keynesian demand management and regulation. As in the third period, Labour's results in this fourth period – of profound and rapid change – have been very mixed.

It was not until its historic election victory of 1997 that New Labour successfully challenged post-1979 Tory hegemony. Thereafter New Labour, under the contrasting personalities of Prime Ministers Tony Blair and Gordon Brown, retained power for thirteen years. In contrast to the BLP, the ALP fared well for most of the 1980s and 1990s, but poorly during the second half of the 1990s and the first six years of the first decade of the new millennium. The Labor Prime Ministers Bob Hawke and Paul Keating adopted a combination of regulatory, 'corporatist' and predominantly neo-liberal policies and between them achieved an unprecedented five successive federal election victories for the ALP between 1983 and 1996.

This was at the time when the Conservatives, of course, ruled supreme in Britain and when many thought that the BLP would never again achieve national office. Significantly, in 1990 the BLP sent its 'rising stars', Tony Blair and Gordon Brown, on a party visit to Australia to learn from the 'third way' successes of Hawke and Keating.[16]

Yet between 1996 and 2007 the Liberals and their Coalition partners exerted a stranglehold on federal power. For much of this period it was the ALP's turn to be in the political doldrums and widely portrayed as being hopelessly divided, out of touch and even in terminal decline.

In the 2007 federal election, however, the ALP successfully reinvented itself as the party of 'the future' and the inclusive, progressive nation. In contrast to Labor, the outgoing Howard government was now portrayed as being outmoded and sectional.[17]

The ALP's electoral record in the states during the fourth period as a whole has been much better than at the federal level. Between 1976 and 2005 the ALP held power for twenty-three years in New South Wales, nineteen years in South Australia, fifteen years nine months in Victoria, fifteen years six months in Tasmania, almost fifteen years in Western Australia and thirteen years seven months in Queensland. In the latter state, a Labor stronghold from 1915 to 1957, Labor had been out of office for over thirty years up to 1989. Moreover, we must remember that, historically, the states have held responsibility for education and health, road and rail transport, urban development and, in part, industrial relations. As Markey has noted, these are all 'major areas of ALP concern'.[18]

As we will see in Part V, a key factor in determining the electoral performance of the BLP and the ALP in this fourth period has revolved around the ways in which they have tackled international developments, their particular manifestations in Britain and Australia, and issues 'peculiar' to these nation-states. Among this very wide and mixed set of developments and issues we may, at this juncture, simply highlight the following: the international economic crisis of the mid 1970s and its effects; 'globalisation' and the transition from Keynesianism to neo-liberalism; the end of the Cold War, the decline of socialism and collectivism; socio-economic restructuring, involving the decline of the 'traditional' male-dominated working class, the rise of a 'new' multi-racial working class in which consumerism, individualism, gender and multi-culturalism figure more prominently; and the increasingly fragile and contingent relationship between class and voting patterns. In recent years the issues of the 'war on terror', 'neo-imperialism', the highly racialised issues of migration, national security and border protection and, of course, the financial crisis and the weaknesses of neo-liberal, deregulated capitalism have been prominent. Increasingly 'professionalised' Labour parties have sought, with very mixed results, to 'modernise' themselves and widen their appeal in order to retain their relevance and standing in this rapidly changing world.

Key arguments

I present three core arguments concerning the influences of nation, empire, race and class upon Labour's electoral performance.

First, I maintain that Labour often performed best at elections both in Australia and in Britain when it successfully presented itself as the true agent of not only its traditional and predominantly white and male working-class constituents and their domestic 'bread and butter' concerns, but also of the wider 'productive' 'people's' modern and reforming interests and ideas, including those of the enlightened, prosperous and progressive nation, Empire and/or Commonwealth. Since the middle years of the twentieth century, this wider 'Labour' public, especially in Britain, has included a significant and mainly working-class black and Asian presence.

Labour's successful electoral appeal to the nation, modernity, progressivism, material prosperity and competent economic management has assumed a variety of forms over time. For example, it was reflected in the popular radical nationalism of the early ALP. This held up 'new world' Australia as a 'beacon' of progress, high living standards, egalitarianism, opportunity, 'mateship' and racial sovereignty. In the spirit of maturing national confidence and self-reliance, it demanded more autonomy for Australia within an enlightened imperial framework. It was also seen in Harold Wilson's and Tony Blair's modernising technological, politico-economic and inclusive national 'crusades' against narrow, exclusive and reactionary British 'traditionalism'.[19]

In their distinctive ways the governments of Whitlam, Hawke and Keating were reforming, radical and 'modern'. They championed multiculturalism as against 'whiteness' and 'homogeneity'; the rights of women and Aboriginals, progressive social-welfare policies and Australian self-respect, pride and independence as against traditional deference towards Britain. While Whitlam's government failed the electoral test of economic competence, albeit in increasingly difficult domestic and external economic circumstances, Hawke and Keating were more successful.

Labour in both Australia and Britain successfully presented itself during the period of World War Two as both the defender of free and democratic nations and the Commonwealth against fascist tyranny and global ambition and – as the representative of what David Marquand has termed the 'progressive conscience' – the initiator of post-war reconstruction and social justice.[20] In Britain the Labour Party's election manifesto of 1959 declared the 'transformation of the old British Empire into the first inter-racial Commonwealth of free nations' to be the 'supreme achievement' of the 1945 Labour government.[21]

Second, Labour has fared least well when it has been widely seen by the electorate as having acquired a combination of negative characteristics. These have included, for example, perceptions of tiredness, running out of ideas, being out of touch and backward looking, divided and incompetent, especially economically. The latter fatally wounded the Whitlam government and, irrespective of questions of fairness and accuracy, those of Brown and Rudd.[22] Labour has also suffered badly when it has been widely seen to be too extreme and even disloyal to the national and imperial interest. As we will observe in Parts III and IV, this was often the case, especially in Australia, during the interwar and post-war periods. Lastly, in both countries anti-Labour forces have repeatedly resorted successfully to the charge that Labour represents the sectional and largely male, 'class'-based interest, rather than that of the 'public' or 'the nation as a whole'.[23]

Third, Labour has traditionally enjoyed little success as an independent political body when it has failed to offer a clear and viable progressive alternative to the policies of the Right. For example, much of the ALP's anti-communism has mirrored that of the Coalition. Moreover, it is the latter rather than the former which has derived by far the greatest electoral benefit from anti-communism. Even Irish Catholics, Labor's mainstay constituents traditionally most opposed to 'atheistic' socialism and communism, deserted in large numbers to the rival and fiercely anti-communist Democratic Labor Party during the Cold War years. They simply did not accept the premise that the ALP's practice matched its anti-communist rhetoric.[24]

As seen in debates in Britain surrounding the public interest and economic policy in the late 1920s and early 1930s, leading Labour figures, such as MacDonald and Snowden, largely echoed the Conservative Party leader Stanley Baldwin's belief that the nation would best be served during the Depression by the political economy of deflation rather than the BLP's 'sectional' and 'selfish' opposition to cuts in unemployment benefit. The latter would result in 'national ruin', according to Snowden.[25] MacDonald also shadowed Baldwin in his identification of the British nation with the rural idyll, reverence towards the monarchy, constitutionalism, toleration, freedom, fairness and social accommodation and consensus versus exclusion and conflict. Largely absent from this viewpoint were radical, oppositional and transforming notions of Englishness and British-ness.[26]

On the basis of their attitudes to economic policy and the public interest it made perfect sense for MacDonald, Snowden and their like-minded colleagues to ally themselves with Conservatives and others in the 1930s National Government rather than remain in the 'sectional' and oppositional Labour Party. The same conclusion may be applied to Joseph Lyons and his like-minded Labor 'rats' who joined the UAP in early 1930s. As we will observe in Part III, conservative and Conservative views of the nation and economic policy prevailed in interwar Britain and Australia.

On one level these examples amount to nothing more than the truism that Conservatives, Nationalists and their allies best and most successfully express conservative views and that labour movement politicians who attempt to imitate them do so at their own peril. Yet on another level matters are far less simple and one dimensional. As demonstrated in the cases of Hawke, Keating and Blair, traditional party divisions have ironically been blurred and sometimes overturned by successful Labour practitioners of the 'Third Way'. In openly accepting and championing the national interest, globalisation, aspects of neo-liberalism, in throwing down the gauntlet to traditional collectivist and class-based Labour and in seeking to capture the middle ground of politics and its constituency of the mainly affluent and 'aspirant', these 'Third Way' politicians stole key aspects of what has often been regarded as the 'natural' electoral and ideological baggage of the Right. The period of New Labour's most emphatic domination of British politics, between 1997 and 2007, witnessed the peculiar spectacle of a Conservative Party desperately trying to prove that it was not a mere shadow of Tony Blair's government.

Finally, it is important to note that while it has been historically important for Labour parties to formulate clear alternatives to the Right, the electoral and wider societal outcomes of these alternatives depend very much upon their viability and their efficacy, especially in terms of economic competence and social benefit. For example, notwithstanding the poverty of his recent economic performance, Gordon Brown's excellent record as Chancellor of the Exchequer under-pinned many of the successes of New Labour between 1997 and 2007.

These arguments are developed in more detail in the chronological Parts II to V below. I turn first, in Part II, to a consideration of Labour's fortunes in its formative years between 1900 and the time of World War One.

Notes

1 James Jupp, 'Saving the Party from Itself', unpublished paper, 2007. I am grateful to Jim Jupp for permission to quote from this paper. James and Markey, 'Class and Labour', 25; *Sydney Morning Herald*, 26, 27 November 2007; *Guardian*, 26 November, 2007 (Richard Flanagan, leader); *Observer*, 3 June 2007 (Will Hutton), 25 November 2007 (Barbara McMahon); Nicholas Stuart, *What Goes Up: Behind the 2007 Election* (Carlton North: Scribe Publications, 2007).
2 *Sydney Morning Herald*, 23, 24 August 2010; *Guardian*, 7, 8 May, 23, 24 August 2010.
3 James and Markey, 'Class and Labour', 25–6.
4 For relevant details and ongoing debates among historians see Kirk, *Change, Continuity and Class*, ch. 8.
5 Neville Kirk, '"Australians for Australia"'; Jacqueline Dickenson, *Renegades and Rats: Betrayal and the Remaking of Radical Organisations in Britain and Australia* (Carlton: Melbourne University Press, 2006).

6 Kirk, '"Australians for Australia"', 105.
7 R.S. Ross, *Revolution in Russia and Australia* (Melbourne: Ross's Book Service, 1920), p. 47.
8 For the interwar Labour Party see, for example, Maurice Cowling, *The Impact of Labour* (Cambridge: Cambridge University Press, 1971); David Howell, *MacDonald's Party: Labour Identities and Crisis 1922–1931* (Oxford: Oxford University Press, 2002); Laybourn, *Century of Labour*; Andrew Thorpe, *A History of the British Labour Party* (London: Palgrave, 2001); Ross McKibbin, 'The Economic Policy of the Second Labour Government, 1929–1931', and 'Class and Conventional Wisdom: The Conservative Party and the "Public" in Inter-War Britain', in his *Ideologies of Class: Social Relations in Britain 1880–1950* (Oxford: Oxford University Press, 1991); Matthew Worley (ed.), *Labour's Grass Roots: Essays on the Activities of Local Labour Parties and Members 1918–45* (Aldershot: Ashgate, 2005); Matthew Worley, 'Building the Party: Labour Party Activism in Five British Counties between the Wars', *Labour History Review*, 70:1 (April 2005), 73–95; Duncan Tanner, 'The Pattern of Labour Politics', in Tanner, Williams and Hopkins (eds), *Labour Party in Wales*, pp. 111–35; Chris Cook, *The Age of Alignment: Electoral Politics in Britain 1922–1929* (Basingstoke: Macmillan, 1975).
9 Andrew Thorpe, *The British General Election of 1931* (Oxford: Clarendon Press, 1991), p. 273.
10 George Orwell, *The Lion and the Unicorn: Socialism and the English Genius*, in Sonia Orwell and Ian Angus (eds), *The Collected Essays, Journalism and Letters of George Orwell*, vol. II, *My Country Right or Left 1940–1943* (London: Secker and Warburg, 1968), pp. 56–109; Angus Calder, *The People's War: Britain 1939–45* (London: Cape, 1969); Steven Fielding, Peter Thompson and Nick Tiratsoo, *England Arise! The Labour Party and Popular Politics in 1940s Britain* (Manchester: Manchester University Press, 1995); Stephen Brooke, *Labour's War: The Labour Party during the Second World War* (Oxford: Clarendon Press, 1992); Caroline Knowles, *Race Discourse and Labourism* (London: Routledge, London, 1992); Peter Clarke, *Hope and Glory: Britain 1900–2000* (London: Penguin, 1996); Geoffrey Bolton, *The Oxford History of Australia*, vol. 5, *The Middle Way 1942–1996* (Oxford: Oxford University Press, 1996 edition); D.B. Waterson, 'Chifley, Joseph Benedict 1885–1951', pp. 412–20 and Geoffrey Serle, 'Curtin, John 1885–1945', pp. 550–8 in *Australian Dictionary of Biography*, general editor John Ritchie, vol. 13, *1940–1980* (Carlton: Melbourne University Press, 1993); Leslie F. Crisp, *Ben Chifley: A Biography* (London: Longmans, 1961).
11 Allan W. Martin, *Robert Menzies: A Life*, vol. 2, *1944–1978* (Carlton: Melbourne University Press, 1999); Allan W. Martin, 'Menzies, Sir Robert Gordon (Bob) (1894–1978)', *Australian Dictionary of Biography* (Australian National University, 2006, online edition, www.adb.online.anu.edu.au/biogs/A150416b.htm); Brett, *Australian Liberals*, pp. 116–42; Ian Hancock, 'The Rise of the Liberal Party', Robert Murray, 'The Split', in Robert Manne (ed.), *The Australian Century: Political Struggle in the Building of a Nation* (Melbourne, Text Publishing, 2001); James and Markey, 'Class and Labour', 25; Frank Cain and Frank Farrell, 'Menzies' War on the Communist Party, 1949–1951', in Ann Curthoys and John Merritt (eds), *Australia's First Cold War 1945–1953*, vol. 1, *Society, Communism and Culture* (Sydney: George Allen and Unwin, 1984); Peter Love, 'The Great Labor Split of 1955: An Overview', in Brian Costar, Peter Love and Paul Strangio (eds), *The Great Labor Schism* (Carlton North: Scribe Publications, 2005).
12 David Anthony Jarvis, 'Stanley Baldwin and the Ideology of the Conservative Response to Socialism, 1918–31' (PhD dissertation, University of Lancaster, 1991); Bruce Coleman, 'The Conservative Party and the Frustration of the Extreme Right', in Andrew Thorpe (ed.), *The Failure of Political Extremism in Inter-war Britain* (Department of History and Archaeology, University of Exeter, 1989), pp. 49–66; Richard Thurlow, *The Secret State: British Internal Security in the Twentieth Century* (Oxford: Blackwell, 1995), especially chapter 4; Kevin Morgan, *Bolshevism and the British Left*, Part One, *Labour Legends and Russian Gold* (London: Lawrence and Wishart, 2006), pp. 13–17, 19–21, ch. 7.

13 Clarke, *Hope and Glory*, chs 8, 9.
14 For Heath's and Thatcher's strong employment of the 'Red Scare' tactic in 1974 and 1979, albeit with contrasting electoral outcomes, see, for example, *Guardian*, 4, 7, 8, 9, 11 February 1974, 2 October 1974, 1 May 1979; *Daily Telegraph*, 1, 2, 4 May 1979.
15 James and Markey, 'Class and Labour', 29; Ross McKibbin, *Classes and Cultures: England 1918–1951* (Oxford: Oxford University Press, 2000), pp. 202–3, 530–6; Gareth Stedman Jones, 'Why is the Labour Party in a Mess?', in his *Languages of Class: Studies in English Working Class History 1832–1982* (Cambridge: Cambridge University Press, 1983); Eric Hobsbawm, *Worlds of Labour: Further Studies in the History of Labour* (London: Weidenfeld and Nicolson, 1984), chs 10, 11.
16 Pierson and Castles, 'Australian Antecedents', 693–4.
17 *Sydney Morning Herald*, 26 November 2007; Paul Kelly, 'Labor and Globalisation', in Manne (ed.), *Australian Century*; Robert Manne, 'From Keating to Howard', in his *Left Right Left: Political Essays 1977–2005* (Melbourne: Black, 2005), pp. 335–77.
18 James and Markey, 'Class and Labour', 25, 27, 29–31.
19 Kirk, *Comrades and Cousins*, pp. 120–9; Nicholas Abercrombie and Alan Warde, *Contemporary British Society* (Cambridge: Polity Press, 2000), pp. 147–51, 425–41; *Guardian*, 11 May 2007 (Polly Toynbee).
20 Bolton, *Oxford History*, ch. 2; *Guardian*, 11 May 2007 (David Marquand).
21 Knowles, *Race Discourse*, pp. 95–6.
22 *Guardian*, 24, 25 June 2010; *Observer*, 27 June 2010; *Sydney Morning Herald*, 27 April, 12, 26 (Ross Gittins), 28 (Phillip Coorey) May, 8, 24, 25 June (Damien Murphy) 2010.
23 McKibbin, *Ideologies of Class*, ch. 9; Brett, *Australian Liberals*, pp. 52–3.
24 Love, 'Great Labor Split'.
25 For Snowden's views and mainly Labour reactions to them see *Manchester Guardian*, 17, 19, 20, 22, 24, 25, 26, 27, 28, 29 October 1931.
26 Ward, *Red Flag and Union Jack*, ch. 9; *Manchester Guardian*, 7 October 1924, 10 June 1929; Cowling, *Impact of Labour*, pp. 359–72.

PART II

The growth of independent Labour

Introduction

The birth and growth of independent labour politics, in the form of the ALP and the BLP, constituted the most significant development in the political history of labour movements in Australia and Britain between the late nineteenth century and the period of World War One. The turn to independent labour politics in these two countries, moreover, was part of an international phenomenon whereby labour movements, albeit unevenly, moved away from reliance upon mainstream 'capitalist' parties to seek 'emancipation' by means of the establishment of their 'own' labour or socialist political organisations. Common or similar international experience, however, also contained within itself many national and other 'peculiarities' and differences. For example, the precocity of the 'new world' ALP may usefully be set against the far more limited progress of the 'old world' BLP. Whereas the former rapidly became a major, arguably the hegemonic, force in Australian politics, the latter's 'rise' was far more limited. From its achievement of minority national office in 1904 to its split over the issue of conscription for overseas military service and subsequent loss of federal power at the end of 1916, the ALP was the main political actor in Australia. In contrast, between 1900 and 1914, and despite making some gains, the Labour Party remained the fourth parliamentary force in Britain, behind the Liberals, the Conservatives and the Irish Nationalists.

The purposes of Part II are to trace and explain the development and fluctuating fortunes of Labour politics. It offers three main conclusions. First, agreement is registered with 'traditionalists' and 'revisionists' that domestic socio-economic and political factors played a key role in the formation and early characteristics of independent labour politics in both countries. Second, it maintains that the neglected forces of nation, empire and race also made a significant, but variable, contribution. Third, this contribution was far more pronounced in Australia than in Britain.

CHAPTER THREE

Chronology, constituencies, impact

Chronology: Britain

The Chartist movement, stretching from the 1830s to the 1850s, may be seen as the first *national* exercise in independent working-class politics of a 'mass' kind in modern Britain.[1] From the demise of Chartism to the end of the century the institutions of the labour movement characteristically supported the radical wing of the Liberal Party and the election of 'Lib-Lab' working-class trade union candidates to parliament. 'Lib-Labism' was particularly strong among 'respectable' skilled artisans and coalminers. The latter group increased from 500,000 to 1.2 million male workers between 1871 and 1911, and by 1908 possessed the largest union in the country, the Miners' Federation of Great Britain, with over 500,000 members.[2] At the same time Conservatism, with its 'populist', religious-sectarian and paternalistic appeals, continued to command much working-class support in some of the Lancashire and Cheshire cotton towns, parts of the industrial areas of Scotland and in ports such as Liverpool and Glasgow.[3]

The ability of workers to influence parliamentary elections, of course, was limited by the nature of the political system. As a result of the Reform Acts of 1867 and 1884 many male working-class heads of household were entitled to vote, and in some parliamentary constituencies 'a considerable majority of the electorate was made up of industrial or agricultural wage-earners'. At the same time, however, 'probably no more than three in five of adult male wage-earners were eligible to vote in the elections of the early twentieth century, and the proportion fell well below this in the poor, central districts of large towns'.[4] Women continued to be excluded from the parliamentary franchise and full membership of the two main party organisations until 1918. While the Representation of the People Act of that year enfranchised women over thirty, it was not until 1928 that all adult women received the vote.[5] The lack of payment for MPs until 1911 and the difficulties involved of being placed on the electoral register, especially if a lodger, itinerant or in receipt of poor relief, constituted further obstacles to the political representation and active involvement of working people. On a wider level, the continued material, ideological and cultural power and influence of the propertied classes, combined with deference and all manner of internal differences and divisions within working-class communities, contributed significantly to working-class and labour movement incorporation into the two-party political system and capitalism itself.[6]

Yet towards the end of the century there were limited and uneven, but unmistakeable signs of reawakened and growing labour movement political assertiveness and independence. In 1888 the Scottish Labour Party was formed. Five years later what was to prove the most influential group of the 'socialist revival', Keir Hardie's Independent Labour Party (ILP), came into existence. Although numerically small, the main socialist groups, the ILP itself, H.M. Hyndman's Social Democratic Federation (SDF), the Webbs' Fabian Society, alongside the propagandistic, educational and 'life-style' Clarion Fellowship of Robert Blatchford, did play an important part in the education and training of 'the movement's' 'militant minority' of political and industrial leaders. They also involved themselves in the struggles of the unemployed and both 'old' (i.e. mainly craft and skilled) and 'new' (predominantly non-skilled) trade unionists and in 'spreading the word' to organised labour's rank and file and the wider public.[7]

Immediate results, nevertheless, were far from impressive. For example, the ILP's figure of 'just over 10,000' paid contributors in 1895 was 'almost halved by 1901', while the SDF, with a total membership of 'around 1,700' in 1902, was 'quite unable to win mass support'.[8] Despite the gains made by both 'old' and 'new' unionism during the 1880s and early 1890s, in the mid 1890s depression and the 'counterattack' by employers and influential judges against trade unionism took a heavy toll. Andrew Thorpe observes that while between 'three-quarters and four-fifths' of the population 'could be described as working class', yet 'only around 13 per cent of those who could have been members of unions were'.[9] For much of the 1890s the Lib-Lab dominated TUC proved unresponsive to socialist appeals for the creation of an independent labour party, while in the 1895 general election one of the foremost champions of such a party, Keir Hardie, lost his parliamentary seat at West Ham South. All the other twenty-seven ILP candidates were defeated.[10]

Despite these setbacks, and the often considerable tensions between middle-class socialists and working-class trade unionists,[11] Keir Hardie's persistence in promoting the idea of a new labour rather than an explicitly socialist party, founded upon an alliance between the trade unions and the socialists, eventually brought dividends. In 1899 the TUC passed a resolution at its Plymouth conference calling for delegates from the trade unions, the socialist groups and the co-operative societies to meet to consider the issue of labour representation. The meeting, held in London in February 1900, and involving all the invited groups apart from the Co-operative Union, created the LRC. The latter was charged with the establishment in parliament of 'a distinct Labour Group . . . who shall have their own Whips and agree upon their policy', but who would also 'embrace a readiness to co-operate with any party which, for the time being, may be engaged in promoting legislation in the direct interest of labour'. In addition, the Group would be 'equally ready to associate themselves with any party in opposing measures having an opposite tendency'.[12]

In placing independent labour politics once again upon the agenda of British politics and in so departing, at least potentially, from total reliance upon the two main parties to represent the interests of the labour movement in parliament, the LRC and its 1906 successor, the Labour Party, effected an important break in British political history. However, as is well documented, the strength, progress and appeal of independent labour politics up to the time of World War One were limited and uneven.

For example, the new organisation was 'tiny'. Only forty-one unions, with a total of 353,070 members, were affiliated to the LRC at its formation. This represented only 17.4 per cent of the total union membership. The most notable outsider was the 'Lib-Lab' Miners' Federation of Great Britain, which switched its allegiance to Labour only in 1908.[13] To be sure, union-affiliated membership of the LRC rose to 861,000 in 1903, while the Labour Party benefited from the impressive increase in trade union membership from around 2.5 million in 1910 to 4.1 million by 1914. By 1915 the vast majority of the party's 2.1 million members (a massive advance upon the 1.4 million of 1910) were affiliated by the unions. The reversal of the 1909 Osborne judgment by means of the 1913 Trade Union Act signified that unions were once again free to provide financial support to the Labour Party. As a consequence the BLP's finances were placed on a firmer footing and new full-time party agents and officers were appointed, mainly at the national level. Yet many unions remained opposed to the 'socialism' of Labour, including the 45 and 40 per cent of miners' union members who voted respectively against affiliation in 1908 and the creation of a political levy to support the Labour Party in 1913.[14]

In the 1900 general election the LRC ran fifteen parliamentary candidates, two of whom, Keir Hardie, the former miner, and Richard

Bell of the Amalgamated Society of Railway Servants, were successful. Although Bell 'moved steadily towards the Liberals, and effectively abandoned the LRC in 1904', the LRC performed well at the next general election in 1906, endorsing fifty candidates and seeing twenty-nine returned to parliament. This performance, hailed by the *Labour Leader* as a 'triumph' and the *Clarion* as a 'revolution', resulted mainly from the fact that Ramsay MacDonald had entered into a secret pact with the Liberals in 1903 in an attempt to minimise direct electoral conflict between the two parties. In the 1906 contest only five Labour seats were gained against Liberal opposition. Labour's successes were most marked in Lancashire constituencies, followed by Yorkshire, the North-East, the London area, Scotland and Wales.[15]

At the general elections of January and December 1910 forty out of seventy-eight and forty-two out of sixty-two Labour candidates were returned respectively. While these figures represented an improvement upon the 1906 result, they did not occasion much rejoicing or keen anticipation of major advances in the immediate future. The return of forty Labour MPs in January 1910 'represented a net loss of five seats on its pre-dissolution strength'. Moreover, 'Labour had little to say that was distinctive from the Liberals' and once again had benefited significantly from the deal with the Liberals to avoid three-way contests.

Labour lost four seats in by-elections between the end of 1910 and 1914. Its performance in local elections, however, was more encouraging. Benefiting from a more extensive local government franchise, Labour made 'a net gain of seats' in 'every year between 1909 and 1913'. The 171 seats gained locally in 1913 contrasted markedly with the 91 won in 1906. Once again the party's main strength was in Lancashire and Yorkshire.[16]

In addition, Labour improved its organisation and strategy, won control of many trades councils across the country and, notwithstanding the widespread nature of patriarchal attitudes and practices within its ranks, made some attempt more fully to involve women in its constituent organisations. Women often played an important part in the socialist societies, in which they enjoyed full membership, while the Women's Labour League acted as an auxiliary of the Labour Party. The latter cooperated with the moderate National Union of Women's Suffrage Societies in pursuit of the demand that women would necessarily be included in a widened suffrage.[17]

On balance, the cause of independent labour politics made undeniable, but limited and uneven, advances in Britain between 1900 and 1914. The Labour Party was a new and partly independent force in British politics and society. By the end of the period it had established a strong base in the trade unions, was improving its organisation and was making an effort to appeal to women. It sought to become the 'natural' party of working-class communities. However, results were limited and mixed. In terms of the national scene, the Progressive Alliance between Labour and the Liberals generally maintained itself, with Labour continuing to play a minor role. On the eve of World War One there was no sign that Labour was about to replace the Liberals and become the main alternative to the Conservatives. In the country it remained very weak in rural areas and its most striking gains in the major urban centres would await the post-war years.[18] It had, however, established a firm industrial base in some parts of the country, especially in Lancashire and Yorkshire, and a tangible, if limited, parliamentary presence.

During the period of mass industrial conflict between 1911 and 1914 some within the movement became frustrated with the limited performance of parliamentary gradualism and advocated a resort to more 'direct' forms of action, especially at the point of production. Yet the Labour Party gave no appearance of being about to go into decline or disappear from the political map. While in 1914 its future progress seemed likely to be 'slow and piecemeal', it had undoubtedly become, in the face of Liberal and Conservative opposition, the main representative of the organised labour movement. Its refusal to adopt an explicitly socialist position, especially one rooted in the notion of 'class warfare', had led to the disaffiliation of the SDF from the LRC as early as 1901 and widespread socialist frustration. However, in many ways its 'labourist' mixture of eclecticism, empiricism and pragmatism were more in touch with the daily realities of working-class life than 'intellectual', 'middle-class' socialism. Finally, its continued presence signified that both 'new' and 'old' Liberalism had failed to prevent the 'rise of Labour' and that the future domination of Liberalism and subordination of Labour could not be taken for granted.[19]

The creation and limited development of the BLP were keenly observed by the Australian labour movement. While criticising the 'knock-kneed and wavering' stance of the Liberal Party towards the South African War, the socialist *Worker*, the 'Official Journal of the Federated Workers of Queensland', warmly welcomed the establishment of the LRC and Labour's participation in the general elections of 1900, 1906 and 1910.[20] The fact that the majority of LRC and Labour Party candidates were unsuccessful was to be expected. The election results were 'simply a commentary on British social and political conditions'. While the more extensive support given by the trade unions to Labour candidates was perceived to underpin the party's growing strength and influence, differences and divisions among 'old' and 'new' trade unionists, trade unionists and socialists, and socialists themselves, were highlighted as being indicative of a divided British working class and its 'imperfect development of class consciousness'.[21] Attention was also drawn to the continuing powers of conservatism, property, inequality and the limited nature of political democracy in the 'old country'. In contrast, the earlier and more extensive achievement of democracy in Australia – manhood suffrage in the 1850s, full adult suffrage in 1902 and 1909 for national and state elections respectively, payment of MPs in all colonies except Western Australia by the late 1880s[22] – combined with higher living standards, fewer established class barriers and more socio-economic opportunities for 'ordinary' men and women,[23] were held to be largely responsible for the more 'advanced' state of independent labour politics, the labour movement and the wider working class in Australia.[24]

Notions of English and British 'conservatism', 'slow movement' and 'backwardness', as compared with Australia's 'progressivism' and 'rapid advancement' to a leading, and perhaps *the* leading, position in the international labour movement stakes, became increasingly widespread among Australian activists between 1900 and 1914. This was the case not only in the eastern and southern states but also in the newly expanding 'frontier' areas of the West. For example, the *Westralian Worker*, the main organ of organised labour in the western goldfields, commercial centres and ports, explained the lack of working-class parliamentary representation in Britain in terms of the powerful influences of tradition, resignation and working-class 'blindness' as to its 'true' interests.[25] In 1894 a Western Australian socialist, Claude Thompson, who worked with 'Clarionettes' in the Manchester region of England, recorded his dismay at Lancashire workers' Liberalism and Conservatism, and their general indifference, indeed 'hopelessness', towards to socialist and independent labour politics.[26] Yet, as noted earlier, Lancashire was more responsive to the appeals of the LRC and the Labour Party than most other areas of Britain. The main hope for the British and other less 'advanced' labour movements was seen by Australian activists to lie in economic determinism: the further development of capitalism would inevitably, if unevenly, lead to the global spread and eventual triumph of class consciousness and socialism.[27]

Chronology: Australia

Australian cockiness towards Britain, of course, was in many respects justified. As briefly indicated earlier, it was, to use Stuart Macintyre's term, the very 'precocity' of its growth and impact between the late 1890s and the time of World War One that underpinned its self-confidence and most impressed the numerous foreign visitors and observers of the Australian labour movement. As Macintyre notes, 'Continental socialists could trace a lineage of more than half a century for their workers' parties and yet they remained on the margin of politics; in Australia Labor had achieved office while still in its adolescence.'[28]

A political movement for democracy, involving 'popular sovereignty as a feature of representative government' and led by 'radical intellectuals', had emerged among the labouring people and the 'middling sort' of professionals, trades people, publicans and shopkeepers in New South Wales at mid century.[29] This did not, however, become the kind of mass, nationally based movement characterised by Chartism in Britain. From mid century onwards, the trade unions, the main organisations of the Australian labour movement, lobbied politicians, factions and the fledgling parties and made political alliances to further their legislative goals. It was during the 1890s and the early 1900s that the crucial developments in the field of independent labour politics took place. Labor parties emerged and developed rapidly in some of the colonies during the 1890s. Following the New Commonwealth's first federal election, in March 1901, and the return of twenty-four Labor candidates, the ALP was formally established as 'a federation of the pre-existing state organizations'.[30]

New South Wales led the way at the state level. Formed in 1891 by the Trades and Labour Council, the New South Wales Labor Party had become by the turn of the century 'one of the major political forces' in the colony and the most important formative influence upon the ALP in terms of internal party discipline and its 'synthesis' of the policies of arbitration, White Australia, the old-age pension and support for smallholders.[31] Between 1898 and 1910 Labor increased its vote in New South Wales from 11.4 per cent to 48.9 per cent. The following seven years saw the ALP in power in the state for an extremely impressive total of six years and two months.[32]

During the 1890s Queensland promised much. Established in 1890, the Labor Party in Queensland 'achieved the first Labor government in the world in 1899, albeit a minority one lasting less than a week'. Although 'close to political power' in 1910, the Queensland ALP failed to maintain its early performance. Beset by internal splits and divisions over its commitment to socialism and the question of political independence versus a Lib-Lab alliance, the party did not attain state office until 1915. However, underpinned by strong support from the mainly rural-based Australian Workers' Union (AWU), miners and others among the rural and urban 'producing classes', the Queensland ALP became more united and held state office continuously from 1915 to 1929.[33]

During the 1890s Labor in Victoria and South Australia 'existed only under the wing of Protectionist liberals, while in Western Australia there was a purely trade union organisation and in Tasmania no organization at all'.[34] In Victoria the strength of the Lib-Lab tradition and its key concern with good relations between 'fair' masters and men, combined with the Labor's weaknesses in rural areas and the debilitating effect of conflicts between Catholics and Protestants upon the party's appeal, ensured that 'the Labor Party's journey to political independence was long and troubled', according to Frank Bongiorno.[35] Before 1924 Labor held office in Victoria for a miserly total of two weeks, in 1913.[36] In South Australia the party's successful expansion of its base from Adelaide to some of the predominantly rural areas of the state ensured that it did not suffer the same fate. In its two periods of office in pre-1915 South Australia, from 1905 to 1909 and from 1910 to 1912, the ALP enjoyed power for a combined total of almost five and a half years. Moreover, it was the ruling political force in that state between 1915 and 1917.[37]

In the new and booming state of Western Australia the growth of trade unionism on the goldfields was crucial to the birth and development of Labor. The latter's electoral fortunes fluctuated during the first decade of the new century, accession to office in 1904 being followed by six years out in the cold. Between 1911 and 1916, however, Labor governed Western Australia for almost five years.[38] Finally, in Tasmania the weakness of trade unionism and the fact that male suffrage was introduced as late as 1901 ensured that the Labor Party's growth was 'slow and uneven': Labor held power there for just over two years between 1909 and 1916.[39]

Labor's progress in the states, therefore, was impressive. By 1911 it held 'nearly half the seats in the six state lower houses, and held power in New South Wales, South Australia and Western Australia'. By 1915 there had been 'a Labor government in every state'.[40]

Yet this considerable feat was surpassed by Labor's spectacular performance at the federal level. The first year in the life of the New Commonwealth saw not only the unexpected return of twenty-four Labor candidates to the first federal parliament and the establishment of the federal ALP, but also Labor holding the balance of power between the Protectionists and the Freetraders. Between 1901 and 1903 the ALP usually gave its support to the protectionist governments of Sir Edmund Barton and Alfred Deakin. After the 1903 election, however, Labor was responsible for the defeat of the Deakin government in a division on the Arbitration Bill. Deakin would not accept Labor's successful amendment that state employees, in the form of railway workers, be brought under the jurisdiction of the proposed federal

Arbitration Court, and resigned in April 1904. The ensuing election resulted in a historic victory for the ALP, the 'first workers' party anywhere in the world to form a national government', albeit a minority one.[41] John Christian Watson, 'a grave and cautious' compositor turned journalist, and 'a man of education and high repute, with a valuable name for honesty', 'constructive' thought, and 'sound finance',[42] became the first Labor Prime Minister. Watson's firmness, pragmatism and moderation allayed mainstream press and establishment fears that he would be unable to control Labor's more 'extreme' and 'revolutionary' elements who would ruinously put 'class before country'.[43]

From the other side of the world the ILP's *Labour Leader* ran an interview with C.H. Chomley, a Free Trader and former editor of the *Beacon*, a Single Tax monthly in Victoria, in order to enlighten its readership about Australian politics and the new Labor government. Chomley insisted upon the moderation of not only Watson, but also his parliamentary Labor colleagues. He also maintained that, as 'traditional Englishmen', Australians were practical rather than theoretical beings. 'Practically', he concluded, 'we are the most Socialistic country there is; but theoretically we do not hold Socialist opinions. We socialise as we go along.'[44]

The liberal *Manchester Guardian*, the conservative *Times* and the revolutionary Marxist *Justice* (the main organ of the SDF), also agreed that Watson and most of his colleagues at the federal level did not pose a fundamental threat to capitalism.[45] In contrast to the *Guardian* and *The Times*, however, *Justice* opposed the ALP's accession to minority federal office as leading necessarily to limited and temporary gains, combined with demoralising and counter-productive compromises, disappointments, defeats and obeisance to capitalist rule. Following Kautsky, *Justice* advised socialist and Labour parties to forego short-term parliamentary gain for the longer-term achievement of 'real' power on the ground and the revolutionary transition to socialism.[46]

The government lasted only four months when Deakin allowed Labor to fall on a clause in the Arbitration Bill dealing with preference to trade unionists. In contrast to *Justice*, the socialist *Worker* maintained that Labor was right to assume federal office, however briefly. The latter provided invaluable practical experience of government and, above all, demonstrated both Labor's impressive *independent* strength and 'its right to the throne'. Conversely, coalition rule was to be avoided as a sign of weakness.[47] The downfall of the Watson ministry was 'not an event greatly to grieve about': Labor should henceforth bide its time in opposition until it could reasonably expect to achieve majority rule.[48]

George Reid, the leading Freetrader and anti-socialist, then served for eight months until he was defeated by the combined forces of

Labor and the Protectionists. Deakin once again assumed office and his second ministry, generally supported by Labor, lasted from June 1905 to November 1908. As Macintyre observes, this was 'the Indian summer of Protectionist liberalism', focused as Deakin's government was upon the achievement of social and economic justice and fairness by means of 'old-age pensions, anti-monopoly legislation, higher tariffs and accompanying legislation intended to guarantee domestic living standards'.[49] Yet, in some ways similar to the growing tensions within Lib-Labism in parts of Britain, it became increasingly obvious that Labor was demanding more, in terms of collectivism and state regulation – 'extending federal powers, strengthening the Arbitration court and regulating living standards'[50] – than the progressivism of Deakin would allow.

When Deakin's government was dismissed in November 1908, Andrew Fisher became the second Labor prime minister of a minority government. Both Hardie and Ramsay Macdonald wrote to congratulate Fisher.[51] The Labor government lasted until June 1909, when it was defeated by the newly created Fusion Party of Deakin and the Anti-Socialists, the erstwhile Freetraders.[52] Deakin took office for the third time and Labor went into opposition for the remainder of the parliamentary session.

In the election of April 1910, however, Labor secured its second and even more historic federal victory. This time it secured a majority in both Houses, an unprecedented feat in the New Commonwealth and the world, for a social-democratic party.

Labor enjoyed federal office until 1913, 'a period of reform unmatched in the Commonwealth until the 1940s'.[53] Having lost by one seat in 1913, the ALP secured a handsome victory in 1914. In October 1915 Fisher resigned as leader, largely on health grounds, and William Morris Hughes became prime minister. During 1915 and 1916 the ALP was afflicted by serious internal differences and conflicts concerning the 'imperialist war', the harsh effects of the War Precautions Act upon radicals and revolutionaries and, above all else, the issue of conscription for overseas military service. Matters came to a head in December 1916, when most of the pro-conscription forces within the ALP, including Hughes, were expelled from the party. In the previous month Hughes had led his supporters out of the Caucus room and formed an interim ministry. He then joined conservative anti-Labor forces to form and lead the Nationalist 'Win-the-War' Party. Having failed to achieve a majority in the Senate, Hughes called an election for May 1917, in which Labor was defeated.[54]

Despite its mounting problems during wartime, the irreparable split over conscription and the loss of office at the end of 1916, the ALP had performed extremely well at the federal level in its first fifteen years of existence. Minority office had been achieved within three years of its formation and majority power within nine. Labor's vote had risen markedly, from 19.24 per cent in 1901, 30.95 per cent in 1903, 36.64 per cent in 1906 to the remarkable 49.97 per cent in 1910.[55] Between 1910 and 1916 Labor enjoyed almost five and a half years of federal rule. By 1910 'Australian Labor had progressed far ahead of all equivalent parties anywhere'.[56] By the end of the war Australians lived in 'the most unionised country in the world, and in the only country where the Labor party had formed majority governments'.[57] The party's seemingly inexorable march to power had also forced a fundamental realignment in domestic politics. From 1909 to World War One previously antagonistic Free Traders and Protectionists combined as 'Fusionists' to wage mainly unsuccessful electoral war in the defence of property, 'choice' and 'individualism' against the 'collectivist tyranny' and 'socialist' threat of ascendant independent Labor.[58]

As in 1904, the ALP's striking progress between the later years of the first decade of the twentieth century and World War One was closely observed and commented upon both at home and abroad. For many advocates of independent labour politics the ALP and its 'Forward March' served as a beacon to the rest of the world. In the eyes of Andrew Fisher and his colleagues, European, British and American labourites and socialists could all learn much from the 'Australian way'.[59] The *Worker* believed that the victory of 1910 was 'without parallel in the history of the working class'. Moreover, given necessary attention to organisation, education and policy – 'freeing the soil to the people', nationalising monopolies, improving living standards and broadening the party's appeal to more women and the 'great unattached army of workers' – Labor's and Australia's achievement of the Co-operative Commonwealth was seen, by the *Worker*, as more or less inevitable.[60] The main voice of radical nationalism in Australia, the *Bulletin*, was similarly enthused by the 1910 election result: 'Between them, Labor and Australia last week won the most brilliant victory that has been recorded since the flag of the Commonwealth waved over a united nation.' The 'Fusionists', including Deakin, had 'sold themselves' to the 'Little Australians', the 'old, resurrected anti-Federal crowd' whose primary, 'parish pump' allegiance was to the states rather than the Commonwealth. As a result, Deakin and Cook had 'stupidly' thrown 'the Australian Nationalists and the Labor Party into one army'.[61] In contrast, the conservative *Australasian*, a fierce defender of 'states' rights' and opposed to Labor's attempts to give more power to the Commonwealth government, dreaded the prospect of a Labor government which would put 'class' and 'machine politics' before 'country' and 'democracy'.[62]

Many British observers and visitors were fascinated by, and many impressed with, Labor's achievements. At the mainstream level both the *Manchester Guardian* and *The Times* recognised that the ALP was becoming a powerful political force in Australia. The former saw the ALP's triumph at the polls in 1910 as an inspiration to labour elsewhere in the British Empire.[63] The latter, much in the manner of the *Australasian*, exhorted Fisher to ignore the 'many members' in his party who looked to the development of the powers of the Commonwealth as a means to 'class-despotism' rather than to 'impartial State initiative and national advance'.[64]

British labour movement responses were overwhelmingly positive. The Webbs, who visited New Zealand and Australia in 1898, constituted the predictable exception. In the patronising manner of 'core metropolitans', they branded the Australian working-class 'colonials' of Sydney as being mainly 'uncivilised' 'backward' and 'largely non-political'.[65] Yet the dominant response was that the ALP, in organisation and outlook, constituted, apart from its protectionism, 'an inspiration' for the BLP.[66] The latter sent messages of congratulation to Fisher upon his short-lived electoral success of 1908–9 and the 'magnificent results' in 1910. Following his visit to Australia, as part of his 'world tour' of 1907–8, Keir Hardie was 'certain' that 'Australasia [*sic*] will be the first country in the world to come under the rule of the working class'.[67] Ramsay MacDonald congratulated Fisher on a 'glorious victory' and eulogised Australia as 'the hope of the coming democracy', while Margaret MacDonald was extremely proud of the fact that many of Australia's victorious labour leaders, at both the federal and state level, had served their formative years in Britain and the British movement and were still on personal terms with activists 'back home'.[68] The *Clarion* saw the Australian 'Socialist' victory of 1910 as marking 'a new fact in the world's history, and one which is certain to be felt in the Old as in the New World'.[69] Even many of those to the left of the Labour Party who were critical of 'labourism' and 'parliamentary gradualism' echoed Tom Mann's view that the causes of labour and socialism were more advanced in Australia than in most of the countries of the world and provided a 'start' or 'platform' for future socialist transformation.[70]

Constituencies

In both Australia and Britain the essential strength of the emergent Labour parties was rooted in the trade unions. Despite the often considerable setbacks of the depressed 1890s, both 'old' and 'new' unionism made considerable headway in Australia and Britain from the later nineteenth century to the immediate post-World War One years. In Britain, the pioneer and 'true home' of trade unionism, total union membership increased from 1,576,000 in 1891 to just over 2 million in 1900, to 4,145,000 in 1914, and then more than doubled to 8,348,000 in 1920. These figures represented increases in trade union density from 10.6 per cent, to 12.7 per cent, to 23 per cent and 45.2 per cent respectively.[71] In Australia there were an estimated 55,900 trade unionists in 1891. This number increased to 97,200 in 1901, about 9 per cent union density, to 302,100 in 1910 and to a remarkable 523,000 by 1914. By the latter date union density in Australia was 33 per cent, as against Britain's 23 per cent. Further evidence that Australia had overtaken Britain as the trade union capital of the world was provided in 1919, when Australia's union density stood at 50 per cent, in contrast to Britain's 43 per cent.[72]

The introduction of the system of compulsory arbitration, one of the pillars of the New Commonwealth, undoubtedly acted as a stimulus to trade union growth in Australia during this period. Compulsory arbitration involved the formal registration of unions with the arbitration courts at the state and federal levels. This amounted to *de facto* state recognition of unions in Australia, whereas in 'voluntarist' Britain union recognition was heavily dependent upon the nature of and fluctuations in market conditions and bargaining power. Compulsory arbitration also facilitated the development of 'new' unions. For example, the shearer-dominated 'new' union, the Australian Workers' Union, rapidly became the wealthiest and most powerful union in the country.

The two other pillars of the New Commonwealth, 'White Australia' and 'New Protection', also increased the potential strength of trade unionism. The former restricted the supply of 'cheap' labour in the market and so, at least in theory, drove up the price of available labour. Significantly, the unions were among the foremost champions of 'White Australia'. Deakin designed 'New Protection' to guarantee a 'living wage' to those workers, increasingly unionised and overwhelmingly male heads of families, who were employed by 'fair employers'. In return the latter would be exempted from the payment of an excise duty on local products. Although an appeal to the High Court resulted in the imposition of this duty being declared beyond the powers of the Commonwealth and therefore unconstitutional, the practice of protection, 'of basing a minimum wage on the cost of living', would become 'generally accepted' in Australia by the 1920s.[73]

Two important differences should be highlighted in terms of the union–party connection in Australia and Britain. First, the system of political parties was far more established in Britain than in Australia. Second, notwithstanding the continuing strength of Lib-Labism in

Victoria, union attachments to the mainstream parties were much stronger in Britain. Like the BLP, the ALP was largely the progeny of the unions. Unlike the BLP, however, the ALP had a much greater opportunity to become the unrivalled political voice of more or less the entire union movement at a very early stage in its development.

This, in fact, is what happened. Despite the existence of a formal 'no politics' rule among the Amalgamated Society of Engineers and other, largely British-inspired, craft and skilled unions in Australia, *both* the 'old' and 'new' Australian unions provided early and over-whelming support for the ALP. As a result there developed extremely close links between the industrial and political arms of labour in Australia: the movement enjoyed 'an enviable degree of solidarity and unity of purpose'. The persistence of union and working-class allegiances to Liberalism and Conservatism, as noted above, meant that both these links and labour movement unity were weaker in Britain.[74]

Like the BLP, the ALP attempted to appeal not only to its core constituency in the unions, but also to other male and female work-ers, small producers and the 'middling' sections of the middle class. The continuing, albeit uneven, strength of popular Liberalism and popular Conservatism, the scarcity of constituency Labour parties with individual membership, the restricted nature of the franchise, the male-dominated character and structures of the BLP and its weakness in most rural areas, as indicated above, severely limited its wider appeal before 1918.

In Australia male trade union domination of the political movement was equally strong. In addition the ALP had a wider social appeal than the BLP. It prided itself, along with its predecessors in the states, upon 'leading the way in demands for the enfranchisement of womanhood in Australia'.[75] Unlike the BLP, the ALP also built up a strong rural constituency. The proportion of the labour force engaged in agriculture around 1900 stood at 8 per cent in Britain and 16 per cent in Australia. Many of those so engaged in Australia were rural workers, small farm-ers and other petty rural producers. The ALP in Queensland and some of the other states derived much of its 'populist' and 'producerist' character from the fact that it made a successful appeal to these rural dwellers. It sought the allegiance of 'all workers – primary producers as well as wage earners' – on the basis of its demands for improved wages and access to land, improved marketing and transport facilities, and curbs, especially by means of taxation, on the powers of the large rural leaseholders, the 'squattocracy'.[76]

As in Britain, socialists were heavily involved in labour politics in Australia, especially as leaders, propagandists and organisers. In both countries, however, socialism in this period remained a minority force, subordinated to the pragmatism and eclecticism of the BLP's and the ALP's ruling common sense.[77] While both parties could draw on an exceptional range and depth of able and committed leaders, both the ALP and the Australian unions were particularly fortunate in recruiting their leaders from a wide pool of very experienced 'old hands', many of whom had 'served their time' in Britain, and native-born 'youngsters', mainly men in their twenties, who were energetic, quick to learn and highly mobile.[78]

Impact

While trade unionism was afforded a recognised place in the system of compulsory arbitration, the labour movement as a whole and its core working-class constituency achieved unprecedented levels of influence and power in the early life of the New Commonwealth. The formation of the latter represented an attempt to overcome the fierce industrial and class conflicts of the 1890s by means of a process of national reconciliation or 'settlement' between the main socio-economic and political forces of the day, capital, including rural capital, and labour, 'rather than the "triumph" of the one over the other'.[79] The key elements of the new system, 'new protection', social welfare provision, with the old-age pension at its core, arbitration and 'White Australia', both reflected the compromise between capital and labour and were designed to promote social stability, consensus and common national purpose. From the very birth of the New Commonwealth, therefore, the labour movement attained major importance as a key player in this process of national reconciliation and in shaping the future of the 'new' nation. The rapid advancement of both the ALP and trade unions between 1901 and 1914 further strengthened organised labour's standing and influence within the national community.

In contrast to the view of some historians that labour was being 'incorporated' into the 'system' as a subordinate force,[80] many contemporaries echoed the sentiment, expressed in 1909 by W.G. Spence, veteran unionist, leading figure in the AWU and a visionary socialist, that 'the Labor Movement has now become an almost dominant factor in the political life of the community'.[81] For example, in 1914 one of labour's fierce critics, C.E. Jacomb, an 'Old Harrovian' who had worked as a fruit grower for six years in Victoria, drew his readers' attention to the 'extraordinary position' achieved by Labour [sic] in 'God's Own Country', and the 'abundance' of socialist demagogues and agitators there. Jacomb concluded that in Australia the 'working man' ruled 'supreme'.[82]

Acutely aware of its importance and growing power within the New Commonwealth, the ALP made a conscious and determined attempt to present itself to the electorate as *the* party of the progressive nation as well as representing the 'white' working class and 'producers'. Far from restricting or 'closing down' its chosen options to the course of narrow 'labourism', concerned wholly or predominantly with the sectional and immediate concerns of trade unionism, the federal ALP set itself up as a transforming and potentially hegemonic force within Australian society as a whole.[83]

We will see the full significance of this transforming vision of 'the national', complete with its practical limits and setbacks, to Labor's electoral performance in the next chapter. At this juncture it is sufficient to note that from the outset the ALP set out to cultivate 'an Australian sentiment' or 'true' 'Australianism' rooted in the creation of a democratic and egalitarian 'new world' society. While maintaining a position within the Empire, this independent, 'enlightened' and 'self-reliant' 'new Australia' would totally reject 'the spirit of the old Crown Colony days, with its utter subservience to and dependence on Downing Street'.[84] In contrast, many of Labor's political enemies were depicted as 'plutocratic Imperialists' who were 'scheming to deprive Australia of its self-governing powers . . . and render it subservient to a ruling class of capitalists and militarists twelve thousand miles away'.[85]

In Britain the situation was quite different. Although growing in numbers and influence, the labour movement remained very much a subordinate part of 'old world' British society and its empire. It was a junior 'estate' of a realm in which the landed interests still exercised formal governmental control in the interests of a hierarchical social order rooted in 'natural' inequality and privilege, paternalism and deference, and opposition to full-blown democracy. Labour sought a more democratic, open and just society, but, unlike the ALP, it was not a serious contender for political and social power. For the most part it adopted a more narrowly corporate, sectional and insular approach than its Australian counterpart.

Notes

1 Dorothy Thompson, *The Chartists: Popular Politics in the Industrial Revolution* (Aldershot: Wildwood House, 1986).
2 Thorpe, *History of the British Labour Party*, p. 22; Kirk, *Change, Continuity and Class*, ch. 8.
3 Kirk, *Change, Continuity and Class*, ch. 8; Kenefick, *Red Scotland!* pp. 13–15; Patrick Joyce, *Work, Society and Politics: The Culture of the Factory in Later Victorian England* (Brighton: Harvester Press, 1980), chs 8, 9.
4 Gordon Phillips, *The Rise of the Labour Party 1893–1931* (London: Routledge, 1992), p. 3.
5 June Hannam and Karen Hunt, *Socialist Women: Britain 1880s to 1920s* (London: Routledge, 2002), ch. 1, pp. 126–8.

6 Ross McKibbin, 'Why was there no Marxism in Britain?', in his *Ideologies of Class*, p. 11; Kirk, *Change, Continuity and Class*, chs 8, 9.
7 Eric Hobsbawm, 'The "New Unionism" in Perspective', in his *Worlds of Labour*, p. 154; John Barnes, *Socialist Champion: Portrait of the Gentleman as Crusader* (Melbourne: Australian Scholarly Publishing, 2006), chs 4–7.
8 Phillips, *Rise of the Labour Party*, p. 6. Kenefick (*Red Scotland!*, p. 75) notes that from the mid 1890s the ILP was 'the leading political organisation associated with the trade union and labour movement in Scotland, with a combined membership greater than . . . the other socialist societies . . . put together'. David Howell's *British Workers and the Independent Labour Party 1888–1906* (Manchester: Manchester University Press, 1984) remains the seminal work on the early ILP.
9 Thorpe, *History of the British Labour Party*, p. 13.
10 *Ibid.*, p. 11.
11 McKibbin, 'Why was there no Marxism', pp. 32–6.
12 Kirk, *Change, Continuity and Class*, p. 287 (Document 14: *Report of the Conference on Labour Representation*).
13 Thorpe, *History of the British Labour Party*, p. 13.
14 Phillips, *Rise of the Labour Party*, p. 23; Kirk, *Labour and Society in Britain and the USA*, vol. 2, *Challenge and Accommodation 1850–1939* (Aldershot: Scolar Press, 1994), p. 243; E.H. Hunt, *British Labour History 1815–1914* (London: Weidenfeld and Nicolson, 1988), pp. 295–6.
15 *Labour Leader*, 19, 26 January, 2 February 1906; *Justice*, 27 January 1906; *Clarion*, 26 January 1906; Phillips, *Rise of the Labour Party*, pp. viii–ix, ch. 3; Thorpe, *History of the British Labour Party*, pp. 14–19; Kenefick, *Red Scotland*, p. 79; Eddie May, 'The Mosaic of Labour Politics, 1900–1918', in Tanner, Williams, Hopkin (eds), *Labour Party in Wales*.
16 Thorpe, *History of the British Labour Party*, pp. 23–5; Phillips, *Rise of the Labour Party*, ch. 5.
17 Hannam and Hunt, *Socialist Women*, ch. 5; Pamela M. Graves, *Labour Women: Women in British Working-Class Politics 1918–1939* (Cambridge: Cambridge University Press, 1994), ch. 1.
18 *Manchester Region History Review*, special issue, *100 Years of Labour 1900–2000*, XIV (2000); Duncan Tanner, *Political Change and the Labour Party 1900–1918* (Cambridge: Cambridge University Press, 1990), Part II; Duncan Tanner, 'The Pattern of Labour Politics, 1918–1939', in Tanner, Williams and Hopkin (eds), *Labour Party in Wales*; Lawrence, *Speaking for the People*, Part II, ch. 9.
19 Kirk, *Change, Continuity and Class*, pp. 196–7.
20 *Worker*, 29 September, 6 October 1900, 20 January, 3 February 1906, 5 February 1910.
21 *Worker*, 29 September 1900, 5 February 1910.
22 James and Markey, 'Class and Labour', 24.
23 Kirk, *Comrades and Cousins*, ch. 2.
24 *Worker*, 20 January 1906.
25 Kirk, *Comrades and Cousins*, pp. 107–8.
26 *Ibid.*, p. 107.
27 *Worker*, 5 February 1910.
28 Macintyre, *Oxford History*, p. 87. See also George E. Boxall, 'Labour in Australia and Britain: A Contrast', *Labour Leader*, 26 January 1906.
29 Terry Irving, *The Southern Tree of Liberty: The Democratic Movement in New South Wales before 1856* (Sydney: The Federation Press, 2006).
30 Macintyre, *Oxford History*, pp. 85–6, 348 (n. 27).
31 Markey, *Making of the Labor Party in New South Wales*, p. 2, ch. 6.
32 James and Markey, 'Class and Labour', 25; Kirk, *Comrades and Cousins*, pp. 103–4.
33 Kirk, *Comrades and Cousins*, p. 103; James and Markey, 'Class and Labour', 25–6.
34 Macintyre, *Oxford History*, pp. 85–6.
35 Bongiorno, *People's Party*, pp. 22, 29.

36 James and Markey, 'Class and Labour', 25.
37 Kirk, *Comrades and Cousins*, p. 104; James and Markey, 'Class and Labour', 25.
38 Kirk, *Comrades and Cousins*, pp. 104–5; James and Markey, 'Class and Labour', 25.
39 Kirk, *Comrades and Cousins*, p. 105; James and Markey, 'Class and Labour', 25; Patmore, *Australian Labour History*, pp. 79–80.
40 Macintyre, *Oxford History*, pp. 86, 95.
41 Kim Beazley, 'Foreword' to Faulkner and Macintyre (eds), *True Believers*, p. xxi.
42 *Bulletin*, 28 April 1904.
43 *Australasian*, 30 April 1904, 16 April 1910.
44 *Labour Leader*, 6 May 1904. For a useful study of Single Taxers with reference to the American Pacific North West see Lawrence M. Lipin, *Workers and the Wild: Conservation Consumerism and Labor in Oregon 1910–30* (Urbana: University of Illinois Press, 2007).
45 *Manchester Guardian*, 25 April 1904; *The Times*, 27 April 1904; *Justice*, 14 May 1904.
46 *Justice*, 14, 21 May 1904.
47 *Worker*, 30 April 1904.
48 *Ibid.*, 20 August 1904.
49 Macintyre, *Oxford History*, pp. 91–2.
50 *Ibid.*, p. 92; Nick Dyrenfurth, '"Vote down the Conspiracy": Labor's View of Fusion', ch. 3, Stuart Macintyre, 'Whatever Happened to Deakinite Liberalism?', ch. 8, in Paul Strangio and Nick Dyrenfurth (eds), *Confusion: The Making of the Australian Two-Party System* (Carlton: Melbourne University Press, 2009).
51 Murphy, 'Fisher, Andrew'.
52 *Worker*, 20, 27 May, 3, 17 June 1909.
53 Murphy, 'Fisher, Andrew', p. 505; Patrick Weller (ed.), *Caucus Minutes 1901–1949: Minutes of the Meetings of the Federal Parliamentary Labor Party*, vol. 1, *1901–1917* (Carlton: Melbourne University Press, 1975), pp. 252–3.
54 Macintyre, *Oxford History*, pp. 167–8, 190.
55 Brett, *Australian Liberals*, p. 19.
56 Ross McMullin, 'Leading the World: 1901–16', in Faulkner and Macintyre (eds), *True Believers*, p. 38.
57 Terry Irving, 'Early Views of Industrial Democracy: Australia, 1914–1921', unpublished paper, 2001, quoted in Kirk, *Comrades and Cousins*, p. 102.
58 Brett, *Australian Liberals*, pp. 20–7.
59 Kirk, *Comrades and Cousins*, p. 108.
60 *Worker*, 21, 28 April, 26 November 1910, 8, 15, 22 May, 5, 26 June 1913.
61 *Bulletin*, 21 April 1910.
62 *Australasian*, 16 April 1910.
63 *Manchester Guardian*, 14, 15 April 1910.
64 *The Times*, 16 April 1910.
65 Kirk, *Comrades and Cousins*, p. 107.
66 *Ibid.*, pp. 107–9; Stefan Berger, 'Labour in Comparative Perspective', in Tanner, Thane and Tiratsoo (eds), *Labour's First Century*, p. 313.
67 Kirk, *Comrades and Cousins*, pp. 109–10; *Manchester Guardian*, 18 April 1910.
68 Kirk, *Comrades and Cousins*, p. 109; *Manchester Guardian*, 15 April 1910. See also Ramsay MacDonald's and 'my wife's' 'heartiest congratulations' to Fisher in November 1908, Fisher Papers, NLA, Series 1, General Correspondence 1885–1940, 2919/1/42.
69 *Clarion*, 22 April 1910.
70 Kirk, *Comrades and Cousins*, p. 110; *Justice*, 23 April 1910 for Ben Tillett on the ALP's victory.
71 Kirk, *Challenge and Accommodation*, p. 65.
72 Kirk, *Comrades and Cousins*, p. 99.
73 *Ibid.*, pp. 98–9; Macintyre, *Oxford History*, pp. 103–4.
74 Kirk, *Comrades and Cousins*, p. 112.
75 See 'Foundation Day' in the *Worker*, 26 January 1927.

76 James and Markey, 'Class and Labour', 28–9; Macintyre, *Oxford History*, p. 87; Pamphlet no. 1, *Compare their Achievements*, and Pamphlet no. 22, *Producers Unite*, Queensland State Labor Party, in Election Pamphlets: ALP, Noel Butlin Archives, Australian National University, Canberra, P5/1/1099.

77 Macintyre, *Oxford History*, pp. 86–8; Thorpe, *History of the British Labour Party*, pp. 9–13.

78 Kirk, *Comrades and Cousins*, pp. 112–20; Stuart Macintyre, 'The First Caucus', in Faulkner and Macintyre (eds), *True Believers*, pp. 21–9; *Labour Leader*, 25 March 1910, 'Will Crooks on his Travels'.

79 Kirk, *Comrades and Cousins*, p. 120.

80 *Ibid.*, p. 121.

81 *Ibid.*

82 See C.E. Jacomb's ironically entitled, *"God's Own Country": An Appreciation of Australia* (London: Max Goschen, 1914), pp. 87–9.

83 Kirk, *Comrades and Cousins*, pp. 121–9; Scates, *New Australia*, pp. 3–11, 207–8.

84 *Worker*, 26 January 1927.

85 Kirk, '"Australians for Australia"', 102. For the view that the ALP 'has always been the most strongly nationalist' of Australia's 'major parties' and 'the most critical of the imperial connection and its implications', see Rawson, *Labor in Vain?*, pp. 4–5.

CHAPTER FOUR

Explanations and characteristics

Traditionalists and revisionists

As well documented by traditionalists and revisionists alike, a combination of domestic 'bread-and-butter' socio-economic, political and cultural factors played a very important role in persuading sections of Australian and British labour to jettison their 'traditional' political allegiances in favour of the adoption of independent labour politics.[1] The main purpose of this section is to provide the reader with a summary of these well-known factors rather than to recount them in full. In the following sections I will address my comparative British and Australian concerns with nation, empire, race and their connections with class, and integrate them into my explanatory framework.

The main concern of the chief protagonists in both countries, the trade unionists, rested with the serious defeats and setbacks inflicted upon them by employers and the state during the 1890s and early 1900s. In Australia the extremely bitter and unsuccessful 1890 Maritime Strike, the pastoral conflicts of the same year, and the profoundly adverse effects of the 1890s depression – the worst of the century, upon levels of employment, living standards and union membership – were instrumental in convincing many trade unionists that industrial activity would have to be supplemented by independent labour political action and more favourable legislation if their grievances were to be successfully resolved.[2]

Likewise in Britain the 1890s depression, the employers' 'counterattack' on trade unionism and legal assaults on the same institutions, culminating in the infamous Taff Vale judgment of 1901, combined with the perceived unwillingness of the established parties sufficiently to redress labour's wrongs and run working-class candidates, were key factors in labour's independent political 'turn'. In awarding strike damages to the Taff Vale Company against the Amalgamated Society of Railway Servants, the Taff Vale judgment was of landmark significance.

It established the principle of union 'agency', whereby unions became legally and financially liable for the actions of their members. As such, it overturned the Acts of 1871 and 1875 which, it was believed, had 'exempted unions from claims for damages'. It was widely seen within the movement as 'an attempt to crush out Trade Unionism by claims upon its funds'. The unintended effect was to galvanise more widespread union support for the LRC.[3]

The object of the LRC's 'Foundation Conference' was to secure 'A resolution in favour of working-class opinion being represented in the House of Commons by men sympathetic with the aims and demands of the Labour movement'.[4] The overwhelming consensus expressed at the annual conferences of the LRC between 1900 and 1905 was that such men should be, in the words of Keir Hardie, 'capable persons' and 'from their own ranks' rather than 'outsiders': they must teach the workers that if they desired social reforms, then 'they must send Social Reformers, not partisans of Liberalism or Toryism, to secure them'.[5] In the opinion of W.J. Davis, President of the Second Annual Conference, workers had suffered from too much 'class' legislation in a parliament 'dominated by the rich' and had sent 'too many landholders and capitalists' to represent them. It was now time to end that process. By means of both its own independent actions and pressure upon the mainstream parties, the LRC would bring about legislation designed to safeguard the position of the unions, to 'redress the grievances under which the workers suffered'[6] and to improve the living and working conditions of its wider, predominantly working-class, constituents.[7]

Both the ALP and the BLP attended first and foremost to the demands of the unions. In Britain, especially in the wake of Taff Vale, top priority was attached to the restoration of free collective bargaining and trade union immunity from legal damages. These objectives were successfully achieved in 1906 when a combination of self-interest and labour movement pressure saw the Liberal government introduce the Trade Disputes Act. This important piece of legislation 'finally restored the unions' right to strike, free from any fear of legal retribution'.[8] In 1908 the promised eight-hours bill for coalminers became law under the Liberals. In the following year, however, the House of Lords' Osborne judgment outlawed union financial contributions to political parties. The party survived this damaging blow, but 'in the short term, many local Labour parties collapsed and Labour candidates at the 1910 elections were desperately short of money'.[9] Fortunately, the potentially disastrous longer-term effects of the Osborne judgment did not materialise. In 1911 the Liberals' introduction of payment for MPs removed the financial burden of MPs' wages from union sponsors. Two years later the Trade Union Act went some way to negating

Osborne by declaring that while the unions would still not be allowed to make political donations from their general funds, they would henceforth be allowed to ballot their members on the creation of a separate political fund. Contributions to the Labour Party could be made from this fund, with members being able to 'contract out' from the 'political levy' if they so wished. In practice 'most of the ballots went in favour of establishing political funds' and the BLP benefited accordingly from the injection of funds provided by the burgeoning wartime and post-war union movement.[10]

In Australia the ALP's primary commitment to the unions was demonstrated by its programmatic support for 'White Australia' and compulsory arbitration. By 1902 the former topped Labor's 'fighting' platform, while the latter came second. In calling for the 'total exclusion of coloured and undesirable races', the ALP aimed to restrict the supply of competitive, 'cheap labour' in the marketplace, while, as noted above, arbitration involved the registration and *de facto* recognition of unions. This provided a fillip to trade union growth and was warmly welcomed by a union movement weakened by the depression and anti-unionism of the 1890s.[11] Labor's determination to extend the protection afforded by the system of arbitration to public employees and to give preference to trade unionists in terms of employment and workplace bargaining rights figured centrally in the federal elections of 1903 and 1904. The issue of preference to unionists was also the crucial factor in triggering the 1914 federal election. Moreover, these two issues constituted important markers of the boundaries between the 'collectivism' of the labour movement and the progressivism of Deakin.

Compulsory arbitration was also supposed to make possible the payment of 'good wages' subject to 'prevailing economic circumstances'. As observed by Macintyre, Deakin's 1905–8 administration went better than this in its adoption of the doctrine of 'New Protection'. As noted earlier, under the latter employers would be excused the payment of an excise duty if they paid their workers 'fair and reasonable' wages. As enshrined in the Harvester judgment of 1907, the President of the Commonwealth Arbitration Court, H.B. Higgins, decided that such wages would be needs- rather than market-based. A wage of 7s per day was decided upon as the minimum amount 'that would enable a worker to live as a "human being in a civilized community" and to keep himself and his family in frugal comfort'. The assumption was that the main 'breadwinner' was the male head of a nuclear family and that women were 'naturally' 'at home' as wives and mothers. While the vast majority of paid women workers were awarded 'a wage sufficient to keep a single person', the male wage covered 'a man, a wife and three children'. Declared on appeal to be unconstitutional, the Harvester 'standard' 'could not be institutionalized' and was patchy in its application before the war. However, within five years of Higgins's judgment 'Labor governments in three states had legislated for the judicial determination of a basic wage'. Arbitration was of 'greatest benefit' to the non-skilled male workers, who usually lacked the bargaining power and union defences of the skilled. In the post-war years protection 'became firmly established as the basis of Australian living standards' for the twentieth century.[12]

Labour's aims to improve the living and working conditions of the wider working class and small producers and to advance the causes of social justice and the full attainment of political democracy were reflected in numerous ways. In Britain between 1906 and 1910 the Labour Party 'campaigned strongly for public programmes to remedy unemployment, and to establish the "right to work"; it sought the amendment of industrial welfare laws concerned with workmen's compensation, factory conditions or hours of work', land nationalisation and the public ownership of the mines and railways.[13] The Liberal 'Welfare Reforms' between 1906 and 1914 – old-age pensions, minimum wages in selected industries, anti-'sweating' measures and state insurance for the sick and unemployed – were designed partly to head off the rise of 'class' politics in the forms of the Labour Party and socialism.[14] At the local level some Labour parties were committed to programmes of 'municipal socialism'. These aimed to improve services in the fields of housing, education and general social welfare and to provide relief 'without pauperisation' for the unemployed. They also sought to extend municipal employment, complete with improved hours of work, union recognition and union rates of pay, and inject more democracy and accountability into matters public and political. Although generally dominated in this period by male trade unionists, local politics also afforded some, albeit limited, scope for the expression of gender- and neighbourhood-based concerns with welfare and maternity issues (public clinics, school meals, scales of poor relief and the like).[15] A minority of women ratepayers held the vote locally, while at the national level the Labour Party advocated adult suffrage rather than the more limited and property-based demand of votes for women.[16]

In Australia the federal ALP had as one of its founding policies 'one adult one vote'. In addition to its active support for 'votes for women', achieved in Commonwealth elections in 1903 and in all the states by 1909, Labor campaigned for the maternity allowance which was 'designed to strengthen the family', old-age and invalidity pensions, and for civil equality between women and men. Late in 1910 the *Worker* both looked aghast at the violence meted out by the authorities towards the suffragettes in Britain and declared Australia to be 'far more advanced' in its general treatment of women.[17] The cause of direct democracy would be strengthened by 'greater use of the referendum'. The causes of socio-economic justice and improved efficiency and wealth would be well served by 'new protection', the nationalisation of monopolies, the creation of a national bank, improved unemployment and accident insurance at state level, the break-up of large estates, a graduated tax on unimproved land and improved infrastructural, organisational and marketing facilities for rural producers, mainly of a state-based and co-operative kind.[18]

In terms of the concrete realisation of demands made by the ALP on behalf of its working-class and 'producerist' supporters, Fisher's 1910–13 administration led the way. Its impressive legislative achievements included maternity allowances, a land tax, amendments to the Arbitration Act and the establishment of a Commonwealth Bank.[19] It failed, however, as a result of the narrowly defeated referenda of 1911 and 1913, in its key aim of seeking enlarged powers for the national government in order to settle industrial disputes and effectively to tackle the growing problem of 'monopolistic' trusts. The latter were seen as the selfish, sectional 'exploiters of society' and, in their control of prices, as artificially inflating the cost of living and 'fleecing the people'. If left unchecked they would, in the manner of the USA, 'enslave' the people and trample democracy underfoot.[20]

The ALP, while taking it for granted that it was *the* party of 'the workers', also presented itself as the *natural* 'people's party', acting not from vested or envious 'class' interest, but out of consideration for interests of the 'progressive Australian nation' as a whole.[21] A special appeal was made to 'housewives and mothers who bore the brunt of high prices'.[22] By nationalising monopolies, Labor would 'initiate the process of taking over for the people the means of life'.[23] Yet these plans remained unfulfilled, as did the aim of formally committing the ALP to the extensive public ownership desired by the socialists in the party's ranks.[24]

Some historians, working within the discrete national frameworks of Britain and Australia, have argued that Labour's, albeit limited, success in appealing to working-class people was further enhanced by a renewed or new sense of class among workers. The nub of this argument, as made most famously by Hobsbawm in relation to Britain, is that the combined effects of a variety of factors led to the 'remaking' of the working class. These comprised accelerated urbanisation and industrialisation, an increase in the size of units of production and the number of workers engaged in manufacturing and mining, growing class-based residential segregation, the increasing commercialisation of leisure and the narrowing of differences among workers in terms of mobility, marriage patterns, income and skill. The 'traditional' working class which emerged was far more united, homogeneous and 'class conscious', in a limited and reformist rather than revolutionary sense, than its fragmented and status-conscious post-Chartist counterpart, according to Hobsbawm. It expressed 'a secular tendency' to join unions and to identify with Labour as a 'class party'.[25] A thesis of class 'making', whereby workers in communities across the country began to 'cohere as a class' in response to socio-economic, political and cultural developments, has also been advanced for Australia, albeit far more sketchily and tentatively in terms of the period in question.[26] In response, critics in both countries have argued that these notions of class 'remaking' or 'making' exaggerate the depth and extent of unity and underestimate sources of difference and division, such as religious sectarianism and gender, at work and in the community.[27]

As a contribution to debate, I strongly endorse the view that the growth of independent Labour should be set within its wider societal context rather than constrained within narrow institutional boundaries of a party-political kind. I also agree with the 'revisionists' that more attention should be paid to political languages and representations than has traditionally been the case.[28] These endorsements underpin the approach adopted here.

I also maintain that, as matters stand, this potentially exciting area of national and cross-national comparative debate, however, has produced largely inconclusive results. Only when scholars have more fully and extensively investigated sources of working-class commonality, similarity, difference, unity and conflict, both nationally and comparatively, will we be in a strong position to make authoritative judgements about the relationship between the rise of Labour and the 'remaking' of the working class in Britain and its 'making' in Australia.

Finally, a favourable conjuncture of structural and experiential forces ensured that the early growth of independent Labour would be much stronger in Australia than in Britain. As highlighted above, economic depression, unemployment, anti-unionism, frustration with existing mainstream political and other institutions, impressive leadership and growing cooperation and solidarity within the labour movement and, more contentiously, growing class consciousness among the wider working class, signified that similar and common stimuli were in evidence in both countries. Yet in key ways the overall politico-economic structures and experiences of Australia and Britain were very different.

For example, the early achievement of political democracy, combined with the more limited, uneven and less 'transforming' growth of industrial capitalism in Australia,[29] meant that, notwithstanding the defeats of the 1890s, the labour movement had the 'nuts and bolts' of its own political agency and independent development to hand, and that the unions had the opportunity to secure a relatively strong bargaining position and platform for future growth within the post-depression economic revival. Their position, of course, was strengthened by arbitration and the other pillars of the New Commonwealth.

As highlighted above, within the framework of the New Commonwealth Labor became a major political player. Its strong racialised, class-based and nationalist appeals, its impressive leadership, the more or less uniform support provided by the trade unions for the ALP and the increasing weakness of the political opposition, augured well for the future. Labor had begun its seemingly inexorable rise to political and social power and its eventual 'social revolution' in Australia.[30] Thus Henry Boote, socialist editor of the *Worker*, regarded the prospect of electoral defeat in the federal election of 1913 as 'no more than a temporary phase in the evolution of our Movement'. The labour movement in Australia had 'reached a stage of progress which has no parallel elsewhere on earth', declared Boote, and the 'fusion' of its political opponents proved that 'they are beaten, and they know it'.[31]

In mid and later Victorian Britain the predominantly craft and skilled unions had won widespread recognition and acceptance. During the same period the limited and slow transition from 'competitive' to 'monopoly' capitalism, combined with the strength and tenacity of labour movement organisations, also meant that, like many of their Australian counterparts, British skilled and craft workers were less 'transformed' and undermined at the workplace than their counterparts in the USA.[32]

At the same time the British labour movement and the working class continued to occupy a subordinate place within a highly 'traditional' political and social system, lacking in democracy, 'openness' and egalitarianism. Although making limited progress, in terms of political independence, the British labour movement was more strongly influenced than Australian labour by established partisan political allegiances and continued to express a more limited, defensive and corporate view of the world. Lacking the hegemonic potential of its counterpart in the antipodes, it also remained more fragmented, both politically and industrially.

Nation, empire, class and race

As noted above, the ALP saw itself from the beginning not only as the party of the workers and the producers, but also as the only 'true' party of the 'progressive new nation'. Although the historiography of Australian labour has traditionally concerned itself mainly with material factors, there has been recognition of Labor's nationalism. This has been accompanied by debate as to whether the ALP's nationalist credentials were mainly of the progressive and transforming radical kind claimed by the party itself.

For example, Don Rawson and Raymond Markey have highlighted both Labor's appeal to small producers and its consequent 'populist' opposition to 'monopolies' and the fact that the 'labourist political consensus', embodied in the policy framework of 'national settlement', had 'the effect of making the ALP the major bearer of nationalism in Australian politics'.[33] For Markey populism of a predominantly progressive but thoroughly racist type had become 'the dominant social force within labour' by 1900. Moreover, the labour movement was relatively cheaply 'incorporated' into the 'the State institution', the 'parliamentary status quo' and capitalism.[34]

In the opinion of D.J. Murphy both the state and federal Labor parties 'became the only mass working-class parties in Australia to succeed because their reforming radical and nationalist aspirations, combined with a willingness to use state power, coincided with the aspirations of the urban and rural working man'.[35] Ross McMullin agreed: 'Labor had developed policies attuned to national aspirations.'[36] For Humphrey McQueen, however, Labor's 'radicalism and nationalism' were 'in every way the logical extension of the petty-bourgeois mentality and subordinated organizations which preceded them'. Labor continued to be mainly 'actively subservient' to 'the outlook of imperialism' and pro-British – 'British race patriotism' was 'widespread among Labor men' – adopted 'democratic militarism' to keep Australia 'white' and was easily incorporated into Australian capitalism.[37] Finally, Terry Irving has painted a more complex and changing picture. 'Labourism' contained within it some of the features highlighted by McQueen and Markey at various points in time, but it was a changing rather than a static bundle of elements. Challenge, conflict, radical nationalism and socialism were necessary constituents in addition to moderation, collaboration, racism and sectionalism. The extent to which the 'progressive' or 'conservative' aspects of 'labourism' have predominated is, concludes Irving, dependent upon specific historical conjunctures.[38]

Basing my findings mainly upon the investigation of primary sources concerning federal elections, I contribute to these debates in four ways in the following sections of this chapter. First, I endorse the crucial importance of nationalism to the ALP. Second, I maintain that this nationalism was predominantly radical in character, although of a reformist rather than revolutionary kind. Third, I demonstrate the ways in which Labor's nationalism was profoundly shaped by the influences of class, 'populist' producerism, race and empire. As noted in Part I, the ALP reconciled its strong and radical, class- and populist-based Australian nationalism with support for the enlightened British Empire and 'white' British-ness. Fourth, I offer the thesis that Labor's nationalism was the key factor in its meteoric rise at the polls.

In terms of the British case, I conclude, mainly on the basis of Labour's programmes in the general elections of 1900, 1906 and 1910, that the issues of nation, empire and race mattered more to the Labour Party than is suggested by the conventional wisdom. With reference to the comparative dimension, I present three arguments. First, in overall terms these issues were more important to the ALP than the BLP. Second, they constituted a more significant aspect of the Labour politics of both countries than traditionalists and revisionists have suggested. Third, as a corollary they should be afforded their due importance in the relevant bodies of national and comparative historiography. I start with Australia.

The Australian case

The newly born federal ALP loudly proclaimed itself to be the foremost representative of Australia as a 'new world' nation. 'By a happy fortune', Australia was 'free of most of the superstitions, traditions, class distinctions and sanctified fables and fallacies of the older nations' and had a 'unique opportunity' to establish a 'Workers' Paradise'. It was a land 'for the people', possessing 'no aristocracy of birth', 'no military caste', 'no state chartered clerical order' and with 'abundant' opportunities for 'opportunity', 'freedom' and 'justice'. It was the mission of the ALP to further promote these opportunities, especially for workers and small producers, to transform Australia into the 'Co-operative Commonwealth' and to act as a 'beacon' or 'exemplar' to all progressives and radicals in the 'old lands'.[39]

The 'manifest destinies' of the labour movement, the workers and the 'new' nation itself were seen as inseparable. As the *Worker* proclaimed, 'the hope of the working class is the Labour party, and Australia's hope is the working class'.[40] Unlike the 'Imperialists', whose primary loyalty lay with Britain, the Empire, the monarchy and the Union Jack, the ALP placed Australia's interests, including loyalty to the Australian flag, 'Australian industries, Australian art, Australian literature, Australian music, Australian philosophy', Australian cricket and other forms of sport as 'first', as 'standing above all others'.[41] The ALP portrayed itself as 'the only truly national party', while the *Australian Worker* saw itself as representing the cause of 'AUSTRALIANS

FOR AUSTRALIA': it had as its sub-title, 'An Australian Paper for Australian People'.[42]

The vital importance of 'the national' to Labor was clearly revealed during federal elections. The top priority afforded by Labor to the 'absolute restriction of alien and inferior races', from the first election of 1901 onwards, signified that the party stood, above all else, for national homogeneity and stability, for 'national character and racial purity'. Labor's election material stated that capitalists' 'greed of gain', in exploiting 'cheap coloured labour', must not be allowed to lead to 'the degradation of Australian character'. Moreover, the 'free admission of coloured peoples' would 'eventually reproduce here the evils from which even prolonged civil war failed to emancipate America', involving 'the descent to their level of our own workers'.[43]

The examples of the 'black labour loving capitalists of the Rand' during the South African War and their post-bellum importation of 'slave' Chinese labour into South Africa were likewise held up in the labour press as examples of international capitalist indifference to the plight of 'white workers' and the national interest.[44] In the 1910 federal election Fusionist candidates and their supporters were often portrayed by their ALP opponents not only as the 'enemies of federation', nationalism and progress, but also as supporters of a 'cheap', 'coloured labour' regime.[45]

Labor's policies on defence and shipping were also framed in terms of the national interest. Compulsory military training for home defence, established by Deakin in 1910, was further developed by Labor in 1911. Fisher's establishment of an Australian navy rather than the financing of Dreadnoughts, and the desire to place coastal trading in Australian hands, stemmed from the overriding desire to put Australia and Australian interests 'first'. In contrast, some of Labor's opponents were seen as putting Britain and the Empire first and Australia second.[46]

The appeal to the national interest was very pronounced during the first majority Labor government. For example, it was strongly reflected in the campaign to expand the powers of the Commonwealth. So long as the Commonwealth was denied the powers over sectional interests, Australia 'cannot be called a Nation in anything other than an embryonic form', declared the Worker. 'NATIONALISM IS THE WAY OF SALVATION FOR AUSTRALIA.'[47] The radical nationalist Bulletin was in full agreement. The ALP had the chance to be 'the National Party for all time' rather than the 'devoted slave of the Parish Pump'. But it must not limit its ambition. It had, for example, to disown those in its own ranks in New South Wales and Western Australia who were defending 'states' rights'. It also had to 'abolish privilege' and 'Fat Landlord' control of the upper houses of the states and promote deserving Australian men, rather than aristocratic Britons, to positions of public prominence.[48]

In practice Labor sought enhanced powers for the Commonwealth to establish a 'National Bank', to 'regulate monopolies and nationalise industries' and to 'give the Commonwealth the same power as the States over labour laws'. Extended arbitration would ensure 'uniform industrial laws' and 'equality of industrial conditions' throughout the country and that living standards would not vary from state to state. 'Scab' states would cease to exist.[49] Labor was successful in realising its first objective in the form of the Commonwealth Bank, but, as a result of the failed referenda of 1911 and 1913, unsuccessful in the other two. It also developed the Australian navy and army, albeit on lines recommended by Britain. Yet primary responsibility for Australia's defence was seen to rest with Australians themselves. The country was not to rely 'abjectly' on Britain.[50]

It is important to remember that, despite significant setbacks, Labor dominated the federal political scene between 1910 and 1914, achieved 'a period of reform unmatched in the Commonwealth until the 1940s', and did well in the states.[51] Its successful appropriation of the language of the national interest undoubtedly contributed substantially to these electoral successes. While Labor regarded itself as the 'true voice' of the nation or 'community' and its manifestoes as 'doctrines of patriotic inspiration',[52] its political enemies were identified with 'sectional' and 'selfish', interest groups. The latter assumed various forms of 'FAT': 'monopolists', 'trusts', 'plutocrats', the 'squattocracy', 'capitalist exploiters', states resistant to Labor's planned expansion of Commonwealth powers and 'Imperialists' and Fusionists scheming to undermine Australia's 'whiteness' and its wishes to be more united internally and have a more independent presence in the Empire.[53] Even in 1914 the surge of patriotic and cross-party support for the war could not conceal the fact to the labour press that 'THE FUSION IS ANTI-AUSTRALIAN THROUGH AND THROUGH'. This was demonstrated in the fact that it was 'the friend and accomplice of the Trusts' that 'disloyally' continued to 'exploit the Australian people' at a time when national unity and common purpose and sacrifice were becoming the orders of the day.[54] It was against these 'anti-social' and 'un-Australian' 'others' that 'truly Australian' Labor defined itself.

It will be readily evident from the examples presented above that Labor's nationalism was highly racialised, classed and inextricably connected with the question of empire. From Labor's perspective, 'whiteness', combined with 'protection' and paternalism towards their 'own' 'coloureds', the Aboriginal people, were part and parcel of what it meant to be an Australian. Labor's siege-like mentality, based not only on economic but explicitly and unapologetically on racist opposition to 'Asiatic' and other forms of 'coloured' immigration and insistence upon a 'racially pure' and 'homogeneous' Australia, would persist well into the post-World War Two period.[55] As highlighted by McQueen and Markey, this was the unpleasant and reactionary face of the Australian labour movement's nationalism.[56]

The fact that Federation took place under the British crown, that the British monarch was Australia's head of state and that the New Commonwealth was part of the British Empire, meant that in Australia attitudes to nationalism were often inextricably tied to questions of empire. While imperial matters per se figured less prominently in terms of federal Labor's electoral agenda than predominantly domestic concerns with nation, class and race, nevertheless, in practice these concerns often could not be isolated from the wider imperial context. For example, Fisher's attitude to coastal shipping, the navy, Dreadnoughts and other defence matters, his support for the war in 1914 and the issue of conscription necessarily involved major questions concerning not only Australian nationalism and 'Australia first', but also the country's rights and responsibilities towards the 'mother country'.

'White Australia' was also part and parcel of wider debates concerning 'race' within the British Empire. Labor criticisms of the latter stemmed in part from its 'mixed race' character and Britain's formal commitments to legal equality and free entry into the mother country for all subjects of the Empire, irrespective of race.[57] As noted in Part I, in its 'whiteness' the ALP sought to be more racially 'pure' than the British. 'Whiteness', of course, was an essential aspect of the ALP's nationalism.

In terms of attitudes towards Britain and the imperial connection, McQueen is right to argue that Australian labour valued the protection afforded by Britain, but that 'they did not always trust Britain to put Australia's interests first'.[58] At the same time, however, he either greatly underestimates or ignores the primary evidence supporting the conclusion that, while holding out the hand of friendship towards British workers and their labour movement, many within the Australian movement remained not only suspicious, but also hostile towards the British upper classes and, in some instances, British imperialism.

The labour movement's criticisms at this period in time were generally of three distinct but at times overlapping kinds. First, there was hostility towards the assumed superiority, arrogance and condescension towards 'colonials' of Britain's upper classes, its ruling elite and their imitators and dependants. For example, the conduct of British officers towards Australian troops and Australia during World War One – their haughtiness, 'little British-ness', their 'lack of recognition' of the Australian soldiers' outstanding contribution to the war effort and their seeming indifference to Australia's primary interests – aroused widespread criticism and outrage.[59] Second, there was a *minority*, left viewpoint expressed, for example, by the *Worker*. This viewpoint offered systemic and mainly unqualified opposition to modern imperialism in general and British imperialism in particular. It saw imperialism, whether in Ireland or India, as a *necessary* feature of capitalist class-based exploitation, aggression, power and domination.[60] Third, the *majority* voice, that of the mainstream ALP and the labour movement as a whole, was far more qualified and conditional. As noted in Part I in relation to 'the British world' perspective, while critical of some aspects of capitalist imperialism, including British imperialism, it saw Australian nationalism as being perfectly compatible with continuing membership of the British Empire.

As expressed by Watson, Fisher and many of their colleagues, this majority viewpoint was extremely critical of Britain's aggressive, exploitative and cruel role in the South African War, demanded the right of self-determination for subject colonies, including 'coloured' ones, and maintained that Britain still had some way to go before fully meeting the ALP's demand that Australia be treated as a self-governing community within the Empire.[61] At the same time, however, it recognised that Australia, despite its wish to become more self-reliant, was still mainly dependent upon Britain for its successful defence, a point made repeatedly by 'Billy' Hughes. The simultaneous rise of Britain's rivals, Germany and Japan, their potential challenge to British imperial hegemony and the potential threat of Japan to Australia greatly reinforced Australian awareness of the overriding need for British protection. Most significantly, notwithstanding his principled opposition to war and militarism in general, Prime Minister Fisher and his party declared their full support for Britain in 1914 and the war effort.[62]

Fisher and his colleagues also saw Britain far more as a practitioner of 'enlightened', rather than 'coercive', imperialism. The 'mother country' was in the process of regarding the White Dominions less as children than as adults within the imperial 'family', as 'deserving' of more respect, independence and autonomy than in the past.[63] The key aspect of this developing policy towards Australia, of course, was seen in May 1900 when Joseph Chamberlain both introduced into the House of Commons a bill to sanction the New Commonwealth and declared that it would not weaken the imperial tie.[64] There followed a marked decline in republican and anti-British feeling in Australia. While the ALP was the only body practically committed to putting Australia 'first', and while Britain was not to be entirely trusted, nevertheless, Fisher and the majority ALP were determined to fight for better representation, more consultation and greater autonomy for Australia *within* the imperial framework. Fisher himself fully agreed to his appointment as Australian High Commissioner in London, hardly the sentiment of an unqualified anti-imperialist! In sum, as maintained by proponents of 'the British world' viewpoint, Labor's nationalism, complete with its selected criticisms of empire, was entirely compatible with overarching loyalty to the British Empire.[65]

Yet matters could and did change somewhat. As we will see in Part III, Labor's divisions and split over conscription in 1916 and 1917, its increasingly anti-war stance and its sharp movement to the left generally, both during and immediately following the war, saw it become more critical of the Empire. At the same time it was criticised by the Right for its new-found 'extremism' and 'disloyalty' to Australia and the Empire. Foremost among Labor's accusers were Protestants who singled out Irish Catholic Australians, and especially the large numbers of the latter present in the ALP, for particular condemnation. In actual fact the vast majority of Irish Catholic Australians actively supported the war effort. While they were prominent in the opposition to conscription, they continued to express multiple views in relation to the British Empire. Most supported Irish Home Rule within the framework of empire, even in the wake of Britain's bloody suppression of the 1916 Easter Rising. Yet they were increasingly targeted as being 'un-Australian', 'Sinn Fein' 'traitors'.[66] As we will observe in due course, the 'politics of loyalism' would undermine the ALP's political hegemony during the interwar years.

Labor's nationalism, of course, was also very strongly informed by class. We have seen that the ALP derived its bedrock support from workers and small producers, and that these supporters and the party were intent upon creating an open, democratic and just 'New World', in contrast and opposition to the stuffy, privileged and hierarchical societies of the 'Old'. These changes were to be achieved by peaceful, gradual and parliamentary rather than revolutionary means. In sum, in its nationalism, its attitudes to imperialism and class-based support and programme, the Australian labour movement was the main force for progressive change in pre-war Australia.

Finally, it is important briefly to ponder the relative influences of nationalism and class on the birth and spectacular electoral successes of the ALP. Australian labour historiography has, on balance, tended to adopt the view that class took precedence over nationalism in terms of the formation and subsequent twentieth-century development of the labour movement. The most recent expression of this viewpoint may be found in Simon Booth's original and splendidly researched study of the cartoons of Melbourne's labour press between 1890 and

1919. Booth's conclusion is that, in the images employed, 'the politics of nation were of secondary importance to that of class, and . . . the nation was used as a frame to present class politics rather than as a politics in itself. The nation was in these images predominantly represented as a site of class exploitation.'[67]

My investigation would suggest otherwise. While bedrock occupational and wider class ties and loyalties contributed significantly to Labor's growing support, it was the party's ability to present itself as the champion of the 'new' radical, 'white' nation, complete with overall loyalty to the British Empire, especially 'white' British race patriotism, which enabled it to capture federal power and hold on to it. In so doing it utilised but transcended the 'politics of class'. In stark contrast, its Fusionist opponents were identified with backward-looking and selfish 'un-' and 'anti-Australian' interest groups.

Yet the story of the relationship between class and nation was far from finished. As we will see in Part III, between 1917 and the 1930s the tables were turned when Australian nationalism became predominantly conservative in character. Labor was now successfully branded by its Nationalist opponents not only as extreme and disloyal, but also as selfish and sectional.[68]

The British case

Unlike the ALP, the BLP had little prospect of achieving national political power in this period and, as such, becoming the official guardian of the national interest. Failing to fulfil its early independent promise, the parliamentary Labour Party remained very much in the shadow of the Liberals. As a result, increasing numbers within the labour movement became frustrated with the 'parliamentary road' and placed more emphasis upon industrial action. Between 1911 and 1914 industrial unrest, along with the issues of Ireland and women's suffrage, dominated the national political agenda. Moreover, the constituency base of the Labour Party was more narrowly rooted in trade unionism than in Australia. So dominated by the unions, and as a corporate and subordinate body in a highly traditional society, the BLP, as reflected in the historiography, remained predominantly concerned with domestic 'bread and butter' issues. Questions concerning the nature and future of the nation and the Empire, including the issue of race, assumed far less immediate and overall relevance to the BLP than its Australian counterpart.

This is not to suggest, however, that these questions were by any means so marginal or insignificant as is often suggested in the literature. For example, imperial and national matters assumed a degree of importance to Labour during the 'Khaki' general election of 1900, which has either been ignored or greatly underestimated in most institutional histories of the party and some of the wider works of social and political history. The former have concentrated upon the grievances of the trade unions and the socio-economic concerns of organised labour referred to earlier. The latter have often taken their cue from Richard Price's claims, made in 1972, that 'indifference' towards British imperialism was accompanied by 'more immediate' concerns with 'social reform' (wages, hours, employment, housing and social-welfare issues) in British 'working-class constituencies' during this election.[69] Yet there is a wealth of evidence about the election in neglected primary sources, such as the socialist, labour and more mainstream press, to demonstrate that this was not the case.

It is, for example, important to recall the fact, largely omitted or marginalised in the historiography, that the LRC was formed and the election took place at a time when Britain was waging, between 1899 and 1902, a major imperialist war against the Boer republics in South Africa. The LRC came into being at the end of February 1900, when 'jingo khaki' fever, involving a considerable amount of violence perpetrated by 'hooligans' against anti-war meetings and speakers in various parts of the country, was at its height.[70] It is the case that the LRC's founding conference concerned itself with the issue of independent labour representation and its socio-economic underpinnings. But it is also worth noting that at this and subsequent conferences opposition was registered to the war and Britain's role in it.[71]

During the election campaign of September 1900, moreover, questions concerning the war, British imperialism and Britain's national standing mattered far more in 'working-class constituencies' and among the LRC's fifteen parliamentary candidates and their supporters than an emphasis upon the overriding importance of 'social reform' would suggest.[72] Practical socio-economic concerns, such as poverty, unemployment, housing, old-age pensions and the public control of monopolies, did figure in the addresses of these candidates, and in some instances, such as the campaign of George Lansbury at Bow and Bromley, occupied pride of place. In overall terms, however, the issues of war and British imperialism were the most pressing concerns of these candidates.[73]

For example, while expressing support for the 'bravery' and 'hardships' of the British 'Tommy' in South Africa, the LRC's candidates also uniformly condemned the war as a 'deception' and a 'fraud'. Support had been 'manufactured' on the basis of the Boers' denial of the franchise to recent British immigrants. But this was a 'cover' for the 'base' motives of 'rapacious capitalists'. 'Greedy financiers' sought to 'annex, plunder and rob' the goldmines and other valuable resources of South

Africa, to unmercifully 'smash' the Boers and to substitute 'enslaved' and 'cheap' 'black' and, at some stage, Chinese labour for well-paid 'white' labour in the mines.[74] There was similarly uniform outrage against the 'atrocities' and 'barbaric' methods of 'militarism' employed by the British in South Africa. The 'insatiable drug' of 'militarism' and 'tyrannical' imperialism was also seen as inimical to progressive causes at home, such as social reform and the further extension of democracy.[75] Despite evidence to the contrary in some constituencies, 'khakimania' was widely held by contemporaries to be the decisive factor in the Conservatives' victory at the election, especially in urban areas.[76]

It is also interesting to note that the war raised important issues for the candidates about their patriotism and nationalism. These issues have been neglected in the historiography.[77] The LRC's candidates strongly rejected the charge levelled against them by pro-war Conservatives and Liberals that they were acting 'cowardly' and 'treasonably'.[78] There was, moreover, unanimity among them that the 'butchery', the 'pillage', the 'English terror at Bloemfontein' and the reduction of large areas of South Africa to a 'charred and blackened waste', were 'dragging Britain's honour into the dirt', 'ruining' her prestige and reputation for toleration, liberty and fairness 'before the whole world' and bringing her empire 'to the very verge of its ruin'.[79]

The candidates and the *Clarion*, *Labour Leader* and *Justice* argued strongly that there was an urgent need for the labour movement to 'rescue' Britain's national honour and reputation from the 'cesspit' into which the war had cast them. Blatchford and others exhorted the radical 'people' to 're-possess' patriotism, 'to take it out of the hands of the heartless bullies who would squander its heart and blood and prostitute its honour to serve their greed and avarice'.[80] Hardie urged his fellow candidates to expend 'restless, untiring effort' to see the country 'rescued from the clutches of the Mammon-inspired war fiend' and so regain the 'respect of the common people of Europe'.[81] For the Executive Committee of the SDF, 'true patriotism' resided 'not in the domination and degradation of others, not in the subjugation of Africa, still less in the manufacture of permanent famine by the bleeding to death of India, but in the education and uplifting of England herself as a nation, in the democratic organisation and social emancipation of yourselves'.[82] These specific expressions formed part of a well-established tradition of radical patriotism in Britain, characterised by the movements of the 'workers' and the 'people' for democracy, decency, reform, social justice and fairness against the forces of 'reaction', 'privilege', 'tyranny' and 'monopoly'.[83]

The version of radical patriotism presented constituted the British equivalent of the ALP's 'true Australianism'. The candidates saw their labour movement as being the 'real' representative of the radical and patriotic nation, as opposed to the landed classes and the industrial, commercial and financial capitalists. They were unsparing in their condemnation of class-based 'coercive' imperialism, not only in relation to the South African War, but also in general. They wished to remove not only nationalism but also imperialism from capitalist control and place it in the hands of the 'progressive' labour movement and the 'radical people'. In these ways nationalism and imperialism would become more 'enlightened', 'democratic' and 'popular' in character.[84]

The next general election, in 1906, was dominated by the issues of free trade versus tariff reform, while those of January and December 1910 revolved around the Irish question, tariff reform and, most crucially, the House of Lords' right of veto after it had rejected the Liberals' budget to introduce new land taxes. The 1906 election resulted in a Liberal landslide, but as a result of the 1910 contests the Liberals were dependent upon Irish and Labour votes in parliament. For its part, the Labour Party lacked a strong and distinctive parliamentary presence and programme. It remained very much in the shadow of the Liberal Party.[85]

Although nationalism and patriotism were not significant issues in these elections, both tariff reform and the constitutional position of the Lords did raise questions concerning special protection and privileges for 'selfish' manufacturing interests and the 'dictatorial' landed Lords at the expense of the wider national community.[86] In both 1906 and 1910 Labour candidates unsuccessfully attempted to elevate class-based issues concerning the 'social conditions of the people', land nationalisation and public ownership of the mines and the railways to a position of central importance as against the 'sham' of free trade versus protection.[87]

Race and empire did figure in the 1906 contest, but mainly in a background capacity. They manifested themselves in lingering debates about the indentured Chinese male labourers first imported into the mines of the Transvaal in 1904. Henry Pelling maintained that while Liberals denounced the 'Chinese labour experiment' mainly on humanitarian grounds (the workers were housed in compounds and lived and worked under 'degrading' conditions), the British labour movement was opposed primarily for economic reasons. The Chinese constituted 'cheap' competition in the labour market and their importation flatly contradicted the Tories' claim that the South African War had been fought to 'open up' South Africa to emigrants from Britain.[88]

Three further claims may be registered. First, there was also considerable labour movement opposition to the fact that the Chinese were 'forced' or 'enslaved' rather than 'free' workers. Second, while some British workers undoubtedly held negative racial stereotypes of the Chinese labourers, the dominant response of the British socialist and labour press was to condemn racist opposition to the Chinese and to advocate the supremacy of class over race. Third, this was in marked contrast to the explicitly racist opposition to the Chinese expressed by the vast majority of labour movement members in South Africa and Australia.[89]

There were no more general elections before World War One. Despite the existence of anti-imperialist and pacifist sentiments within its ranks, the British labour movement, like its Australian counterpart, gave its majority support to the war effort. The interests of the movement, the working class, the nation and the Empire demanded that 'democracy' and 'freedom' be defended against 'Prussian' 'autocracy' and 'tyranny'.[90]

Conclusion

Part II has set new and neglected questions to the evidence concerning the influences of nation, empire and race upon the birth and early development of independent labour politics in Australia and Britain. I have argued, on the basis of a reading of the secondary and, in many cases neglected, primary sources, that these influences were both more significant and closely intertwined with class, gender and politics than suggested in much of the relevant nationally based and comparative literature. Moreover, both the structural locations and historical experiences of labour movements and workers within their respective national and imperial contexts underpinned the fact that the influences of nation, empire and race were more profound in the Australian case. As we will observe in Part III, from the time of World War One to the eve of World War Two these influences not only continued strongly to inform the character and development of both the Australian and British labour movements in general, but also played an important part in determining the contrasting fortunes of labour politics. Whereas the BLP rose to national prominence and office, the pre-war political rule of the ALP was sharply reversed. It is to a study of these developments that I now turn.

Notes

1 Scates, *New Australia*, pp. 76–82; Patmore, *Australian Labour*, pp. 80–1; Thorpe, *History of the British Labour Party*, ch. 1; Hilson, *Political Change and the Rise of Labour*, chs 2, 3.
2 Markey, *Making of the Labor Party*, chs 5, 6; Macintyre, 'First Caucus', p. 26.
3 Hunt, *British Labour History*, p. 315; *Labour Party Foundation Conference and Annual Conference Reports 1900–1905*, Hammersmith Reprints of Scarce Documents no. 3 (London: Hammersmith Bookshop Ltd., 1967), p. 60.

4 Kirk, *Change, Continuity and Class*, Document 14, 'The issue of Labour Representation', p. 287.
5 *Labour Leader*, 21 April, 22 September 1900.
6 Kirk, *Change, Continuity and Class*, p. 290.
7 *Labour Party Foundation Conference*, pp. 64–5.
8 Phillips, *Rise of the Labour Party*, p. 17.
9 Thorpe, *History of the British Labour Party*, pp. 23, 26.
10 Phillips, *Rise of the Labour Party*, pp. 26–7.
11 Macintyre, *Oxford History*, p. 102.
12 *Ibid.*, pp. 103–4, 111.
13 Phillips, *Rise of the Labour Party*, pp. 16–17; *Labour Leader*, 7, 21 January 1910.
14 Kirk, *Change, Continuity and Class*, pp. 192–8.
15 Neville Kirk, '"Traditional" Working-class Culture and "The Rise of Labour": Some Preliminary Questions and Observations', *Social History*, 16:2 (May 1991), 203–16; George Lansbury, *My Life* (London: Constable and Company, 1931), ch. 8.
16 For debates among socialists concerning adult suffrage and votes for women see Hannam and Hunt, *Socialist Women*, ch. 5; Lansbury, *My Life*, ch. 8; Dr. Marion Phillips, 'The Democratic Appeal of Women's Suffrage', *Labour Leader*, 16 December 1910.
17 *Worker*, 26 November, 10 December 1910.
18 For Labor's demands and platforms see Macintyre, 'First Caucus', p. 18; Macintyre, *Oxford History*, p. 111; *Manchester Guardian*, 14, 15 April 1910; *Justice*, 23 April 1910; James and Markey, 'Class and Labour', 31–3; *Compare their Achievements; Producers Unite; Bulletin*, 5 May 1910 for accident insurance for miners and their dependants in New South Wales.
19 Macintyre, *Oxford History*, p. 94.
20 *Worker*, 15, 22, 29 May 1913; *Australian Worker*, 20, 27 August 1914.
21 McMullin, 'Leading the World', p. 38; *Worker*, 7, 14 April 1910, 8, 15 May, 5 June 1913; *Westralian Worker*, 8, 22 April 1910.
22 *Worker*, 15, 22 May 1913.
23 *Ibid.*, 14 January 1911.
24 James and Markey, 'Class and Labour', 32–3.
25 Eric Hobsbawm, 'The Making of the Working Class 1870–1914', in his *Worlds of Labour*, p. 194.
26 Macintyre, *Oxford History*, pp. 48–56; Kirk, *Comrades and Cousins*, pp. 119–20.
27 Kirk, *Change, Continuity and Class*, pp. 214–25; Kirk, *Comrades and Cousins*, p. 120; Macintyre, *Oxford History*, pp. 48, 67–8.
28 Worley, 'Building the Party', 74–5; Lawrence, *Speaking for the People*, ch. 3.
29 Kirk, *Comrades and Cousins*, pp. 91–100.
30 *Worker*, 26 June 1913.
31 *Ibid.*, 5 June 1913.
32 Kirk, *Challenge and Accommodation*, ch. 1.
33 Rawson, *Labor in Vain?*, pp. 4–5; Markey, *Making of the Labor Party*, pp. 13–15, 314–16.
34 James and Markey, 'Class and Labour', 32; Markey, *Making of the Labor Party*, p. 316.
35 D.J. Murphy (ed.), *Labor in Politics: The State Labor Parties in Australia 1880–1920* (St Lucia: University of Queensland Press, 1975), p. 10.
36 McMullin, 'Leading the World', p. 39.
37 McQueen, *New Britannia*, pp. 11, 16–24, 220–1, 236.
38 Terence H. Irving, 'The Roots of Parliamentary Socialism in Australia, 1850–1920', *Labour History*, 67 (November 1994), 97–109; Terence H. Irving, 'Labourism: A Political Geneology', *Labour History*, 66 (May 1994), 1–10; Kirk, *Comrades and Cousins*, pp. 122–3.
39 *Worker*, 5 January 1901.
40 *Ibid.*, 29 January 1910.
41 Kirk, '"Australians for Australia"', 102.

42 *Ibid.*
43 See W.G. Spence's address to Sydney's Darling electorate in the folder '1901 Federal Election Ephemera. Candidates A–Z'. See also the folder '1903 Federal Election Ephemera – Parties. Labor Party', in Federal Election Ephemera, National Library of Australia, Canberra, Petherick Reading Room, MS 2247771.
44 *Worker*, 30 March 1901, 2 April 1904.
45 *Westralian Worker*, 8 April 1910; *Worker*, 7 April 1910.
46 *Bulletin*, 5 May 1904, 21 April 1910; *Australasian*, 30 April 1904; *Labour Leader*, 25 March 1910.
47 *Worker*, 14 January 1911.
48 *Bulletin*, 21 April 1910; *Worker*, 21 April 1910.
49 Murphy, 'Fisher, Andrew', p. 506; *Worker*, 14 January 1911.
50 Macintyre, *Oxford History*, pp. 140–1; *Worker*, 27 August 1914; *Australian Worker*, 27 August, 3, 10 September 1914.
51 Murphy, 'Fisher, Andrew', p. 505.
52 *Worker*, 8 May 1913.
53 See, for example, *Westralian Worker*, 8, 22 April 1910; *Worker*, 7, 14 April 1910, 8, 15, 29 May, 5, 26 June 1913; *Australian Worker*, 3, 10 September 1914.
54 See the articles by Boote in the *Australian Worker*, 20, 27 August, 3 September 1914.
55 Neville Kirk, 'Traditionalists and Progressives: Labor, Race, and Immigration in Post-World War II Australia and Britain', *Australian Historical Studies*, 39:1 (March 2008), 53–71; Kirk, *Comrades and Cousins*, pp. 129–31, 202–3.
56 McQueen, *New Britannia*, chs 2, 5; Markey, *Making of the Labor Party*, ch. 10, p. 314; Kirk, *Comrades and Cousins*, pp. 129–31, 202–5; Lake and Reynolds, *Drawing the Global Colour Line*, ch. 6. For an unsuccessful attempt to cast Labor's attitude to 'White Australia' as predominantly progressive see Keith Windschuttle, *The White Australia Policy* (Sydney: Macleay Press, 2004).
57 Clark, *History of Australia*, vol. V, pp. 131–2 190–1, 206–7; Kirk, *Comrades and Cousins*, pp. 127, 202–3.
58 McQueen, *New Britannia*, p. 18.
59 Macintyre, *Oxford History*, pp. 128–9, 180–1.
60 Kirk, *Comrades and Cousins*, pp. 126–8; *Worker*, 2 April 1901, 6 August 1904.
61 Kirk, *Comrades and Cousins*, pp. 168–9, 203–4; Kirk, '"Australians for Australia"', p. 104; *Worker*, 5, 12 January 1901.
62 Macintyre, *Oxford History*, pp. 138–41, 152; Day, *Fisher*, pp. 289–304.
63 Kirk, *Comrades and Cousins*, pp. 169, 171; Gavin Souter, *Lion and Kangaroo: The Initiation of Australia* (Melbourne: Text Publishing, 2000), ch. 1.
64 Clark, *History of Australia*, vol. V, p. 175.
65 Kirk, *Comrades and Cousins*, pp. 126–9, 168–71.
66 Macintyre, *Oxford History*, pp. 165–6, 172–3; Campbell, *Ireland's New Worlds*, pp. 156, 161–2, 168–70, 174–7, 180.
67 Simon Booth, 'Picturing Politics: Cartoons of Melbourne's Labour Press, 1890–1919' (PhD dissertation, University of Melbourne, 2008), p. 137.
68 For the increasingly conservative nature of Australian nationalism and charges of Labor extremism and disloyalty during the period of World War One see *1914 Federal Election Ephemera: Liberal and Farmers' Candidates, 1917, Parties: ALP, National Party*, in Federal Election Ephemera, National Library of Australia, Petherick Reading Room, MS 2247771.
69 Richard Price, *An Imperial War and the British Working Class* (London: Routledge and Kegan Paul, 1972); Morgan, *Hardie*, p. 178, for the essential 'insularity' of British labour which the South African War 'did not seriously modify'.
70 *Labour Leader*, 3 November 1900; *Justice*, 7 April, 11 August, 3 November 1900.
71 Kirk, *Change, Continuity and Class*, p. 292; *Labour Party Foundation Conference and Annual Reports*, pp. 44, 65.
72 For an emphasis upon the electoral importance of the war see Henry Pelling, *Social Geography of British Elections 1885–1910* (London: Macmillan, 1967), p. 18; Pelling,

'British Labour and British Imperialism', pp. 92–5; Paul Readman, 'The Conservative Party, Patriotism and British Politics: The Case of the General Election of 1900', *Journal of British Studies*, 40:1 (January 2001), 107–45; Paul Readman, 'The Liberal Party and Patriotism in Early Twentieth Century Britain', *Twentieth Century British History*, XII (2001), 288–302; *Manchester Guardian*, 5, 9, 10, 15, 17 October 1900; Engelken, 'Labour Movement and the Chinese Labour Question', pp. 120–5.

73 *Justice*, 7 April, 11 August, 8, 22, 29 September, 6, 13 October 1900; *Clarion*, 6 October 1900; *Labour Leader*, 22, 29 September, 6, 20, 27 October, 3, 10, 17 November 1900.

74 *Justice*, 6, 13, 20 January, 24 March, 29 September, 27 October 1900; *Labour Leader*, 21 April, 27 October 1900; *Clarion*, 13, 27 January, 10 February, 3, 10, 24 March, 4 August 1900; Pelling, 'British Labour and British Imperialism', pp. 83–7.

75 *Labour Leader*, 3, 10 November 1900; *Clarion*, 29 September 1900; *Justice*, 29 September 1900.

76 *Labour Leader*, 22, 29 September, 13, 20, 27 October, 3, 10, 17 November 1900; *Justice*, 6 October 1900; *Manchester Guardian*, 10, 15, 17 October 1900.

77 For exceptions to this neglect see, for example, Cunningham, 'Language of Patriotism'; Samuel, *Patriotism*; Taylor, 'Patriotism, History and the Left'; Ward, *Red Flag and Union Jack*, pp. 64–71.

78 *Justice*, 13 January, 1, 22, 29 September 1900; *Clarion*, 3 November 1900.

79 *Labour Leader*, 3, 10 November, 22 December 1900; *Justice*, 6 January, 7 July, 25 August 1900.

80 *Clarion*, 13, 27 January, 3 March 1900.

81 *Labour Leader*, 22, 29 September, 3, 10, November, 22 December 1900.

82 *Justice*, 13, 20 January 1900; *Labour Leader*, 3 November 1900; *Clarion*, 13, 27 January, 3 March 1900; Robert Blatchford, *Merrie England* (London: Clarion Press, 1908).

83 Ward, *Red Flag and Union Jack*, ch. 1.

84 *Ibid.*, pp. 69–70. For British socialists' systemic and experiential critiques of imperialism see Kirk, *Comrades and Cousins*, pp. 166–90.

85 Pelling, *Social Geography of British Elections*, pp. 21–2. See also *Justice*, 29 January 1910 for the SDF's view that in its dependence upon the Liberals, the Labour Party, 'as an independent force', had 'committed suicide'. For a defence of the BLP see MacDonald's article, 'What's the Matter with the Party?', *Labour Leader*, 18 March 1910.

86 *Labour Leader*, 12 January 1906, 14, 21 January, 30 December 1910; *Justice*, 6 January 1906.

87 *Labour Leader*, 12, 19 January 1906, 7 January, 16 December 1910.

88 Pelling, 'British Labour and British Imperialism', pp. 96–9.

89 Kirk, *Comrades and Cousins*, pp. 164–5, 185–7, 190–1, 201–4; *Labour Leader*, 30 June, 6 October 1905, 12 January 1906; *Justice*, 25 February, 30 December 1905, 31 March 1906; Engelken, 'Labour Movement and the Chinese Labour Question', pp. 134–79.

90 Jay M. Winter, *Socialism and the Challenge of War: Ideas and Politics in Britain 1912–1918* (London: Routledge and Kegan Paul, 1974), ch. 7.

PART III

The politics of loyalism

Introduction

The interwar years constituted a chastening experience for the ALP.
The party's pre-war ascendancy was overturned by the Nationalists
in 1917 and, with the exception of Scullin's 1929–31 Labor administration, the Right, in the form of the Nationalists and their successors,
the Nationalist-Country Party coalition and the United Australia Party
(the latter including Labor 'rats'), ruled the federal political roost up
to 1941. Although Labor's performance at the state level was better,
it failed to match both its own pre-war record and that of the Right
during the interwar period. Despite the continuing militancy and
strength of the trade unions up to the Depression and from 1934 onwards,
the labour movement's unity and boundless confidence of the pre-war
years gave way to introspection, pessimism and the bitterness resulting from the major internal splits over conscription in 1916 and 1917
and economic policy in 1930 and 1931. As the *Australian Worker*
declared in 1937, in the 'fervor of youth', the 'gospel of mateship and
its application to the industrial and social life of the nation' had been
'continually in our thoughts' and 'the Co-operative Commonwealth
was a constant vision before us'. Now, however, that 'fervor' had
'faded' and 'in the struggle with stern realities the ideal has been thrust
aside and sometimes forgotten altogether'.[1] The hegemony of the Right
and the subordination of the labour movement constituted the dominant
political reality of interwar Australia.

This was also the case in Britain. The interwar period is conven-
tionally regarded as marking the true 'Rise of Labour', as compared
with its limited and uneven development during the pre-1914 years.
The BLP achieved national office for the first time in 1924, albeit in
a minority capacity, and in so doing replaced the Liberals as the main
opposition to the Conservatives. Labour made further organisational
and electoral gains between 1924 and 1929. As a result of the general
election in the latter year another minority Labour government took
office.[2] However, Labour's interwar rise was limited. Notwithstanding
post-war militancy and the General Strike, the trade union movement
was on the defensive for most of the period. Much in the same way
as the ALP, the Labour Party split over economic policy and fared
disastrously in the 1931 election. In the 1935 election Labour 'took a

larger share of the popular vote than ever before but won a mere 154 seats'. Gains made at the municipal level in the same year provided scant compensation for another national failure and there was precious little evidence that Labour was mounting an effective challenge to the National Government in the years immediately preceding the outbreak of World War Two.[3] Moreover, the interwar period as a whole belonged to the Conservative Party and the Conservative-dominated National Government. The Conservatives, 'either independently or in governments they dominated, were in office for 17 of the 20 years', and enjoyed 'huge parliamentary majorities'.[4]

As noted in Part I, traditional and revisionist explanations of Labour's fluctuating fortunes in the two countries have revolved mainly around socio-economic and political factors. With specific reference to the interwar years, Labour's rise in Britain has been attributed to the party's attempt to widen its appeal beyond its core and mainly male trade union constituency to a wider cross-section of the community, including women and sections of the mainly urban lower and middle classes. Towards this end Labour campaigned not only to improve male living standards, but also to secure improvements for families and communities in terms of housing, education and health.[5] Labour also attempted to present itself as the 'natural' party of both the largely urban working class and the wider hard-working or 'productive people'.[6] Important organisational and ideological changes, such as the establishment in 1918 of constituency-level parties, with the opportunity for individual membership, and a new party programme, 'Labour and the New Social Order', plus improved finances, publicity and local leadership, were 'arguably ... integral to the widening of its electoral appeal and the cultivation of Labour's identity in a number of British communities'.[7]

In terms of wider societal factors, the labour movement's majority support for the war effort, its involvement in and the successes of wartime collectivism and planning and the creation of a mass electorate in 1918 have also been seen as conducive to Labour's rise.[8] On the negative side, Labour's failure to deal successfully with the Depression and unemployment between 1929 and 1931 and its split over economic policy in 1931 brought to an end its national electoral successes of the post-war period. In the interwar period as a whole, but especially during the 1930s, the Conservatives' ability to capture most of the middle-class, including ex-Liberal, vote, roughly half of the working-class vote,[9] its wide cross-class appeal to women and its highly effective negative portrayal of the organised working class as sectional, sullen, greedy, aggressive and in many instances rough, impolite, scrounging and generally lacking in independence and respectability, ensured that Labour's rise was limited and Conservative hegemony complete.[10]

[92]

In Australia the conventional literature has drawn attention both to the continuing strength of trade union support for the interwar ALP and the latter's special appeal to the material interests of the manual, and especially male, working class and small urban and rural producers. At the same time, however, it has also highlighted the party's disastrous splits over conscription in 1916 and economic policy in 1931, and the growing self-confidence and cross-class appeal of Nationalist and Country Party politicians, especially to women, and their successful opposition to industrial militants and other 'extremists', 'revolutionaries' and 'disloyalists'.[11]

Despite their many strengths, neither traditional nor revisionist accounts of Labour's mixed political fortunes in Australia and Britain during the interwar period have, in overall terms, incorporated the key concern of this chapter – the politics of loyalism to nation and empire – *fully* into their explanatory frameworks. To be sure, a concern with the issue of loyalism has been far more prominent in the Australian than the British literature. For example, Stuart Macintyre and others have shown that on several occasions from 1917 to the early 1930s Nationalist politicians successfully smeared the ALP as disloyal and revolutionary.[12] At the same time, however, the relevant body of Australian historiography as a whole has been concerned far more with the Right's employment of the 'red Scare' tactic to discredit the revolutionary Left and other elements of the labour movement, than the extent and frequency with which the Nationalist Right sought to so discredit the mainstream ALP. These gaps in our knowledge are compounded by the fact that the ALP's reactions and the outcomes of these contests have received even less attention.[13] In sum, there is scope to investigate the Australian dimension of loyalism in a more systematic and detailed fashion for the period as a whole than has so far been the case.

The same conclusion applies even more forcefully to Britain. It is the case that historians have demonstrated the importance and success to the Tories of their interwar appeals to the public/national interest, patriotism and anti-socialism.[14] Yet, as in the Australian case, Labour's responses have been neglected. Moreover, the issue of loyalism has, at best, been marginal to and, at worst, completely ignored by *labour historians'* accounts of the electoral fortunes of the interwar Labour Party.[15] Finally, detailed and systematic historiographical attention to the *comparative* Australian–British aspect of loyalism is conspicuous by its absence.

The purposes of Part III are to correct this neglect and advance the thesis that the politics of loyalism played a significant and necessary, but not in itself, sufficient part in bringing about the electoral and wider social hegemony of the Right and the subordination of Labour and labour movements in interwar Australia and Britain. I also maintain that, while present in both countries, the tarring of mainstream labour with the brushes of extremism and disloyalty was more pronounced, persistent, fiercely contested and successful in Australia than Britain, while anti-socialism was a powerful force in both countries. In putting forward these arguments I am seeking to enrich rather than discount both traditional and revisionist explanations.

Before moving to the substantive demonstration of my case in chapters 5 and 6, it is important to alert the reader to two issues which inform the chapters conceptually, methodologically and empirically. First, I am concerned to explore the extent to which there existed shared and contested definitions and practices of loyalty to nation and empire, or a mixture of these, as between mainstream Labour and its political opponents in both countries. Second, I employ the term 'the politics of loyalism' both generally and specifically. My general usage refers to attitudes and practices towards nation and empire and the often closely related issues of socialism, class and race. My particular usage concerns the examination of the nature, extent and success with which sections of the Right in both countries sought to tar the ALP and the BLP with the brush of 'alien', and especially 'Bolshevik' disloyalty and extremism. As we will see below, there were often considerable overlaps between the two usages.

Chapter 5 focuses upon the context, chronology and extent of tarring and anti-socialism in the two countries. Chapter 6 considers Labour's responses and electoral outcomes. The conclusion summarises the case for the importance of the politics of loyalism, both on its own terms and in relation to traditional and revisionist explanations.

Notes

1 *Australian Worker*, 'TWENTY YEARS AFTER', 3 November 1937.
2 Thorpe, *History of the British Labour Party*, 1997 edition, ch. 3.
3 *Ibid.*, ch. 4; Ben Pimlott, *Labour and the Left in the 1930s* (Cambridge: Cambridge University Press, 1977), Introduction.
4 Ross McKibbin, 'Class and Conventional Wisdom: The Conservative Party and the "Public" in Inter-War Britain', in his *Ideologies of Class*, p. 260; McKibbin, *Classes and Cultures*, p. 530.
5 Worley, 'Building the Party', 74–5, 83–4, 90.
6 For Labour's problematic attempts to present itself as the authentic voice of local communities up to 1914 see Lawrence, *Speaking for the People*.
7 Worley, 'Building the Party', 74.
8 McKibbin, 'The Franchise Factor in the Rise of the Labour Party', in his *Ideologies of Class*.
9 McKibbin, 'Class and Conventional Wisdom', p. 287.
10 *Ibid.*, especially pp. 270–5, 283–5.
11 Kirk, '"Australians for Australia"', 95, 108 (references in note 4); Macintyre, *Succeeding Age*, pp. 227–8, 243–50; Stuart Macintyre, *The Reds: The Communist*

Party of Australia from Origins to Illegality (St Leonards: Allen and Unwin, 1998), pp. 154–8, 214–15; Brett, *Australian Liberals*, pp. 59–60, 66, 91, 105–7.

12 Macintyre, *Succeeding Age*, pp. 190–1, 196–7, 227–8, 244–50, 273–4; Kirk, '"Australians for Australia"', 95.

13 *Ibid.*

14 McKibbin, 'Class and Conventional Wisdom'; Ward, *Red Flag and Union Jack*; Cowling, *Impact of Labour*; Jarvis, 'Stanley Baldwin'; Coleman, 'Conservative Party'; Cook, *Age of Alignment*.

15 For a good summary of the somewhat narrow and insular conceptual, methodological and substantive concerns of these accounts see Worley, 'Building the Party'.

CHAPTER FIVE

Anti-socialism and the tarring of Labour

The context: World War One and its aftermath

Key events and processes of World War One and the post-war years shaped the development and character of the Right's anti-socialism and the attempt successfully to portray Labour as disloyal and extreme. Within this context Australia and Britain underwent both shared and distinct experiences. For example, although the domestic mobilisation of physical and human resources for the war effort was more extensive and profound in Britain than in Australia, both countries suffered from war-induced human death, suffering, trauma and grief on an unprecedented scale. The modern era's first 'total' war resulted in the death of 745,000 of Britain's men (the 'lost generation') and the wounding of 1.6 million others out of approximately 5 million serving soldiers and a total population of over 40 million.[1] In Australia the 400,000 or so men who enlisted for active service constituted about one-third of the able-bodied male population out of the country's total enumerated population of 4,941,000 in 1914 (the latter excluded about 100,000 Aboriginals). Of these 400,000 a staggering total of 60,000 died, while many more were maimed. In truth 'the mythology of Anzac and the vaunted ferocity of the Australian warrior obscured the unpleasant fact that Australia's payment in lives was relatively among the combatants' highest'.[2] Unlike the European powers, this was also Australia's first large-scale external war.

Australia, moreover, was bitterly divided by the conscription issue and the future conduct of the war effort. The failure of the conscription referenda in 1916 and 1917 was accompanied by the irrevocable and disastrous split in the ALP and the mainly enforced departure from the party of pro-conscription and pro-British leaders such as 'Billy' Hughes. There subsequently occurred a fundamental realignment in Australian politics, with ex-ALPers and anti-Labor figures coming together in the Nationalist Party, formed in 1917, in order to 'Win the War'. In turn, during the following year, while the war was still taking place, the ALP supported a negotiated peace and subsequently adopted a formal commitment to peace. As we will see below, as a result of these policies the ALP was fiercely accused of disloyalty to the war effort, the 'Diggers', the country and the Empire.

As noted in Part II, this accusation was directed especially against the ALP's large Irish Catholic constituency. Despite the latter's plurality of views towards the relationship between Ireland and Britain, including majority support for Irish Home Rule *within* the British Empire, Britain's brutal suppression of the Easter Rising of 1916 was followed by the growth of anti-British sentiment among Australia's Irish Catholic communities. It was, moreover, accompanied among the population at large by anger and hostility towards British officers' incompetence, snobbery and indifference towards the Diggers' contribution to the war effort.[3]

There also existed strong anti-conscription and pacifist voices in Britain, especially among members of the Independent Labour Party and the Liberal Party. However, the majority voice in the Labour Party and the trade unions supported conscription as a necessary means in the fight for 'democracy' against 'autocracy', while labour leaders became actively involved in the war effort at local and national level. British society and the BLP as a whole were less divided by the conscription issue and the pursuit of the war to a successful conclusion than were their Australian counterparts. In turn, it was far more difficult for the Right in Britain to construct an anti-loyalist case against mainstream Labour. To be sure, Labour and Liberal opponents of conscription and pacifists were heavily defeated at the 'coupon' general election of 1918. MacDonald and Snowden and virtually all the leaders of the pre-1914 Liberal Party, including Asquith himself, suffered this fate at the hands of 'patriots'. However, for the Labour Party as a whole the election resulted in 'solid advance': the number of returned Labour Members rising from forty-two in December 1910 to sixty.[4]

The fact that the majority of the Labour Party had consistently supported the war also meant that the returning soldiers and sailors were far less likely to vent their anger and frustration against Labour than were their counterparts in Australia. The albeit short-lived National Union of Ex-Servicemen (NUX) was established early in 1919 as the socialist 'agent of a reformist labour movement'. Its purposes were 'the reintegration of soldiers into the civil order of a democratic polity' and the formation of an effective organisational counterweight against fears that 'radicalized ex-servicemen might be mobilized against the Left by right-wing extremists'. Once these fears failed substantially to materialise, 'the work of the NUX was done'. Its successor, the

[97]

hardy British Legion, formed in 1920, was free to meet the needs of the returned men on a non-political, if socially conservative, basis.[5] In contrast, as we will see below, the main ex-servicemen's organisation in Australia, the Returned Soldiers' and Sailors' Imperial League of Australia (RSSILA), was closely associated with the Right in opposition to the ALP and the Left.[6]

As the war progressed, widespread support was accompanied by a growing sense of dissatisfaction and frustration among large sections of both the Australian and British populations. This resulted from a combination of factors. These included war weariness, price inflation, high rents, declining real wages, the increasingly centralised and bureaucratic workplace and leisure-based controls and restrictions imposed on the labour movement and the wider population (dilution, the right to strike, the opportunity to drink and so on), profiteering and perceived inequalities of sacrifice and reward. The limited and uneven extent to which workers and returning service personnel were rewarded for their massive wartime sacrifices and heroism in the immediate post-war period of promised 'Reconstruction' further added to popular discontent. The outcome, in Australia, Britain and many other countries was a vast outpouring of popular protest.

At times this assumed a reactionary form, as seen in the 'race riots' against black, Arab, Chinese and African seamen in British ports in 1919 and the 'Red Flag Riots' against Russian revolutionaries and more mainstream members of the labour movement involved in a civil liberties march in Brisbane in the same year. In the former case 'intense competition for jobs' and racism were much in evidence, while in the latter opposition to Bolshevism, its symbol the Red Flag (the carrying of which was still banned under the provisions of the draconian War Precautions Act) and allegedly 'pro-Bolshevik' ALPers and trade unionists were to the fore. In both cases 'loyalist' soldiers and sailors played the main role, whether in attacking the persons, property and buildings of people of colour, revolutionaries and other labour movement activists.[7]

At the same time, however, the returned service personnel constituted a highly volatile and unpredictable element in post-war society. There were fears in official circles that if not quickly and adequately rewarded for their patriotic efforts and sacrifices, often combined with physical injury and mental suffering, they might easily 'get out of hand' and even, as in Russia, fall under the 'evil influence' of radicals and revolutionaries.[8] In fact, these fears were largely unrealised in both countries. Yet there were disturbances on the part of the returning men in Britain around 'the inadequacies of the demobilization plan', the provision of jobs and other forms of material security for them and their dependants. These included 'The Great Mutiny' of January 1919, when 2,000 servicemen in Folkestone demonstrated against delays in their demobilisation and 'freedom'.[9]

In Australia serious conflicts took place between the authorities and returned soldiers and sailors during the huge peace celebrations in 1919. In that country those who had fought in the war returned to a conflict-ridden, 'bleak and confusing' society in which they faced criticism as well as praise for the war, in which they were all too often uncertain of finding secure employment and in which some of them faced discrimination in the job market because of 'incomplete training, interrupted by the war, or incapacitation'.[10] The most serious disturbances, in Melbourne during July, involved four days of clashes between armed police and large crowds in which the returned men were prominent, the shooting and killing of a returned soldier, several injuries and arrests, and a physical attack on the offices of the state government during which the Nationalist Premier, Lawson, was injured. Significantly, officers of the RSSILA both admitted that the more 'misguided' of their members were heavily involved in the disturbances and claimed that the 'demagogues' and 'revolutionaries' – 'traitors to Australia and its soldiers during the war' – who were in the vanguard of the maritime strike then gripping Melbourne were 'only too eager to make use of the soldiers, and to sneak behind them when trouble comes'.[11]

For the most part wartime and post-war popular protest assumed a radical and, in a minority of instances, even potentially revolutionary form. This was seen in a massive upsurge in industrial militancy and political radicalism in both countries, including the New South Wales General Strike in 1917, the growing popularity of the 'One Big Union' idea among Australian trade unionists, rent strikes and other forms of collective action on 'Red Clydeside', post-war industrial 'unrest' and militancy in both countries in which ideas of workers' control, inter-union solidarity and nationalisation gained popularity, and formal commitments to socialism on the part of the BLP, in 1918, and the ALP, in 1921. On a wider canvas the Russian Revolution of 1917, combined with the formation and spread of communist parties, gave a massive boost to revolutionaries and radicals worldwide and filled defenders of the status quo with dread and loathing.[12]

In this very tense situation and despite differences of response both within and between the ruling groups in Australia and Britain, the state, many employers and the political Right adopted a battery of repressive measures in order to defeat 'IWWers' (members of the revolutionary syndicalist organisation, the Industrial Workers of the World), 'Bolsheviks' and 'Sinn Feiners'. The aim was to restore order, security, stability and the force of tradition in what had become a highly unstable and threatening world.[13] Equally, indeed probably more frightening to conservatives worldwide was the fact that the post-war popular insurgency and the prospect of social transformation were truly international in character. For example, governments 'toppled all over Europe', and there was acute concern over the continued health and prospects of the British Empire in Ireland, India and elsewhere. Much of this 'unrest' was perceived to be guided by the 'conspiratorial hand' of international communism. A concerted and unrelenting international response was required to smash the threat. World War One was to be succeeded by a new war, the first 'Cold War' against the 'Bolshevik menace'.[14]

Australia: from World War One to the Depression

In Australia it was not only the revolutionary Left, but also the ALP and the rest of the mainstream labour movement which became prime targets of the Right. The essence of the charge levelled against them by the Nationalists and their allies, including leading figures in and much of the membership of the RSSILA, was that the post-war Australian labour movement had cast aside its pre-war 'moderation' and 'respectability' and, bereft of staunchly pro-Empire leaders such as Hughes, had both moved rapidly to the left and become the tool of 'alien Reds'. Moreover, the latter process was taking place more by design than by accident: 'knavish' ALP leaders at all levels knowingly 'associated with and encouraged' the 'extremists'.[15] In addition the 'Reds' and their labour movement 'dupes' were intent upon enlisting the support of 'coloureds' internationally in order to destroy 'traditional' White Australia.[16]

Instances abound of the smearing of Labour and the labour movement by the Nationalists, the Country Party, the United Australia Party and mainstream conservative newspapers such as the *Sydney Morning Herald*. Selected examples are given in this section and the following chapter of the 'loyalist' propaganda material offered by members of these organisations. As a preface to this material, it should be noted that the organisations cited sought for the most part to achieve their goals peacefully and constitutionally, although at times with the 'necessary' resort to 'legitimate' force. As such, they did not usually endorse the resorts to violence and 'circumscribed tyranny' advocated by the proto-fascist paramilitary Diggers' Clubs portrayed by D.H. Lawrence in his 1923 novel, *Kangaroo*, set largely in Sydney, and sometimes practised by sections of the extreme Right in Australia.[17]

I begin by considering some of the key issues contained in the collection of pamphlet and other election material put out by the National(ist) Party in New South Wales in the run up to the federal election of December 1919. The collection is dominated by allegations that the labour movement in both New South Wales and the other states had been taken over, in the face of rank-and-file innocence and ignorance but with the cognisance and complicity of supposedly moderate leaders, by 'IWW', 'Bolshevik' and 'Sinn Fein' 'enemy agents and sympathisers'. In the eyes of their right-wing accusers, Irish Catholic Australians and 'their' labour movement were in total agreement with Archbishop Daniel Mannix of Melbourne, 'Irish Australia's most effective leader', in being anti-British, anti-empire and anti-Australian. No attention was paid by these right-wing propagandists, either in 1919 or into the 1920s, to the continuing 'multiple voices' of Australia's and the ALP's Irish Catholics towards 'the disruption of the empire', the partition of Ireland and the 'descent into civil war'.[18]

Material concerning the election in Broken Hill highlighted the Labor candidate's 'Stop the War' campaign, his 'Waving the Red Flag' – 'I respect no country and no flag, and the only country I will ever fight for is the red flag of the working class' – his 'alliance' with the revolutionary IWW and his support for the release of imprisoned IWWers. Voters in Broken Hill were urged to support 'THE NATIONAL CANDIDATES and Save the Country from the "Go Slow" and "Sabotage" evils'.[19]

In Melbourne the Nationalists exhorted the electorate to 'Vote the Mannix-Ryan Combination OUT!' because it 'stands for Sinn Fein', support for De Valera and his advocacy of 'a German invasion of England' and the overthrow of British 'foreign tyrants'.[20]

A letter in the collection, written by Prime Minister W.M. Hughes, expected 'every loyal Australian' to vote for the Nationalists in opposition to 'the enemy within our gates'. While not directly naming the ALP and the mainstream trade union movement as parts of 'the enemy within', Hughes left no doubt that this was now the case.[21]

The labour movement's specific opposition to conscription and its overall lack of 'genuine commitment', indeed mounting 'treachery', to the Diggers and the war effort figured prominently not only in Hughes's letter, but also in the collection as a whole. For example, Captain Harris, a Nationalist candidate in Paddington, Sydney, accused the Sydney Labor Council of 'disloyalty' in its adoption of resolutions, in May 1918, refusing 'TO TAKE PART IN ANY RECRUITING CAMPAIGN' and calling upon 'workers of this and other belligerent countries to urge their respective Governments to immediately secure an armistice on all fronts and initiate negotiations for peace'. These resolutions both reflected the ALP's commitment to peace by negotiation and anticipated its adoption, in the summer of 1918, of a formal anti-war position. An outraged Harris pointed out that this was also the time when General Haig sent 'the most memorable message in English history' to the Allied troops in France: 'With our backs to the wall, each must fight to the end. There must be no retirement.' The Labour's Council's resolutions, allegedly endorsed by his ALP opponent, L.J. O'Hara, signified 'treachery' to the Allies, to the heroic Diggers with their 'backs to the wall' and support for the 'Russian Bolshevists' who had 'deserted' the Allied cause and made peace with the German enemy, according to Harris.[22]

There was unanimity among Nationalist voices in the collection concerning labour movement 'hypocrisy' towards the returned soldiers and sailors. From allegedly being branded by sections of that movement during wartime as 'SIX-BOB-A-DAY MURDERERS', the returned men were now being hailed by the post-war labour movement as 'OUR GALLANT CHAMPIONS OF LIBERTY', and asked to join the movement and vote Labor out of both material self-interest and class solidarity. Yet contrary to the ALP's claim that it was most committed to meeting the returned men's needs for decent jobs, wages and social-welfare provision, the Nationalists were quick to point out that the labour movement supported preference in employment for trade unionists rather than the returned soldiers and sailors. The latter were urged to 'VOTE FOR HUGHES THE SOLDIERS' REPRESENTATIVE', the champion of 'Preference to Returned Soldiers in all Government Employment', 'INCREASED PENSIONS', 'THE MOST LIBERAL GRATUITY IN THE WORLD' and the 'saviour' of 'THE WHITE AUSTRALIA POLICY'. However, 'ABOVE ALL', they must 'VOTE FOR AUSTRALIA', 'the land which you saved', and 'let those who opposed you in the War, who let 60,000 of your pals die . . . be utterly condemned'.[23]

An equally emotive appeal was made to the 'WIVES, MOTHERS, SISTERS' of 'Australians Who Went and Fought for Home and the Flag'. Major Shillington, ex-Vice President of the RSSILA, and the Nationalist candidate for Petersham in Sydney, asked them to remember that 'The National Party was true to you and your soldier lads right through', whereas Labor 'contained all the "disloyal" and treacherous elements'.[24] Propaganda of this kind made an important contribution to the easy Nationalist victories in the federal elections of 1917 and 1919.

Shillington's appeal to women underlined the important general fact that the politics of loyalism were highly gendered in character. We have seen already at various points in this study that the ALP prided itself upon being the leading progressive voice in relation to the 'emancipation of women'. It had, of course, been a keen supporter of the enfranchisement of women. At the same time, however, it was fiercely patriarchal in its defence of the notion of the 'male breadwinner' and the belief that men constituted the 'natural' leaders of the party and the unions. Truly independent women found a more congenial home in feminist and socialist circles in both Australia and Britain.

The Right also opposed the notion of the economically independent and sexually liberated woman. At the same time, however, it maintained that as the 'true' guardians of the home, the family and children, women, and especially Protestant women, were in charge of institutions vital to the preservation of social and political stability, consensus and order. As such, they constituted a crucial element in the fights against extremism, disorder and disloyalty.

This was clearly revealed in the case of 'the largest and most enduring liberal organisation before the formation of the Liberal Party' in 1944–45, the increasingly autonomous and influential Australian Women's National League (AWNL). Formed in 1904 'as part of an anti-Labor movement by the Victorian Employers' Federation', the AWNL adopted a 'fighting platform' to 'support loyalty to the throne; to combat State socialism; to educate women in politics; to preserve the purity of home life'. Socialists, perceived as the dominant force in the ALP, were portrayed as 'the enemies of family life', the advocates of 'free love' and as, at root, anti-imperial, anti-monarchical republicans. In essence they were 'un-Australian' and 'un-British'. Increasingly their primary loyalty was seen to lie with an 'alien' and 'extreme' force, the newly created Soviet Union.

During the interwar period the AWNL maintained its independent existence and large membership (around 30,000 during the 1930s) and supported 'the party that stood in opposition to Labor – whatever its name and whoever its leader'. As such, it constituted a significant basis of autonomous women's support for the Right. In 1944 Menzies persuaded the AWNL to merge with his 'recreated Liberal Party', but the league agreed only on the basis that the Women's Section in the new party 'retained its own secretary and organisational structure, as well as achieving equality for women in the party as a whole'. In contrast, women in the male-dominated ALP were portrayed as being 'marginalised and largely powerless'.[25] As we will see in due course, building upon their late nineteenth- and early twentieth-century experience in the Primrose League, women in Britain would provide a similarly important base of support for the anti-socialism, patriotism and imperialism of the 'loyalist' interwar Conservative Party.[26]

By the early 1920s there was general agreement on the constitutional Right that the electorate and the population as a whole were faced with the stark choice between a more or less fully 'Bolshevised', 'disloyal' and anti-imperial ALP and the secure, patriotic, democratic and home-grown Nationalist Party and its successor in government, the Nationalist-Country Party coalition.

The inflammatory election propaganda put out by the National Party in 1922 demonstrates this point. For example, Labor was portrayed as a 'Devilfish' which had abandoned its reforming 'Australian' past in favour, 'AS ITS MAIN OBJECTIVE', of a 'SCHEME DIRECTLY MODELLED ON THE SOVIET SYSTEM OF COMMUNISM'. 'Proof' of this lay in its adoption of the 'socialisation' plank in 1921 – formally committing the party to 'the socialisation of industry, production and exchange' – and widespread post-war support in the labour movement for 'revolutionary class hatred and industrial warfare'. 'New' Labor was now 'dominated by revolutionary Communists', by men who 'have no love for Australia or the British Empire', who preach 'hatred, upheaval, chaos' and who 'wish to introduce into Australia foreign doctrines such as have brought bloodshed, starvation and economic ruin to Russia'. 'Communist Bosses' were also seen as the wire-pullers behind the ALP's intention to reduce interest on war loans and savings bank accounts to the financial detriment of 'hundreds of thousands of earners of small incomes'.

In contrast the Nationalists portrayed themselves as guaranteeing 'SAFTEY FIRST', 'sound government and a fair deal for every class' and 'unswerving loyalty and devotion to His Majesty the King and the British Empire'. The Empire was the embodiment of 'freedom and the Brotherhood of Nations'. It constituted 'the only bulwark to-day between world-revolution and civilising democracy'. As such, it was imperative to safeguard its present and future inviolability against the ALP's 'disruptive' advocacy of 'self-determination' for Ireland and Australia.[27]

The politics of loyalism in Australia at this time were both highly symbolic and fiercely contested in character. This was seen dramatically in the 'battle of the flags'. The Labor 'Devilfish' raised the spectre of the 'tentacles' of 'REVOLUTIONARY COMMUNISM' and its puppet ALP 'clutching at the nation's flag' and replacing it 'with a RED one'. The identification of the Red Flag with Bolshevik subversion and disloyalty had been at the centre of the 'Red Flag Riots' in Brisbane in March 1919 and Sydney in May 1921.

As briefly noted above, in the former case returned soldiers attacked revolutionaries, many of them Russian, who were carrying the banned Red Flag. There ensued three nights of rioting on the part of 'loyalist' forces who wrecked the Russian Hall, seriously injured nineteen policemen and attacked a building housing the ALP's *Daily Standard* newspaper, which was 'accused of being pro-Bolshevik'. Prime Minister

Hughes 'expressed unabashed delight at hearing how the soldiers had dealt with the Bolsheviks', while the conservative *Brisbane Courier* 'exulted' in the 'wild and thrilling magnificence' of the rioting. In turn, the ALP in Brisbane clearly distanced itself from the actions of the revolutionaries, highlighted its constitutionalism and the 'peaceful attainment of its political objective', and abhorred the 'direct' and 'mob' actions of the revolutionaries and their returned soldier assailants respectively. E.G. Theodore's state Labor government subsequently imprisoned fifteen men 'simply for displaying red flags'.[28]

On 1 May 1921, in Sydney, revolutionary communists and their supporters marched behind the Red Flag, which was no longer banned by law, and held a meeting on the Domain to celebrate not only the achievement of the Eight Hour Day, as was the tradition, but also international working-class solidarity, especially with communists in Russia and elsewhere. During the meeting clashes broke out with a small group of returned soldiers. In the course of these some of the soldiers attempted to pull down the Red Flag and hoist a Union Jack in its place. They were unsuccessful, but in the ensuing melée a torn piece of the Union Jack was 'hoisted alight on the end of a stick by some person in the crowd and burned'.

This led to a massive conservative backlash. In 'a demonstration of loyalty unprecedented in Australia', between 100,000 and 150,000 'patriots' from all over New South Wales responded by taking part in a rally in Sydney a week later to pledge allegiance to the Union Jack, 'the priceless symbol of the freedom of our British institutions, of the democratic spirit of our British constitution, of empire unity, and of all the common ties of race and blood'. The meeting resolved that neither the 'red flag' nor 'any other emblem of revolution' 'shall . . . be exhibited in this state'.

During this 'Orgy of Patriotism' there took place fights between the Left and Right, the burning of a Red Flag, the 'tearing down' and trampling underfoot of the Australian flag and a physical attack upon an ALP platform and its own returned soldier speakers. The meeting declared the Union Jack to be 'the flag for Australia', and, 'in view of the dangers threatening the Commonwealth and the State', advocated the 'eradication' from Australia of 'all enemy agents and sympathisers who are out to disrupt the integrity of the Empire'. Further verbal and physical exchanges between 'loyalists' and 'revolutionaries' occurred during the following week.[29]

As in Brisbane two years earlier, there followed recriminations between, on the one hand, the Nationalists and their allies and, on the other hand, the ALP and its supporters. For example, the *Sydney Morning Herald* blamed the ruling ALP authorities for the 'disloyalty' and 'disorder' (the same charge had been made by the *Brisbane Courier* against Premier Theodore and the ruling ALP in Brisbane). Rather than permitting the march, meeting and the carrying of the Red Flag on May Day, the authorities should have banned them as being offensive to 'all law-abiding people', 'antagonistic' to Australian nationalism and 'destructive' of 'the British Empire and of its emblem, the Union Jack', according to the *Herald*. Furthermore, instead of describing the loyalist meeting as 'mob rule', the ALP should have joined the *Herald* in celebrating the eruption of 'a great, luminous flame of patriotism'. However, in the opinion of the newspaper and prominent Nationalists, Labor's failure to do so lay in the fact that it, and especially its supine leaders in Sydney, had been 'captured' by its 'extremist wing' of 'Bolsheviks' and 'Sinn Feiners'.[30]

As in Brisbane, leading spokespersons of the ALP in Sydney totally rejected these allegations. They pointed out that their party had not been associated with 'the Communists' in 'any way' during May Day and subsequent events, and that it unreservedly condemned 'mob violence' and the revolutionary road for Australia.[31] In addition to insisting upon the party's impeccable constitutional and peaceful credentials, including the rights of free speech and lawful assembly, they strongly maintained that it was the ALP and its members, rather than the 'sham nationalists' of the National(ist) Party, who were the 'real' patriots, the 'true' 'Australians for Australia'.[32]

Henry Boote, the outstanding editor of the Sydney-based *Australian Worker*, criticised the *Sydney Morning Herald* and the Right for their attempt to 'push forward the Union Jack' as *the* flag commanding their allegiance as Australians. This attempt constituted an act of 'disloyalty to the Australian people', according to Boote, because while the Union Jack 'is the emblem of the Empire' and while Australia 'is part of the Empire', it also 'has its own national individuality and its own national flag'. Boote concluded that in largely ignoring the place and role of the Australian flag in arguments about loyalty and disloyalty and in 'exalting the Union Jack above it', the *Sydney Morning Herald* and the Right in general were subordinating the national and patriotic to the imperial, and in large measure anti-Australian, British interest.[33]

Lastly, ALPers defiantly pointed out that allegiance to the Red Flag was by no means the sole preserve of revolutionary communists. For example, in Australia and Britain it was symbolic of organised workers' commitment to non-revolutionary labour movements and 'the international emancipation of the workers'. It represented loyalty to *both* the domestic and international workers' movement and the nation. A 'symbol of common faith', it was 'superior to the national welfare without being in the least antagonistic towards it'. It was thus beholden upon all 'true' democrats to tolerate widespread and varied allegiance to flags and other 'sacred symbols'.[34] The attempt on the part of the Nationalists and the RSSILA to ban the Red Flag constituted a glaring example of their 'Prussianism', of their concerted attempt to use the 'affront to the Empire Flag' cynically and falsely 'to discredit the Australian Labor Party' and to fasten 'un-Australian' and 'imperialistic' 'despotism and militarism' upon the country in the name of stability, order and security.[35]

The Right's extensive tarring of the ALP and its general resort to 'Prussianism' bore only limited electoral fruit in the immediate term. In the 1922 federal election the ALP won three more seats than the Nationalists. This underscored the fact that the politics of loyalism did not constitute either the sole or sufficient explanation of electoral trends in these years. However, the Country Party's fourteen seats and its subsequent willingness to form a coalition with the Nationalists ensured another defeat for Labor. The one mitigating factor for the latter was that formation of the coalition was conditional upon Hughes's resignation. In this way the ALP's most prominent 'rat' and one of its fiercest critics, was forced from power.[36]

In the longer term, however, Labor satisfaction was short lived. The coalition government went on to achieve clear victories in the federal elections of 1925 and 1928, albeit with a much reduced majority in the latter. In the 1929 election the ALP achieved an isolated federal success under the leadership of James Scullin and his successful defence of two key pillars of the New Commonwealth, the system of federal arbitration and the 'Australian standard' of comparatively high wages and good working and living conditions. This defence was conducted against Prime Minister S.M. Bruce's radical-reactionary plan to hand most responsibility for arbitration back to the states in order to reduce the incidence of industrial conflict and the power of trade union 'oligarchs' and to deflate the economy.[37]

Bruce lost the election in 1929 because of a widespread perception that he had become too extreme, too sectional and partial towards the interests of capital and too unmindful of cherished national traditions and institutions. Yet in the previous two elections he had successfully presented himself as the champion of the national interest against the 'selfishness', 'extremism' and 'disloyalty' of the labour movement. The elections of 1925, 1928 and indeed 1929 were set against the shaping background of extremely fierce, bitter and long industrial battles on the waterside and in the timber and coalmining industries. In the face of these conflicts, declining profit margins and, by the late 1920s, the onset of the Depression, the Nationalist-Country Party coalition sought to cut labour costs, 'tame the unions', legalise lock-outs, increase strike penalties, deport foreign-born 'undesirables' and increase the surveillance and censorship of 'labour'. In the eyes of the latter they were 'repressive', 'vindictive' and 'authoritarian' tools of reactionary capital.[38] In their own eyes they were the 'saviours of the nation'.

This was clearly seen in 1925 when coalition leaders turned the federal election into an 'anti-communist' crusade. Bruce warned that, 'in a very critical hour in our national history', the unions had been 'captured by "wreckers who would plunge us into the chaos and misery of class war"', and of the urgent need to 'cut out of our National life' the 'canker of these men advocating Communistic doctrines'.[39] Tom Walsh and Jacob Johnson, both foreign born and respectively ex-communist president and secretary of the Seamen's Union, were made scapegoats for the disruption of maritime transport and sentenced to deportation under the amended Immigration Act. The High Court rejected the attempted deportation as being unconstitutional, but this did not quell Bruce's fury. The Prime Minister both declared his general support for trade unionism and condemned the 'supineness' [sic] of its leaders who were allowing the movement to be 'used to-day by extremists for the purpose of defying Governments, and dictating to them'. In this 'critical' situation, concluded Bruce, the government itself was obliged to take the lead in 'saving' both the union movement and the country at large from 'the disasters and sufferings which the few extremists in our midst are desirous of bringing upon it'.[40]

Once re-elected, the government earnestly set about the process of redemption. This was particularly so in the case of the new Attorney-General, John Latham. Latham's personal papers bear full testimony to the crude and paranoiac, but determined and ruthless, anti-communist and anti-radical mindset that informed government thinking at the very highest level and anticipated the Cold War and McCarthyism of the 1950s. In his unpublished typescript, 'The Communist Menace in Australia', Latham called upon Australians to 'WAKE UP' and 'clear Australia from the blight which is already sapping its life blood'. That 'blight', of course, was the 'international conspiracy' and 'worldwide threat' of 'Communism' – that 'subtle and sinuous menace'. 'Acting under . . . orders' from their 'masters in Moscow' and 'little dreamed of by the public and even by members of many trade unions', Australian communists were engaging in 'silent and unseen propaganda, ceaselessly working and poisoning far below the surface' in their 'germ cells', in order to 'enslave and destroy Labour and to pave the way for . . . the coming of the revolution', according to Latham. Furthermore, although small in numbers, the Communist Party had 'many adherents and dupes', and was 'slowly but surely gaining control of the unions and emulating the small but effective group which ruled the Bolshevik government in Russia from the outset'.[41]

In Latham's opinion the ALP was faced with a simple choice: to 'acknowledge their obedience to the Communist Party or to give it unequivocal official denial and to prove by its actions as well as words where and for what it stands'. As matters stood, and notwithstanding the ALP's proscriptions against communists, the fact that Jock Garden continued to be secretary to the New South Wales Labour Council and a leading member of the Communist Party signified, for Latham, that it was 'futile for Labour to deny its kinship with the Communist Party'. It was the duty of all patriotic citizens to rally behind the Nationalist cause, expose and oppose the ALP's and the trade unions' disloyalty and extremism. Once again, there was perceived to be no scope for equivocation or the adoption of a 'middle way' between the Nationalists and communism.[42]

The charges levelled by Latham against the labour movement continued to be the common currency of the Right for the remainder of the decade. For example, during the state election in New South Wales in 1927 T.R. Bavin, the Nationalist candidate, declared that the 'priceless heritage of our race' – 'our parliamentary institutions and the system of representative, responsible government' – was 'at stake' because the Labor opposition and the trade unions were increasingly under the control of forces which 'repudiate any obligations of loyalty to the British Empire'.[43] Bavin won the subsequent election and the *Sydney Morning Herald* congratulated the electorate on stopping 'the stone of unloosened Communism', which had grown beyond the control of the Labor Premier, Jack Lang, and which might otherwise 'have speedily become an avalanche and wrecked the state'.[44] A year later, with the federal election taking place against the background of repressive anti-union legislative measures, claims of labour disloyalty to the nation, empire and White Australia and allegiance to 'Moscow and Shanghai' and 'black, brown and brindle' socialist internationalism, appeared regularly in the press.[45]

In 1929 Bruce claimed that the 'death blow to Federal arbitration' had been 'struck by the extremists who have been allowed to occupy positions of power and authority within the Labour movement'.[46] *Victory*, the newspaper of the National Party of New South Wales, declared that Australians had to choose between 'the rule of law' and 'the rule of the irresponsible trade union leaders who have encrusted themselves on the Labour Party'. The latter were 'wreckers' who, 'following blindly . . . the Russian-Mongol Reds', would jettison White Australia and 'put the black hand of misery and ruin all over Australia', with wages 'equivalent to husks of rice' and 'the smell of an oil-rag'.[47]

On this rare occasion, however, scaremongering failed to return the coalition to federal office.

Britain: from World War One to the Depression

I will turn to the story of tarring and anti-socialism in 1930s Australia in due course. Before doing so, it is necessary to trace parallel developments in Britain from the time of World War One to the Depression and see how they compare with those in Australia during the same period. In this context it is useful to note three comparative conclusions which emerge from the evidence presented both above and below.

First, although tarring of the mainstream labour movement with the brushes of disloyalty and extremism was certainly present in Britain from the years of wartime through the decade of the 1920s, in overall terms it was less marked and sustained than in Australia. Second, it was also, again in overall terms, less aggressive, uncompromising and indiscriminate in its application in Britain. Third, at the same time tarring in Britain formed part of the development of a much wider anti-socialist current of thought and feeling which strongly informed many aspects of the life of the country, including its daily cultural and social experiences and 'commonsense', as well as its formal and more narrowly defined political institutions and electoral contests. As Ross McKibbin has so persuasively argued, it was the daily 'commonsense' of the 'un-British' or at least 'un-English' nature of the 'socialist other' that did so much to underpin the hegemony of both conservative 'ways of being and seeing' and Conservatism in interwar Britain.[48]

In the later years of World War One and the immediate post-war period the BLP was not subjected to the charge of 'disloyalty' to anything like the same extent and intensity as was the ALP in Australia. As noted earlier, the support of the majority of the British labour movement for conscription and bringing the war to a successful conclusion, combined with the active involvement of prominent labour leaders in the institutions of the state and civil society set up to promote the war effort, meant that there was far less scope for either the Right or the returned soldiers and sailors to tar the labour movement with the brushes of pacifism, defeatism and disloyalty. The Labour Party in Britain emerged from the war far more united, expectant and confident of the future than its fundamentally split and beleaguered counterpart in Australia.[49] The different wartime experience of British labour also helps to explain why Britain did not experience a post-war 'battle of the flags', at least on the Australian model and scale, and why the British Legion and its members, in contrast to the RSSILA, did not ally itself closely with a right-wing political party.

Even during the period of post-war insurgency and crisis the author-ities increasingly realised that blanket condemnation and the 'Red' tarring of the whole labour movement, in accordance with the wishes of some of the more extreme elements in the Conservative Party and beyond, would both be misplaced and probably make matters worse. While there was unqualified opposition to the 'wild men' of the move-ment, there was also a growing appreciation of the fact that many trade union leaders exerted a moderating influence upon their members and were totally opposed to the prospects of social breakdown and revolution. The employment by the state, the Coalition and employers of a mixture of coercion and conciliation contributed greatly to the successful defusion of the post-war crisis. For example, while there was firm resolution against the threat of revolution, of a ready resort to strike breaking, industrial and political 'blacklisting', espionage and pro-capitalist propaganda, there also existed a preparedness to recognise unions, to find allies among trade union leaders and to promote limited social reform and industrial welfare and recreation schemes.[50] This provided a marked contrast to the process whereby the Right more or less uniformly tarred the entire labour movement in Australia.

This is not, however, to suggest that commonalities and similarities between the tarring of the labour movements of Australia and Britain as disloyal and extreme were either absent or negligible. For example, in similar fashion to the Australian federal elections of 1917 and 1919, the 'coupon'[51] general election of 1918 in Britain, the first election conducted on the basis of universal adult male suffrage, was dominated by the issue of 'patriotism'.

The election resulted in a landslide for the Conservative-dominated Coalition which had actively pursued the war effort and which exploited 'the wave of patriotic sentiment that followed the end of the war'. In contrast, 'The Liberal pacifists were totally obliterated', the Independent Liberals 'massacred' and the 'pacifist' wing of the Labour Party suffered 'almost total defeat'.[52] The latter included defeat at the polls for two of Labour's most prominent leaders, the ILPers Ramsay MacDonald and Philip Snowden.[53] The facts that the Labour Party's formal, if vague, commitment to a socialist objective in 1918 coincided with the rise of Bolshevism and that, like their counterparts in Australia, many British labour movement activists and leaders welcomed the Bolshevik Revolution as marking the dawn of a new era of equality and 'true' workers' democracy, were eagerly seized upon by sections of the Right. Conservatives attempted to 'establish an organic link between Marxism-Leninism and the British Labour Party'. The latter was seen as 'an integral part of a worldwide revolu-tionary movement', complete with support for nationalist groups and independence in Ireland and India.[54] Moreover, these developments presented the Conservative Party with a very favourable opportunity to make political capital out of Labour's support for the 'Reds' at a time of serious industrial crisis and when it feared for its continued popularity within the new setting of mass democracy.[55]

Beyond the Conservative Party, the Anti-Socialist Union (ASU), formed in 1908 and including among its ranks several individuals who were also members of the former organisation, 'made every effort' to draw a close association 'between communism and a more socialist-orientated Labour Party'. It attempted to show that Bolshevik agents were 'actively engaged in fomenting unrest in Britain' and that 'the Labour Party encouraged the Russian Bolsheviks, and obstructed every foreign policy of our government which might possibly operate unfavourably to the world revolution plans of the tyrants'.[56]

It is a well-established fact among historians that the tarring of the Labour Party with the Red brush was most pronounced during the general election of 1924. The previous two elections, in 1922 and 1923, had been dominated by other issues. The 1922 contest followed the break-up of the Coalition. It resulted in a 'severe Liberal defeat', especially among the Coalition Liberals. Labour, however, made 'dramatic gains in the industrial regions', especially on Clydeside, and grew nationally 'from a relatively ineffective … force to the position of a vigorous and determined opposition'. The Conservatives, freed from the Coalition, won 'with a clear majority of seats'.[57] During the contest Labour campaigned hard on the 'Condition of the People' socio-economic question and on peace and reconciliation, rather than aggression, revenge and exclusion, in an extremely unstable post-war Europe. It also claimed that the rich should meet their obligations towards social stability and improved living standards. It proposed a capital levy in order to redeem the War Debt and so to reduce the high taxation associated with the payment of interest on the debt.[58]

In response, Winston Churchill, Lloyd George and other prominent politicians accused Labour of now being under the control of 'wilder, more violent and irresponsible' young men who had 'voted down the older wiser heads' and who were seeking to 'drive capital away', 'as in Russia', and so bring about 'national ruin'. Labour was also charged with support for revolutionary, unconstitutional and illegal measures and of representing the 'selfish' class interest rather than that of the nation as a whole.[59]

Key figures in the Labour Party, including the then leader J.R. Clynes and MacDonald, who would resume the party leadership in 1924, offered an immediate and unqualified counterattack. There had been 'unparalleled misrepresentation of the programme and purposes of the labour Party': Labour was 'constitutional', 'patriotic', a 'critical' opposition and 'a possible alternative government' and the representative of the national interest and 'all classes'. The capital levy was defended on the grounds that the privileged and propertied possessed not only rights, but also obligations towards the interests of society as a whole. The proposed levy was thus defended in the national interest rather than out of class envy and revenge or any general communistic levelling intent.[60]

Labour leaders feared that sections of the political establishment and the Tory press were intent upon unfairly 'playing the red card'. These fears were reinforced in the weeks immediately following the election when the recently elected leader of the Conservative Party, Bonar Law, briefed some sections of the press, but not the Labour Party's *Daily Herald*, that a 'Red Plot' lay behind the marches and demonstrations of the unemployed in London and that the police would be armed to prevent a 'riot'.[61] As the Liberal *Manchester Guardian* observed, Bonar Law had 'blundered' in his lack of honesty and accuracy.[62]

The tarring of the Labour Party played an insignificant part in the election of December 1923. This was the election in which Stanley Baldwin, who had replaced Bonar Law as the Conservative leader, fought unsuccessfully in favour of Protection. Baldwin's government was succeeded by a minority Labour government in January 1924. This, of course, was the first time Labour had held the reins of national power. This was a historic moment for the party and its supporters even though it was dependent upon Liberal support. Unfortunately for Labour, its period in office lasted only until the next general election, of October 1924. On this occasion the tarring of Labour proved to be the decisive factor in its defeat.

Much in the manner of Labor in Australia, by 1924 the Labour Party in Britain had clearly dissociated itself from and become a firm opponent of 'revolutionary' and 'dictatorial' communism and the Communist Party. Despite early enthusiasm for the Bolshevik Revolution among its members, Labour had come to see communism as being at odds with its own constitutionalism and gradualism. The Communist Party's attempts to affiliate to the Labour Party in Britain the early 1920s had been successfully rebuffed and the party was now giving serious thought to the ways in which it could deal successfully with the problem of individual Communists who had been elected, in the trade unions and other constituent bodies of the party, as delegates to Labour conferences.[63]

Yet even before 1924 the Labour Party's attempts to distance itself from communism met with 'considerable scepticism' on the part of many Conservatives and ASU members.[64] This 'scepticism' was trans-formed into open and widespread disbelief by a series of issues and events during the brief lifetime of the Labour government. For example, a conflict arose as to whether allegiance to the Red Flag, the 'workers' flag', was compatible with loyalty to the nation and empire and British 'freedom', as argued by Labour, or, as claimed by Churchill and others, whether it signified Russian 'slavery'.[65] Conflict also resulted from the government's proposed treaty with and loan to Russia in order to boost trade and prosperity and bring Russia into 'the family of nations', and its decision to withdraw the prosecution against J.R. Campbell, the editor of the communist *Workers' Weekly*, who had urged troops not to fire on strikers. MacDonald, the Prime Minister, adopted a conciliatory approach to Russia as part of a general strategy to heal wartime and post-war wounds in Europe by means of patient negotiation, arbitration and inclusion. He also maintained that the prosecution of Campbell, especially if unsuccessful, would draw more attention to and probably increase the popularity of the communist cause in Britain. In addition, communism would be driven underground and so make official scrutiny and control more difficult.[66]

Labour's attempts to defuse matters only succeeded, however, in making them much worse. In October the government resigned and called a general election in response to a successful Liberal motion to set up a committee of inquiry into the 'Campbell affair' as 'a matter of confidence'. The ensuing general election campaign was dominated from beginning to end by the 'Red Scare'. Although there was debate among the candidates about unemployment and other social issues, it was barely audible amidst the general clamour that the Labour Party had been effectively 'captured' by 'the Reds', the 'wild men', the 'extremists'.

Churchill and Lloyd George were among the leading and most vociferous accusers. Thus, 'a body of extremists' had 'forced MacDonald's hand' and the Prime Minister was 'too afraid' to stand up to them. His party wanted to 'abolish capital and overthrow the existing order of society', 'interfere with the course of justice' and the 'time honoured' independence of the judiciary (in the Campbell case) and make a treaty and offer a loan to a Bolshevik government committed to 'revolution' and 'revolutionaries', 'autocracy' and the 'crushing' of 'the last embers of liberty in Georgia'. In addition, in the event of the Russians defaulting on the repayment of the loan, the British taxpayers would be liable for payment. This was at a 'time of hardship' at home and 'when we have not got enough to develop our own Empire'.[67]

Churchill further denounced the 'wickedness' taking place in Russia, appealed to the country 'not to put on her shield' the 'foul Red Flag of the Communist Revolution' and concluded that 'if we are to be ruled by the Socialists' then 'at least let us have the headquarters in London and not in Moscow'.[68] Lloyd George exhorted Liberals to 'fight the extremists of the Socialist Party' and to stand 'shoulder to shoulder' with Conservative colleagues. Otherwise 'it will not be long before the existing order is overthrown'. The success of this exhortation was revealed in the widespread and frequent formation of anti-socialist electoral alliances and pacts by Liberals and Conservatives, especially in municipal politics, throughout the 1920s.[69]

The most significant feature of the election campaign was that these allegations, condemnations and exhortations were not confined to Churchill, other 'Diehards' in the Conservative Party, the conservative press and other renowned anti-socialists, such as Lloyd George. Rather they were expressed, with a rare depth, breadth and ferocity, by politicians and press organs from right across the political spectrum and the country as a whole.

Two examples may serve to underline this point. First, the *Manchester Guardian*, committed to both liberalism and the Liberal Party, and yet mindful of the fact that the Labour Party 'is a composite party', the 'bulk 'of it being composed of 'elements of active Liberalism or Radicalism', nevertheless declared, 'On the other hand, there is a minority of doctrinaire Socialists, some of them hardly distinguishable from Communists, who exercise within the party an influence altogether out of proportion to their numbers.' The party had effectively been taken over by these 'extremists'. The *Guardian* also disagreed with Labour's 'political motive' in interfering in the Campbell case and its 'extraordinary eagerness' to 'conclude a treaty on almost any terms with the Russian communist Government' and 'their willingness to run all risks in defence of it'. As seen in the earlier unsuccessful efforts of Lloyd George, the Liberals 'also want a treaty' with Russia, but 'not on any terms', according to the *Guardian*.[70]

Second, Stanley Baldwin, while cutting a relatively moderate figure, emphasising the importance of improving social conditions and urging 'working men' to 'take their proper place in the ranks of our party', was also very critical of Labour's 'insolence' in 'looking to Russia', rather than Britain and its history, 'for a gospel suitable for the most progressive people'. In Baldwin's opinion, Britain should not make a treaty with a country committed to 'world revolution'. Revolution in Britain would mean, as in the Russian case, 'starvation for the mass of the people'. Baldwin warned Labour that 'before it could ever hope to secure power in this country', it would have to 'purge itself of the Communist hindrance', 'this foreign, anti-English element.[71]

In the immediate term the 'bombshell' of the Zinoviev letter meant that Labour simply did not have time to heed Baldwin's advice. The culmination, rather than, as argued in parts of the historiography, the central feature, of a campaign already thoroughly 'swamped' by the 'Red Scare', the letter was published in the *Daily Mail* on 25 October, only four days before polling day. Purportedly signed by Zinoviev, the President of the Soviet Presidium and Arthur McManus of the British Communist Party, it contained instructions to 'British subjects' to 'work for the violent overthrow of existing institutions in this country' and the 'subversion of His Majesty's armed forces as a means to that end'. The letter had supposedly been sent in mid-September and reached MacDonald around 10 October. The latter, however, was awaiting proof of its authenticity before bringing the matter into the public domain. MacDonald's credibility was badly damaged not only by his procrastination but also by the fact that it was the Conservative *Mail*, rather than himself, which first brought the letter to public attention. 'While not definitely committing himself', MacDonald suggested that the letter was 'a forgery', 'the work of political conspirators against Labour'. In any event, coming on top of the barrage of anti-Labour propaganda, the Zinoviev letter merely sealed Labour's fate.[72]

The election thus saw the triumph of 'the politics of extremism'. The Conservatives came out clearly on top and the Liberal Party suffered 'virtual destruction'. The Labour Party experienced mixed fortunes. Although it lost power and saw its seats fall from 191 in 1923 to 151 in 1924, its overall vote increased by over 1 million, it made impressive gains in industrial constituencies and it saw itself, and was seen by the Australian labour movement, as the ascendant force of 'progress and democracy' in British politics.[73] At the same time the party was left to heed the lessons of 'tarring'. In the future it would present itself, in the face of mounting criticism from the ILP and other sectors of the Left,[74] even more strongly as the party of the consensual nation, enlightened empire, constitutionalism, moderation, responsibility and respectability.

The election campaign of 1924 bore a striking similarity to those in post-war Australia described earlier, in terms of the acute, unremitting and extensive ways in which mainstream labour was tarred with the 'Red' brush. Leading figures in the Australian labour movement, so used to being 'smeared' as 'Reds' by their opponents at home, quickly and correctly identified the key role of the employment of the 'Political Bogey Man', while also exaggerating the significance of the Zinoviev letter, in the British election. The British party was advised by Queensland's Labor Premier, Theodore, to 'mind its own business, to deliver its own goods and not to associate with any other party'.[75]

Although quick to accept such advice, the post-1924 Labour Party soon discovered that moderation, in itself, did not guarantee that tarring would automatically be put to rest. Two years later, during the General Strike, the labour movement was widely portrayed as being unconstitutional and motivated by sectional greed rather than the national interest. Despite the obvious moderation and constitutionalism of many of its leaders, labour was widely accused of having been taken over by the 'wild men' taking their orders from Russia, 'with cautious Labour MPs and trade unionists forced to follow their initiatives'. The Labour Party was believed to be insufficiently tough in its actions against communist 'infiltrators' (although now barred as candidates and party members, communists could still attend Labour conferences as union delegates), while in Bermondsey, Battersea, Hull and some other parts of the country the cry was raised that Labour had 'put the Red Flag before the Union Jack'.[76]

Between the end of the General Strike and the Depression the direct tarring of labour declined markedly. This resulted partly from the increasingly defensive position and far more moderate and conciliatory character of the trade union movement as a whole. This was a period in which the economy was generally depressed, in which trade union membership fell to below the five million mark in the wake of the General Strike (the acute fall in 1926 was part of an almost continuous membership decline in British trade unionism, from the historic high point of 8,348,000 in 1920 to a low of 4,392,000 in 1933[77]) and in which the state and employers adopted a combination of punitive and conciliatory measures towards industrial labour.[78] In addition, communist influence in the trade union movement fell steeply. The failure of the 'direct action' methods of the General Strike gave moderate union leaders a golden opportunity to increase their own powers and to 'root out' dissident voices.

This set the tone for the 1930s, when the dominant trade union leaders, Ernest Bevin and Walter Citrine, prided themselves upon their anti-communism and 'statesman-like' behaviour. Expelled from the unions and the Labour Party in increasing numbers, communists also distanced themselves from the mainstream labour movement as a result of their allegiance to the Moscow-imposed 'class against class' line from 1928–29 onwards. The Communist Party's membership declined from 12,000 in 1926 to just over 2,000 in 1930.[79] Now far more moderate, both absolutely and in relation to its Australian counterpart, the post-1926 British trade union movement thus constituted a far less likely and successful target for 'red' baiters.

A shift in political emphasis – from the politics of loyalism to a central concern with mounting economic and social problems – also helped to ease matters. The general election of 1929 was dominated by Labour and Liberal claims that the Conservatives had failed to solve the key problems of unemployment at home and the firm establishment of peace and reconciliation in Europe. Between the elections of 1924 and 1929 Labour had achieved important by-election successes. As a result of the 1929 election it captured the very impressive total of 287 seats, as against the Conservatives' 255 and the Liberals' 57. The Brisbane-based *Worker* ran the headline, 'TORIES ROUTED IN BRITAIN', and editorialised that the incoming minority Labour government had a 'great opportunity' to launch a successful fight against 'War, Armaments, Unemployment and Poverty'.[80] Significantly, Labour had won an election in which 'red baiting' paled into insignificance in comparison with socio-economic issues.

The triumph within the Conservative Party of Baldwin's accommodating strategy towards mainstream labour at the expense of the uncompromisingly 'red-baiting' approach of Churchill, Sir William Joynson-Hicks and other party 'Die-Hards', also contributed significantly to the decline in the tarring of labour. Baldwin succeeded Bonar Law as leader of the Conservative Party and Prime Minister in 1923. After the election debacle of 1923, which temporarily placed his political standing and future in some jeopardy, Baldwin went on successfully to mould the Conservative Party around his 'straight and honest', 'reliable and solid' personality and centrist political philosophy until his retirement from the party leadership in 1937. As noted above, in 1924 Baldwin had given notice that it was important to welcome the moderate labour leaders and their supporters into the loyalist, constitutionalist fold and actively to seek their cooperation in opposing and defeating 'extremists' and promoting social reform. The Conservative triumph in the 1924 election, Labour's replacement of the Liberals as the main opposition to the Conservatives, the failure of the General Strike and the labour movement's increasing moderation, all gave added impetus to Baldwin's earlier resolve. During the second half of the 1920s Baldwin's policy of 'taming', accommodating and subordinating the 'labour interest' within the body politic and civil society in Britain, achieved dominance within both Conservative and wider governing circles.[81] This stood in marked contrast to the far more confrontational and uncompromising stance adopted by Bruce and the Nationalist-Country Party coalition in Australia.

Baldwin's position and approach, however, were by no means entirely accommodating or 'soft'. While holding out tactical and strategic olive branches to MacDonald and other moderates, Baldwin also adopted an uncompromisingly hostile stance towards 'socialism', including the socialism of British labour. As a 'traditionalist' and 'One Nation'

Conservative, whose English-ness was cast largely in rural terms, Baldwin was part of a wide current of thought and feeling which saw socialism as being irredeemably 'foreign', 'alien', 'un-English', 'un-British' and 'anti-imperial'. The product of 'de-humanising' mass industrialisation and urbanisation, socialism was portrayed as a uniform 'system' of 'abstract' and 'mechanical' thought, standing in direct opposition to 'English' 'commonsense', 'empiricism' and 'pragmatism'. It lacked the 'human' or 'common' touch. The 'English genius' for 'compromise', 'toleration', 'eccentricity', 'individualism' and a sense of humour and modesty was alien to its 'ideological', 'absolutist' and 'uncompromising' ways. Socialism was equated with political and industrial 'slavery', 'bureaucracy', 'financial chaos', 'paralysed distribution and production'. In post-revolutionary Russia it was also intent upon 'destroying' the family and religion and promoting 'atheism', 'free love' and the 'nationalisation of women'. It was beholden upon all 'true patriots' to ensure that 'socialism' never achieved the upper hand in Britain.[82] By the end of the 1920s it was not only Baldwin's accommodating strategy towards labour but, as noted earlier, anti-socialism which was in the political and social ascendancy in Britain.

Britain and Australia: the 1930s

Despite electoral successes in 1929, neither the BLP nor the ALP was able to withstand the whirlwind of the Depression. By the end of 1931 both parties had split irrevocably on the issue of deflationary versus expansionary economics and had failed to solve the key problem of unemployment. The dominant perception in both countries was that Labour's 'sectional' approach was inadequate to meet the size of the task at hand. As a result, appeals to the 'national' rather than the 'sectional' interest proved to be irresistible.[83] In both countries 'National' governments were voted into office with very large majorities and remained in office throughout the decade. From an electoral point of view the 'Red decade' was dominated by conservative governments.

Conservative political hegemony was particularly marked in Britain. The 1931 election resulted in a 'crushing victory' for the National Government, with 554 MPs returned, 470 of them Conservatives, and a 'disaster' for Labour with a miserly 52 MPs (including six unendorsed, mainly ILP, candidates). The fact that Labour received 29.3 per cent of the votes cast, as opposed to the 37.1 per cent of 1929, was scant consolation. In the general election of 1935 Labour received a slightly higher percentage of the vote than it had done in 1929 – 38 versus 37 per cent – but it won only 154 as opposed to 287 seats. Between 1935 and 1940 there were few, if any, signs that Labour would become the governing party in the foreseeable future, while Conservatives continued to dominate the National Government.[84]

In Australia the Nationalists' ability to retain federal office from 1931 onwards was also impressive. In practice, however, their hold on power was much less secure than that of the National Government in Britain. Following its heavy defeat at the hands of United Australia Party in December 1931, the ALP improved its performance at the election of 1934, when the UAP was forced into an alliance with the Country Party in order to protect its small electoral advantage over the ALP in the House of Representatives. Notwithstanding continuing disunity in New South Wales, Labor's improvement continued in the 1937 federal election under the inspirational leadership of John Curtin. It became even more marked in the 1940 federal contest. As a result of the latter, the ALP received thirty-six seats in the House of Representatives as compared with the UAP's twenty-three and the Country Party's fourteen. The balance of power was held by two Independents. Prime Minister Robert Menzies' invitation to the ALP to join an all-party war administration was turned down by John Curtin. Labor would bide its time before seizing the main chance at the most opportune moment.[85]

In comparison with the period from World War One to the Depression, the Red card and the politics of loyalism to nation and empire were played less often and extensively against mainstream Labour during general elections in Britain and federal elections in Australia in the 1930s. This resulted largely from four factors. First, as noted above, in both countries the Right was in electoral control nationally throughout the entire period from 1931 to 1940, and in comparison with earlier years the electoral threat from Labour at the national level was contained more easily, albeit far more so in Britain than in Australia. Second, politics in general revolved far more around socio-economic issues at home and the threats of war and fascism abroad than questions of loyalty to nation and empire. Fascist Germany and Italy, including their supporters and sympathisers abroad, replaced Communist Russia as the main bogeymen of Britain, the USA and Australia. Third, mainstream labour movements were increasingly fragmented, divided and predominantly moderate and centrist. As such, they constituted less of a threat to the status quo, and as a consequence it was less necessary for the Right to discredit them by means of the Red brush than in the highly charged years from 1918 to the mid 1920s in Britain, and from 1916 to the Depression in Australia. Fourth, it was the Left in both countries, engaged in united and popular front activities in support of socialism and internationalism and in opposition to fascism, war, unemployment, imperialism, conservative forms of nationalism and the 'rights of property', which bore the brunt of continuing anti-Red propaganda and action. This latter process assumed a more confrontational and coercive character on the part of the establishment in Australia. Although the Left was influential in terms of ideological, cultural, unemployed and industrial struggles, it exerted very limited influence upon the dominant features and practical politics of the British and, to a lesser extent, Australian labour movements.[86]

For most of the 1930s these movements, albeit more so in Britain than in Australia, were largely preoccupied with the defensive task of repairing their severely damaged resources and morale. In both cases there was the pressing concern to restore unity in the wake of the disasters and deep splits of 1929–31. In practice they were also far more intent upon securing immediate and short-term improvements in living and working conditions than challenging capitalism. Notwithstanding the agitational vitality of the Left, mainstream labour, especially in Britain, was for the most part under the effective control of moderate and pragmatic trade union leaders. The latter were less concerned to mount all-out offensives against employers than to restore their pre-Depression strength, standing and membership levels. This was particularly the case in Britain, where industrial militancy fell away and 'the only two large-scale strikes of the thirties resulted in victory for the employers'. In Australia, the same defensive mainstream trade union tendencies were evident, but within the context of a much quicker, stronger and more extensive post-Depression revival in the fortunes of both trade unionism and industrial militancy. In that country the 'number and duration of industrial disputes increased steadily from a low-point in 1933 to a new peak in 1938'.[87]

The British general election of 1935 and the Australian federal elections of 1934 and 1937 were dominated by domestic economic and social issues and the increasing rise and threat of fascism abroad. On these occasions Labour politicians demanded improvements in unemployment, unemployment insurance, housing and social welfare provision at home and asked whether the fight against fascism and war would best be served by 'softly-softly', anti-conscriptionist and even (in the case of Australia) 'isolationist' rather than more aggressive, 'hands on' means. These issues greatly overshadowed the less immediate concerns of loyalty to nation and empire.[88]

A key feature of both the BLP's and the ALP's moderation lay in their continuing and resolute opposition to communism. Although British and, to a much greater extent, Australian communists continued to play a role in trade unionism and the industrial struggles of workers, their parties remained small (from around 2,000 to 4,421 paper members between 1931 and 1939 in Australia, and from just over 2,000 in 1930

to just under 20,000 by 1939 in Britain) and their overtures for affiliation to and joint action with mainstream political labour received
short shrift. The BLP and ALP expelled communists and communist
sympathisers from their ranks.[89]

It was within this determining context of the hegemony of the
Right, the weakness and moderation of mainstream labour, the marginal influence of the Left and the changing international and national
political agendas, that we must place the declining influence of the
politics of loyalism upon the fortunes of mainstream labour during
the 1930s. To argue in this way, however, is not to suggest that these
politics exerted little or no influence. Rather, it is to maintain that
their effects were both more variable and, in overall terms, less profound
in terms of 1930s mainstream labour than they had been in the period
of war, turbulence and left-wing revolt and revolution from World
War One to the Depression.

At times, however, they continued to be of considerable importance.
This was the case in both Britain and Australia during the crucial
elections of 1931. Although historians have rightly claimed that the
latter revolved mainly around issues of political economy, they have
often neglected the fact that the politico-economic issues and debates
in question often necessarily involved contested notions of loyalty to
nation and empire.[90]

In the run up to polling day in Britain Labour was widely and
repeatedly accused, by Baldwin and Labour's 'renegades' as well as
'extreme' Tories, of pursuing its own sectional interest in opposing cuts
in unemployment benefit and employment, rather than seeing them
as unwelcome but vital measures to prevent a further run on and the
collapse of the pound sterling – 'to the bottomless pit' – the 'cancellation' of 'all the savings of the people' and national 'ruin' and 'disaster'.[91]
Philip Snowden's letter, sent to all candidates of the National Labour
Party, declared that it was the 'solemn duty of every patriotic citizen
to put the welfare of the nation before party considerations', that it
was vital to take 'necessary and unpleasant measures' and 'save the
unemployed from an even worse plight'. It also condemned both
the 'ruinous' and 'vast' increases in national expenditure proposed in
the Labour Party Manifesto and 'the cowardice and untrustworthiness
of men who ran away from their national duty in the hour of crisis'.
These very same Labourites had 'themselves arranged and approved
these "cuts" up to the point when their courage failed them', according
to Snowden.[92]

Although the issue of loyalty to the national interest greatly
overshadowed the spectre of the 'Red' menace, the latter made a well-
publicised appearance during the election. It issued not only and

predictably from the Conservative right, but also more dramatically and vituperatively from Snowden. He stigmatised Labour's programme for 'increased expenditure', the nationalisation of the banks and finance houses and 'derelict industries' as 'not Socialism' but 'Bolshevism run mad'.[93] Countercharges were made by three of Labour's biggest guns, Clynes, Henderson and Citrine. They accused Snowden of 'hypocrisy' in that both he and MacDonald were 'heavily responsible' for the nature of past and present Labour policy. They maintained that Labour was opposed to both inflationary and deflationary solutions for the crisis, and that it advocated a balanced budget without a reduction in unemployment benefit. They were also insistent that it was opposed to the dictation of government policy by any 'outside interest', including both financiers and the trade unions, and that it put 'national wellbeing before private advantage'. The 'national wellbeing' embraced peace, cooperation, disarmament, security and support for the League of Nations in international affairs.[94]

Snowden accepted none of this. He responded by defending his advocacy 'for forty years' of 'sane and evolutionary' rather than 'revolutionary' socialism. He repeated the accusations that TUC 'bosses' were 'dictating' Labour's policy and that the 'Labour leaders who deserted their posts' in the country's hour of need could not 'be trusted with serious responsibility'. They would 'destroy' confidence 'at home and abroad' and 'plunge the country into irretrievable ruin' for workers as well as capitalists. In the process they would also undermine the basis for socialist advance, according to Snowden. For both the latter and MacDonald strongly believed that socialism in Britain would develop out of 'social amelioration' and improved working-class conditions rather than capitalist economic collapse and working-class impoverishment. He did not wish to see 'the work of a lifetime' brought to 'rack and ruin' by Labour's 'Bolshevism'.[95]

Snowden's charge against his erstwhile colleagues and comrades was in fact preposterous. As the *Manchester Guardian*'s American correspondent dryly observed, it seemed 'hardly appropriate' to level the charge of Bolshevism against 'patriotic and constitutional' Labour and it was difficult to see 'Mr. Snowden . . . tarring and feathering Mr. Henderson'.[96] Yet, while preposterous, it served its intended political purpose to discredit Labour in the eyes of the electorate. In its editorial, 'The case of Mr. Snowden Apostate?', the *Guardian* declared that Snowden had become 'the idol of the Conservative press', and more contentiously, his 'bitter attacks on former colleagues' constituted 'the trump card of the Conservatives in the election'.[97] In the 'shortest, strangest and most fraudulent election campaign of our times', the country had been 'swept' by 'fear', 'panic' and 'hysteria'. Labour had successfully been portrayed as 'Lenin in lamb's clothing', and a 'sweeping victory' for the 'Coalition' as 'the only thing that stood between us and national bankruptcy'.[98]

The National victory on a loyalist ticket received the stamp of royal approval. Late in 1931 King George V's Private Secretary, Lord Wigram, wrote to Sir Philip Game, the British-born governor of New South Wales, 'it is a great experience to live in such stirring days. The people at home responded magnificently as soon as they realised that the fate of the country was at stake . . . the Labour Party and Trade Unions have been utterly discomforted'. Labour had paid the price for the 'fact of the matter' that 'our standard of living is too high, our wages too high and trade unions too spiteful and hindering'. The introduction of a tariff would be necessary to 'reduce' high wages. The victorious 'Coalition' had 'weathered all storms which Winston and other reactionaries have worked up against them' and there was now 'a God-given opportunity for the component parts of the Empire to come together, with the King at the head, economic union and an Imperial currency', concluded Wigram.[99] In marked contrast, the Australian labour press condemned the 'TRAITOROUS ACT' of MacDonald, Snowden and their colleagues in 'succumbing' to 'THE MONEY POWER', the 'love of power and the flattery of the great'.[100]

The interlocking issues of loyalty to nation and empire and the 'Red Scare' were even more pronounced during the bitterly contested Australian federal election of December 1931. As in Britain, the question of cuts in expenditure as the necessary solution to the Depression dominated the Australian contest. The recently formed UAP, with prominent Labour 'rat' Joseph Lyons at its head, won a landslide victory on the programme of 'sound finance', economic salvation and conservative loyalty to nation and empire.

Lyons, the former Treasurer of the ALP, had left the party in protest against its alleged inflationary folly. Within the ALP, Prime Minister Scullin occupied a 'centrist' position on the issues of cuts, expansion and deflation, while Curtin and Theodore favoured a more expansionary approach. Further to the left, Jack Lang, the dominant Labor figure in New South Wales, was the most outspoken ALP critic of the British and Australian 'Money Power' or 'Money Monopoly'.

In this instance the latter was personified by Sir Otto Niemeyer. On his visit to Australia in 1930, as the representative of the Bank of England and effectively the British government, Niemeyer demanded that Australia adopt a deflationary policy, including large cuts in public expenditure, in an attempt to resolve its financial and underlying economic and social problems. This demand was accepted by the state premiers in the Melbourne Agreement. However, it fundamentally

divided the labour movement. Although a specially convened conference of the unions and the ALP 'called on the Scullin government to
resist cuts and mobilize credit', Scullin, 'along with the Labor premiers
of South Australia and Victoria, regarded his hands as tied'. It was in
the face of subsequent government drift and Scullin's reinstatement
of Theodore as a treasurer committed more to economic expansion
than contraction that Lyons, 'appalled by the prospect of inflation',
resigned.

Meanwhile, Lang, having won a landslide victory in New South Wales
in 1930 on the basis of his defence of Australian 'self-government'
and the 'Australian standard' of wages and living conditions against
the cuts and 'groveldom' to Britain, proposed to stop interest payments
to London. Most of the ALP 'recoiled in horror from proposals tanta-
mount to debt liquidation and debauchment of the currency'. In March
1931 the ALP expelled Lang's New South Wales branch. Two months
later the Scullin government ended 'more than twelve months of
prevarication' by 'capitulating' to the Premiers' Plan of cuts in government expenditure, an increase in taxation and the sop of a reduction
in internal interest rates.[101]

Against this complex and turbulent background of policy inconsis-
tency, divisions, plots, resignations and expulsions and the continuing
failure of the Scullin government to solve the country's economic
problems – complete with an unemployment figure in excess of 25 per
cent and a cut in financial support for pensioners – the result of the
election was never in doubt. As Macintyre observes, 'Campaigning on
a platform of sound, honest finance which would restore the honour
and credit of the country . . . Lyons swept the polls'.[102] The UAP had
successfully branded the ALP not as only hopelessly divided, economically 'irresponsible', 'crazy' and 'inflationary', but also as both
antagonistic and 'disloyal' to the 'true' interests of Australia and the
Empire and, as in the 1920s, beholden to the 'Reds'. Whereas the UAP
portrayed itself as representing the 'great moderate section of the Australian people', the ALP was once again cast in the role of an extremist
force dominated by 'outside bodies', although, 'of course, the Labour
leaders deny this'. Henry Boote concluded that Labor lost the election
so badly largely due to the fact that the UAP and the press 'frightened
the people with the direful vision of a communist dictatorship' and
the 'downfall of the British Empire'.[103] Much as in the case of the
British Labour Party, the mainstream ALP's protestations of financial
'soundness', national 'responsibility' or 'true Australianism', anti-
Bolshevism and general moderation, fell largely on deaf ears.[104]

As noted above, the elections of 1931 constituted a watershed in
the history of the politics of loyalism in both Australia and Britain.

Secure in its political and wider societal hegemony and faced with a demoralised and relatively weak labour opponent, especially in Britain, the post-1931 Right had far less need to tar mainstream labour with the brushes of 'Red' disloyalty and extremism than in the 1920s. However, the Left and its supporters, both actual and potential, continued to be so tarred. For example, in November 1932 Wigram declared to Game that the 'so-called' Hunger Marchers congregating in London – 'wretched men and women' who, nevertheless, 'really did not look to be suffering from lack of either food or clothing' – were the 'dupes of Communist Organisations'.[105] In the aftermath of the 1931 election the Lyons government 'mobilized against the communist menace'. Its 'repressive conformity' and 'intolerance' were applied sweepingly and allowed 'any troublemaker to be labelled a "Commo"'.[106] Labor's alleged links with Communists resurfaced during the federal election of 1937.[107]

Finally, as we will observe in more detail in the next chapter, contested notions of nation and empire continued to be an important constituent of Australian, but far less so British, politics in the post-1931 period. Leading ALPers continued to express a class-based form of radical nationalism and qualified anti-imperialism which found only a faint echo among their counterparts in Britain. In the eyes of Curtin, the Lyons government of 1937 continued to be 'subservient' towards the 'Money Power' at home and the 'the abject tool' not only of 'the Tory government of Britain', but also of the 'plutocrats' and war-mongering 'Brasshats' of both countries'.[108]

Arguments

It is useful at this juncture briefly to pause in order to pull together the arguments presented above. First, I have argued that in both Australia and Britain anti-socialism and the tarring of mainstream labour with the 'Red' brushes of disloyalty and extremism were widespread, persistent and effective, both during federal and general elections and, more extensively, in the interwar period. Second, as such, they played a key role in the hegemony of the Right and the subordination of Labour and wider labour movements. Third, tarring and anti-socialism were most marked and successful during two periods of extreme social tension: World War One and its aftermath of turbulence, domestic conflict and international revolution and counter-revolution; and the Depression years, when the very existence and future of capitalism were thrown into doubt.

Fourth, the tarring of labour was more evident and sustained in Australia than in Britain. The reasons for this lay in the historically more militant, successful and threatening character of the labour movement in Australia;[109] the more exposed and vulnerable geo-political position of Australia in relation to the threats of communist and 'coloured' influence and 'invasion'; and the more confrontational and less accommodating stance adopted towards labour by the dominant fractions of the ruling class in Australia.[110]

Fifth, in the changed national and international interwar context of instability, crisis and conflict, the Right, in both Australia and Britain, was very successful in appropriating the languages and practices of loyalty to nation and empire. It portrayed itself as the defender of order, tradition, stability, security and moderation against the Left's and labour's alleged disloyalty, extremism and the promotion of sectionalism, greed, conflict and instability. Many electors now identified loyalism and democracy as inseparable from the Nationalist cause in both Australia and Britain.

Yet this is by no means the end of the story. However unsuccessful at the national and federal levels, mainstream labour both contested charges of disloyalty and extremism and attempted to lay them at the door of the Right. Labour's response to the Right was far more challenging in Australia than Britain. It is to an examination of this response and its impact at the state, regional and local levels that I turn in Chapter 6.

Notes

1 Arthur Marwick, *The Deluge: British Society and the First World War* (London: Macmillan, 1975), pp. 17, 290; Eric Hobsbawm, *Age of Extremes: The Short Twentieth Century 1914–1999* (London: Abacus, 1995), ch. 1.
2 Harold Thornton, 'Red Flag over Johannesburg: Australia and the Rand Revolt of 1922', *Journal of Australian Studies*, 18 (May 1986), 19–29; Bill Gammage, *The Broken Years: Australian Soldiers in the Great War* (Canberra: Australian National University Press, 1974).
3 Campbell, *Ireland's New Worlds*, pp. 167–70; Macintyre, *Succeeding Age*, chs 7, 8.
4 Cook, *Age of Alignment*, pp. 8–9.
5 David Englander, 'The National Union of Ex-Servicemen and the Labour Movement, 1918–1920', *History*, 76:246 (1991), 24–42.
6 Gregson, 'Footsoldiers for Capital'.
7 John Stevenson, *British Society 1914–45* (Harmondsworth: Penguin, 1984), p. 97; Jacqueline Jenkinson, 'The Glasgow Race Disturbances of 1919', in Kenneth Lunn (ed.), *Race and Labour in Twentieth-century Britain* (London: Frank Cass, 1985), pp. 43–67; Jacqueline Jenkinson, 'The 1919 Race Riots in Britain: A Survey', in Rainer Lotz and Ian Pegg (eds), *Under the Imperial Carpet: Essays in Black History 1780–1950* (Crawley: Rabbit Press, 1986), pp. 182–207; Neil Evans, 'Regulating the Reserve Army: Arabs, Blacks and the Local State in Cardiff, 1919–45', in Lunn (ed.), *Race and Labour*, pp. 68–115; Raymond Evans, *The Red Flag Riots: A Study of Intolerance* (St Lucia: University of Queensland Press, 1988); Raymond Evans, 'Red Flag Riots, 1919', in Raymond Evans and Carole Ferrier (eds) with Jeff Rickert, *Radical Brisbane* (Carlton North: The Vulgar Press, 2004), pp. 167–74; Raymond Evans, '"Agitation, Ceaseless Agitation": Russian Radicals in Australia and the

Red Flag Riots', in John McNair and Thomas Poole (eds), *Russia and the Fifth Continent: Aspects of Russian-Australian Relations* (St Lucia: University of Queensland Press, 1992), pp. 126–71; Don. W. Rawson, 'Political Violence in Australia', *Dissent: A Radical Quarterly*, 22 (Autumn 1968), 18–27.

8 See, for example, Englander, 'National Union', 27–28; *Argus*, 24 July 1919. The volatility and socio-political behaviour of returned soldiers and sailors in the immediate post-war years constitutes an interesting and potentially very fruitful topic of cross-national comparative research.

9 Stevenson, *British Society*, p. 97; *Herald*, 11, 18 January 1919.

10 Bobbie Oliver, *War and Peace in Western Australia: The Social and Political Impact of the Great War 1914–1926* (Nedlands: University of Western Australia Press, 1995), p. 145.

11 *Argus*, 19, 21, 22, 23, 24 July 1919; *Age*, 21, 22, 23, 28 July 1919; *Worker*, 24 July 1919.

12 Stevenson, *British Society*, pp. 85–102, 117, 195–202; Chris Wrigley, 'The Trade Unions between the Wars', in Chris Wrigley (ed.), *A History of British Industrial Relations*, vol. 2, *1914–1939* (Brighton: Harvester Press, 1987); James Hinton, *Labour and Socialism: A History of the British Labour Movement 1867–1974* (Brighton: Wheatsheaf Books, 1983), ch. 6; James E. Cronin, *Labour and Society in Britain 1918–1979* (London: Batsford, 1984), ch. 2; Kenefick, *Red Scotland!*, chs 4, 5; Frank Farrell, *International Socialism and Australian Labour: The Left in Australia 1919–1939* (Sydney: Hale and Iremonger, 1981), pp. xi, 169, 229; Macintyre, *Succeeding Age*, pp. 163–4, 170–1, 183–5; Macintyre, *Reds*, ch. 1, pp. 47–8.

13 Stevenson, *British Society*, pp. 74–7, 97–102; Arthur McIvor, 'Political Black Listing and Anti-Socialist Activity between the Wars', *Society for the Study of Labour History Bulletin*, 53:1 (1988), 18–26; Thurlow, *Secret State*; Macintyre, *Succeeding Age*, pp. 169–74, 188–91; Thornton, 'Red Flag', 19; Humphrey McQueen, 'Shoot the Bolshevik! Hang the Profiteer! Reconstructing Australian Capitalism 1918–21', in E.L. Wheelwright and Ken Buckley (eds), *Essays in the Political Economy of Capitalism*, vol. 2 (Sydney: Australia and New Zealand Book Company, 1978), ch. 7.

14 Thornton, 'Red Flag', 19, 25, 27; Miriam Dixson, 'Reformists and Revolutionaries: An Interpretation of the Relations between the Socialists and the Mass Labor Organisations in New South Wales, 1919–27, with Special Reference to Sydney' (PhD dissertation, Australian National University, 1965), p. 119; Jarvis, 'Stanley Baldwin', p. 201; Cronin, *Labour and Society*, ch. 3.

15 See, for example, the charges of association and collusion with revolutionaries laid against ALP leaders during the Red Flag Riots in the *Sydney Morning Herald*, 3, 4, 9, 10, 13, 14, 16 May 1921; Evans, *Red Flag Riots*; Rawson, 'Political Violence', 19–22; *Worker*, 27 March, 3, 10, 24 April, 8 May 1919; *Australian Worker*, 3 April 1919, 12, 19 May 1921.

16 See, for example, D.H. Lawrence, *Kangaroo* (New York: Penguin in association with Heinemann, 1980 edition, first published 1923), p. 208.

17 See the 'Thematic Section', entitled 'The "Extreme Right" in Twentieth Century Australia', in *Labour History*, 89 (November 2005), 1–123.

18 National Party, New South Wales, 'Pamphlets etc.', 1919, Mitchell Library (Q329.21N); Campbell, *Ireland's New Worlds*, pp. 168–82.

19 'P.L.L. and I.W.W. The Broken Hill Baby Proves the Alliance', in National Party, New South Wales, 'Pamphlets etc'.

20 'Wake Up, Australia! The Mannix-Ryan Combination Stands for Sinn Fein', in *ibid.* Dr. Mannix enjoyed huge popularity among his flock and was intensely disliked by Protestant Imperialists. A 'true' patriot, he opposed conscription, was fiercely critical of British policy towards Ireland, supported Sinn Fein and subscribed to the notion that 'Australia is first, and the Empire is second'. T.J. Ryan was an anti-conscriptionist, Premier of Queensland, Chair of the Irish Race Convention and, like Mannix, a supporter of the republican Eamonn de Valera. See Macintyre, *Succeeding Age*, pp. 172–3, 187, 194; Campbell, *Ireland's New Worlds*, pp. 180–1.

21 See Hughes's letter, dated 9 December 1919, in National Party, New South Wales, 'Pamphlets etc'.
22 'What Did O'Hara's Party Say', in *ibid*.
23 'A Tell-Tale Difference'; 'Diggers! Labor asks for your Votes!'; 'Diggerettes from Labor's Collection'; 'Soldiers! Will You Stand for This?'; 'A Few Personal Points for Soldiers Only'; 'Ask the Labor Candidate, Does He Support Preference to Returned Soldiers?'; 'No State is Doing so much for Returned Soldiers as NSW', in *ibid*; Rawson, 'Political Violence', 19; Oliver, *War and Peace*, p. 145.
24 'Wives, Mother, Sisters of Australians', National Party, New South Wales, 'Pamphlets etc'.
25 Marian Quartly, '"Politics among the People": Political Housekeeping and Fusion', in Strangio and Dyrenfurth (eds), *Confusion*, pp. 162–87; Brett, *Australian Liberals*, pp. 60, 117.
26 Jon Lawrence, 'Class and Gender in the Making of Urban Toryism, 1880–1914', *English Historical Review*, 108:428 (July 1993), 629–52.
27 See *The December 16 Devilfish*, in 'Federal National Party, How to Vote Pamphlets, 1922', Mitchell Library (Q329.2N); *Labor and Loyalty*, in 'New South Wales, Elections. Leaflets etc. 1922', Mitchell Library (Q329.1N); Clark, *'Old Dead Tree and the Young Tree Green'*, pp. 190–1.
28 Evans, *Red Flag Riots*; Evans, 'Red Flag Riots, 1919', p. 174; Evans, '"Agitation, Ceaseless Agitation"', pp. 149–64; Rawson, 'Political Violence'; McQueen, 'Shoot the Bolshevik!; *Australian Worker*, 3 April 1919.
29 For different accounts of the events and the principal actors see *Communist*, 1, 6, 13, 20, 21 May 1921; *Sydney Morning Herald* 2, 3, 4, 5, 6, 7, 9 May 1921; *Australian Worker*, 12, 19 May 1921; *Worker*, 19 May 1921; Tony Laffan, 'The Protestant Independent Labour Party of New South Wales, 1923–1929', *Hummer*, 3:9 (Summer 2002–3), 16–24.
30 *Sydney Morning Herald*, 3, 4, 9, 10, 13, 14, 16 May 1921.
31 *Australian Worker*, 12, 19 May 1921.
32 Kirk, '"Australians for Australia"', 102.
33 *Australian Worker*, 12 May, 2 June 1921.
34 *Worker*, 29 April, 6 May, 8 July 1920, 19 May 1921; *Australian Worker*, 21 November 1918, 29 April 1920; Elizabeth Kwan, 'The Australian Flag: Ambiguous Symbol of Nationality in Melbourne and Sydney, 1920–1921', *Australian Historical Studies*, 26:103 (October 1994), 280–303.
35 *Australian Worker*, 12, 19 May 1921.
36 Macintyre, *Succeeding Age*, p. 197.
37 *Ibid*., pp. 246–50; Patmore, *Australian Labour*, p. 85; Raymond Markey, *In Case of Oppression: The Life and Times of the Labour Council of New South Wales* (Leichardt: Pluto Press, 1994), pp. 255–6.
38 Macintyre, *Reds*, p. 102; Macintyre, *Succeeding Age*, p. 228; Patmore, *Australian Labour*, p. 85; Bede Nairn, *The "Big Fella": Jack Lang and the Australian Labour Party 1891–1949* (Carlton: Melbourne University Press, 1986), p. 101.
39 Macintyre, *Reds*, p. 102; Patmore, *Australian Labour*, p. 85.
40 Macintyre, *Reds*, p. 102. For Bruce see the pamphlet entitled, *The PM's Dandenong Speech*, 9 September 1925, in Sir John Latham Papers, NLA, MS 1009/27/115–162, folder 4, pp. 1–2, 5–6, 9, 14.
41 John Latham, *The Communist Menace in Australia*, Latham Papers, 1009/27/120– 162, folder 4, pp. 1, 128, 140, 156–7, 160; Markey, *In Case of Oppression*, p. 246.
42 Latham Papers, 1009/27/120–162, folder 4, p. 161. See also Latham Papers, 1009/27/120–162, folders 1, 2, 3, 5, 6 for Latham's further thoughts on the 'Communist Menace' in Australia and other countries, including Britain. For Latham's views on the labour movement and the defence of Australia see Latham Papers, 1009/26, folder 9.
43 National Party, New South Wales, *The National Policy: Speech Delivered by Hon. T.R. Bavin, MLA at Chatswood Town Hall*, 8 September 1927, Mitchell Library.
44 *Sydney Morning Herald*, 12 November 1927.

45 See, for example, the editorial in the *Sydney Morning Herald*, 13 November 1928.
46 National Party, New South Wales Elections, *The Government Policy: Speech Delivered by Rt. Hon. S.M. Bruce*, 18 September 1929, Mitchell Library. See also National Party, New South Wales Elections, *Speech by T.R. Bavin, New South Wales Premier*, 18 September 1930, Mitchell Library.
47 *Victory*, 9, 10, 11 October 1929.
48 McKibbin, 'Class and Conventional Wisdom'; McKibbin, *Classes and Cultures*, pp. 202–4, 295, 529–31.
49 Although there were significant divisions in the British labour movement between pro- and anti-war elements, these were not so profound as to lead to an Australian-style split in the party. See Hinton, *Labour and Socialism*, pp. 100–2.
50 Hinton, *Labour and Socialism*, pp. 115–17; McIvor, 'Political Black Listing'.
51 As explained by Cook (*Age of Alignment*, p. 6, n. 7), the 'coupon' was 'a letter of support' signed by the Conservative and Liberal Coalition leaders, Bonar Law and Lloyd George, 'sent to each favoured candidate'.
52 Cook, *Age of Alignment*, pp. 3–9.
53 In 1914 'the great majority of ILP members, and five of the seven ILP-sponsored MPs', had not gone along with the Labour Party's support for the war. Much of their opposition to both the war and conscription was based upon pacifism. MacDonald, who resigned as the party's leader 'in order to be free to oppose the war', nevertheless established a position, in the Union of Democratic Control, 'independent of the pacifist ILP'. He maintained both that 'we must go through' with the war and that 'the mind of peace' must be safeguarded during the conflict. See Hinton, *Labour and Socialism*, pp. 100–1; Kevin Morgan, *Ramsay MacDonald* (London: Haus Publishing, 2006), ch. 4.
54 Jarvis, 'Stanley Baldwin', pp. 113–14, 201–10.
55 David Jarvis, 'British Conservatism and Class Politics in the 1920s', *English Historical Review*, CXI (1996), 59–84; Jon Lawrence, 'The Transformation of British Public Politics after the First World War', *Past and Present*, 190 (February 2006), 185–216; Andrew J. Williams, *Labour and Russia: The Attitude of the Labour Party to the USSR 1924–34* (Manchester: Manchester University Press, 1989), pp. 6–7; Coleman, 'Conservative Party', pp. 55–6.
56 Kenneth D. Brown, 'The Anti-Socialist Union, 1908–49', in Kenneth D. Brown (ed.), *Essays in Anti-Labour History: Responses to the Rise of Labour in Britain* (Basingstoke: Macmillan, 1974), pp. 234–61, especially pp. 253–4.
57 Cook, *Age of Alignment*, pp. 16–26; *Manchester Guardian*, 17 November 1922; Kenefick, *Red Scotland!*, pp. 190–1.
58 *Daily Herald*, 14, 15 November 1922. See also George Lansbury's articles in the *Daily Herald*, 22, 24, November, 2 December 1922.
59 *Manchester Guardian*, 14, 15 November 1922.
60 *Manchester Guardian*, 20, 21 November 1922; *Daily Herald*, 17, 21 November 1922; Cowling, *Impact of Labour*, pp. 178–80.
61 *Daily Herald*, 23, 27, 28 November 1922; *Manchester Guardian*, 21, 23 November 1922.
62 *Manchester Guardian*, 23 November, 1922.
63 Andrew Thorpe, '"The Only Effective Bulwark against Reaction and Revolution": Labour and the Frustration of the Extreme Left', in Thorpe (ed.), *Failure of Political Extremism*, pp. 19–20; *Manchester Guardian*, 8 October, 7, 15, 17 November 1924; Kenefick, *Red Scotland!*, pp. 196–7.
64 Jarvis, 'Stanley Baldwin', p. 122; Brown, 'Anti-Socialist Union', p. 253.
65 Jarvis, 'Stanley Baldwin', pp. 222–3.
66 *Manchester Guardian*, 7, 8, 9, 16 October 1924.
67 *Ibid.*, 2, 7 October 1924; Kenefick, *Red Scotland!*, pp. 193–4.
68 *Manchester Guardian*, 8, 10 October, 3, 4 November 1924.
69 *Ibid.*, 15, 28 October 1924; Sam Davies and Bob Morley, *County Borough Elections in England and Wales 1919–1938: A Comparative Analysis*, vol. 1, *Barnsley–Bournemouth* (Aldershot: Ashgate, 1999), pp. 63, 339, vol. 2, *Bradford–Carlisle*

(Aldershot: Ashgate, 2000), pp. 313, 530; Sam Davies and Bob Morley, 'The Politics of Place: A Comparative Analysis of Electoral Politics in Four Lancashire Cotton Textile Towns, 1919–1939', *Manchester Region History Review*, Special Issue, *100 Years of Labour 1900–2000*, XIV (2000), 63–78.

70 *Manchester Guardian*, editorials 6, 16 October 1924.

71 *Ibid.*, 3, 20, 21 October 1924.

72 *Ibid.*, 25, 26, 27, 28, 29, 30, 31 October, 1, 3, 5 November 1924. *New Leader*, 31 October, 7 November 1924; Cook, *Age of Alignment*, pp. 300–1, 305–9.

73 Cook, *Age of Alignment*, pp. 300, 301, 308, 310–15; Thorpe, *British Labour Party*, p. 60; *Manchester Guardian*, 25, 27, 28, 30 October, 3, 7 November 1924; *New Leader*, 31 October 1924. For positive Australian labour movement attitudes towards MacDonald (especially his foreign policy initiatives concerning peace, reconciliation and disarmament), the Labour government, the election and Labour's future see *Worker*, 3, 24, 31 January, 7, 21 February, 16, 23, 30 October, 6 November 1924; *Australian Worker*, 23 January, 5 November 1924.

74 During 1924 the ILP generally supported MacDonald's European policy, but was increasingly critical of the government's support for 'coercion in India', its hostility to Russia in the wake of the Zinoviev letter, its condemnation of Communists as 'enemies' and its growing moderation and 'timidity'. While opposed to the communists' support for revolution and their lack of respect for 'democracy' and 'constitutionalism', the *New Leader*, the organ of the ILP, could not bring itself to regard them as labour's 'enemies' in 'the sense that Conservatives are our enemies'. The proposed solution was to 'ignore them'. See, for example, *New Leader*, 31 October, 7, 14, 21 November, 1924. Two years later the ILP attacked labour leaders such as J.H. Thomas who 'dreaded' the General Strike. In the same year MacDonald's attack on the ILP's 'Living Wage' policy met with the retort that he was more interesting in 'managing' rather than 'transforming' capitalism. See *New Leader*, 12 March, 21, 28 May 1926. For communist criticisms of Labour's 'servility to capitalism', its 'anti-working class mentality' and its cry, 'MACDONALDISM MUST GO!' in 1924, see *Workers Weekly* 3, 10, 31 October 1924.

75 *Worker*, 23, 30 October, 6 November 1924; *Australian Worker*, 5 November 1924.

76 Brown, 'Anti-Socialist Union', p. 254; Paul Ward, 'Preparing for the People's War: Labour and Patriotism in the 1930s', *Labour History Review*, 67:2 (August 2002), 174; *Australian Worker*, 19 May 1926 (for Bermondsey and Battersea); *Daily Herald*, 22 November 1926; G.A. Phillips, *The General Strike: The Politics of Industrial Conflict* (London: Weidenfeld and Nicolson, 1976); Andrew Thorpe, *The British Communist Party and Moscow 1920–43* (Manchester: Manchester University Press, 2000), Introduction; David Howell, 'Diary of a Somebody', *Twentieth Century British History*, 5:1 (1994), 125. For an earlier example of the 'Battle of the Flags', at Thaxted in 1921, see Michael Tyldesley, 'Jack Bucknall (1888–1954): A Particular Kind of Socialist', *Labour History Review*, 67:2 (August 2002), 205–20.

77 Kirk, *Challenge and Accommodation*, pp. 307–8, 318–20, 350–4; Kenefick, *Red Scotland!*, pp. 198–200.

78 Punitive measures were expressed in the Trade Disputes and Trade Unions Act of 1927. This Act banned general and sympathetic strikes, outlawed the closed shop in public sector employment and did not allow civil service and local government workers to join unions which could affiliate to the TUC and which compelled union members to 'contract out' of support for the Labour Party. Conciliation was reflected in the short-lived Mond-Turner talks of 1928–29 which sought to promote industrial collaboration and peace but which 'broke down before resolving any major issues'. See Kirk, *Challenge and Accommodation*, pp. 318–23; Cronin, *Labour and Society*, pp. 46–7, 94–5.

79 Thorpe, *British Communist Party and Moscow*, p. 1. As Kevin Morgan and Matthew Worley have argued, despite the 'Class against Class' policy and the formal anti-communism of mainstream labour, there was not complete *closure*. There continued to exist some, if not many, examples of ties and points of accommodation between communists, other sections of the Left and the labour movement during

the late 1920s and 1930s. See Matthew Worley, *Class Against Class: The Communist Party in Britain between the Wars* (London: I.B. Tauris, 2002), Introduction; Morgan, *Labour Legends*, pp. 12–13, 19–21, ch. 7. On a wider front, there exist sharp disagreements among historians concerning the extent to which the British Communist Party maintained its independence towards the Comintern. See Thorpe, *British Communist Party and Moscow*, Introduction; Worley, *Class Against Class*, Introduction; Alan Campbell and John McIlroy, 'The Last Word on Communism', *Labour History Review*, 70:1 (April 2005), 97–101; Morgan, *Labour Legends*, ch. 7, afterword.

80 *Worker*, 5, 12 June 1929. See also *Australian Worker*, 5 June 1929, *Manchester Guardian*, 1, 4, 5 June 1929.

81 Despite the fact that many within the Conservative Party resented Baldwin's unsuccessful resistance to punitive action against the trade unions in the wake of the General Strike, his support of votes for women under thirty and other progressive measures. See Stuart Ball, *Baldwin and the Conservative Party: The Crisis of 1929–1931* (New Haven: Yale University Press, 1988), pp. 4–11; Jarvis, 'Stanley Baldwin', pp. 123, 126; *Manchester Guardian*, 5, 11 November 1924; Cronin, *Labour and Society*, ch. 3; Thurlow, *Secret State*, pp. 135–43.

82 Ball, *Baldwin and Conservative Party*, pp. 9–10; Jarvis, 'Stanley Baldwin', pp. 58–60, 135–42, 161–2, 174–6, ch. 3, Conclusion; David Jarvis, 'Mrs Maggs and Betty: The Conservative Appeal to Women Voters in the 1920s', *Twentieth Century British History*, special issue, *Conservatism in the Twentieth Century*, 5:2 (1994), 129–52.

83 Philip Williamson discounts the importance of notions of the 'national interest' and 'patriotism' as 'leading explanations' for the responses of the actors in Britain's political and economic crisis of 1931. This is because 'everyone' claimed to be acting in the national rather than the sectional interest. Although this was arguably the case, Williamson's argument begs the central question as to why a conservative definition of the national interest, subscribed to by MacDonald, Snowden and Thomas as well as leading Conservatives such as Baldwin, became, from a Gramscian perspective, hegemonic, or the ruling 'commonsense' among contemporaries. See Philip Williamson, *National Crisis and National Government: British Politics, the Economy and Empire 1926–1932* (Cambridge: Cambridge University Press, 1992), p. 17; Ward, *Red Flag*, p. 198.

84 Thorpe, *History of the British Labour Party*, pp. 77–8; Thorpe, *British General Election 1931*, Conclusion.

85 Macintyre, *Succeeding Age*, pp. 273, 297–8, 331; *Australian Worker*, 27 October 1937. Curtin, an admirer of Roosevelt's 'New Deal', was elected leader of the ALP in 1935. Curtin's main concerns as leader in the years before World War Two were to promote improvements in Australians' working and living conditions, unity and compromise in a party bitterly divided by the experiences of Jack Lang's split from the mainstream ALP in New South Wales and conflicting Catholic and left perspectives towards Spain and Italy. As we will see in chapters 6 and 7, a lifelong opponent of imperialism, war and conscription, Curtin became a highly successful and popular prime minister who introduced conscription and actively pursued the Allied cause during World War Two. See Geoffrey Serle, 'For Australia and Labor: Prime Minister John Curtin', John Curtin Prime Ministerial Library, Perth, 1998.

86 Thurlow, *Secret State*, p. 137; Ward, 'Preparing for the People's War', p. 176; Pimlott, *Labour and Left*, p. 5; Farrell, *International Socialism and Australian Labour*.

87 Wrigley, 'Trade Unions between the Wars', ch. 2; Pimlott, *Labour and Left*, p. 2; Macintyre, *Reds*, pp. 331–40; Markey, *In Case of Oppression*, chs 5, 6; B.J. Costar, 'The Great Depression: Was Queensland Different?', *Labour History*, 26 (May 1974), 32–48; John McCarthy, 'Unions and the United Australia Party: New South Wales, 1932–39', *Labour History*, 2 (May 1971), 17–24.

88 For the 1935 British general election see *Australian Worker* 13, 20, 27, November, 16 December 1935; *Worker*, 19 November 1935; Thorpe, *History of the British*

Labour Party, pp. 86–94. For the 1934 and 1937 federal elections in Australia see *Australian Worker*, 11, 18 July, 22 August, 19 September, 1934, 22, 29 September, 27 October, 3, 10 November 1937; *Worker*, 5, 19 September, 3 October, 1934, 21 September, 26 October, 2, 9, November 1937. In both labour movements there continued to be deep fears about 'militarism', 'rabid jingoism' rearmament, 'preparation for war' and conscription. See, for example, *Australian Worker*, 6, 20 March, 9 October, 13, 27 November 1935, *Worker*, 19 November 1935; Pimlott, *Labour and Left*, p. 4; Ward, 'Preparing for the People's War', 172–3, 178.

89 Pimlott, *Labour and Left*, pp. 5, 42–58; Ward, 'Preparing for the People's War', 176; Thorpe, *British Communist Party and Moscow*, p. 1, chs 7–9; Worley, *Class Against Class*, pp. 8–11; Craig Johnston, 'The Communist Party and Labor Unity, 1939–1945', *Labour History*, 40 (May 1981), 77–92; Macintyre, *Reds*, pp. 92–4, 179, 197, 274, 293–6, 311, 329, 340–6, 351, 419. See *Worker*, 23 November 1937, for condemnation of Stalin's purges in Russia.

90 See the references to Williamson and Ward in note 83 above. Thorpe, *British General Election 1931*, pp. 230–4.

91 *Manchester Guardian*, 24 October (letter from H. Richardson), 25 October (Baldwin), 26 October 1931 (letter from J.A. Hobson).

92 *Manchester Guardian*, 17 October 1931.

93 *Ibid.*, 19 October 1931.

94 *Ibid.*, 21, 24, 25 October 1931.

95 *Ibid.*, 25 October 1931.

96 *Ibid.*, 27 October 1931.

97 *Ibid.*, editorial, 20 October 1931.

98 *Ibid.*, editorials, 27, 28 October 1931.

99 See Game, Sir Philip – Papers 1930–34. Correspondence with King George V, 1930–34 (hereafter Game Papers), Roll no. CY 3207, microfilm, Mitchell Library, Sydney. Letters dated 23 December 1931, 26 January 1932.

100 *Australian Worker*, 26 August, 21 October, 4 November, 9 December 1931; *Worker*, 2, 16, September, 14, 28 October, 4 November 1931.

101 Macintyre, *Succeeding Age*, pp. 257–72; Kirk, '"Australians for Australia"', 104.

102 Macintyre, *Succeeding Age*, p. 273.

103 *Australian Worker*, 16, 23, 31 December 1931; *UAP Speakers' Handbook*, Melbourne, 1937, Mitchell Library.

104 *Australian Worker*, 9, 16 December 1931; *Worker*, 2, 16 December 1931.

105 Game Papers, letter from Wigram to Game, 7 November 1932.

106 Macintyre, *Succeeding Age*, p. 307.

107 *Australian Worker*, 22, 29 September, 27 October, 3, 10 November 1937; *Worker*, 21 September, 26 October, 2, 9 November 1937.

108 *Australian Worker*, 22, 29 September 1937.

109 Coleman argues ('Conservative Party and Extreme Right', p. 56) that had a 'hard left' been 'more influential and successful' in interwar Britain, then 'almost certainly a more significant "hard right" would have developed in reaction against it'.

110 For traditions of accommodation and recognition in Britain see Eric Hobsbawm, 'Trends in the British Labour Movement since 1850', in his *Labouring Men: Studies in the History of Labour* (London: Weidenfeld and Nicolson, 1974).

CHAPTER SIX

Labour responses and political outcomes

Responses

In both countries mainstream labour strongly rejected the Right's charges that it was disloyal and extreme. Far more so in Australia than in Britain, it also offered alternative and competing definitions of the national and imperial interest. In both countries Labour prided itself upon its constitutionalism, its gradualism, its attachment to both class-based, progressive nationalism and internationalism and its opposition to communism, revolution and fascism. The ALP closely linked its radical nationalism to qualified anti-imperialism and mounted a fierce critique of the Right. It responded to the latter's charges of disloyalty and extremism by claiming that it was the party of 'true Australianism' in opposition to the 'Imperialism' and 'bogus' nationalism and loyalism of the 'Nationalists'. Moreover, the latter were seen as raising false charges against the labour movement in order to mask their 'real' purpose of imposing 'Prussianistic Imperialism' upon Australia. This comprised 'despotism', 'militarism' and the 'strangling of our liberties for British Imperialism'.[1]

The response of the BLP was much softer, moderate and defensive. In a marked departure from the tradition of 'radical patriotism', it increasingly tended to shadow Conservative, and especially Baldwin's, definitions of the nation and patriotism. Situated at the geographical core rather than on the periphery of empire, it also predominantly embraced 'enlightened' imperialism rather than anti-imperialism.

The BLP and the ALP were united by a common, strong and consistent commitment to the liberties, traditions and values of British-inspired 'popular constitutionalism'.[2] This commitment involved core beliefs in parliament, the peaceful and gradual 'parliamentary road' and the full democratic franchise, the rights to speak and act freely within the law, including the freedoms to strike and hold minority and oppositional views, respect for and toleration of opposing viewpoints and practices, the right of lawful assembly and the display of 'sacred' symbols such as flags.

In accordance with these views the ALP and the BLP condemned the Nationalists' and some Conservatives' intolerance of the Red Flag, their narrow identification of the national interest with the Union Jack and, on occasion, their 'repressive' and 'coercive' attitudes and actions towards the lawful assemblies and industrial actions of members of the labour movement. Condemnation of the 'Prussianistic' Nationalists and their allies, especially among the returned soldiers, was particularly strong during the 'Red Flag Riots', strikes and other forms of workers' protest in Australia. In Britain there was criticism of the 'intolerant' and 'repressive' methods favoured on occasion by Churchill and his supporters in the Conservative Party. This manifested itself, for example, during the 1924 election campaign and the 1926 General Strike.[3] However, the Conservatives' predominant constitutionalism and moderation, championed so well by Baldwin, as compared with the far more ready resort of the Nationalists, the Coalition and the UAP in Australia to open physical confrontation with the forces of the labour movement, meant that in Britain the BLP was more restrained and moderate in its critique of its political opponents than was the ALP.

Attachment to popular constitutionalism and the associated virtue of gradualism did, however, lead both the ALP and the BLP strongly to dissociate themselves from and to condemn the revolutionary, 'divisive', 'foreign' and 'dictatorial' methods of the communists. As noted in the previous chapter, initial enthusiasm for the Russian Revolution and the achievements of Lenin and the Bolsheviks in ending Czarist 'tyranny' and promoting 'real freedoms' soon gave way to disillusionment and condemnation.[4] There was general agreement among Labourites in both countries that while revolutionary tactics and strategy might have a place in an autocratic country like Russia, they did not in democratic and constitutional Australia and Britain. In these countries reforms and eventually socialism were to be achieved by tried and trusted peaceful, evolutionary and constitutional methods. 'Ours will be a Revolution of peace', proclaimed Boote, for in democratic Australia it was 'enough to cast a vote'.[5] The importation of the 'Russian model' into Australia by misguided revolutionaries was not only at odds with indigenous traditions, but was also highly damaging to the causes of the labour movement and democracy. In their advocacy of confrontation and violence and their view of parliamentary institutions are a mere fig leaf for brutal class rule, the communists were seen to be inviting a repressive and coercive backlash of the Right against all 'progressive forces'.[6]

In sum, the ALP and BLP were adamant that the Right's central charge – that they had succumbed to extreme and disloyal 'alien' Bolshevism – was completely false. Their cherished commitment to popular constitutionalism signified that they were the 'true' democrats and respecters of indigenous traditions and methods.

In keeping with the latter, the ALP continued its pre-war tradition of presenting itself as the main representative of 'true Australianism'. In contrast to the 'disloyal' Nationalists and UAPers, the 'plutocratic Imperialists', it claimed to put the Australian rather than the British or Imperial interest 'first'.[7] The notion of 'Australia first' was also highly symbolic in character. Boote condemned the Right's 'disloyal' attempt to present the Union Jack, the 'emblem of the Empire', as the 'Australian Flag', and so 'exalt' the interests of the Empire above those of 'our Commonwealth'. 'Some Nationalists', furthermore, went so far as to 'despise the Australian Flag, and all that it signifies as the emblem of a great and free nation'.[8]

In opposition to the Nationalist charge that it had abandoned its reforming goals in favour of new-found extremism, the ALP reaffirmed its 'traditional' commitments to the creation of a more equal, just and democratic 'Workers' Paradise'. The socialist commitment of 1921 was seen to be a logical development in the party's 'traditional' fight for justice.[9] Although the imminence and outbreak of World War Two would effect a radical shift in ALP policy to support for rearmament and the war effort, for most of the interwar period the party was progressively opposed to war, militarism and conscription and committed to reconciliation, peace, arbitration and disarmament on the international front.[10] Against the accusation that it was a sectional rather than a national body, the party sought to appeal not only to its traditional constituency among the organised workers, but also to the wider working class, small producers and others among the 'middling sort' in society. As noted earlier, the ALP attempted, with very limited success, to appeal to returned soldiers.[11]

The ALP was also proud of its past achievements. It claimed to have played a 'leading role' in the New Commonwealth in terms of the introduction of 'White Australia' – the protector of national 'homogeneity', 'racial purity' and high wages – Arbitration, the enfranchisement of women and the maternity bonus, the national bank, an 'independent' defence programme and the campaign to have Australian citizens appointed as state Governors 'in lieu of imported British aristocrats'.[12] In the past, present and future it was also committed to 'fostering the genius of our own country' by means of the promotion of all things Australian.[13]

The insistence on 'putting Australia first' was a consistent feature of ALP ideology in the 1930s as well as the 1920s. Reference was

made in the previous chapter to the fact that in the 1931 election
Lyons and the UAP were accused of 'selling out' Australia's interests
to the deflationary British 'imperialists' and 'plutocrats'. The same
and similar criticisms constituted an important aspect of the ALP's
ideology during Curtin's period as leader from 1935 onwards. For
example, during the 1937 election Lyons' support for the low tariff
was seen by Curtin as 'un-Australian' in that it provided insufficient
protection for the country's secondary industries. Australia's primary
producers were also portrayed by the ALP as suffering unnecessarily
as a result of low prices for their products and the high cost of borrowing. In these and other ways Lyons was practising policies designed
to meet the interests of the 'Money Power', of domestic and overseas
'exploiters and investors'. His government was 'servile', a 'flunkey', the
'abject tool of the Tory government of Britain', according to Curtin.[14]

For most of the interwar period the ALP adopted a more critical
attitude to Australia's relationship with Britain and British imperialism
in general than between 1900 and the outbreak of World War One.
As noted earlier in Part III, this mainly resulted from the party's move
to the left in the later stages of the war and immediate post-war years.
It was also because the ALP sought clearly to differentiate its proud,
independent nationalism from the 'deference' of its political opponents
during the 1920s and much of the 1930s. Thus, whereas the Nationalists
were believed to 'grovel' to their British 'master', the ALP placed a
premium upon self-reliance, self-respect and class-based mutuality.
The assumption often prevailed within the ALP that the very nature
of the imperial tie, rooted in both systemic and experiential British
domination and Australian subordination, meant that British interests
usually took precedence over those of Australia. There existed 'utter
incompatibility' between Australian radical nationalism and British
imperialism, according to the *Australian Worker*.[15]

Yet, as in the pre-war period, the *Australian Worker*'s viewpoint
was an exaggerated and misleading reflection of the mainstream ALP's
attitudes and practices towards the British Empire. On balance, a far
more qualified conclusion is in order. For example, the ALP maintained
its central commitment to the notion of Australia as a self-governing
nation *within* the British Empire. Furthermore, during our period the
British Empire evolved into the British Commonwealth and in
the process became, at least formally, more equal than in the past. The
landmark Balfour Declaration of 1926 stated that Britain and the
Dominions were henceforward to be 'autonomous communities within
the British Empire, equal in status, in no way subordinate to one
another . . . though united by a common allegiance to the Crown'. For
the first time Australia would formally be free to conduct her own

foreign policy and not automatically be bound by treaties drawn up by the British government.[16] The 'gradual rise of Labor to governmental control in various parts of the Empire' also raised the possibility that imperialism would become more 'enlightened', 'peaceful', 'democratic' and less 'plutocratic' and 'jingoistic' in character.[17] The ALP continued to place great store on its historically close ties with workers and the labour movement in Britain and its 'British' 'whiteness'.[18]

In contrast, however, to the predominantly shared and consensual emphases of 'the British world' perspective,[19] the interwar ALP, on balance, emphasised more the tensions and conflicts between Australia and Britain than aspects of unity and harmony. For example, in the early 1920s the Labor government in Queensland expressed 'outrage' at the denial of local democracy and the 'tyranny' and 'blackmail' visited upon it by an alliance of some of the state's conservative pastoralists and the British government. The latter both denied Queensland a loan and placed an 'economic blockade' against it lasting almost four years.[20]

The appointment of wealthy and conservative Britons, as opposed to native-born white males, to state Governorships also generated much Labor hostility, as did Prime Minister Bruce's 'anti-Australian' appointment of a British naval officer to command the Australian navy.[21] Similarly the ALP's attack on state upper houses – 'either nominated or elected on a restricted franchise' – arose not only from a commitment to the achievement of 'full' democracy, but also from continued opposition to a symbol of British aristocratic, monarchical and imperial rule.[22]

The 'real' effects of the Balfour Declaration were also believed to be far less profound in practice than in theory. Many within the ALP detected continued British 'rule' over Australia in the guises of 'equality' and 'autonomy'. This was reflected in various ways. For example, there was the continuing economic power of Britain and her 'plutocrats' over Australia, the latter's reliance on Britain for defence purposes and the practical 'impossibility' of Australian neutrality in the event of a British declaration of war. Britain's 'dumping' of her unemployed on Australia during the 1920s also met with fierce criticism.[23]

In 1930 King George V was extremely reluctant to allow Scullin to appoint Sir Isaac Isaacs as the first Australian-born Governor General. The King backed down only after months of wrangling and in the face of Scullin's threat to call an election on the issue.[24] Two years later Jack Lang, the premier of New South Wales, was dismissed by the state's British-born Governor, retired Air Vice-Marshall Sir Philip Game. Although the latter declared that Lang had acted illegally in his refusal to pay money to the Commonwealth in order to meet interest payments to British bondholders, the 'populist' Lang saw himself as standing up for labour and 'the Nation' against the British and Australian 'Money Power'.[25] As noted briefly in Chapter 5, Curtin continued to express the belief that the UAP, in both its economic and foreign policies, was sacrificing the principle of 'Australia first' upon the altar of Empire loyalism. He also believed that J.H. Thomas, as Dominions Secretary, 'was definitely and almost instinctively hostile to Australia', as was the National Government in Britain generally.[26] However, as will see in the next chapter, the outbreak of World War Two and Curtin's wartime experiences as prime minister saw the ALP adopt a far more friendly attitude towards Britain and the Commonwealth.

The ALP also expressed strong criticisms of British imperialism in general. The departure of pro-British voices from the party and the leadership in 1916 and 1917 gave more prominence to the large number of ALPers who saw imperialism, including British imperialism, as a *system* rooted in militarism, exploitation, 'territory grabbing', 'race aggrandisement', the 'subjugation' of colonial peoples and denial of their 'right of self-determination'.[27] While defending 'White Australia', Curtin, Boote and many others supported the principle of self-determination not only for 'white' countries such as Ireland, but also for India, Egypt and China, countries 'where civilisation is much older than in Europe'.[28] Monarchy was viewed as an 'anachronism' of a 'barbarous past', even though individual monarchs might display pleasing personal characteristics. Monarchs were also 'mere figureheads' and 'puppets' of the capitalist imperial machine.[29] Empire Day was largely ignored or opposed by the labour movement because of its close association with Protestant Imperialists.[30] These criticisms were made most vociferously between World War One and the early 1930s. As noted earlier, during the later 1930s questions of war and fascism took precedence over the pros and cons of imperialism.

In comparison with the ALP, the BLP offered a far more muted and moderate challenge to the Right's definitions of nation and empire in Britain. The Labour Party, of course, did present a more 'classed' and progressive view of the nation than the Conservatives. In the manner of the ALP it both advocated the achievement of socialism by gradual means and claimed to represent all 'productive' social elements rather than just sections of the working class. MacDonald's policy of promoting peace and reconciliation in 1920s Europe rather than the alleged stance of some Tories for prolonged conflict and aggression also met with warm praise from Curtin and other leading ALPers.[31]

In terms of the key question of nation and empire, the clear and unambiguous differences and conflicts between the ALP and the

[139]

Nationalists in Australia, however, assumed a far more blurred and at times barely existent form between Labour and the Conservatives in Britain. Above all, as shown by Paul Ward, in the 1920s MacDonald and his colleagues abandoned 'radical patriotism' in favour of 'a consensual view of Britain, and its political behaviour'. Their overriding concerns were to demonstrate Labour's respectability, moderation and responsibility, its 'fitness to govern', its clear opposition to the communists and 'direct action', and its respect for and abidance by established traditions, habits and the fundamental features of the social system – parliament, the House of Lords, the monarchy, the Empire, the 'rights of property' and so on.[32] MacDonald's romanticised view of 'the nation' and 'Englishness' – 'love of the soil . . . our villages, our cottages . . . the patriotism of the old gentry and nobility' – bore a striking resemblance to Baldwin's rural idyll.[33]

The full extent of the appeal of the constitutional monarchy and tradition to MacDonald was demonstrated in 1930 during the dispute surrounding the appointment of the Australia's Governor-General. Scullin's view was that the advice he had given to King George in his capacity as the Prime Minister of Australia acting in consultation with his ministers would, in the newly 'autonomous' Commonwealth, take precedence over the advice given by ministers in London. The latter practice belonged to an 'unenlightened' imperial past when the metropolitan interest ruled over the 'colonial'. However, MacDonald and Thomas advised Scullin to abide by established tradition. The highest priority should be attached to the wishes of the King 'inasmuch as Governors-General are the personal representatives of the monarch'. In the event, of course, Scullin was successful in pressing the priority of 'local conditions' and 'local sentiment' over those expressed in London.[34] MacDonald was not pleased. He concluded that Scullin had 'jumped the pitch' and that 'the conduct of some of these Dominions is getting intolerable'.[35]

MacDonald's 'sell out' to 'the nation' in 1931, the seemingly untouchable power of the National Government, the labour movement's internal differences and the fact that its priorities lay elsewhere, meant that the BLP did not mount either a strong or effective challenge to Conservative and conservative notions of the nation and empire during the 1930s. To be sure, leading figures in the Labour Party continued to highlight the 'Englishness' of their socialism, and, as in Australia, the arrival of World War Two would once again place questions and contested notions of the nation and patriotism at the centre of politics. However, during the 1930s it was the Scots, the Welsh and, in both Britain and Australia, the communists who most concerned themselves with issues of radical nationalism.[36]

The view that 'the British national interest' should at all times prevail over 'local' interests and causes, including demands for self-determination, determined mainstream Labour's attitudes to foreign policy and empire, whether in Ireland, India or elsewhere, throughout the interwar period.[37] Notwithstanding the continued anti-imperialism expressed by some within the BLP and on the Left,[38] the dominant commitment within the party was one of support for MacDonald's 'imperial standard' or 'enlightened' imperial and Commonwealth rule.[39] Leading Labour figures, even those who entertained some misgivings about the compatibility of imperialism and democracy, expressed the view that Britain was 'the best-fitted power to rule an empire, because its history had been linked to the advancement of political institutions based on liberty'. The main tasks facing Labour were to rid the British Empire of any lingering connotations of coercion and repression, and further to promote MacDonald's enlightened 'imperial standard', economic development and the 'gradual extension of self-government'.[40] As we will see in Part IV, by the 1950s Labour had come to see the transformation of the Empire into 'the first inter-racial Commonwealth of free nations' as the 'supreme achievement' of the 1945 Labour government.[41]

In conclusion, the more moderate views expressed by the BLP towards nation and empire, as compared with its Australian counterpart, derived partly from the belief of the former that national office could be achieved for the first time and in the foreseeable future only on the basis of clear and unambiguous commitments to respectability, responsibility and due regard for established traditions, power structures and social relationships. They also issued from the fact that, although it occupied a subordinate and contradictory position with the metropolitan heartland, the BLP nevertheless adopted many of the dominant attitudes and practices of the ruling power towards empire and imperial relations. In contrast, and notwithstanding its country's growing formal autonomy within the Empire, the ALP continued keenly to resent Australia's lack of 'real' power, equality and opportunities in relation to the ruling British nation and its 'plutocratic' masters.

Outcomes

This chapter has so far highlighted the hegemony of the Right, the subordination of Labour and the important role played by the politics of loyalism in these outcomes. It has also noted that, especially in Australia, Labour attempted to mount an effective challenge and present an alternative to the Right's charges of disloyalty and extremism. In the changed context of interwar political, social, economic and cultural developments, however, Labour's overall challenge failed to win the day in terms of both federal elections in Australia and general elections in Britain. By the 1930s the dominant 'spirit of Australianism' had been transformed from the radical and in some respects anti-imperial force of the pre-World War One period to one synonymous with conservatism and conformity.[42] In Britain, Labour's moderate and 'responsible' attitudes to nation and empire largely shadowed those of Baldwin. It was no great surprise that MacDonald and his colleagues joined Baldwin in the centrist National Government. The remaining task, undertaken in this final section, is briefly to evaluate the extent to which the hegemony of the Right and the subordination of Labour were replicated at the state and local levels.

The bare answer is that, although mixed, Labour's electoral record at the state level in Australia and the local level in Britain offered limited compensation for poor federal and national results. Queensland was the ALP's flagship state. Apart from the years between 1929 and 1932, the ALP held continuous office in that state for the entire interwar period. Between 1916 and 1940 Labor held power for thirteen years in Western Australia, eleven in Tasmania, seven in South Australia, six in New South Wales and a mere four in Victoria. In overall terms the ALP's electoral record in the states throughout the interwar years was both less impressive than in the pre-1916 period and inferior to that of the Right, albeit less so than federally.[43] In Britain Labour's impressive local rise was seen in its achievement of office in increasing numbers of the urban, manufacturing and mining centres of the country, especially in the west of Scotland, South Wales and the north of England. Outside of Norfolk, where agricultural trade unionism was relatively strong, the party continued to perform poorly in most rural areas, especially in the face of the continuing power of Conservatism, paternalism, deference and traditional religion.[44]

There is some evidence to suggest that an appeal to the tenets of 'true Australianism' both characterised and brought mixed fortunes for the ALP at the state level. As noted earlier, in both Queensland and New South Wales the party fought for local democracy and put 'Australia first' in its relations with Britain and British and Australian 'imperialists' and 'plutocrats'. Throughout the states the ALP was also careful clearly to dissociate itself from the communists and the charge of extremism. Both these policies brought electoral rewards, especially during the 1920s, but in most states, and especially during the Depression and beyond, the results were very mixed. As at the federal level, Labor's radical nationalism in the states as a whole failed to act as an effective counterweight to the Right's conservative nationalism and 'patriotic' allegiance to Britain. It was also the case that Labor

[142]

politics in the states were dominated far more by immediate socio-economic issues concerning working and living conditions and questions of organisation, finance, leadership, tactics and strategy and the balance of social and political forces, than by the seemingly more remote issues of nation and empire.[45]

The same conclusions may be drawn for Britain. Past and current research suggests both that when and where they did arise at the local level the issues of nation, patriotism and empire were mainly appropriated by the Right (although there is scope for more research into this much neglected area),[46] and that in general terms these issues were overshadowed in local politics by 'bread and butter' matters. For example, Labour's main local concerns lay with health, housing, jobs and general improvements in living and working conditions, with growing appeals to newly enfranchised women voters, especially around social welfare issues, and with attempts firmly to root itself in the life of these localities as the voice of the 'community' and the 'people'.[47] Yet at both the local and national levels the BLP generally failed to offset the 'huge' Conservative lead among women voters. As in Australia, large numbers of 'respectable' women in Britain saw themselves as the guardians of hearth and home and the 'natural' supporters of the 'true' party of patriotism, the public interest and beneficent imperialism. In Britain this was primarily the Conservative Party.[48]

In both countries, therefore, the importance attached to the politics of loyalism is partly related to questions of place and space. A focus upon local politics and elections, and even Labour politics within a purely national context, reveals far less about the issues and importance of nation and empire than does concentration upon the cross-national comparative and imperial dimensions of Australian and British history.

Conclusion

Despite complexities and variations in terms of national, federal, state and local politics and election results, the politics of loyalism to nation and empire played an important, but historiographically neglected, part in bringing about the political hegemony of the Right and the subordination of Labour in interwar Australia and Britain. At the same, however, other factors undoubtedly influenced the mixed electoral fortunes of Labour. These ranged from internal differences and fundamental splits within the labour movement's ranks to the material, political and cultural factors which have figured so prominently in the traditional and more recent historiography.

The existence and varied influence of a multiplicity of factors, however, should neither obscure nor detract from the often considerable influence upon Labour's electoral performance of the issue of loyalism. As we will observe in Part IV, the question of loyalty to the nation, combined with mounting anti-communism, would dominate Australian and significantly influence British politics between the 1940s and the 1970s.

Notes

1 *Worker*, 8 July 1920; *Australian Worker*, 12, 19 May 1921.
2 Paul Pickering, 'Popular Constitutionalism in Colonial Radicalism', paper presented to the symposium, 'The People and their Rights: Notions of Rights and Popular Sovereignty in the British World since 1790', Institute of Commonwealth Studies, London, October 2002.
3 *Australian Worker*, 29 April 1920, 12, 19 May 1921; *Worker*, 29 April, 6 May, 8 July 1920, 19 May 1921; *Manchester Guardian*, 8, 10, 30 October, 3 November 1924. The *Worker*, 30 October 1924, quoted Colonel R.A. Crouch, 'a well-known Victorian Laborite' [*sic*] as saying, 'The Tories sing "God Save the King" at the opening and close of all their meetings, and use the Union Jack as their own property, as quite becoming the real British patriots.' For Bertrand Russell's view of the Union Jack as 'the symbol of pomp' and the generator of 'the emotions which lead us to cause misery to countless millions in Asia and Africa' see *New Leader*, 21 November 1924. For further debate about allegiance to the Union Jack and the Red Flag see *New Leader*, 14, 28 November 1924; *Worker*, 6 November 1924. For 1926 see Phillips, *General Strike*; Keith Laybourn, *The General Strike of 1926* (Manchester: Manchester University Press, 1993), Introduction, ch. 6. For the close connections between the celebration of Empire Day, the Conservative Party, the Union Jack and anti-socialism see Jim English, 'Empire Day in Britain, 1904–1958', *The Historical Journal*, 49:1 (March 2006), 247–76.
4 *Manchester Guardian*, 7, 8 October, 7 November 1924 (MacDonald), 15, 17 November 1924 (Clynes); *New Leader*, 3 October, 21 November 1924; Morgan, *Labour Legends*, p. 13; *Worker*, 27 March, 17, 24 April, 31 July 1919, 1, 8 November 1923, 1 February 1924, 25 February, 27 October 1926, 11 May, 28 September, 23 November 1927, 15 August, 5 December 1928; *Australian Worker*, 1, 22 May 1919, 10 March 1921, 27 October 1926, 30 January 1929, 19 February 1930. For continued praise for the economic and social achievements of Russia see the article, 'TWENTY YEARS AFTER', in *Australian Worker*, 3 November 1937.
5 *Australian Worker*, 16 September 1920, 15 November 1922, 27 October 1926.
6 *Australian Worker*, 16 September, 14 October 1920.
7 *Australian Worker*, 12 May, 2 June 1921, 8 December 1926.
8 *Australian Worker*, 12 May, 2 June 1921.
9 Macintyre, *Succeeding Age*, pp. 229–33; *Australian Worker*, 16 September 1920, 17 May 1923, 12 May 1926, 7 May, 10 December 1930; *Worker*, 15, 22 July, 19 August 1920.
10 Kirk, '"Australians for Australia"', 99–101.
11 *Ibid.*, 101–2.
12 Neville Kirk, 'Traditionalists and Progressives: Labor, Race and Immigration in Post-world War II Australia and Britain', *Australian Historical Studies*, 39:1 (March 2008), 53–71; *Worker*, 26 January 1927.
13 *Australian Worker*, 2 June 1921; Australian Labor Party, *Manifesto of the Australian Labor Party to the People of the Commonwealth*, 1919, pp. 6–7.
14 *Australian Worker*, 22, 29 September 1937.
15 *Ibid.*, 2 June 1921.
16 Dennis Judd, *Balfour and the British Empire: A study in Imperial Evolution 1874–1932* (London: Macmillan), pp. 319, 327–8.

17 *Australian Worker*, 19 May 1921; *Worker*, 2 June 1926.
18 *Australian Worker*, 19 May, 2 June 1921, 27 May 1925.
19 See Bridge and Fedorowich (eds), *British World*; Kirk, *Comrades and Cousins*, pp. 128–9; Ward, 'Two Kinds of Australian Patriotism'.
20 Tom Cochrane, *Blockade: The Queensland Loans Affair 1920 to 1924* (St Lucia: University of Queensland Press, 1989); *Worker*, 22 July, 19 August, 2, 16 September 1920.
21 *Worker*, 15, 22 July 1920; Bede Nairn, *The 'Big Fella'*, p. 99; *Australian Worker*, 16 January 1929.
22 Macintyre, *Succeeding Age*, p. 233; *Westralian Worker* (Curtin), 4 April 1924.
23 *Westralian Worker*, 3 December 1926, 1 April 1927, 1 June, 3 August 1928; *Worker*, 29 September, 27 October, 22, 29 December 1926, 1 February, 9 May 1928; *Australian Worker*, 13 January, 27 October 1921, 10 November, 1, 8 December 1926, 26 January 1927, 11 November 1931.
24 James Henry Scullin Papers 1929–1939, National Library Australia, MS 356, 1 folder (hereafter Scullin Papers); *Australian Worker*, 7, 14 May, 10 December 1930; *Worker*, 10, 17 December 1930; *Bulletin*, 30 April, 10 December 1930.
25 Game Papers, Letters from Wigram, 7 June, 18 July, 30 August, 7 October 1932; Frank Cain, 'NSW Labor Governments at the Hands of their hostile British Governors', in Greg Patmore, John Shields and Nikola Balnave (eds), *The Past is Before Us: Proceedings of the Ninth National Labour History Conference* (Sydney: Australian Society for the Study of Labour History, 2005), pp. 63–70.
26 *Worker*, 26 November 1935.
27 *Worker*, 19 August 1920, 6 April 1927; *Australian Worker*, 29 July 1920, 5 November 1924, 29 May 1929.
28 Frank Anstey and John Curtin, *The Heritage*, 1930, http://johncurtin.edu.au; *Westralian Worker*, 4 February, 1 April 1927, 1 June 1928; *Worker*, 8 July, 28 October 1920, 26 May 1921, 19, 26 January, 9, 23 February, 30 March, 6, 13 April 1927; *Australian Worker*, 14 November 1918, 6, 20 May, 17 June, 15 July, 19 August, 2 December 1920, 31 March 1921, 28 April, 8 December 1926.
29 *Worker*, 13, 27 May, 10 June, 15 July, 5 August 1920, 6, 13 April 1927; *Australian Worker*, 15 April, 6 May, 3, 10, 17 June, 1 July 1920, 26 January, 11 May 1927, 25 June 1930; Kevin Fewster, 'Politics, Pageantry and Purpose: The 1920 Tour of Australia by the Prince of Wales', *Labour History*, 38 (May 1980), 59–66.
30 Macintyre, *Succeeding Age*, p. 133; Maurice French, 'The Ambiguity of Empire Day in New South Wales, 1901–21': Imperial Consensus or National Division?', *Australian Journal of Politics and History*, XXIV:1 (April 1978), 61–74; Stewart Firth and Jeanette Hoorn, 'From Empire Day to Cracker Night', in Peter Spearritt and David Walker (eds), *Australian Popular Culture* (Sydney: George Allen and Unwin, 1979), ch. 2; *Australian Worker*, 26 May 1926, 1 June 1932.
31 See Curtin in *Westralian Worker*, 15 February, 12 September, 17 October, 7 November 1924, 12 October 1928; *Australian Worker*, 5 November 1924, 29 May 1929; *Worker*, 12 June 1929.
32 Ward, *Red Flag*, ch. 9. For ILP support for MacDonald and his view of the national interest in 1924 see *Manchester Guardian*, 17 October 1924.
33 *Manchester Guardian*, 7 October 1924; Ward, *Red Flag*, pp. 172–6.
34 Scullin Papers, 'Letter/Cablegram sent by Scullin to the Secretary of State for Dominion Affairs', 16 and 17 May 1930, 'Reply from the Secretary of State for the Dominions', 23 April 1930, pp. 2–3. See also Malcolm MacDonald MP, 'The Imperial Conference, 1930', *Labour Magazine*, IX:8 (December 1930), 339–43; Ward, *Red Flag*, pp. 182–4.
35 Ramsay MacDonald Papers, John Rylands Library, Deansgate, University of Manchester, 23 April 1930, RMD/1/14/46. I am grateful to Kevin Morgan for this reference.
36 Ward, *Red Flag*, pp. 197–8, 199 (n. 14); Ward, 'Preparing for the People's War', pp. 172–5; Macintyre, *Reds*, pp. 315–19.
37 Ward, *Red Flag*, pp. 184–7.

38 Pimlott, *Labour and Left*, ch. 5; Ward, 'Preparing for the People's War', p. 177; Howe, *Anticolonialism*, ch. 2; Kirk, *Comrades and Cousins*, pp. 166–90; *New Leader*, 31 October 1924; *Herald*, 11 January, 8, 22 February, 15, 22, 29 March, 1, 9, 16, 19, 21 April 1919, 3, 4 December 1926.
39 Howe, *Anticolonialism*, pp. 47–8; *New Leader*, 19 March 1926.
40 Ward, 'Preparing for the People's War', 177–8.
41 Knowles, *Race Discourse and Labourism*, pp. 95–6.
42 McQueen, 'Shoot the Bolshevik!'.
43 Kirk, '"Australians for Australia"', 105.
44 Ward, *Red Flag*, pp. 176–7; Cook, *Age of Alignment*, pp. 8, 22–3, 50, 311–14; Worley (ed.), *Labour's Grass Roots*; Davies and Morley, *County Borough Elections*, for numerous examples of Labour's growing strength in urban, manufacturing and mining areas. For Sheffield, 'the first city to come under Labour control', in 1926, see Helen Mathers, 'Preparing for Power: the Sheffield Labour Party 1890–1926' and John Rowett, 'Sheffield under Labour Control', 'Conference Report', *Bulletin of the Society for the Study of Labour History*, 39 (Autumn 1997), 12–13; Nicholas Mansfield, *English Farmworkers and Local Patriotism 1900–1930* (Aldershot: Ashgate, 2001).
45 Kirk, '"Australians for Australia"', 105–7.
46 Davies and Morley, 'Politics of Place'; Davies and Morley, *County Borough Elections*, vol. 1, pp. 224, 337–402, 467–9, 477–8 for the instructive examples of Birmingham, Blackburn, Bury and Bolton; Mike Savage, *The Dynamics of Working-Class Politics: The Labour Movement in Preston 1880–1940* (Cambridge: Cambridge, University Press, 1987).
47 Lawrence, *Speaking for the People*, ch. 9; Worley, 'Building the Party', 74–5, 82–4, 88, 90; Davies and Morley, *County Borough Elections*, for a predominantly materialist interpretation, albeit enriched by the issues of gender, ethnicity and religion, of municipal politics in England and Wales. Davies and Morley also usefully highlight the extent to which the Conservatives contested Labour's claim to be the 'natural' representatives of the 'people's' 'bread and butter' issues. 'Spendthrift' Labour was frequently taken to task by local Tories who prided themselves on their overriding commitment to 'economy'. See, for example, *County Borough Elections*, vol. 1, p. 465, vol. 2, pp. 530, 605.
48 McKibbin, 'Class and Conventional Wisdom', p. 285; Jarvis, 'Mrs Maggs and Betty'.

PART IV

Mixed fortunes: from the 1940s World War to the 1970s class war

Introduction

During the period covering the 'unity' years of World War Two, the divisions of the Cold War, the economic boom of the 1950s and 1960s and the escalating economic problems, social conflicts and crises from the mid 1960s to the end of the 1970s, the BLP and the ALP experienced mixed fortunes in terms of both overall development and electoral performance.

In contrast to the disasters of the 1930s, spectacular successes at the polls were registered in both countries during the wartime and immediate post-war years. For example, following its successful participation in the wartime coalition government, the Labour Party in Britain unexpectedly won a landslide victory at the general election of 1945 and formed the first majority Labour government in the country's history. It also won, albeit very narrowly, the next election in 1950 and lost in 1951, despite receiving 'a record number of votes' (48.7 per cent of all votes) ever cast for 'a single party'.[1] During these years (1945–51) the trade unions were strong and total membership of the Labour Party reached its peak of 1 million in 1951–52. The party not only demonstrated formidable strength among urban working-class, and especially male, voters, but also reached out with considerable success, especially in 1945, to a wider, male, female and middle-class constituency of the 'progressive people'.[2]

The wartime and post-war years in Australia also saw continuing trade union strength being accompanied by a sharp upturn in the fortunes of the ALP following its long periods out of federal office during the interwar years. Curtin, who became Prime Minister in 1941, proved to be a highly determined, effective and popular war leader. The ALP won an important federal victory in 1943, its first since 1929. Thereafter it successfully conducted Australia's war effort and achieved further federal success in 1946. At the state level Tasmania, followed by New South Wales, led the electoral way. In these two states Labor enjoyed continuous control from 1934 to 1969 and from 1941 to 1965 respectively. Moreover, Labor remained in office in Queensland from 1932 to 1957 and in Western Australia from 1933 to 1947 and from 1953 to 1959. In contrast, South Australia was entirely barren territory for the ALP between 1933 and 1965, while in Victoria the party experienced only six and a half years in power between 1930 and 1955. In overall terms, however, the ALP fared much better at the state level from the 1940s to the 'Great Split' of 1955 than it had during the interwar period.[3]

Yet, as the experiences of wartime and post-war reconstruction gave way to the Cold War and the long period of economic boom, so were Labour successes thoroughly overturned by a resurgent Right. In Britain the Conservative Party enjoyed thirteen years of unbroken parliamentary rule between 1951 and 1964 and managed to recapture much of its 'natural' middle-class support. Although the ALP reached its historic membership peak of 75,000 in 1954, and although it came close to federal election victories in 1954 and 1961 and often won a majority of the votes cast in federal elections between 1951 and 1961, the mid-century years belonged firmly to the Liberal-Country Party coalition. The latter, counting upon the bedrock support of the 'forgotten' middle classes and influential elements in rural society, chalked up the remarkable record of being in federal office for the entire period between 1949 and 1972. The ALP did eventually return to power in the 1972 election under the charismatic leadership of Gough Whitlam. Whitlam, however, was defeated in 1975 and Labor did not return to federal office until 1983.

At the state level, the years from the mid 1950s to the early 1980s constituted a more mixed but in overall terms very disappointing experience for Labor. Although results in Tasmania (largely throughout) and South Australia (from 1965 onwards) were impressive, Queensland (from 1957) and Victoria (from 1955) were Labor wastelands until the 1980s. The ALP generally performed badly in Western Australia from 1959 to 1983. Its twenty-four years' hold on power in New South Wales, from 1941 to 1965, was broken for ten years between 1966 and 1976. However, it then held office for almost thirteen years between 1976 and 1988.[4]

Lastly, in 1960s and 1970s Britain the Labour Party attempted to tackle the country's increasingly severe economic and social problems with mixed success. It fought back against mid-century Tory hegemony to enjoy two periods of office, from 1964 to 1970 and from 1974 to 1979, a total of almost eleven years, before succumbing to the force of Margaret Thatcher in 1979.

The purposes of Part IV are to chart further and explain the various twists and turns in Labour's electoral performance sketched above, to critically engage with, fill gaps in and so enrich the nationally focused traditional and revisionist literature, and to add a new, predominantly comparative, but also trans-national, dimension to our knowledge and understanding of this period. The chapter maintains that Labour's mixed electoral, institutional and social fortunes resulted, in both Australia and Britain, from the successes and failures with which it addressed four broad sets of issues during the period under review. As we will see below, these comprise not only 'traditional' material and 'revisionist' gender and political factors, but also race, nation, empire and commonwealth. The thesis presented is that while a sufficient explanation of Labour's mixed fortunes must embrace this whole range of issues, explanatory priority should be attached to a combination of the following: trends in living standards; the balance of the forces of unity and disunity in Labour's ranks; the politics of economic management, particularly questions of competence, success and failure; a commitment and appeal to the social forces of the modern, progressive nation; and the issue of loyalism to the nation and the Commonwealth.

The first group of issues revolves around the discrete, but closely interconnected, factors of class, nation, gender, race and commonwealth. I argue that Labour electoral and social successes, as in the 1940s and at various points in the 1960s and 1970s in both countries, were most marked when it successfully presented itself not only as the representative of the 'bread and butter' concerns of the male, urban and trade union sections of the working class, but also as a party 'truly' representative of the wider interests of the progressive nation, with an appeal to women, rural dwellers, the more forward-looking sections of the middle class and increasingly, but in a very limited way, from the 1960s onwards, to a 'multi-cultural' constituency. From the 1950s onwards we may detect a general trend for Labour's 'traditional' male, working-class vote to decline, although at some elections and other specific points in time this trend was limited, uneven and even reversed. However, the very fact of its existence and accelerating importance over time forced the Australian and British labour movements to give increased attention to organised labour's actual and potential constituency.[5]

In the 1940s and 1950s Labour also attributed great importance to and took much credit for the growth of a more enlightened British Commonwealth, especially in terms of developing equality of status among the Commonwealth's member countries and decolonisation in India and elsewhere. The British, rather than Australian, labour movement also took pride in the creation of the first multi-racial commonwealth. While the former movement remained committed, up to the 1960s, to Britain's 'open door' policy for all intending imperial migrants to the 'mother country', irrespective of race, the latter remained steadfast in its support for 'White Australia' and the notions of racialised citizenship and national homogeneity.

As maintained by 'British world' scholars, the British 'embrace' of Australia and a shared sense of British-ness between the two countries declined irreversibly from the later 1950s onwards. Despite continuing

Labour and nationally based Commonwealth ties and connections, the place of the Commonwealth in Labour politics in both countries became of much diminished significance in the face of more pressing foreign policy matters and commitments. As a result of the Cold War and the shifting geo-politics of the Asia-Pacific region, Australia, including its labour movement, moved closer to the United States as a means of defence against the rapid spread of communism in the region and the seeming threat of invasion from the 'North'. At the same time there existed strong feelings within the Australian labour movement of anti-Americanism, based largely upon the role of the United States as the pre-eminent western 'Cold War warrior' and its threats to world peace and security, and in favour of a more independent-minded foreign policy in which, until the end of the 1950s, 'undue' dependence on the United States would be avoided by a defence partnership with Britain. There was also growing Australian resentment of the fact that Britain was seen increasingly to attach more importance to entry into the European Economic Community (EEC), as a perceived solution to the country's mounting political and economic ills, than to ties with Australia and the rest of the Commonwealth.

Paradoxically, Labour's 'New Britain' of the 1960s and beyond would endorse both openly racist immigration controls and domestic 'race relations' legislation in the putative interests of racial equality, social stability and harmony. In contrast, by the early 1970s Australia and the Australian labour movement had formally ended their long commitment to 'White Australia' in the interests of economic growth, trade and the promotion of anti-communism and more friendly relations with their Asian neighbours. There was also growing, but limited, labour movement and wider support for the political and civil rights of Australian Aborigines and women.

Attention to this first set of issues has been extensive, but also, in important respects, limited and uneven among historians and other social scientists. For example, I observe that while there has been considerable combined historical, political and sociological attention to Labour's declining appeal among white working-class males, especially in Britain, there has been far less published interest in the gendered, racialised, non-urban and cross-class dimensions and limitations of that appeal. Similarly, while Labour's progressive nationalism has figured prominently in parts of the relevant British literature concerned with politics in the 1940s, especially in relation to the 1945 election, and in the Australian literature for the same decade and the Whitlam government, 1972–75, nevertheless, it has been generally either underplayed or neglected for Labour in Britain during the 1960s, often in favour of a more or less all-consuming 'traditional' concern with the subject matter of Labour and the economy. It has also been somewhat neglected for Australian Labor during the 1950s and 1960s. While Australian historians have shown more interest than their British counterparts in Commonwealth ties, relations and developments between Australia and Britain in this period, the Labour aspect of this comparative and trans-national subject area has been mainly overlooked. This last point leads me to note a more general picture of comparative neglect, or more accurately absence, in relation to most of the factors comprising this first set of issues. The aim is to make a contribution towards correcting these deficiencies.

The second set of issues revolves around what may be termed the politics of Cold War loyalism to nation and commonwealth. The reader will observe that this concern with loyalism represented a continuation and development of the dominant theme of interwar Australia, as discussed in Part III. In its Cold War form, loyalism had both external and internal aspects. Externally, the onset and development of the Cold War raised pressing international concerns about peace, security, stability and defence in an increasingly divided world, faced for the first time with the possibility of nuclear Armageddon. For both Britain and Australia, including their respective labour movements, relations not only within the Commonwealth but also, increasingly and more importantly, with the United States, the Soviet Union, their competing global 'spheres of influence', and Communist China, were of new-found importance. For example, many within early 1950s Australia accepted Liberal Prime Minister Menzies' fervent beliefs that the communists were intent upon global expansion and domination, that a third World War was imminent, that Australia would be isolated and invaded and that Australian Labor was too 'soft' on communism adequately to defend the nation and to make a serious contribution to the defence of the Commonwealth and the 'Free World'.

Internally, the Cold War resurrected, even more strongly and extensively than the first 'cold war' of the interwar years, charges that both communism and socialism were synonymous with collectivist tyranny and incompatible with individual and social freedom and choice. Once again mainstream labour movements were tarred with the brushes of alien extremism and disloyalty to the nation, the Commonwealth and other 'free world' countries. In Australia, moreover, this process of tarring issued not only from establishment figures 'from above', but also from the large and increasingly organised group of anti-communist Catholic trade unionists and ALP members 'from below'. This group was at the centre of the 1955 Split.

I argue that, as in the interwar period, the tarring of Labour from the late 1940s to the late 1960s was more extensive, persistent, aggressive and successful in Australia than in Britain. I endorse the viewpoint, expressed in the general historiography, that anti-communism pervaded Australian society in this period, often in the highly racialised form of fears of domination and invasion by communist Asian and Chinese 'hordes'. I use neglected and under-studied primary sources to support Stuart Macintyre's claim that the inability of Labor to 'resist the demands of the international Cold War contributed to its fall in 1949 and kept it out of office over the next two decades'.[6] Yet I also agree with Macintyre that, while significant, particularly from the Split onwards, Cold War loyalism's influence upon the ALP's electoral performance at the state level was more limited and uneven than in the sphere of federal politics.[7]

In putting forward this argument I seek to correct an imbalance in the existing labour historiography. Although some Australian labour historians of this period have set the development of the labour movement within its wider social context, the dominant focus has been set rather narrowly upon the internal development of the labour movement's industrial and political institutions. While the latter has necessarily included reference to the politics of communism and anti-communism *within* those institutions – most prominently the events leading up to and including the Split – it has not paid sufficient attention and attributed due significance to the crucial role played by the wider politics of the Cold War, both institutional and non-institutional in character, in severely damaging the political fortunes of Australian labour from the late 1940s to the late 1960s.

I argue further that the domination of Labour's and the wider political agenda by the politics of the Cold War meant that for most of the period under review the ALP was unable to draw sufficient national attention to its historiographically somewhat neglected proposed programme of socio-economic reforms in the pre-Whitlam years. Had it been able to do so, then its chances of electoral success would have improved markedly. Only when the suffocating politics of the Cold War began to wane from the later 1960s onwards was Labor, in the form of Gough Whitlam, able to create sufficient space in which to achieve electoral success on the basis of its extensive progressive and nationalist reform programme.

In terms of the largely absent comparative dimension, I maintain that while the external aspects of the politics of Cold War loyalism were equally important in Britain, they occasioned, on balance, less political and social conflict and division in that country than in Australia. For example, notwithstanding important points of difference and division, there existed a broad consensus among the mainstream British political parties concerning Britain's stabilising and containing external roles in the Cold War world. Internally, the issue of communism, while divisive, did not lead to conflict in the BLP and the wider labour movement on anything approaching the Australian scale. And although anti-socialism was a marked and persistent feature of anti-Labour propaganda and action in both countries, the 'tarring' of the labour movement as 'Red' and disloyal was far more marked in Australia. The Communist Party of Australia (CPA) was also both more subservient to the Soviet 'line' in the 1950s and, at crucial points in time, more militantly influential in the unions and industrial disputes than the more independent and moderate Communist Party of Great Britain (CPGB).[8]

Lastly, in terms of the comparative aspect, I claim that in Britain the overriding political concern of the period as a whole, for both successive governments and the labour movement, rested far more with economic matters, particularly with immediate economic problems and those consequent upon its long-term decline from its nineteenth-century position of global hegemony, than with the dominant issue in Australia of Cold War loyalism. At the same time I show that economic matters impinged on politics in important ways in both countries. This was seen, for example, in the fact that the mid-century economic boom contributed significantly to the hegemony of the Right in both countries, and that from the mid 1970s onwards the adverse domestic effects of the international economic crisis and the collapse of the post-war Keynesian demand-management paradigm, preoccupied politicians in Australia, Britain and many other countries.

Yet there were also important economic differences between Britain and Australia which meant that acute and systemic economic problems dominated national political discourse to a much greater extent in the former than in the latter. For example, the 'total' experience of World War Two imposed severe strains on the British economy and hampered its post-war recovery. In contrast, in Australia the war provided the platform for rapid post-war growth, as opposed to 'recovery', by greatly increasing the need for local capacity and so benefiting substantially Australian manufacturing industries. Furthermore, the shared experience of economic boom during the 1950s and for part of the 1960s could not conceal major structural and conjunctural differences and problems in the political economies of the two countries. Above all, Britain was faced with the seemingly insoluble problem of how to manage and reverse its 'decline', especially in relation to its overseas competitors, while maintaining its world role and status in a period of decolonisation. This issue of 'overload' and the related problems of low investment, low productivity, the continuing decline of the staple export industries and too heavy a reliance upon the financial and (increasingly) services sectors, combined with resistance to change in an increasingly outmoded class-based society ('traditionalism'), alleged 'bloody-mindedness' on the part of sections of the labour force, especially the unionised parts, and escalating industrial and class conflicts, preoccupied British politicians and dominated British elections from the early 1960s to 1979. In turn the BLP, during both these years and the period of post-war recovery, was, on balance, more interested in material 'bread and butter' issues and related industrial and class-based problems than was the federal ALP. Until the easing of the Cold War during the late 1960s the federal ALP was forced time and again to confront *the* issue of overriding national importance: the politics of Cold War loyalism.

During the same period of time the 'young', 'up and coming' Australian economy was in far more robust health than its 'old' and declining British counterpart. Although Australia continued to be highly dependent upon foreign capital and technology, the war, as noted above, had stimulated the growth of the country's secondary industries. In the post-war years Australia not only enjoyed a more profound, extensive and longer-lasting growth in living standards and home ownership than Britain, but also benefited immensely from booming world demand for agricultural commodities in the later 1940s and 1950s and minerals in the 1960s.[9] To be sure, Australia was faced with mounting economic problems during the second half of the 1970s (they would become all consuming of politics during the Hawke-Keating Age, 1983–96), but in the 1970s they were less systemic, less long-term and certainly less productive of socio-political conflict than in Britain. From the late 1960s to the mid 1980s Britain experienced levels of industrial and class conflict and general instability unmatched in Australia.

The British labour and more general British historiography has reflected this dominant 'bread and butter' concern with the domestic economy. At the same time it has mirrored the Australian historiography in its general neglect of the comparative UK–Australian dimension of the politics of Cold War loyalism. As documented in the chronological sections below, there have been frequent references in the relevant British literature to persistent anti-socialism, to the 'totalitarian' and 'gestapo' tarring of the Labour Party by some Conservatives during the 1945 election, to the 'Red' smearing of parts of the labour movement at various points during the Cold War and to conflicts around communism within that movement. Some historians have also made reference to the charges of extremism and disloyalty directed by sections of the establishment and the Conservative Party against militant trade union leaders and members of their rank and file during the turbulent 1970s. Conversely, the historiography has either omitted reference to or underplayed the important extent and frequency, and albeit variable successes, with which the Conservative Party smeared the mainstream Labour Party as Red, extreme, alien and disloyal to the nation and 'Free World' during most of the 1970s decade.

Part IV adds new material to the national and comparative pictures. In terms of the latter, the reader's attention is drawn to the central importance of shifts and continuities in geo-politics in shaping the character, similarities and differences of the politics of the Cold War in Britain and Australia. Above all, 'exposed' Australians were far more concerned with the regional advance and threat of communism, both externally and internally, to the security of their country than were the more nuclear-protected and secure Britons. After all, in contrast to the Asia-Pacific region, communism had ceased to advance in Europe by the 1950s. Feelings of exposure, threat and even a siege mentality were largely responsible for the development of the dominant Cold War 'warrior' mentality in Australia as contrasted with the less aggressive and paranoid response in Britain. The key issues of geo-politics and the mentalities they spawned are set into engagement with other contributory factors, including 'hard' and 'soft' establishment policies and traditions, of exclusion and containment, towards the 'Red' 'other'.

Third, as will be evident from the concern with economic matters above, and as reflected extensively in the domestic Australian and British historiography (the comparative aspect, once again, is not addressed), economic trends, the politics of economic policy and management – especially questions of competence, success and failure – and the associated issues of industrial and wider class relations significantly influenced Labour's fortunes. For example, in both countries it was overwhelmingly the Right that successfully took the credit for and reaped electoral benefit from the post-war boom. Yet we will also see that matters were more complicated at the state level in Australia. While the Australian Commonwealth largely controlled the economy by this period of time, the states retained important aspects of control and influence in relation to 'major areas of ALP concern' such as health and education, road and rail transport and shared responsibility with the Commonwealth for industrial relations matters.[10] In some of the states the ALP's successful attempts to represent and improve the socio-economic conditions of workers and to work closely with the trade unions redounded to its electoral benefit throughout the period. At the same time, however, I observe that the divisive politics of Cold War loyalism ended the ALP's electoral influence in states such as Victoria and Queensland for many years to come, following the 1955 Split.

During the 1960s and 1970s the picture, both nationally and comparatively, becomes more variable. For example, in the 1970s voter perceptions of 'responsibility' for economic crisis and chronic class conflict worked to the benefit of both Labour in Britain in 1974, the Tories in 1979 and, as a result of Whitlam's economic failures, Malcolm Fraser in Australia in 1975. (In the 1983 federal election Fraser's failures to resolve growing economic problems and social divisions would be fully exploited by the triumphant ALPer, Bob Hawke, campaigning on a platform of national 'Reconciliation, Recovery and Reconstruction'.)

In bringing my comparative concerns to bear on this third set of issues I highlight the ways in which both Labour and the Right, but more so the latter, were quick to portray their economic policies as being in the interest of the national community as opposed to the 'sectional', and often 'class-based' loyalties of their opponents. As observed especially in the revisionist literature, the reasons for variable political outcomes must be sought not only in the 'raw material' of socio-economic factors but also in the spoken, written and symbolic ways in which politicians, political parties and the media attempted to shape voter behaviour by taking credit for economic policies which, even if 'painful' and 'unavoidable' in the short term, were designed to bring about longer-term and 'sustainable' 'success', 'modernisation', security, stability and social harmony. (This would be particularly the case in 1980s Britain under Margaret Thatcher and Australia under Hawke and Keating.)

Fourth, as in 1916 in Australia and 1931 in Britain and Australia, the extent to which Labour could maintain its unity in the face of internal party differences and conflicts exerted an important influence upon its fortunes. Once again an extensive, nationally based literature is not accompanied by a relevant comparative focus. In attending to this deficiency I observe that while both parties were largely united in the period of World War Two, they were increasingly divided during the 1950s. The Australian Split of 1955, however, was far more complete and had far more lasting damage upon the fortunes of the ALP than did conflicts between the Gaitskellites and Bevanites upon the BLP. Yet from the late 1960s onwards there developed significant differences and conflicts both within and between the political and industrial wings of the British labour movement. These became particularly acute during the 'Winter of Discontent', 1978–79 and, as we will see in Part V, exerted a profoundly debilitating effect upon the BLP's fortunes between the early 1980s and the mid 1990s.

The four sets of issues constitute the core focus of Chapters 7 to 9 below. I start with Labour's high expectations of the 1940s and end with the dashed hopes and fears of the late 1970s.

Notes

1 Fielding, Thompson and Tiratsoo, *England Arise!*, pp. 191–209; Clarke, *Hope and Glory* (2004, Penguin edition), pp. 237–40.
2 Fielding, Thompson and Tiratsoo, *England Arise!*, pp. 212–14; McKibbin, *Classes and Cultures*, Conclusion; James and Markey, 'Class and Labour', 29.
3 James and Markey, 'Class and Labour', 25.
4 Hancock, 'Rise of the Liberal Party'; Brett, *Australian Liberals*, ch. 6; James and Markey, 'Class and Labour', 25, 29; Sean Scalmer, 'Crisis to Crisis: 1950–66', in Faulkner and Macintyre (eds), *True Believers*, p. 104; *Worker*, 31 May 1954; *Australian Worker*, 2 November 1955, 26 November 1958, 20 December 1961.
5 Andrew Scott, *Fading Loyalties: The Australian Labor Party and the Working Class* (Leichhardt: Pluto Press, 1991), chs 2, 3; Scott, *Running on Empty*, ch. 3; Fielding, *Labour and Cultural Change*, especially Conclusion. Both Scott and Fielding conclude that while not the 'inevitable result of cultural change' (Fielding, p. 230), Labour's 'generally unimpressive' election results in this period resulted partly from the 'traditionalism' (my term) of its internal culture and its consequent failure to relate more fully and successfully to the changing composition of the electorate and the wider population.
6 Stuart Macintyre, *A Concise History of Australia* (Cambridge: Cambridge University Press, 2006), p. 209. See also Scott, *Running on Empty*, pp. 49–51.
7 Macintyre, correspondence with the author, 4 October 2009.
8 See the illuminating comparative study of the Communist Party of Great Britain and the Communist Party of Australia by Phillip Deery and Neil Redfern, 'No Lasting Peace? Labor, Communism and the Cominform: Australia and Great Britain, 1945–50', *Labour History*, 88 (2005), 65.
9 I am grateful to Stuart Macintyre and Sean Scalmer for these insights into the nature and development of the Australian economy.
10 James and Markey, 'Class and Labour', 27.

CHAPTER SEVEN

Labour successes: the 1940s

Britain

The experiences of World War Two, especially the mass suffering and sacrifices made, combined with the widespread expectation that the post-war years would usher in a more civilised world and major improvements in people's lives, worked to Labour's benefit. As we have seen, Britain first 'total' war, between 1914 and 1918, had played an important part in the Labour Party's youthful 'rise'. But this process became even more pronounced during World War Two, when the mature Labour Party both became a key player in Winston Churchill's wartime coalition government and attained majority office for the first time as a result of the general election of 1945.

To be sure, Churchill had been an extremely popular war leader and confidently expected the Conservative Party and his caretaker 'National' government to reap their reward at the 1945 election.[1] In the opinion of the *Manchester Guardian*, the 'general feeling' just before the July election was that the Tories would win, but that it would be a 'close' result.[2] Yet this opinion underplayed the fact that, according to the young Gallup polls, 'Labour had enjoyed a sizeable lead over the Conservatives since 1943, and one which had steadily increased over the period up to the election.'[3] In the event, much to Churchill's anger and the surprise of 'most observers', Labour won a historic victory. It achieved an absolute parliamentary majority of 146 seats (a swing of about 12 per cent), while the Conservatives suffered their third-worst general election defeat in their history, behind those of 1832 and 1906. Labour increased its vote from 8,325,000 in 1935 to almost 12 million, and its percentage of the vote stood at 47.8 as against the Conservatives' 39.8 and the Liberals' 9.0 (the Communist candidates won 0.4 per cent). Moreover, while Labour had consolidated its strength in Scotland and Wales and run candidates in Northern Ireland, it was in England 'that the great landslide had taken place'.

This was especially the case among the urban working-class nationally, rural workers and small producers in Norfolk and the professional middle class in the suburbs of the traditionally Conservative home counties. All these groups were radicalised by the wartime experiences of service to the common cause, shared suffering, mounting grievances and the desire to create a better post-war world for all 'useful' Britons.[4] As Ben Chifley, the ALP's successor to Curtin, declared in a message to Attlee, Labour's success constituted a 'magnificent achievement', while for the *Worker* it was a vote for a 'New World'.[5]

Of particular relevance to this study is the fact that Labour achieved its landslide victory in the face of a determined and concerted Conservative attempt to smear its socialism as being, by its very nature, totalitarian, tyrannical and alien. Smearing was, indeed, the key characteristic of a Tory election campaign dominated by the long-standing and aggressive anti-socialist Churchill in his radio broadcasts and speeches to audiences across the country, and the equally outspoken anti-socialist Lord Beaverbrook, the Conservatives' other 'major touring speaker'. More generally, most Conservatives were 'content to follow' Churchill's extremist lead, to appeal to the national interest and to adopt the cult of personality by beseeching the electorate to 'Vote National – Help him finish the job'.[6]

In directing their anti-socialism uniformly and crudely against the Labour Party, Churchill and Beaverbrook stood in contrast to Stanley Baldwin, the dominant figure in interwar Conservatism. As we saw in Part III, while similarly defining socialism as 'un-English' and 'un-British', Baldwin nevertheless adopted a far more subtle and differentiated approach towards the Labour Party's 'socialism' than the 'Diehard' Churchill. Although the labour movement's 'wreckers' and 'militants' were condemned by Baldwin and Churchill alike, the former successfully sought both to enlist the support of MacDonald and other labour movement moderates in the common fight against extremism and, as leader, to keep the more extreme anti-socialist elements in his own party, including Churchill, in check. The key difference by the time of the 1945 election was that the extremist figure of Churchill was now in control of the party and set the Conservatives' agenda.

As is well known, in his election broadcasts and speeches Churchill resorted to the well-worn propagandistic theme that socialism, including Labour's socialism, was a 'continental' import, alien to British traditions, values and ideas. It was alleged that Labour's collectivism, 'totalitarianism', its potential embrace of 'violent revolution' (in the event of the failure of peaceful and gradual parliamentarianism) and its 'abject worship of the state' were 'abhorrent' to 'British' freedoms, constitutionalism, individualism, enterprise, toleration and dissent.

On this occasion, however, the demonic alien force was not Soviet Bolshevism, but Nazi Germany. Labour would 'have to fall back on some form of Gestapo' to enforce its will of total state 'prescription' and 'regimentation'.[7] Beaverbrook, in turn, claimed that Professor Harold Laski, Chair of Labour's National Executive Committee, sought to substitute the 'dictatorship' of his committee for the democratic rule of the parliamentary party. As such, Laski allegedly aimed at nothing less than 'the destruction of the Parliamentary system of Great Britain'.[8] In anticipation of New Right propaganda during the Thatcher years, Conservative spokespersons drew liberally on the ideas of Friedrich von Hayek, the Austrian-born economist who had been a professor in London since 1931, to argue that Labour was paving the way to 'serfdom'.[9]

According to the *Manchester Guardian*, Attlee, Bevin and other leading figures in the Labour Party appealed, in contrast, to 'reason, not to prejudice and fear' and convincingly denied all these 'desperate' and 'preposterous' 'scares', 'smears' and 'diversions' from the real issues at hand.[10] As former members and colleagues of Churchill in the wartime coalition, they were very disappointed and annoyed that he was impugning their proven patriotism and their commitments to freedom and democracy against the totalitarian threat presented by both fascism and communism. They were also dismayed by the fact that he was 'allowing Beaverbrook to dominate the Conservative campaign' and that, while a great national war leader, he was improperly seeking to exploit that reputation for sectional, party-political ends.[11] As the *Guardian* declared after Churchill's first broadcast, 'It is ludicrous to hold up the men with whom he has been working in amity as dangerous revolutionaries ready to employ a Gestapo or to ignore the experience of Socialist Governments in the Dominions and elsewhere which have managed to rule without any of the Hayekian horrors of totalitarianism.' The newspaper's conclusion was that, 'The voice we heard last night was that of Mr. Churchill', the 'great leader in war of a united nation', but 'the mind was that of Lord Beaverbrook'. Interestingly, Churchill's wife and 'at least one daughter' were 'outraged by the Gestapo speech and the attacks thereby on Attlee'.[12]

In his response to the broadcast Attlee regretted the 'travesty' of Labour Party policy presented by Churchill. He highlighted the fact that his party had played a key role in the fights for freedom and democracy, as seen most recently in the 'great war for democracy'. He also maintained that in British history the employment of secret police and repression had been most marked during Lord Liverpool's Tory government after the Napoleonic Wars, and that capitalist 'freedoms' traditionally included exploitation, unemployment, poverty, 'freedom for the rich and slavery for the poor'. Far from being truly representative of the nation, the Conservative Party 'remains, as always, a class party', argued Attlee.[13] He also mounted a strong defence of the home-grown nature of the Labour Party's socialism. Churchill had 'forgotten' that 'Socialist theory was developed in Britain long before Karl Marx, by Robert Owen'. He had also 'forgotten' that 'Australia, New Zealand, whose peoples have played so great a part in the war, and the Scandinavian countries, have had Socialist governments for years'. There were 'no countries in the world more free and democratic', according to Attlee.[14]

In conference with President Truman over the atom bomb later in 1945, Attlee both flatly denied that Socialists of the British kind were enemies of 'the freedom of the individual, of speech, religion and the press', and portrayed the Labour Party as a champion not only of British, but also of traditional American liberties. Thus, 'We in the Labour Party declare that we are in line with those who fought for the Magna Charta [sic], and habeas corpus, with the Pilgrim Fathers, and with the signatories of the Declaration of Independence.'[15]

Attlee and his colleagues also drew the public's attention to past Tory failures, especially their 'reactionary' and discredited socio-economic, defence and foreign policies of the 1930s. Unemployment and hunger had blighted the decade of the Conservative-dominated National Government, while the misjudgement of Chamberlain at Munich and the weakness of Tory appeasers in general had placed the country in great danger.[16] Their 'guilt' was placed in stark contrast to Labour's 'patriotism'. The latter was reflected in Labour's strong commitment to social reform and, by 1939, its recognition of the necessity of rearmament and the fight against Germany. Tory wavering, weakness and failure in the face of the growing Nazi threat underpinned Labour's refusal to serve in a coalition government in 1939.[17] Moreover, the collectivism and comradeship necessary to win another 'total' war convinced Labourites that socialism was not only morally but also practically superior to free-market capitalism. Labour's keynote socialism of the 1945 election was 'derived from the lessons of war', especially the need 'to use controls and public ownership to plan the economy in the national interest'. Labour would introduce nationalisation, pragmatically and selectively as opposed to ideologically and uniformly, in order to increase industrial efficiency, improve overall economic performance and so build a solid economic platform upon which to build better housing, full employment and a welfare state rooted in the principle of universal access and provision.[18] 'At long last', it appeared that the Labour Party 'had been awarded a mandate to legislate socialism, something which practically nobody at the time had expected to happen'.[19]

These contrasting party records meant that while the Conservatives 'held out no hope for the future' and were not fit for the task of 'bold' post-war 'reconstruction', progressive and patriotic Labour was ideally equipped to build the 'New Order'.[20] As the prominent Conservative writer Peregrine Worsthorne wrote of the 1945 election some two decades later,

> An overwhelming majority of the electorate recalling slump, unemployment, appeasement and war under the Tories, accepted the Socialist doctrine of State ownership and the ethos of comradely fellowship as the right and decent way to run the affairs of this country.[21]

Moreover, for some Labour leaders, if less so for the more 'parochial' electorate at large, this was to be a 'New Order' not only at home but also in the creation of a more 'benign', 'enlightened' and 'democratic' British Commonwealth.[22]

In truth, Labour won the 1945 election because Attlee's pragmatic socialist message was far more in touch with what the *Manchester Guardian* termed the 'silent revolution' in people's experiences and expectations than was Churchill's stale, out-of-touch and distasteful resort to smearing.[23] The latter also flew in the face of the fact that Russia enjoyed widespread popularity in Britain during the war as a result of its key role in turning the tide against Hitler. As Arthur Mann, former editor of the Conservative *Yorkshire Post*, wrote in his post-election analysis,

> The election has proved conclusively that the 'red bogey' no longer holds any terrors for the British people who have seen the hostile critics of the Soviet regime confounded by the magnificent spirit of the Russian resistance.[24]

While admiration for the Russian war effort and sympathy for the massive suffering and sacrifices of the Russian people increased the appeal of the British Communist Party – membership rose from 'a maximum of 18,000' to 50,000 in 1944 – it benefited the Labour Party even more. As observed by Henry Pelling, 'many people could maintain that the Labour Party represented the British form of socialism, whereas Communism was the Russian form'.[25]

In their revisionist account of the Labour Party and popular politics in the 1940s, Steven Fielding, Peter Thompson and Nick Tiratsoo maintain that Labour's successful appeal to the largely 'apathetic' electorate of 1945, including sections of the middle class, was based far more on its advocacy of practical 'bread and butter' reforms, revolving around housing, employment and social welfare, than its 'vision' of transforming 'ethical socialism'. While not underestimating the undoubted appeal of these reforms, it would, nevertheless, appear to the present writer to be mistaken to set up a simple dichotomous model of *either* 'apathetic' pragmatism *or* ethical socialism. The weight of evidence would suggest that there was a conscious swing to the left in 1945, and that this comprised *both* pragmatism *and* the hope for a better, fairer future, a 'New World', in which planning, nation-alisation, cooperation, equality of sacrifice in the national interest and the reward of 'fair shares' would constitute, at least in the immediate term, essential parts.[26] It is true that Labour's appeal to the middle classes, especially in the South, in addition to its very strong showing among its 'traditional' working-class base (strengthened by the wartime restoration of 'the old staple industries to full employment') was extremely important.[27] Peter Clarke, for example, argues that 'the breadth of Labour's constituency', putting a 'clear 10 per cent on its pre-war share of the vote', constituted 'the key to its victory'.[28]

In turn, Labour's widened appeal meant that it had become the voice of the new progressive nation. In 1945 the Labour Party, recon-struction, reform, socialism, the 'people' and the 'national interest' had become inseparable, indeed synonymous. The Labour Party had, for a time at least, 'rid itself of that air of being a sect or faction, an estate of the nation'. It had come to 'command the whole array', or at least the 'useful' and 'productive parts' of 'the people and nation'.[29] As observed in parts of the relevant secondary literature, but underesti-mated by the 'apathy school' and meriting more explanatory emphasis in the overall historiography, the appeal of Labour to a radical and progressive form of 'national unity' constituted the key to its triumph in 1945.[30] In contrast, as astutely observed by Mann, notwithstanding the 'immense prestige and popularity of Mr. Churchill', the Conser-vatives had failed to respond to and articulate 'national feeling'. They had undertaken an unsuccessful negative and tired campaign to discredit their opponents in a 'wild and irresponsible' manner. They had failed to adopt 'an attractive programme of practical reconstruction and reform' and remained by and large the sectional representatives of property and privilege.[31]

Labour's reforms and its articulation of the spirit of progressive nationalism continued to exert a powerful appeal in the country up to and including the next general election of 1950. By the end of 1946 Labour controlled fifty-two out of eighty-three county boroughs, com-pared to fifteen before November 1945, and its membership 'continued to grow at an unprecedented rate'. Its slogan of 'no return to the 1930s', combined with its welfare reforms and commitments to full employ-ment and the provision of decent education and housing for all, were manifestly popular with the public. Indeed the Conservatives soon came to accept the main features of the post-war welfare state, while at the same time becoming increasingly critical of the continuing controls and regulations of 'state socialism'. In the face of growing evidence that the public was, at best, lukewarm towards further nationalisation, the Labour Party's emphasis from 1947 onwards shifted from more 'socialism' to the 'consolidation' of its early post-war 'planning' and 'reforming' achievements.[32]

It was by no means all plain sailing for Labour. In the 1947 local elections the Conservatives registered a decisive victory, and there was growing discontent around continuing austerity, government-imposed controls and restrictions and the 'dearth of consumer goods and foodstuffs'. Increasing numbers of the middle class, and women across the classes, desired less of Labour's 'fair shares' and wartime-induced controls and more of the individual freedoms and choices associated with peacetime. This emerging, highly gendered 'consumerist' consciousness and support for the notion of a 'property-owning democracy', including home ownership as the basis of 'good citizenship', would become marked features of both mid-century Britain and Australia. Increasingly, and notwithstanding Labour attempts to appeal to consumers, 'consumerism' and home ownership sat uneasily, in the eyes of many voters, with Labour's emphases upon production, collectivism, state provision, renting, 'dependency' and regulation. They became strongly associated with both the 'libertarian' and 'respectable' aspects of Conservatism and Liberalism and their appeals to women as purchasers, mothers, housewives and the bedrocks of citizenship, stability and order.[33]

On balance, however, Labour remained relatively optimistic about its continued 'forward march' in the later 1940s. Notwithstanding growing criticisms, it was keeping down the cost of living, helping families with food subsidies and in general terms doing a very creditable job of helping the British economy to recover strongly from the 'shambles' it was in at the end of the war.[34] The general election of February 1950 gave limited support to this optimism. A massive 84 per cent turn-out, up by 10.5 per cent on 1945, saw Labour returned to office, albeit with a greatly reduced overall majority, from 146 seats in 1945 to 8. Labour support slipped by 2 per cent from 1945, while the Tories increased their share of the vote by 4 per cent.[35] The Communist Party failed to capitalise upon its popularity during the war. While 21 Communist candidates had polled 64,000 votes in 1945, the 100 candidates who stood in 1950 received fewer than 100,000 votes. No Communist candidate came 'faintly near victory', not even the two retiring Communist MPs.[36]

In 1950 the election revolved around the Labour government's post-war record and future promises on 'fair shares', economic recovery and growth. There also arose the issues of the current state of the economy, including the absence of industrial conflict on the scale of the immediate post-World War One years, the avoidance of a return to the poverty, unemployment and inequality of the 1930s, the ability successfully to 'deal with' Stalin, to strengthen international peace and security and questions of individualism and freedom versus collectivism and state controls. In contrast to the 1945 election, Labour's leaders were keen to play down the issues of nationalisation and socialism.[37]

While some Conservatives branded Labour's 'state socialism' as 'alien' and 'incompatible' with democracy and freedom,[38] there was no concerted attempt during the 1950 contest to tar the mainstream Labour Party and the trade union movement as 'totalitarian' and by implication 'un-English' or 'un-British' on anything like the scale of Churchill's ill-fated campaign of 1945. The Tories were doubtless mindful of the fact that Churchill had failed spectacularly, while Churchill himself increasingly played down the confrontational 'class warfare' line in favour of a more conciliatory Disraelian, 'One Nation' approach. This was reflected in Churchill's increasing mid-century advocacy of peaceful industrial relations and his advice to Conservative-voting workers to join a trade union. Similarly, neither did attempts to tar Labour as 'Red', nor divisive party-political aspects of the politics of the Cold War, apart from Churchill's claim that he was best equipped to negotiate with Stalin, appear as prominent issues in the election campaign.[39]

This state of affairs stood in marked contrast to the situation in Australia. As we will see in Chapter 8, the Australian federal election of 1949 marked the beginning of a determined and successful attempt by the Liberal-Country Party coalition to make the politics of the Cold War, especially the 'Red' nature of the ALP, the key issues in elections. This was to be the case for the next twenty years.

Australia

The single-minded pursuit of the war effort, the championing of progressive national and class interests and post-war reconstruction also constituted the key factors in the sharp upturn in the ALP's wartime and immediate post-war electoral fortunes.[40]

As we saw in Part III, the ALP was out of federal office for most of the interwar years and its record in the states, although better than at the federal level, was patchy. Yet the unifying dynamism and renewed sense of common purpose provided by the new leader, John Curtin, from 1935 onwards, augured well. Furthermore, from the later 1930s the ruling UAP began to 'disintegrate'. It was both bitterly divided by internal conflicts and, as in the case of the National Government in Britain, unprepared and weak in the face of the growing Nazi menace. The UAP's leader, Joseph Lyons, had provided a measure of stability and trust, but his death in 1939 further accelerated his party's demise. After the 1940 general election, Robert Menzies, the new leader of the UAP, became Prime Minister in a hung parliament. With the new government dependent upon the votes of two independents, Menzies invited the ALP to take part in a coalition or national government. Curtin, however, declined the invitation, so continuing Labor's traditional opposition to coalitions. In 1941 Menzies was 'dumped' as Prime Minister by his own party. He was succeeded as Prime Minister by Arthur Fadden, Deputy Prime Minister and leader of the Country Party. After two months, however, Fadden's weak government fell and Curtin became Prime Minister. Thereafter Australia's war effort was conducted not by a coalition government, as in the British case, but by Curtin's ALP.[41]

The results were most impressive. Curtin had trodden softly in his early period as leader, in the face of strong differences between Catholics and the left in the ALP towards Spain and Italy and the strong feeling in his party in favour of international peace, self-defence and opposition to involvement in another overseas war. Curtin himself, of course, had been very much to the fore in the interwar period in his commitments to international reconciliation and arbitration, labour and socialist internationalism, anti-imperialism, disarmament and peace.[42] Up to the late 1930s, and despite strong left-wing opposition within its ranks, the ALP had officially backed the government's policy of support for British appeasement. Yet, as noted by Geoffrey Serle, by early 1939 Curtin was 'unhappily recognising the inevitability of war and that isolation and concentration on self-defence were not enough'. In the face of Hitler's invasion of Poland, the German offensive in western Europe and the 'Battle of Britain' in 1940, Curtin 'weaned the Labor Party from the pacifist and isolationist ideals of earlier years' and prepared it, 'at least to some degree' for war.[43]

During the war Curtin became an extremely effective and popular leader of Australia, being widely hailed as the 'saviour of the nation'.[44] In marked contrast to the ineffectual and vacillating leaders of the UAP he was strong, determined and clearly focused upon equipping the country for war and securing victory. The fierce anti-conscriptionist of World War One improved home defence and successfully withstood his party's opposition to conscription to secure support for the deployment of Australian forces beyond Australian territory. His government adopted 'systematic planning', including 'far-reaching' controls of industry, employment, wages, prices and rents, in order to place the economy on a secure war footing and begin planning for a more civilised post-war world.[45]

The latter, arguably, was underpinned more by the New Deal progressivism of Franklin Roosevelt and the ALP's historic 'mission' to 'civilize capitalism' than by an explicit commitment to socialism, even the socialism practised in the immediate term by the 1945 Labour government in Britain. As Geoffrey Bolton observes, although committed to 'planning', Curtin 'had promised not to nationalize any industries during the war, and although conservatives feared, and socialists demanded, a great growth in government ownership after the war, Labor's leaders were in general cautious about taking on new commitments'.[46] Ben Chifley, Curtin's successor as Prime Minister, was fiscally conservative. The High Court, many states, special interest lobby groups (including the medical profession), religious divisions (especially around education) and unsuccessful referenda in 1944, 1946 and 1948 put a further, if limited, brake upon the extension of Commonwealth powers and the creation of a comprehensive and universal, as opposed to a patchy and selective, welfare state in the post-war years. At the same time, however, the referenda did confirm some Commonwealth powers in social services, and Chifley created new public industries and attempted to nationalise the banks.[47]

Claiming that 'Australia looks to America', Curtin worked closely with the Americans to counter the Japanese threat in the Pacific. Following their attack on Pearl Harbor in December 1941 and their capture of Singapore in February 1942, the Japanese launched air attacks on Darwin and other towns in northern Australian centres. In the wake of the fall of Singapore, and in ways reminiscent of World War One, Curtin criticised Churchill for subordinating Australian interests to those of Britain: the latter's failure to defend Singapore constituted an act of 'inexcusable betrayal' and 'Australia's Dunkirk'.[48] Curtin's priority was to bring home Australian troops to defend the country against the Japanese, while Churchill wanted them to remain in Burma, Java and Sumatra. Maintaining that the imperial interest was of paramount importance and that 'there was no such thing as a separate Australian interest', Menzies 'privately implored Curtin to obey Churchill', according to Serle. Curtin, however, both suspected that Churchill regarded Australia as 'expendable' and expressed overriding commitments to 'Australia' and 'Labor' rather than the Empire. As Serle further notes, 'Curtin was a natural Australian who had been impervious to Imperial ideology.'[49]

Curtin henceforth 'proclaimed the Battle for Australia' and looked to the United States rather than Britain to repel the Japanese advance in the Pacific and drive what the *Australian Worker* termed 'the

Japanese Yellow Peril' from 'the foreshores of Australia'.[50] Curtin's independent nationalism later led Gough Whitlam, who had served in the air force in the Pacific, to declare that 'Australian nationalism was born, not with the Anzac landing, but with the response of the Curtin Labor government to the external threat to our security'.[51] Australian forces were placed under the command of MacArthur, the American general, in order to counter Japanese expansion in the Pacific. Although the Japanese were probably more interested in isolating rather than invading Australia, Curtin's strategy worked. Australian troops played the main role in the expulsion of the Japanese from Papua New Guinea in 1942. Thereafter, concludes Macintyre, 'the Australians were relegated to an auxiliary role in the Pacific war effort'.[52]

Notwithstanding his dominant attachments to the Australian nation, its labour movement and its organised working class, his long-standing opposition to imperialism and his serious disagreement with Churchill over the fall of Singapore, Curtin came, as a result of his wartime experiences, to develop a far more positive view of the British Commonwealth than in the pre-war period. In the process his commitments to Australian nationalism, Britain and the Commonwealth became perfectly compatible. As Serle observes, 'he had come to consider that the Empire/Commonwealth was more of a potential force for good in the post-war world than he had believed'.[53] This view, including an increasingly far more positive attitude towards the British monarchy than earlier in the century and consistent support for 'British' popular constitutionalism and 'race patriotism', was shared by Chifley, his successor as ALP leader, Dr Herbert Vere Evatt and the other leaders of the mainstream post-war labour movement.

It is true that periodic tensions and conflicts occurred during the 1940s and 1950s, well before Britain began its 1960s 'turn' to Europe, as seen most prominently in the unsuccessful application for membership of the EEC between 1961 and 1963. These revolved around areas of continued economic dependence, instances of Britain's 'arrogance' and 'condescension' towards the 'colonies' and its failure sufficiently to consult with and heed the advice of Australia's leaders. Important examples of the latter include Churchill's actions over Singapore and, in 1945, the exclusion of Australia from the crucial meetings at which Britain, the United States and the Soviet Union had decided to set up the United Nations (UN), the successor to the League of Nations. Britain and other western imperial powers, furthermore, did not always take kindly to the Australian labour movement's support for national independence movements in the region and elsewhere in the world. They regarded Evatt as a 'loose cannon', even though he would have largely been happy for the European powers to re-establish their imperial rule in the post-war period if they had been able and willing to do so.[54]

Yet for most of the time during the 1940s and 1950s consensus prevailed over conflict. During the period of World War Two, of course, the battles against expansionary European fascism and Japanese militarism and the defence of democracy and 'British freedoms' occupied centre stage in people's lives in Australia as well as in Britain. Interwar Australian criticisms of the coercive aspects of British imperialism increasingly faded into the background. Australian labour leaders, such as Curtin and Evatt, were fully cognisant of the fact that leaders of the Labour Party in Britain were, at least in thought if not always in deed,[55] seeking to rid the British Commonwealth of its past reputation for imperialistic oppression and exploitation and render it more democratic, open and attentive to the voices and independent aspirations of its constituent national parts. Leaders of both the ALP and the BLP also sought to strengthen ties between the two parties and their respective countries.[56] Of key importance was Curtin's insistence that his country's increasingly close relationship with the United States would not be at the expense of Australia's 'traditional links or kinship with the United Kingdom'. He remained grateful for the support given to Australia by Britain as well as the United States during the war, worked amicably with Britain's political leaders, visited London in 1944 in connection with the Prime Ministers' Conference and expressed 'loyalty to the Throne'. He recorded that the 'discussion of mutual problems' with the British government during the war had 'emphasised the strength and value of our associations'. He concluded, 'We have, as Mr. Churchill has expressed it, become better members of the British Commonwealth by becoming better Australians.'[57] Churchill reciprocated by declaring that, although 'virtually unknown' in Britain at the start of his visit in 1944, Curtin had created a 'profound impression' in his capacity as a national leader. Upon Curtin's death in 1945 Churchill declared that the 'Empire' had lost 'one of its foremost and able statesmen', while Morgan Phillips, the Labour Party's secretary, paid 'tribute to this great man of the people . . . to his untiring and selfless devotion to the cause of socialism and progress' and to his 'great service' not only to Australia, but also to 'the whole British Commonwealth'.[58] During the war and in the 1950s Evatt also staunchly supported Australia's membership of the Commonwealth 'family' based upon cherished 'British freedoms' and Britain as 'a refuge against intolerance and tyranny', a 'fair deal for all' and the 'saviour of the world' in 1940. He also appealed to 'the glorious traditions of our race' in attacking Menzies' attempt to ban the Communist Party.[59]

[171]

Lastly, in the post-war world the ALP combined gratitude to the United States for its support in defence matters with an unwillingness to become too dependent upon a country increasingly committed to a war against communism. While also strongly anti-communist, the ALP believed that over-reliance on the United States would be detrimental both to Australia's independence in foreign affairs and to progressive reform at home. The ALP thus sought to exert Australian influence through the means of the UN and to use a 'revived' British Commonwealth as a 'counterweight to American dominance' and the sterling bloc as 'a defence against US economic hegemony'.[60]

As demonstrated in the elections of 1943 and 1946, Curtin's and Chifley's initiatives proved to be very effective. The ALP's landslide victory in August 1943 marked 'the most spectacular two-chamber victory since the coming of federation'. The party won 'forty-nine seats against twenty-three in the House of Representatives and twenty-two against fourteen in the Senate (the first Labor Senate majority since 1914)'.[61] The new Senate included Labor's first woman federal member, Dorothy Tangney, an engine driver's daughter and a graduate. The outcome of the election also signalled the death of the UAP and the establishment by Menzies and his colleagues of the new Liberal Party in 1944 and 1945. As a significant pointer to its future success, the Liberal Party jettisoned the narrow, business-based appeal of the UAP in favour of a national approach to the 'forgotten' lower-middle class, the more affluent middle classes and 'respectable' women of all classes.[62] Yet in the immediate term it was the ALP which continued to enjoy success at the polls. In the next federal election, in September 1946, Chifley, a working-class-born locomotive engineer, secured for Labor a second term of government 'for the first time ever, and an unassailable majority in both houses'.[63]

As widely acknowledged at the time, the ALP's victories in 1943 and 1946 were built upon the successful realisation of its pledge to gain 'Victory in War and Victory for the Peace'.[64] By the time of the 1943 election Labor could contrast the 'inability' of Menzies and Fadden to 'rise to the occasion' when the nation was in 'deadly peril' with Curtin's demonstrable successes in rallying 'all sections of the community into one great organisation', equipping the country for war and securing support from the United States in the fight against the Japanese while also retaining close ties with the British.[65] Labor's war record, a reflection of its enduring commitment to 'the Australian sentiment', effectively undermined the charges made by its opponents during the election campaign that it was 'anti-British', 'dominated by Communists' and 'isolationist'.[66] During the 1946 campaign, the ALP insisted, in the manner of its British counterpart in 1945, that there would be no return to the miseries of the 1930s and that it possessed a 'proud record of achievement' in terms of its goals to provide full employment, keep price inflation and rents in check, avoid food short- ages (in contrast to most of the other countries affected by the war) and improve social welfare provision. Labor asked for, and duly received, a mandate from the electorate to 'Carry on for Australia' and build the new social order.[67] As in the case of the BLP in 1945, the ALP's appeal to the national interest was vital to its success. 'ONCE MORE', observed the *Worker*, *'THE PEOPLE OF AUSTRALIA HAVE LINKED THE NATION'S DESTINY WITH LABOR'*.[68]

In sum, notwithstanding the considerable power and spoiling tactics of the High Court and other socio-political forces opposed to 'big' Com- monwealth government, Labor was successful in taking bold wartime initiatives and putting into place a post-war reform programme 'without precedent in volume, scope and substance'.[69] Health, education, social welfare benefits in the form of 'child endowment, widows' pensions, unemployment, sickness and funeral benefits, and a spouse's allowance for invalid and old-age pensions', employment and housing were all major beneficiaries. Above all, the pledge to full employment was at the centre of Labor's post-war vision and policy ('the complement of its weak provision of direct welfare payments'). These improvements took place either as a result of direct Commonwealth spending or as increased government subsidies to the states, to the private sector and to private individuals as a contribution to the costs of medical insurance and care.[70]

To be sure, there were limitations. As noted above, Australia's immediate post-war welfare system was less comprehensive in scope and universal in provision than its British counterpart, although, in contrast to the latter, the former was non-contributory. Furthermore, the 'new' order was still highly racialised. Although Chifley sought to cultivate good relations with newly independent India and Pakistan from 1947 onwards, and Arthur Calwell, as Minister for Immigration, allowed in non-Anglophone immigrants and European refugees, the post-war Labor government would not allow Asians into Australia and deported some of those already in the country. It remained steadfast in its commitment to 'White Australia' and its concomitant 'national homogeneity'. It also made very limited efforts to improve the socio- economic and political lot of Aboriginals. The Commonwealth Nationality and Citizenship Act of 1948 did include Aboriginals as Australian citizens. But the voting rights of Aboriginals were either non-existent, as in Queensland and the Northern Territory, or in practice very restricted, as in New South Wales and Western Australia. So, lacking the vote, and constituting only 1 per cent of the population, Aboriginals were largely irrelevant to the ALP's electoral strategy.[71]

To the surprise and consternation of many contemporaries, Labour's post-war successes proved to be short lived. As a result of the next federal election, in 1949, Labor was cast out of office and remained in the federal political wilderness for the next twenty-three years. In Britain the period of exile, from the election of 1951 onwards, was shorter – thirteen 'wasted years' as opposed to twenty-three. But the blow to the Labour Party's self-confidence and optimism about the movement's and the country's forward progressive march was very damaging. It is to an examination and explanation of Labour's years 'out in the cold' in both countries that I turn in Chapter 8.

Notes

1 *Manchester Guardian*, 28 June, 2 July 1945.
2 *Manchester Guardian*, 28 June 1945; Henry Pelling, 'The 1945 General Election Reconsidered', *The Historical Journal*, 23:2 (1980), 408; Orwell and Angus (eds), *Collected Essays of George Orwell*, vol. III, *As I Please 1943–1945* (London: Secker and Warburg, 1968), pp. 380–1, 395.
3 Brooke, *Labour's War*, p. 322.
4 Alan Sked and Chris Cook, *Post-War Britain: A Political History* (London: Penguin, 1993), pp. 15–16; Pelling, '1945 General Election', 413; McKibbin, *Classes and Cultures*, pp. 528–36; Stedman Jones, *Languages of Class*, pp. 243–6; Fielding, Thompson and Tiratsoo, *England Arise!*, pp. 62–3.
5 See *Daily Mail*, 27 July 1945 in 'Press Cuttings, General Election 1945', LP/ELEC/1945/2, Labour History Archive and Study Centre, Manchester (hereafter LHASC); *Worker*, 30 July, 6 August 1945.
6 Sked and Cook, *Post-War Britain*, p. 21.
7 *Ibid.*, pp. 20–1; *Manchester Guardian*, 5 June 1945.
8 Sked and Cook, *Post-War Britain*, p. 21; *Manchester Guardian*, 21, 22 June, 2 July 1945.
9 *Manchester Guardian*, 6 June 1945. This issue of the newspaper also contained a statement by Hayek declaring that he was an economist, not a politician, that he had no connection with the Conservative Party, and that he had written his *Road to Serfdom* 'essentially to persuade the Socialists to act wisely'. His conclusion, however, was that 'I do not seem to have succeeded in that'.
10 *Manchester Guardian*, 6, 30 June, 2 July 1945. See also *Daily Herald*, 5 June 1945 in *Press Cuttings, General Election, 1945*, for criticism of Churchill's 'cheap' electioneering tricks and Conservatives' past praise of Mussolini and other dictators.
11 *Manchester Guardian*, 21, 28, 30 June, 2 July 1945.
12 *Manchester Guardian*, 6 June 1945. I am grateful to Chris Wrigley for the reference to the reaction of Churchill's wife and daughter.
13 *Manchester Guardian*, 6 June 1945.
14 *Ibid*; Ward, 'Preparing for the People's War', 174–7, 180–1.
15 As reported in the *Australian Worker*, 21 November 1945.
16 *Manchester Guardian*, 27 July 1945; Pelling, '1945 General Election', 411–12; Clarke, *Hope and Glory*, p. 215.
17 Ward, 'Preparing for the People's War', 180–2.
18 Brooke, *Labour's War*, pp. 323–5.
19 Sked and Cook, *Post-War Britain*, p. 16.
20 *Manchester Guardian*, 27 July 1945; Clarke, *Hope and Glory*, p. 215.
21 *Sunday Telegraph*, 3 April 1966 in 'Press Cuttings, 1966 Election', LHASC.
22 Ward, 'Preparing for the People's War', 177–8, 180. George Orwell was probably right in his assessment that 'on the whole' people voted Labour 'because of the

belief that a Left government means family allowances, higher old-age pensions, houses with bathrooms etc rather than from any internationalist consideration'. See Orwell and Angus (eds), *Collected Essays of George Orwell*, vol. III, p. 394.

23 *Manchester Guardian*, 27 July 1945.

24 See his letter to *The Times*, 31 July 1945.

25 Pelling, '1945 General Election', 412.

26 Fielding, Thompson and Tiratsoo, *England Arise!*, pp. 212–18; *Manchester Guardian*, 27 July 1945; *Worker*, 30 July, 6 August 1945; *Australian Worker*, 1 August 1945; Brooke, *Labour's War*, p. 327; McKibbin, *Classes and Cultures*, Conclusion; James Hinton, '1945 and the Apathy School', *History Workshop Journal*, 43 (Spring 1997), 266–73. Interestingly, George Orwell's position was mixed. On the one hand, he observed a 'slide to the Left', as manifested in his belief that 'at most 50 per cent could be considered as outright votes for Socialism, and about another 10 per cent as votes for nationalisation of certain key industries'. On the other hand, the 'mood of the country' seemed to him to be 'less revolutionary, less Utopian, even less hopeful, than it was in 1940 or 1942'. See Orwell and Angus (eds), *Collected Essays of George Orwell*, p. 395.

27 McKibbin, *Classes and Cultures*, p. 531.

28 Clarke, *Hope and Glory*, p. 215; Stedman Jones, 'Why is the Labour Party in a Mess?', p. 243; Brooke, *Labour's War*, p. 326.

29 R.B. McCallum and Alison Readman, *The British General Election of 1945* (London: Frank Cass, 1964), pp. 266–7.

30 See, for example, *ibid.*, pp. 266–7; Hinton, '1945 and Apathy School', 271; Stephen Brooke, 'Labour and the "Nation after 1945', in Jon Lawrence and Miles Taylor (eds), *Party State and Society: Electoral Behaviour in Britain since 1820* (Aldershot: Scolar Press, 1997), pp. 153–75; Brooke, *Labour's War*, pp. 311–17; Ward, 'Preparing for the People's War', 180–2.

31 *The Times*, 31 July 1945. See also *Daily Herald*, 1 August 1945 in 'Press Cuttings, General Election 1945', LHASC.

32 Fielding, Thompson and Tiratsoo, *England Arise!*, pp. 170–5; 'British General Election, 1950, Press Cuttings', LP/ELEC/1950/3, LHASC, *The Times*, 3 February 1950, *Daily Telegraph*, 4 February 1950; Kenneth O. Morgan, *The People's Peace 1945–1990* (Oxford: Oxford University Press, 1992), p. 84.

33 Brooke, 'Labour and the "Nation"', *passim*; E.H.H. Green, 'The Conservative Party, the State and the Electorate, 1945–64', in Lawrence and Taylor (eds), *Party State and Society*, ch. 7; Brett, *Australian Liberals*, pp. 59–64, 123, 127, 138–9. I am grateful to Melanie Nolan for drawing my attention to the international post-war connection between women, gender and consumerism.

34 Brooke, 'Labour and the "Nation"', 161–2; Peter Howlett, 'The War Economy' and Catherine R. Schenk, 'Austerity and Boom', in Paul Johnson (ed.), *Twentieth Century Britain: Economic Social and Cultural Change* (Harlow: Longman, 1994).

35 Clarke, *Hope and Glory*, p. 237.

36 *Manchester Guardian*, 25 February 1950.

37 Fielding, Thompson and Tiratsoo, *England Arise!*, pp. 191–5; Ron Noon, 'The Litigious Consequences of Mr. Cube', *North West Labour History*, 31 (2006–7), 60–4; 'British General Election, 1950, Press Cuttings', LP/ELEC/1950/3, LHASC, *Daily Herald*, 4, 16, 17, 20, 25 February 1950, *The Times*, 3, 25 February 1950, *Daily Telegraph*, 25 February 1950.

38 'British General Election, 1950, Press Cuttings', *Daily Telegraph*, LP/ELEC/1950/3, LHASC, 4 February 1950.

39 *Ibid.*, *Daily Telegraph*, 21 February 1950; Chris Wrigley (ed.), *British Trade Unions 1945–1995* (Manchester: Manchester University Press, 1997), pp. 5–6, 44–6.

40 See, for example, Macintyre, *Concise History*, pp. 192–6; Bolton, *Oxford History*, ch. 2; Allan W. Martin, 'The Politics of the Depression', in Manne (ed.), *Australian Century*, pp. 114–18; Serle, 'Curtin, John'; Graham Freudenberg, 'Victory to Defeat: 1941–49, in Faulkner and Macintyre (eds), *True Believers*, pp. 76–89; Patmore, *Australian Labour*, pp. 89–91.

41 Brett, *Australian Liberals*, pp. 114–15; Martin, 'Politics of Depression', pp. 116–18; Serle, 'Curtin, John'; David Day, *John Curtin: A Life* (Pymble, NSW: Harper Collins, 2008).
42 Kirk, '"Australians for Australia"', 99–100, 103–4; Hon. Barry O. Jones MP, 'Curtin's Tradition and the Party's Future', Anstey and Curtin, *Heritage*, at http://www.john.curtin.edu.au.
43 Serle, 'For Australia and Labor'; Serle, 'Curtin, John'.
44 Serle, 'For Australia and Labor'; Serle, 'Curtin, John'; Australian *Worker*, 11 April 1951.
45 Macintyre, *Concise History*, p. 196; Bolton, *Oxford History*, ch. 2.
46 Bolton, *Oxford History*, pp. 27, 29.
47 *Ibid.*, pp. 27–47; Francis G. Castles, *The Working Class and Welfare: Reflections on the Political Development of the Welfare State in Australia and New Zealand 1890–1980* (Sydney: Allen and Unwin, 1985), Preface, pp. 22–4; James and Markey, 'Class and Labour', 33.
48 Macintyre, *Concise History*, pp. 192–4.
49 Serle, 'For Australia and Labor'.
50 *Australian Worker*, 11 April 1951.
51 Serle, 'For Australia and Labor'.
52 Macintyre, *Concise History*, p. 194.
53 Serle, 'For Australia and Labor'; Ward, *Australia and the British Embrace*, pp. 16–17.
54 Macintyre, *Concise History*, pp. 209–10; Rawson, *Labor in Vain?*, pp. 112–15; correspondence from Stuart Macintyre, 4 October 2009.
55 John Saville, *The Politics of Continuity: British Foreign Policy and the Labour Government 1945–46* (London: Verso, 1993), chs 2, 3.
56 See, for example, Evatt's speech to the 1942 Labour Party Conference, reported in *Labour Party Annual Report* (London: Transport House, 1942), pp. 97–8 and J.S.M. Middleton Papers, LHASC, Manchester, JSM/INT/ASA/10, pp. 195–7.
57 See under the heading 'General Elections 1943', the 'Statement of Policy by the Prime Minister', made by Curtin 26 July 1943 at http://www.john.curtin.edu.au.
58 See Middleton Papers, JSM/INT/ASA/31ii, JSM/INT/ASA/31.
59 Ward, *Australia and the British Embrace*, pp. 16–20; *Labour Party Annual Report, 1942*, p. 97; *Australian Worker*, 24 October 1951.
60 Macintyre, *Concise History*, p. 209; Rawson, *Labor in Vain?*, p. 112; Bolton, *Oxford History*, pp. 47–54; correspondence from Stuart Macintyre, 4 October 2009.
61 Martin, 'Politics of the Depression', p. 117.
62 Hancock, 'Rise of the Liberal Party', pp. 121–7; Brett, *Australian Liberals*, pp. 116–20; Margaret Fitzherbert, *Liberal Women: Federation – 1949* (Leichardt, NSW: The Federation Press, 2004), pp. 242–3.
63 Brett, *Australian Liberals*, p. 117; Waterson, 'Chifley', pp. 412–18.
64 *Australian Worker*, 4 August 1943, 25 September 1946; *Worker*, 23 September 1946.
65 *Worker*, 23 September 1946; *Australian Worker*, 4, 25 August 1943, 12 November 1958.
66 *Worker*, 9 August 1943.
67 *Worker*, 2, 9, 16, 23, 30 September 1946; *Australian Worker*, 25 September 1946.
68 *Worker*, 30 September 1946; *Australian Worker*, 2 October 1946.
69 Freudenberg, 'Victory to Defeat', pp. 81, 83.
70 Bolton, *Oxford History*, pp. 29–43, 74–5; Correspondence from Sean Scalmer, 5 October 2009.
71 Bolton, *Oxford History*, pp. 38–9; Kirk, 'Traditionalists and Progressives', 56.

CHAPTER EIGHT

Out in the cold

Australia

Overview

I suggested in the Introduction to Part IV that the politics of Cold War loyalism both dominated Australian society for twenty-years from the later 1940s and constitute a large part of the explanation for the ALP's political weakness, particularly at the federal level, and the hegemony of the Right during this period of time. I maintained further that, while recognised in parts of the relevant literature,[1] these broad claims have not been fully acknowledged in much of the more narrowly focused, institutional labour historiography.[2]

As an essential part of the politics of the Cold War, the Right once again tarred the mainstream labour movement as subscribing to the 'alien', 'extreme' and 'totalitarian' doctrine of socialism and, whether as fools or knaves, being variously 'Red' or the accomplice and/or dupe of 'conspiratorial', 'disloyal' 'tyrannical' and 'wrecking' communists. As in the interwar years, the 'politics of loyalism' constituted a key aspect of the tarring process. Labor was once again accused of being disloyal to the nation and the Empire. But in the years of the Cold War the accusation of also being insufficiently committed to the US-led defence of the 'Free World' was added to the charge sheet. As we will demonstrate below, the process of post-war tarring was undertaken even more extensively and intensively than during the interwar years as a whole.

In response, Labor loudly and persistently denied these allegations. It reaffirmed its independent 'true Australianism' and its support for the 'enlightened' Commonwealth. It also reaffirmed its total support for democracy, constitutionalism, parliamentarianism, gradualism and outright opposition to 'despotic' and 'alien' revolutionary communism. Despite this defence, Labor's and the wider labour movement's position was compromised by what was viewed by many members of the public, including Catholics within the labour movement, as its weak, vacillating and divided stance on communism. As we will see below, ties between communist and Labor trade unionists, and the actions of Evatt in relation to Menzies' attempted ban of the Communist Party and the Petrov affair, were cited as prominent examples of Labor's 'complicity' with and/or 'softness' towards communism. As a result, Labor failed to mount a successful counter-attack on the Right. The latter was widely seen as the only effective means of defence against the internal and external communist threat.

Labor's case was not helped by the outlook and activities of the CPA. The communists declared their undying allegiance to the Stalinist Soviet Union and, from the end of 1947 onwards, their equally strong opposition to the 'class collaborationist' ALP. Communists also established a very strong position in the trade unions during the 1940s. Worker dissatisfaction with the pegging of their wages, rather than the actions of communist militants, constituted the root cause of the post-war upsurge in worker dissatisfaction, militancy and industrial conflict. There is some evidence to suggest that this dissatisfaction, in combination with widespread working-class anger and bitterness towards the ALP's strike-breaking activities during the 1949 coal strike, contributed to Labor's federal election defeat in 1949.[3] Yet, as high-profile leaders and participants in key industrial disputes, communists constituted an easy target for the revived Right, which won the crucial 1949 election largely on the platforms of anti-socialism and anti-communism. Having once realised the electoral success of the politics of tarring in that election, Menzies and his colleagues resorted consistently to the 'Red Scare' tactic in federal elections up to the election of 1966.

Labor's cause was also seriously damaged by the profound divisions and conflicts within the labour movement around the issue of communism. With Catholic anti-communists to the fore, these internal conflicts reached levels unknown since the splits of 1916 and 1931. They caused the ALP's Split in 1955 and the formation of the rival Australian Labor Party (Anti-Communist), which became the Democratic Labor Party (DLP) in 1957. For the next ten years the split 'Labor' vote, with a voting system that allowed DLP supporters to direct preference votes for the ruling Liberal-Country Party coalition, contributed greatly to the ALP's electoral woes. As a result of the Split, membership of the ALP declined 'significantly' – from around 75,000 in the mid 1950s to 45,000 by the end of the decade. The continued running of 'unity' tickets between ALP and communist trade unionists in union elections, in the face of official ALP opposition, during the second half of the 1950s and the disastrous 'Vietnam' election of 1966 also revealed the serious divisions within the ALP's ranks and exposed it once again to charges of being dominated by communists or their sympathisers internally and incapable of meeting the communist threat externally. The ALP lost a further 20 per cent of its membership between 1966 and 1970.[4]

What follows below is a more detailed demonstration of the case made briefly in this Overview.

Key developments

Up to the middle of 1947 the Chifley government prospered. Federal authority was growing, 'though slowly and unevenly' in the face of High Court hostility and failed referenda to increase the powers of the Commonwealth. The key power it gained was exclusive control of income tax, and hence revenue. The post-war Australian economy was booming, largely on the back of rapidly expanding exports. There was unease about rising inflation, but this was low by international standards. Chifley, however, was concerned to ensure that Labor's social service reforms would not be placed in jeopardy by rising prices, increasing wage demands, unemployment and high interest rates. The overriding concern of the Chifley government was to 'maintain a firm hold on the economy'.[5]

In an attempt to achieve this goal the government tried, once again unsuccessfully, to gain federal control of rents and prices through the referendum of 1948. It also sought to maintain stability and control by means of the central banking system established in 1945. When the requirement that local authorities had to 'transact their business exclusively with the Commonwealth Bank' – an aspect rather than the core feature of that system – was challenged by the High Court in 1947, Chifley overreacted by announcing that his government 'would nationalize the entire banking system'.[6] This unwise decision gave the opportunity for Menzies, the anti-Labor sections of the media, the private banks and their employees, along with increasing numbers of the population chafing against continuing Labor controls and regulations, to vent their anger against 'socialism' and express their strong desire for more market-based individualism and 'freedom'. Labor's proposed nationalisation of the banks, along with the unpopular decision to legislate to restore petrol rationing, formed an important part of the backdrop to the election of 1949.

The election, following one of the most bitterly contested and 'divisive' campaigns in Australia 'since that of 1917', resulted in a landmark victory for Robert Menzies, his new and dynamic Liberal Party and their Country Party partners. The coalition achieved a majority of twenty-seven seats over Labor in the House of Representatives. It also won every state in the Senate except South Australia, but Labor secured a Senate majority of eight. In total the combined non-Labor vote in the country reached 50.3 per cent, a 'result not bettered' until the '"Vietnam" election of 1966'.[7] A 'revitalised' Menzies was rightly jubilant. After his 'humiliating rejection' by the UAP in 1941, his creation, the broadly based Liberal Party, now commanded 39.4 per cent of the vote, a rise of 6.4 per cent on 1946.[8] In marked contrast, Chifley and the ALP were despondent. Many within and around the party had confidently predicted a Labor 'landslide' in 1949.[9]

While not wishing a return to the laissez-faire capitalism of the pre-war years and while committed to a measure of government inter-vention in the economy to maintain full employment and improved social services, Menzies nevertheless was fundamentally opposed to state socialism. He maintained that the 1949 election marked the 'climax' of the 'struggle for freedom'. In the manner of Churchill and other 'libertarian' Conservatives in Britain, he claimed that 'a vote for Labor was a vote for socialism' and that socialism was *necessarily* 'totalitarian' in character. The ALP's proposals for bank nationalisation, petrol rationing and other forms of 'bureaucratic controls' were all portrayed as steps 'further towards the development of a totalitarian state'.[10] Menzies promised to reverse them, to promote tax cuts and voluntary health schemes, to develop a contributory system of national insurance to cover sickness, to ban the Communist Party, to enforce secret ballots in relation to strikes and to introduce compulsory military service. Committed to this 'moderate' mixture of public and private provision, Menzies condemned the ALP's 'extreme' proposal for bank nationalisation as symptomatic of its sharp turn to the left – from the reform of capitalism to an attempt to establish 'Socialism in our time'. Menzies maintained that this would lead to the creation of the 'Master State' in which, as in the other 'monstrous totalitarian States which have disfigured the history of the twentieth century', free enterprise and 'all free choice will have gone'.[11] Menzies and his colleagues also charged socialism with a catalogue of familiar vices such as lack of independence, initiative and enterprise, the promotion of dependence and laziness, 'cynicism about spiritual values' and opposition to the Empire. In a manner reminiscent of Sir John Latham, whom Menzies had succeeded as Attorney-General in 1934, they saw socialism as an 'alien and deadly growth' whose 'mental and spiritual infection' had to be destroyed in Australia 'while there was still time'.[12]

They also viewed socialism and the politics of the ALP as being identical. In a highly charged speech delivered some three weeks before the election, Arthur Fadden, leader of the Country Party, asked voters to consider their 'final choice'. Did they prefer 'a government pledged to foster and defend the philosophies of expanding freedom for the individual', or 'a government pledged to make you a pawn of a powerful State by a process of dictatorship, control and conscription'? If, by any chance, they chose the latter, 'then your ballot paper will truly be your last will and testament, disposing in your own lifetime of your liberties and your property, and condemning your children and your children's children to the living death of socialist regimentation'. Fadden, moreover, saw the ALP's commitment to socialisation as 'identical in every way with the avowed objectives of the Communist Party'. Both parties 'worship the ideal of an all-powerful State' and both 'openly boast that the Communist Manifesto of Karl Marx is the fountainhead of their joint inspiration'. Did voters really welcome 'the grim spectre of total socialisation grinning from behind the Iron Curtain of Mr. Chifley's soothing words'? Did they really wish to throw away the 'free democracy' gained in two world wars in favour of the 'planned slavery of ruthless dictators and Godless creeds'?[13]

As in the interwar years, the ALP rejected such charges outright. They were 'wild, irrelevant and untruthful appeals to fear'. It placed its faith in the voters' capacity to set 'reason' above 'fear'. It highlighted Labor governments' successes in wartime and peacetime and their representation of the 'people' rather than the 'money power'. It warned against the danger of a 'plutocratic' Menzies government returning the country to the 'grim depression years'. It emphasised the honest and upright personal qualities of Chifley. It also reiterated its opposition to capitalist exploitation and oppression, its commitments to economic growth and social justice, to the judicious use of public and private means to achieve a better society, to its unqualified defence of freedom, toleration and democracy and its condemnation of all forms of tyranny, including communism.[14] Yet, in the context of growing public dissatisfaction with Labor's collectivism, it was Menzies' anti-socialism which struck the most responsive chord. This context, of course, was very different from Britain in 1945, when 'planning' was popular and when Churchill's 'totalitarian' smearing of Labour failed spectacularly.

Menzies' bid for power received a major boost from two other sources. First, by the time of the December election the Cold War had intensified internationally. Not only had the Soviet Union successfully detonated an atom bomb – so ending the American atomic monopoly – but Stalinist regimes had been imposed upon eastern Europe, 'Germany was divided and the American airlift to Berlin to break the Soviet blockade signalled the heightened confrontation a cross the Iron Curtain'. Closer to home, the Communists now ruled China, the Dutch had been overthrown by Indonesian nationalists, the independence movement in East Asia had developed an 'irresist-ible' momentum, there was insurgency in Malaya and the imminent threat of a major conflict in Korea.[15] Little wonder that Menzies and his colleagues were seriously alarmed by the probability of further communist and anti-western advances in the region, including the possible invasion of Australia, and the prospect, indeed 'imminence' and 'inevitability', of World War Three.[16]

Like Latham in the 1920s, Menzies had come to see communism as a 'set of evil ideas' which were 'quite foreign to our civilisation, traditions and our faith'. It promoted 'class war', 'envy', 'malice' and 'hatred'. It was a 'disease' that was threatening to become globally, regionally and locally pandemic. Given the hardening of the Cold War and the growing threat of another world war, the CPA had come to constitute 'a fifth column for a potential enemy', according to Menzies. Previously opposed to the outlawing of the CPA under conditions of peacetime for the reason that a ban would simply drive communism underground, Menzies now changed his tune. The CPA's ban by the UAP in 1940 had been lifted conditionally by Evatt in 1942, but, with the New South Wales Liberal party to the fore, there developed an irresistible momentum to re-impose it.

It was, furthermore, Menzies' resolute belief that the fight had to be conducted by the coalition rather than by Labor. For, as in the 1920s and whether by accident or design, the ALP, already sharing with the communists a belief in 'totalitarian collectivism', was inca-pable of grasping the true nature of the communism and acting with the necessary unity and urgent 'resolve' against it. Despite forming, under British supervision, the anti-communist Australian Security and Intelligence Organisation (ASIO) early in 1949, Chifley and his colleagues persisted, according to Menzies, in falsely and naively regarding com-munism as 'just some variant of democratic political philosophy', rather than as being 'debased, treasonable, utterly undemocratic ... a subversive conspiracy'. For the electorate to vote Labor would amount to national capitulation and suicide.[17]

Second, the growing strength of communism domestically during the 1940s and divisions within the labour movement's ranks added fuel to the fire. Following Stalin's turn against Hitler, the Communist parties of both Australia and Britain benefited in unprecedented ways from the active involvement of their comrades in the wartime fight against fascism. The membership of the CPA increased dramatically, from 3,569 in 1938 to its historical peak of 22,052 in 1944. The party gained parliamentary representation in 1944 when Fred Paterson, a barrister, won a state election in Queensland. In overall terms, however, it remained electorally insignificant. But this could not detract from the marked successes enjoyed by the party in the workplace and in the trade unions. Alastair Davidson estimates that the CPA 'may have been supported' by 'nearly 40 per cent of unionists' (as against the more conservative estimate of 25 per cent) by 1945, while Deery and Redfern observe that the party had 'majorities or near-majorities on numerous state and provincial Trades and Labour Councils, had its resolutions adopted at the 1945 Congress of the Australian Council of Trade Unions and was able to dictate the policies of the trade unions which covered every basic industry at the federal level except the Australian Workers' Union'.[18]

This unprecedented position of industrial strength bred heightened confidence. The CPA came to believe that it could successfully challenge the ALP and the moderate trade union leaders for control of the labour movement. This turn away from a collaborative united-front policy, to a desire to challenge and 'liquidate' the reformist ALP, became inevitable when the slavishly pro-Soviet CPA was instructed to adopt the new anti-Labor line by the Cominform, established in 1947. In language reminiscent of the 'class against class' phase of the late 1920s and early 1930s, the ALP was labelled a 'traitor' to the working class, a 'bogus' party, an 'anti-labour force' committed to 'the continuance and maintenance of the capitalist order'. Chifley's government had proved the 'bankruptcy' of reformism and social democracy. By sending in troops to break the coal strike of 1949 and arresting leading communists, it was moving 'a stage nearer the fascist state'.[19]

In turn, the ALP ratcheted up its continuing condemnation of Soviet communism as being 'imperialistic', 'even war-mongering' and practising 'slavery' in its labour camps, and the CPA as 'repugnant to all democratic ideals', 'alien', 'traitorous', 'disruptive' and 'wrecking' in relation to the existing labour movement.[20] These mounting ALP criticisms were a part of its wide-ranging counter-attack on the CPA from 1945 onwards. In that year the ALP sponsored and supported the formation by 'loyal' trade unionists of Industrial Groups designed to combat communism in the workplace. Rapidly growing in strength and appeal, especially among anti-communist Catholic trade unionists, the Groups' main goal was to 'displace communist union officials with "trusted" members of the ALP'.[21]

Matters came to a head during the extremely bitter national coal stoppage from the end of June to mid-August 1949. In the post-war years communists had played a prominent part in a wave of strikes in the transport, metal and mining industries. Strikers were determined to defend and improve wages and conditions in the face of rising inflation and the Chifley government's determination to enforce wage 'restraint'. Chifley wrongly saw the 1949 strike, in which communist activists once again played a key role, not only as 'a threat to the Government and a challenge to the State', but as an 'illegitimate' industrial dispute. He described it as 'a political conspiracy inspired by the Communist Party to cripple the economy, discredit the arbitration system and destroy social democracy'. Interestingly, as noted by Phillip Deery, it coincided with the dock strike in England, and both strikes were viewed by the ALP leadership as being part of 'a carefully orchestrated world-wide communist plan to undermine post-war economic recovery in Western [sic] countries' and the fortunes of democratic labour movements and their parties.[22] Chifley sent in the troops to break the strike in the coalfields, an unprecedented practice in peacetime Australian history, confiscated the union's assets, imprisoned its leaders and authorised raids on the CPA's offices. He succeeded in the face of much opposition, bitterness and disillusionment on the part of the mining communities, who had very legitimate 'bread and butter' grievances.[23]

Notwithstanding Chifley's actions during the coal strike, Menzies and his colleagues persisted in their tarring of mainstream labour. To them the very presence and strength of communists within the unions, and labour divisions around communism, including instances of co-operation between CPA and ALP activists during the coal and other strikes, constituted further 'proof' that Labor was ill equipped to deal with not only the external but also the internal communist threat. Labor had 'refused to stand up to the Communist menace' and the Chifley government was 'really only the instrument and obsequious servant of the very extremist Communist unionist [sic] leaders who determine . . . internal and external policy at their will'.[24]

Chifley, his colleagues and the labour press once again offered outraged denials and reaffirmed their anti-communist credentials. For example, they maintained that, as demonstrated by the government during the coal strike, only Labor and its loyal unions were close and tough enough on the ground to root out communist militants and exclude them from union office.[25] In addition, they extended a warm welcome to the jailing of Laurence Sharkey, secretary of the CPA, and other communists in both Australia and Britain on charges of sedition. 'At last', declared the *Australian Worker*, 'the democracies are giving these disrupters and disloyalists a taste of their own medicine – although admittedly not as drastic as the blood-thirsty sentences handed out to democrats in European countries dominated by Communists.'[26]

In truth, however, given the prevailing national mood of pervasive anti-communism, Menzies, rather than Chifley, appeared to be the true champion of the 'loyalist' national interest. Three months after the Labor government defeated the coal strike, Menzies won the election on the basis of his crusade against socialism and communism.

Far from relenting, this crusade intensified during 1950 and 1951. Immediately following the election, Menzies grew more urgent in his insistence that another world war was inevitable, that conditions of wartime effectively existed and that, as a consequence, the Communist Party, as the 'tool' of the aggressive Soviet enemy, must be banned as soon as possible. The CPA was part of a 'world-wide movement' of 'a treasonable or subversive nature'.[27] His fears of communist expansion became even more 'frenzied' when North Korea invaded the South in June 1950. Two months earlier the government had introduced a bill to outlaw the CPA. The ALP was initially united in its opposition to the bill, not because of any sympathy for communists, but because it threatened to undermine civil rights, the time-honoured and 'priceless' British heritage of 'liberty and freedom'. The proposed legislation 'would shift the burden of proof to require citizens who were declared to be communists to demonstrate that they were not'. As a result of the declaration the named person 'could be dismissed from the public service and disqualified from trade union office', while 'failure to cease activity in a banned organisation' would constitute 'a crime punishable by up to five years imprisonment'.[28]

In addition to subverting the principle of being innocent before being proved guilty, the bill, in the eyes of many within the trade unions and the ALP, would be a forerunner to bans on trade unions, political and other organisations not to the liking of the conservative government.[29] 'British' principles of freedom of expression and action, toleration and dissent within the law were thus seen to be in serious jeopardy. Many accused Menzies of employing 'Hitlerite' methods. Evatt, who succeeded Chifley as ALP leader upon the latter's death in 1951, described Menzies' 'police state', 'pro-fascist' and 'McCarthyite' methods and proposals as an attempt to 'destroy the whole democratic fabric of justice and liberty'. They were 'utterly un-British'. They constituted the 'very antithesis', as noted above, of 'the glorious traditions of our race'.[30]

The attempted ban experienced a chequered history. Within the labour movement divisions began to appear between those who were opposed to the bill being passed without the amendments designed to safeguard civil liberties and those who were in favour of its unrestricted passage. Catholics and the Australian Workers' Union, still Australia's largest union, were prominent among the latter group. Those in favour of amendments won the first battle, but the government rejected all Labor's amendments and planned for a double-dissolution election in the event of the Labor-controlled Senate's supporting the proposed amendments. Following a series of strikes against the bill and a threat by waterside workers to refuse to load ships carrying supplies to Korea, Menzies reintroduced the bill in September. This followed his announcements that Australian forces had reached Korea and that Australians 'must immediately prepare themselves for the possibility of a third world war'. As Frank Cain and Frank Farrell declare, 'The stage had thus been set for a "war crisis" election in which the issue of banning the CPA would be seen as an extension of the sacrifices necessary to meet Australia's commitments in Korea'.[31]

In this context of mounting anti-communist hysteria, Labor lost its nerve and its unity. In the face of deep divisions within the movement, a second meeting of the ALP's federal executive decided that the bill would be allowed through without amendments. Menzies immediately described Labor's delaying tactics as 'a great service to the Communists' and declared that the divided ALP executive had reached its decision 'not because it is in favour of it, but because it is frightened to risk its political skin on the issue'. Some labour movement critics had 'practically followed the communist line', according to Menzies, in their opposition to the bill.[32]

The bill became law in October and raids were carried out against the CPA. This, however, was not the end of the matter. The new law was immediately challenged in the High Court by the CPA and ten unions. Evatt, no lover of communism but acting in his legal capacity (he was a former High Court judge), accepted a brief on behalf of the communist-controlled Waterside Workers' Federation. Despite being attacked by the Catholic-dominated executive of the Victorian ALP and other labour-movement anti-communists for giving 'aid and comfort' to the communists, he was successful. The High Court ruled that the legislation was unconstitutional, 'since the country was not at war'.[33]

Following the announcement of the Court's decision, in March 1951, Menzies called a federal election on the issue of the 'communist menace'. Labor attempted to concentrate the voters' minds on economic issues, especially the government's failure to control the cost of living. Inflation was very high (around 20 per cent) and constituted a major obstacle to the government's attempt to increase defence spending in preparation for World War Three. And although Australia suffered far less than Britain from post-war austerity, its post-war affluence did not begin in earnest until the mid 1950s. Labor also argued that a ban would merely drive communism underground, that the only lasting answer lay in an improvement in living and working conditions, so depriving communism of its support, and that, as demonstrated in its effective history of anti-communism from post-World War One onwards, that it was the party best equipped to realise this goal. The ALP, declared Evatt, was 'democratic, national and constitutional', 'absolutely opposed to Communism which is totalitarian in method and anti-democratic in character'.[34]

Menzies, however, would not be sidetracked from the centrality of his anti-communist election message. Leading Country Party and Liberal members promoted anti-communism 'as a national creed', highlighted the divisions within the ranks of the labour movement on the communist issue, condemned Labor's 'wavering' and procrastination around the Communist Party Dissolution Bill and attacked Evatt as Australia's foremost 'Communist collaborator'. Battle had been joined in earnest to defeat 'an armed conspiracy directed from Moscow'.[35]

Menzies once again won the propaganda battle. As a result of the election the government won control of the Senate and retained an, albeit reduced, majority in the House of Representatives. Menzies' promised referendum on banning communism was held in September 1951 and was widely expected to be successful. To his considerable credit, Evatt led the fight against the government's 'totalitarian' proposal and once more staunchly defended 'traditional' 'British' and 'Australian' freedoms, liberties and toleration. The referendum lost, but the 'No' majority was less than 0.5 per cent (2,317,927 against 2,370,009). As Macintyre observes, 'if just 30,000 voters in South Australia or Victoria had voted Yes rather than No, the proposal would have succeeded'.[36]

During the following two years, however, the ALP made a serious comeback. Evatt, as party leader, successfully cultivated the right-wing 'Groupers' and mounted a strong attack on the government's economic policies, especially its failure to control inflation. In the run up to the next federal election, held in May 1954, Labor was confident that Evatt's promise of a 'New Deal' policy for Australia, including equal pay for equal work and a pledge to abolish the means test on pensions, would win the day.[37] In 1953 it had exploited the government's 'inept handling of inflation' to perform well in state polls and at the half-Senate election, in which it harvested 50.6 per cent of the vote. In the May 1954 election it also did well. It won over 50.03 per cent of the votes cast, but Menzies scraped home with a sixty-four to fifty-seven majority.[38]

Menzies' victory resulted from a combination of factors. Evatt was ridiculed by his opponents for not costing his means test proposal, while he was criticised by his colleagues for his failure to communicate and delegate properly. In making a serious attempt to cultivate the support of the right-wing 'Groupers' in Victoria and elsewhere, he also managed to alienate sections of the left in the ALP. As an ominous portent for the post-election period, 'divisions over communism and Catholicism were still building within the party'. The anti-communist 'Groupers', largely inspired by the B.A. Santamaria's Catholic Social

Studies Movement, were increasingly successful in winning control of the Industrial Groups, in considerably weakening the communist 'Anti-Christ' in the unions and in gaining leading positions within the ALP.[39] In turn, Catholic priests and other prominent supporters of 'the Movement' directed their fire against not only communists in the labour movement but also some anti-communist trade unionists and ALPers, including, most prominently, Evatt, on suspicion that they were either too 'soft' on communism or 'fellow travellers' and even 'undercover agents'. In response to this complicating factor, some mainstream anti-communist trade unionists and ALPers, embracing both Catholics and non-Catholics, feared that 'the Movement', an 'outside influence', was improperly seeking to enforce its will upon and ultimately take control of their labour movement. In addition, 'much of the Movement's industrial program', advocating 'increased production, piece work, and wage increases tied to productivity', was 'distinctly unacceptable' to many unionists and their unions. As a result, already debilitating divisions within the ranks of labour were further deepened and complicated: Catholics and anti-communists were now to be located, in both 1954 and the Split of the following year, on both sides of the growing divide.[40]

Menzies' cause was helped by two further developments. First, there was the pre-election visit by the Queen to Australia, between February and April 1954. This was the first visit by a reigning British monarch to the country. The young Queen Elizabeth was rapturously received by huge crowds throughout the country. During the two months of 'Queen mania' millions of Australians turned out to greet 'their monarch', to 'wave flags wildly and cheer themselves hoarse'. Those who managed to 'get a clear view' of the Queen 'just stared and stared'. A month after the end of the tour a poll 'showed that 75 per cent of Australians had seen the queen at least once'. According to the *Bulletin*, Labor members, 'fire eating' and 'Red republicans to a man [sic] a few years ago', were among 'the most ardent strugglers to be near the Royal person'.[41]

The significance of the hugely successful visit was twofold. First, it demonstrated the continuing allegiance of the vast majority of Australians to the throne, Britain, racialised British-ness and the Commonwealth. The *Worker* and the *Australian Worker* offered a 'warm', 'hearty' and 'genuine' welcome to the Queen and boasted that the visit would allow her to appreciate the true extent and depth of the 'white men's achievements' effected by the labour movement in 'young' Australia.[42] Second, although elite attempts to equate loyalty to the Queen with conservatism were contested by the ALP, it is probably the case that the visit and the abundance of patriotism and national unity on display redounded more to the benefit of the party in government than the Opposition. Menzies, his wife, Dame Pattie Menzies, and his colleagues certainly attempted to 'cash in' on the visit by repeatedly highlighting their loyalty to the monarch, the Commonwealth and Australia.[43]

Second, there was the 'bombshell' of the 'Petrov affair'. On 13 April, the day before parliament was due to rise for the election, Menzies announced that Vladimir Petrov, an official at the Soviet Embassy in Canberra, was seeking political asylum in Australia. Petrov's wife was subsequently rescued at Darwin airport from the clutches of two Soviet 'comrades' who were about to 'escort' her back to Moscow. Petrov claimed to have in his possession information from a 'communist spy ring in Australia that included diplomats, journalists, academics and even members of the staff of the leader of the Labor Party'.[44] Evatt, who had not been informed of Menzies' announcement, was furious. He suspected that there was a conspiracy on the part of the government, the ASIO and Santamaria to smear Labor and so keep it from office. It has subsequently been shown that such a conspiracy did not exist.[45]

There is, however, no doubt that Petrov's defection and his allegations harmed the cause of Labor. They added more fuel to the intensive smearing campaign directed by the Right and 'the Movement' against Labor during the election campaign. Evatt in particular was singled out for special treatment. He was accused of being 'A Red' and of associating with communist 'fellow travellers'. The *Worker* declared that while Menzies himself 'disclaims McCarthyism', he leaves it to his supporters to 'smear' and 'slander' – a charge repeated by Evatt. Evatt responded to the accusations of Fadden and his colleagues with vigour: 'if they impute to me, who fought Communism and Russian Imperialism, if they impute to me any sympathy with Communism, they are the vilest liars in the world'.[46] Significantly, the labour press saw the 'personalisation' of issues and the 'vilification' of Evatt as the decisive factor in the closely fought election. They had effectively detracted from the 'real' issue in the election campaign, Labor's socio-economic 'New Deal'.[47]

In August and September 1954 Evatt, in his capacity as a barrister, appeared before the royal commission set up to investigate Petrov's claims. He defended his three personal staff accused of supplying information to the Soviet embassy. At the same time, however, he went public in his allegations of a conspiracy theory. Early in September the judges barred Evatt from the hearings, on the grounds that he had 'compromised his responsibilities' as a barrister by also putting forward his views as leader of the Opposition.[48] In the following month, and anxious about mounting opposition to his behaviour within the ALP, he drafted a press statement in which he made public his allegation of conspiracy against him by the 'Groupers' and Santamaria's 'Movement'. He strongly criticised the actions of 'a small minority group of members, located primarily in the State of Victoria, which has, since 1949, become increasingly disloyal to the labour movement and the Labour leadership'.[49] This was a declaration of open war against the 'Groupers'. It was followed, in March 1955, by the decision of a special ALP federal conference in Hobart to withdraw support from the 'Groupers'. Thereupon seven Victorian members of the House of Representatives and a Tasmanian senator 'quit the ALP to form the Anti-Communist (later Democratic) Labor Party'. The 'Great Split' had arrived and 'the breakaways feuded venomously with the Evatt party for much of 1955'.[50]

It was Evatt, however, who 'most damaged his credibility as leader'.[51] In September the royal commission reported that, while the documents supplied by Petrov were authentic, it was 'unable to furnish the basis for a single prosecution'. Without consulting his colleagues, Evatt naively and impulsively stated in the House that he had written to V.M. Molotov, the Soviet foreign minister, asking about the authenticity of the documents. Molotov had replied that they were not authentic.

Pandemonium then broke out. Evatt had effectively accepted the word of a member of a 'semi-hostile totalitarian foreign government above the findings of three Australian judges'.[52] Menzies and his colleagues declared that Evatt's mind was manifestly 'unbalanced', filled with 'fantasies', 'delusions' and 'obsessions'. His intention was to 'cry down decent and patriotic Australians and to build up a Communist fifth column'. In the event of becoming prime minister he would 'seek to destroy the Australian Secret Service' because he is 'on the side of the Communists'.[53] Evatt's and the ALP's responses – that they were the true representatives of democracy, the nation and constitutionalism and that nowhere else in the Commonwealth 'would you find such long-sustained political smearing of an opponent as that employed by the Menzies government' – cut little ice.[54]

Menzies called an election for December. It revolved almost entirely around the personality and political sympathies of Evatt. As noted by Robert Manne, 'The Cry of Molotov was everywhere'.[55] Helped by the 'splitters' in Victoria, who ran candidates against 'Evatt Labor', the Liberals won easily.[56] Once again, the politics of communism, complete with emphases upon loyalty and disloyalty to nation and Commonwealth, had carried the day.

Between 1955 and the mid 1960s the issue of loyalism and the ruling coalition's continuing campaign against what the *Australian Worker* termed 'socialistic tigers and Bolshevik bogeys'[57] continued to hold sway in Australia. This was the case even though, following Stalin's death in 1953, the Cold War had eased somewhat, and from the early 1950s onwards the ACTU was once again firmly under the control of the anti-communists.[58] The 'Great Split' spread from Victoria to New South Wales in 1956, although it was contained and ALP unity maintained in the latter, and to Queensland in 1957.[59] With the ALP often pitted against anti-communist 'Labor' and the second pre-ference votes of the latter being cast in favour of the ruling coalition 'over the next nine years Menzies was only ever in electoral trouble once'.[60] That was in 1961, when his record for 'sound economic stewardship' faltered. In the face of rising unemployment, the ALP campaigned vigorously in favour of its programme of full employment, economic stability, improved social welfare provision, especially for married women with children, and national development to 'rehabilitate' the economy. In the event, Labor received more votes than the combined coalition forces, but Menzies was returned with a majority of one in the House of Representatives.[61]

Labor's attempt to prioritise socio-economic issues was also evident in the elections of 1958 and 1963 (the latter for the House of Repre-sentatives). Extended social welfare provision and 'Putting the Family First' figured prominently in both election campaigns. Labor promised improved family income and social welfare (child endowment rises and the introduction of a 'complete national health service', including 'dental, optical, and deaf-aid treatment'), lower living costs, increased opportunities for home ownership and a decent education. These were part and parcel of what Evatt and his successor from 1960 onwards as party leader, Arthur Calwell, termed the 'modernisation' of the economy, including the development of the North, and improved social opportunity in contrast to Liberal 'lethargy and complacency'.[62]

By 1963 there were also signs that the ALP was beginning to give some attention to modernising itself 'on the lines of the British Labor [sic] Party'. This would involve not only economic regeneration and greater equality of opportunity, but also attempts to widen the ALP's traditional basis of support and leadership beyond the ranks of male trade unionists.[63] Yet both elections were lost, far more narrowly and disappointingly in 1963 than in 1958.

The high priority attached to socio-economic issues bore electoral success, albeit of a limited and uneven kind, at the state level. As noted in the Introduction to Part IV, although the Commonwealth controlled the economy, there were aspects of industrial relations, social welfare and transport over which the states retained varying degrees of control and influence. In those states in which Labor con-tinued to enjoy electoral success, it was often upon the basis of its continuing efforts to work closely with the trade unions in improving workers' and small producers' living standards and working conditions. This was certainly the case in New South Wales, where the ALP enjoyed an unbroken period of office between 1941 and 1965 and then regained power for a further twelve years in 1976.[64] Much the same was true in Queensland, where the ALP was in power for the entire period between 1932 and 1957, mainly on the basis of meeting the material needs of rural and urban workers, small farmers and selectors, small business people, public servants and Catholics. In the 1950s the Gair government in Queensland introduced 'significant' industrial reforms, including improvements in sick and long-service leave and annual leave for public servants, invested in developmental projects for the state and controlled prices in order to increase real wages.[65]

The remarkable 'generation of Labor rule' in Tasmania between 1934 and 1969 was rooted in the promotion of economic development, 'a fair go for the ordinary bloke', opposition 'somnolence', 'the production of jobs not socialism' and maintaining good relations with the Catholic church.[66] More variable ALP poll successes in Western Australia, Victoria and South Australia were likewise closely related to relations with the unions and material factors such as workplace safety issues, education, community welfare, paid public holidays, public works programmes, low-interest loans and infrastructural economic development. Labor's electoral performance in these three states was also affected by the character and achievements of the political opposition, the nature of the electoral system and the socio-economic and religious character of the electorate.[67] In sum, at the state level the politics of the 'hip pocket' played a key part in ALP successes and the character of politics as a whole.

Labor also attempted in these years to resurrect its nationalist 'true Australian' and Commonwealth credentials. The labour press continued to celebrate 'Australia Day' on 26 January each year. It criticised the Liberals' 'endeavour to hide our convict heritage', their ties with 'MONOPOLY', their 'groveldom' to the British and, in contrast to Curtin-inspired Labor, their lack of 'independence' in matters of defence and their overall lack of 'effective national leadership' and 'unity'.[68] While 'True Nationhood', according to the *Worker*, had 'developed' under the young Commonwealth, 'we were not really "ourselves" until we fought for and won the right to determine our own affairs as a member of the British Commonwealth of Nations'. Australia had also become, largely as a result of the efforts of Labor under Evatt, a 'young' but 'wide-awake' member of the UN.[69]

Yet, neither Labor's 'advanced' socio-economic programme nor its strong attachment to the progressive nation and Commonwealth was able to counteract the continuing negative effects of the politics of the Cold War. These comprised profound labour-movement and working-class divisions around communism, religion and control of organised labour. To be sure, the electoral effects of the Split upon the ALP were uneven at the state level. For example, while they were neutralised in New South Wales and Tasmania and limited in Western Australia, they were a disaster for the ALP in Victoria and Queensland right up to the 1980s.[70]

At the federal level, however, they were uniformly negative. Reference has been made above to the fact that the ALP was now faced at elections not only by the coalition, but also by the anti-communist DLP. During the 1958 campaign Menzies continued to highlight Labor divisions and to tar successfully. He condemned 'unity' tickets between ALP and CPA union activists. These had developed after 1951, when the CPA moderated its attitude towards the ALP and Australia's 'Path to Socialism', the unions and mass strikes. Benefiting from increased worker militancy, anti-'Grouper' and anti-'Movement' sentiment, the CPA improved its standing, up to 1957, among trade unionists and won back leadership positions in unions such as the important Miners' Federation.[71] The Prime Minister also criticised Labor's views about Communist China as being 'in the very teeth of American opinion' and saw Labor's strong allegiance to the UN as operating too often at the expense of 'due' loyalty to the United States. Archbishop Mannix, a champion of the DLP, declared that 'every Communist sympathiser desired Dr. Evatt's success' in the campaign.[72]

Towards the end of 1961 Labor boasted of its successful fight against communists in the ports of the country. Yet 'Red smear' leaflets, prepared 'by the Tory and DLP campaign committees', continued to be 'hurled' at the ALP 'during the last week of the election campaign'.[73] Two years later, Menzies charged the ALP with abandoning its overseas responsibilities by wishing to withdraw troops unilaterally from newly formed Malaysia, while the DLP continued 'disgracefully' to accuse the party of inaction in the face of the 'threat of Communism'.[74]

In 1966, in the face of conflicting Labor attitudes towards the conflict in Vietnam and Calwell's promise to bring back to Australia 'all conscripts then serving anywhere overseas', Labor's seeming lack of resolve to support the Americans and 'hold the line' against the further spread of communism in South-East Asia resulted in electoral disaster and internal party acrimony.[75] At the November federal election Labor received its worst beating 'since 1931'. This led the *Worker* to declare that the ALP now 'totters on the brink of oblivion'. This right-wing labour newspaper maintained that 'far left', 'anti-American' 'extremists' and 'wreckers', with their 'loyalties' lying elsewhere, 'beyond Australian shores, to the pernicious dialectics of a Godless creed', now dominated the party. 'To opt out of Vietnam', declared the *Worker*, and 'run away from the onward march of militant communism was seen by the voters for what it was . . . They rejected it, and . . . thank God they did.'[76] The *Worker* was continuing, 'from within', the anti-communist crusade so long conducted by Menzies 'from without'. The latter, 'The Grand Old Man' of the Empire, had retired earlier in the year, at the age of 71. From 1966 until Gough Whitlam's Labor victory in 1972, Menzies' successors as leader of the coalition and Prime Minister, Harold Holt, John Gorton and William McMahon, continued to carry the anti-communist torch.[77]

Explanations

Geo-political concerns largely underpinned the outstanding success with which the Right exploited the Cold War politics of loyalism in Australia. Above all, as noted in the Introduction to Part IV, there existed the widespread and chronic fear that Australia was about to become a victim of Communist expansion in the Asia-Pacific region. From the post-war years onwards the 'traditional fear' of being 'swamped' by Asian 'hordes' was 'fused with fear of militant communism'.[78] As observed above, Menzies successfully and repeatedly tarred Labor as divided, weak and complicit in relation to communism, as being incapable of playing, whether in terms of domestic or foreign policy, a full part in the fight, led by the United States, against the 'alien' communist 'menace'. Having played the anti-communist and anti-socialist cards decisively in the crucial 1949 election, so ending Labor's 1940s successes, Menzies realised that they were the key to future coalition victories. He played them liberally and consistently thereafter.

We have also seen that Labor's attempts to overcome the Right's barrage of 'Red' smears were unsuccessful. Notwithstanding its repeated anti-communist statements and its protestations of loyalty to the independent nation and the Commonwealth and its commitments to democracy and constitutionalism versus communist and other forms of totalitarianism, Labor failed to convince the public that it could translate its words into united, determined and successful action.

It was compromised, for example, by communist and non-communist trade unionists working together, especially during strikes, and their adoption of 'unity' tickets in elections. It was further weakened by the charge levelled against it by many of its Catholic members that it was either 'Red' or insufficiently hard on communism.

These same members, along with Menzies and his colleagues, were also extremely critical of what they saw as Evatt's pro-communist stances during the period of the Communist Party Dissolution Bill and the Petrov affair. In truth, Evatt was a well-intentioned defender of civil liberties and an anti-communist. But his actions, especially with regard to the charge of disloyalty against the 'Groupers' in 1954, subsequent events leading to the 'Great Split' and his letter to Molotov, were ill-considered, naive and unintentionally disastrous in their consequences. He effectively handed over much ammunition to those who saw him and Labor as 'disloyal' communist 'fellow-travellers'. Conflicting ALP policy statements on, and acute intra-party divisions over, the Vietnam War were largely responsible for the party's dreadful performance in the 1966 election.

Labor failed, therefore, to present itself as a consistent, united and unqualified opponent of communism. The Right was quick to exploit these facts. Anti-communism, rather than the ALP's appeals to progressive independent nationalism and socio-economic reform, became the critical touchstone of patriotism.

Yet the politics of Cold War loyalism and the divisions they engendered constituted a large, rather than the complete, part of the explanation for the hegemony of the Right. As noted earlier, economic factors were also very important. We have indicated that in some states the ALP continued to use the 'hip pocket' issue to its electoral advantage. At the federal level, however, it was Menzies and his allies who successfully took the credit for the post-war boom from the mid 1950s onwards. In a very real sense they were lucky in that, unlike in Britain, the war had provided a stimulus to industrial growth in Australia and Chifley had undertaken much of the necessary groundwork of post-war reconstruction. In turn, rapidly and consistently expanding world trade and the creation of a stable international monetary system gave a great boost to Australian exports, particularly wool, in the post-war world.[79]

The period between 1946 and the early 1970s constituted an Australian 'golden age'. It was an 'era of growth unmatched since the second half of the nineteenth century'. The population 'almost doubled', while 'economic activity increased more than threefold'. An annual growth rate of 'over four per cent' was 'maintained throughout the 1950s and into the 1960s'. In addition there was 'full employment, higher productivity, improved earnings, a pattern of sustained improvement that no-one could recall'. 'Between 1945 and 1965' real average weekly earnings 'increased by more than 50 per cent, and the five-day working week became the norm along with three weeks of paid annual leave'.[80] Home ownership, standing at 53 per cent in 1947, increased 'to an unprecedented 70 per cent by 1961', while by the early 1960s 'one in five' Australians owned a car. Consumerism in general and suburbanisation mushroomed. Industrial relations were characterised more by stability and peace than instability and conflict. Excessive demand and periods of inflation accompanied by credit squeezes became far more characteristic of the economy than pre-war under-consumption and deflation.[81] Enhanced social stability and security, rooted in religion and the nuclear family, became the norm. It was within this context that Menzies' notion of citizenship as constituting 'freedom from threat' took firm root. And it was 'freedom from subversive communist activity' that made the strongest appeal.[82] In overall terms, therefore, it was the Right which clearly benefited most from the politics of the 'hip pocket'.

Britain

Overview

The politics of Cold War loyalism were also an important part of Britain's post-war history. In contrast to Australia, however, they did not constitute the main explanation of Conservative success and Labour failure between 1951 and 1964. They were also far less productive of divisions and conflicts among the main parties in Britain. Anti-socialism persisted in Britain, although it was stronger between 1945 and 1955 than during the nine years thereafter. Of key significance in Britain was the fact that the BLP, working closely with predominantly right-wing trade union leaders, and the Conservative Party were largely united and equally determined in their anti-communism in terms of both domestic and foreign policy. As a result of this, the BLP was not compromised and smeared, either as an extreme and disloyal 'Red', or as a communist 'fellow-traveller', to anything remotely like the extent suffered by the far more fragmented and divided ALP.[83]

Two brief examples may serve to demonstrate this point. First, no equivalent mainstream British Labour leader was subjected to a smearing campaign of the intensity and unrelenting kind directed against Evatt. Second, in contrast to federal elections in Australia, general elections in Britain during the 1950s and 1960s were dominated far more by economic concerns than by issues of anti-communism and the 'extremism' and 'disloyalty' of Labour. In overall terms Britain's political priorities up to the mid 1960s lay not in the tarring of the BLP, but with economic performance and living standards, the continuing status of the country as a major world power, the future of the multi-racial Commonwealth and the question of entry to the EEC.

The mainstream British labour movement's overwhelming and unqualified anti-communism also meant that there was far less scope for the significant development of voices 'from within' critical of and seeking to challenge the existing leadership. For example, while in Britain Catholics were also prominent among labour-movement anti-communists, they were far less likely to attempt to smear Labour's mainstream leaders than were their counterparts in Australia. Even when undertaken, such attempts were far less successful in Britain than in Australia. By the end of the decade those pro-Soviet British labour movement voices of 1945 had also largely entered the dominant pro-American Labour Party fold. As a major consequence, the British labour movement was far less divided by the politics of the Cold War than was its Australian cousin. There was simply no British equivalent of the 'Great Split'. The main divisions within the BLP revolved not around communism but around 'traditional' and 'revisionist' attitudes towards the economics and politics of socialism, nuclear weapons and Labour's future advance.

The CPGB, furthermore, was also less influential in post-war trade unionism and more independent minded, moderate and, in important ways, part of an indigenous radical tradition to a greater extent than was its more Moscow-oriented Australian counterpart. Industrial relations in Britain during the crucial years of the late 1940s were also far more peaceful than in Australia and afforded, with the exception of the London dock strike of 1949, far less opportunity for communist activists to play a leading role in industrial conflicts.

Although there were widespread fears and anxieties concerning communist aggression and expansion in both Britain and Australia during the late 1940s, these 'settled down' more quickly and extensively in Britain. Whereas Menzies continued to play the role of a Cold War warrior, by the early 1950s both Conservative and Labour politicians were more concerned to combine determined ideological anti-communism with the need for negotiation, caution, containment and pragmatic 'commonsense' in their dealings with Stalin and other major Communist figures. The goal was to achieve and preserve peace, stability and security in an increasingly dangerous world. The unreservedly hostile and aggressive approach of 'McCarthyite' Americans and Australians was seen as 'unhelpful' to this process of negotiation and accommodation.[84] This inter-party British consensus on communism represented the resumption of the tradition established by Baldwin and MacDonald in the interwar years of common Conservative and Labour opposition to 'alien' extremism and disloyalty. In this very important sense, Labour and the Conservatives were allies rather than opponents.

I attribute British difference to the following factors. First, there is once again the major importance of geo-politics. In overall terms British politicians were far less afraid of communist 'engulfment' and invasion than were their Australian counterparts. While communism was advancing in the Asia-Pacific region in the 1950s, it had ceased to advance in Europe after 1948. Britain also came to possess the direct 'protection', along with the United States and the Soviet Union, of the atom bomb.

Commitment to the development of an independent British atomic bomb programme had been made by a secret Labour cabinet committee as early as 1947. Bevin, Attlee and Morrison saw possession of an independent nuclear deterrent as 'commensurate with Britain's great-power status and moral influence in the world'. The disarmers offered the counter-argument that unilateral disarmament would 'represent a moral example to others, thus recapturing Britain's fading power in world affairs'.[85] Yet the ruling political common sense in 1950s Britain was that possession of the bomb served as an effective deterrent against further Soviet aggression and the outbreak of another global war. (As an ally of Britain and the United States, Australia, of course, received indirect 'protection'.) In addition, within Britain the CPGB was increasingly seen more as an irritant than a as serious threat to the established order of things. Much-diminished fears of an external communist 'takeover' and its internal threat, combined with pragmatic self-interest, were largely responsible for the development of the more accommodating and cautious approach to communism noted above, even though the UK spent much more on defence as a whole than did Australia.

Second, the developing consensus on communism was part and parcel of the growth of wide inter-party support in Britain for the fundamentals of the post-war system of the welfare state, the mixed economy and Britain as a great power, including its role as an 'enlightened', 'sensible' and 'responsible' leader of the Commonwealth. The fact that this broad consensus contained within it points of inter-party difference and conflict does not negate the fact and importance of its existence.[86] There also existed, of course, a measure of support for the post-war system in Australia. For example, despite his criticisms of socialism and his support for voluntarism and individualism, Menzies favoured a strong public sector. However, we may reasonably argue that during the 1950s and early 1960s consensus was more extensive in Britain. This is reflected in the far more harmonious nature of party politics in that country as contrasted with the deep conflicts between the ALP and the ruling coalition in Australia.

Third, as noted above, the more united and unequivocal anti-communism of the BLP, as compared with the ALP, greatly reduced the possibility of a major labour-movement rupture taking place around the issue of communism, while mainly 'bread and butter' matters dominated elections in Britain.

Key developments

The purpose of this section is further to develop and substantiate the points made in the Overview. I turn first to the issue of anti-communism.

On balance, the Labour Party and the Conservatives saw themselves far more as allies rather than antagonists in the national and international fight against communism. While 'libertarian' anti-socialism by no means disappeared from Conservative thought and action after the failure of Churchill's crusade against socialist/Labour 'totalitarianism' in 1945, it became less important thereafter in terms of political contests between the parties. From the formation of the Cominform in 1947 and its instructions to Communist parties to turn against democratic socialism, to the general hardening of the Cold War in the years between 1948 and 1950, leading Labour politicians expressed, along with their Conservative colleagues, increasing fears and anxieties about communist aggression and adopted correspondingly 'hard-line' attitudes and responses. Churchill, Attlee and their Labour and Conservative colleagues joined the 'English-Speaking Peoples' in Australia and elsewhere in the world in the global fight against 'communist aggression'.[87] In contrast to Australia, however, there would be no attempt in Britain to ban communist organisations.

Even before 1947 Ernest Bevin, Labour's Foreign Secretary, not only shared with Churchill and Eden a deep mistrust and loathing of communism but was also far more ideological and less accommodating towards communism and the Soviet Union than his generally more pragmatic Conservative allies.[88] By 1948–49 heightened British fears of and extreme hostility towards what was perceived as aggressive and expansionary Soviet-dominated European communism had become the norm. Labour's Denis Healey maintained that 'all the Red Army needed in order to reach the North Sea was boots'.[89] Herbert Morrison, a leading figure in the labour movement, described communists in the wake of their overthrow of the democratic government of Czechoslovakia as 'Fifth Columnists', 'men who owe loyalty not to their country but to a foreign power', while the BLP's Morgan Phillips, the *Daily Herald* and Attlee variously saw them as 'totalitarian fanatics' intent upon waging a 'war' against the Labour Party, attempting to 'wreck' its achievements and sow 'chaos' and 'disorder' in the wider society in order to facilitate their violent rise to power.[90]

During the 1949 London Dock Strike, the 'longest and most politically important of the post-war period', the Labour government accused the communists prominent in the unofficial strike committee of 'manipulating' the dockers and the strike 'for political reasons'. They were allegedly seeking to 'sabotage' the Marshall Plan and Britain's economic recovery. They even sought to 'take over the country' and set up a 'Communist dictatorship controlled from Moscow'. In actual fact the 15,000 dockers who were on strike for a month had rational material grievances and flatly rejected the charges that they didn't and that they had fallen for a 'communist conspiracy'. Arthur Deakin, General Secretary of the TUC, nevertheless stuck firmly with the 'conspiracy' line, as did Prime Minister Attlee. The government declared a state of emergency and sent over 12,000 troops into the port to break the strike. They eventually succeeded, although the returning dockers were neither 'defeated nor repentant'. The Attlee government's Emergency Powers were employed again in 1950 when ten striking gas workers were first sentenced to imprisonment but later fined.[91] The trade union and Labour Party leaders also joined with the Conservatives in adopting the Cold War mentality of seeking to steer independence and other movements, including trade unionism, in the colonies and beyond in 'responsible', non-communist directions.[92]

Labour's repression of communism and rank-and-file radicalism was not confined to the London docks and the gas industry. As is well known, Attlee initiated a purge in the civil service, while three allegedly 'crypto-communist' Labour MPs were expelled from the BLP in 1948–49.[93] The late 1940s also marked 'an intensification of Cold War hostility in the unions'. 'New or continuing bans of varying kinds' were widely applied in an attempt to 'reduce the numbers of Communists holding office, and prevent unions from adopting CP policies'. Catholic activists 'provided significant opposition locally and nationally to Communists in several unions', while the TUC was also 'deeply involved'. Although badly shaken by the onslaught, the CP 'proved remarkably resilient'. As often the most active champions of workers' economic concerns, British communists, in the manner of their Australian counterparts, continued to receive active support in a minority of workplaces during the 1950s.[94]

By the early 1950s few, therefore, could doubt the emergence of a strong inter-party consensus around anti-communism and the profound anti-communism of the labour movement itself. Unlike Australia, there was little or no basis in fact for opponents outside the movement or anti-communists within to tar the mainstream movement with the brushes of communism and disloyalty. By that point in time, moreover, several well-publicised examples of communist aggression and hostility, combined with the implementation of the Marshall Plan, had also brought most members of the British Labour Left into 'the Anglo-American Cold War pen'. No longer did they claim, as in 1945, that friendship with the Soviet Union was 'the key to peace'.[95]

The fact that by the early to mid 1950s the CPGB had come to be seen far less as a major threat than as a relatively minor nuisance to the status quo in Britain also helped Labour's cause. As we have seen, in Australia the episodes of the Communist Party Dissolution Bill, the Petrov affair and the federal elections of 1951, 1954 and 1955 revolved around the purported dangers posed by communism to national security and Labour's alleged 'collaboration' with communism. In Britain the situation was very different. The national spotlight was not focused upon Labour 'complicity', and, while not invisible, the early- to mid-1950s CPGB simply did not command the same kind of widespread attention and the same degree of hostility as its Australian counterpart.

Like the CPA, the CPGB had seen a serious decline in its membership and influence since the mid and late 1940s. Its official membership fell from 45,435 in 1945 (it had peaked at 56,000 in 1942) to 38,853 in 1950 and more steeply thereafter. Following its poor showing in the 1950 election, when all of its 100 candidates were defeated, it fared even worse in 1951, when it ran only 10 candidates, all of whom were unsuccessful. As indicated above, it retained a limited presence in the workplace. It also had influence at the leadership level in a minority of unions, most prominently those of the dockers, the miners, especially in South Wales and Scotland, and the electrical workers.[96] In contrast to the CPA, the CPGB, while critical of the established labour leadership from the end of 1947 onwards, had never been in a comparable position of strength in the unions and in strike-prone post-war industries to realistically expect that it could successfully challenge that leadership for control of the movement as a whole. In truth, the CPGB was far less openly hostile to the BLP than the CPA was to the ALP before 1951. It was also much less enamoured of the anti-Labour Cominform line, had more of an independent presence and by 1951 was officially committed to the moderate, peaceful and gradual 'parliamentary road to socialism'.[97]

Lastly, the CPGB, notwithstanding its ultimate loyalty to and domination by Moscow, also continued, in part, to be the product of an indigenous tradition of British radicalism.[98] The CPA, of course, also drew on local traditions and promoted Australian culture.[99] In overall terms, however, the CPGB could not realistically be seen as an 'alien import' to the same extent as the more Moscow-dominated CPA.

Attention to the British general election contests of 1951, 1955 and 1959 bears out the view that the tarring of Labour as an extreme and disloyal 'Red' or communist 'fellow traveller' both was far less marked in Britain and did not contribute significantly to Labour's electoral defeats. Yet, as demonstrated below, we must add the qualification that anti-socialism was the key issue in the 1951 contest and also figured significantly in that of 1955. The Conservatives' successful management of the economy, their wide social appeal and material prosperity dominated the elections of 1955 and 1955. Concerns with the national and Commonwealth interest, alongside questions of peace and security, were present throughout.

In the October 1951 election the Labour Party received 48.8 per cent of the vote, the party's 'highest ever percentage of the vote'. Yet the Conservatives, with 48 per cent of the vote, were victorious. They won 321 seats as compared to Labour's 295. The fact that the 'virtually bankrupt' Liberal Party could put up 'little more' than 100 candidates and that Liberal voters were, in contrast to 1945, moving against Labour's collectivism, worked to the benefit of the Conservative Party. The latter also clawed back some of the middle-class vote temporarily lost to Labour in 1945. Yet Labour managed to secure 'a higher share of the working-class vote than ever before'. Support for Labour among women was 'almost back to the level of 1945', but male support 'was still below the level achieved in 1945'.[100] Labour was not too disappointed. It had achieved 'Victory in votes' and, as observed in the Australian labour press, had achieved much in its post-war periods of office. It confidently expected to regain power in the near future.[101]

The election took place against a worsening economic background. The outbreak of the Korean War and rearmament had resulted in an increase in the cost of living. Both Labour and the Conservatives alerted voters to the fact that the country faced 'urgent' economic problems and that 'no easy promises' were to be offered. The Conservatives in fact were about to be returned to power 'in the midst of the worst balance of payments crisis since the war'.[102] Churchill declared that in order successfully to overcome 'these troubled times' the country needed 'a strong progressive Government', able to 'unite the nation instead of dividing it'. The 'Socialists' of the Labour Party once again were portrayed as being too 'divisive', too sectional and class based in their appeal to achieve this unity. In contrast, as Churchill would repeat during the 1955 contest, the Conservative Party was 'the one party' intent upon the 'reconciliation' and 'representation' of 'all classes'.[103] The Conservatives thus sought to recapture the patriotic nationalism, 'the language of the people', so successfully appropriated by Labour in 1945. As the 1950s progressed this 'people' would be cast far less in terms of their role as producers than as consumers and owners of property.[104]

Churchill also exhorted the voters to elect a government capable of fully stimulating 'our national qualities of thrift, hard work and enterprise'. Only by returning to these practices would the country regain its prosperity. Labour's continuing commitment to government controls and restrictions was seen as the very antithesis of the personal 'freedoms', 'independence' and 'initiative' so 'essential' to the economic growth and prosperity demanded by the Conservatives. The Conservatives thus 'vigorously opposed Labour plans to make the wartime emergency powers permanent'. By the time of the election Labour had effectively abandoned any plans for further nationalisation in the interest of 'consolidation'. It still wanted, however, to retain powers to 'regulate production, distribution and consumption', in order to 'defend full employment, 'fair shares' and avoid inflation. Churchill condemned 'war-time controls in time of peace' as 'evil', while permanent controls 'amounted to a blank cheque for totalitarian government'.[105] Labour vigorously contested these claims. It highlighted its positive record of achievement since 1945, was proud of its record on nationalisation and claimed that a vote for the Conservatives would signal a return to the problems and evils of the 1930s.[106] The issues of Conservative individualism and anti-socialism and Labour collectivism and socialism stood at the centre of the election.

The issue of individualism versus collectivism was also highly gendered.[107] The BLP, like the ALP, cast its appeal largely to men as producers and women as housewives, and sought to improve wages and social welfare provision accordingly. The Conservatives sought to capture the votes not only of housewives 'whose everyday experience of queues, shortages and ration books made the critique of controls immediate and pertinent', but also those of both sexes as consumers seeking to maximise their purchasing power and freedom of choice within the marketplace.[108] As noted in Chapter 7, the Right's consumerist appeal in both Britain and Australia, however, was directed particularly at women. There is, furthermore, evidence to suggest that Conservative and Liberal opposition to continued Labour 'austerity', 'fair shares' and restrictions met with an increasingly favourable response during the 1950s on the part of the middle classes and women across the British and Australian class structures. The 'most substantial margin' in male and female voting patterns in Britain between 1950 and 1966 revealed itself in the 1955 general election, 'when Labour's vote among women was thirteen points behind the Conservatives'. Labour's suspicion of 'consumerism' was also probably rooted in its traditional nonconformist and 'rational' opposition to 'frivolous pleasures', as contrasted with the Tories' traditional defence of the 'people's' more robust, expansive and hedonistic pastimes.[109]

Questions of foreign policy also featured prominently in the 1951 election, even though the Tories 'did not enjoy their customary advantage on defence and international issues'.[110] There was inter-party agreement that the health of the Commonwealth and Britain were inseparable, although Labour derived special pleasure from 'the growth of self-government in India, Pakistan and Ceylon' and the fact that 'the old hard line between Dominion and Colony is slowly melting away'.[111] Notwithstanding its mainstream commitments to the atom bomb and rearmament, Labour sought to gain an advantage over the Conservatives by suggesting that their 'warmongering' constituted a threat to the extremely fragile peace. Churchill, however, counter-attacked effectively by proclaiming his 'personal mission and long-held ambition' to 'make an important contribution to the prevention of a third world war' and the urgent need to establish 'a good working agreement with Soviet Russia by negotiation'.[112]

The only significant occasion when Labour was 'tarred' as being partly 'Red' was during the latter stages of the election campaign. Attlee referred to a 'whispering campaign' to the effect that, if he lost the election, he would be replaced by Aneurin Bevan, 'who is a communist'. Attlee quickly put an end to the rumour by declaring that he would not resign and that Bevan was not a communist. Yet the Conservatives continued to highlight Bevan's lack of 'respect' for Attlee as manifested in his resignation from the Cabinet in April 1951 over the rearmament issue and increased National Health Service (NHS) charges.[113]

Bevan's resignation and the formation of a new parliamentary group-ing, the 'Bevanites', augured badly for Labour unity. For the remainder of the 1950s there developed frequent and often bitter divisions within the party over foreign and defence policy and the domestic 'way forward'. While the Bevanites wanted more socialism, the 'revisionists', headed by Attlee's successor as leader, Hugh Gaitskell, maintained that economic growth, increased prosperity and the decline of class consciousness among manual workers and class conflict in general, meant that the politics of nationalisation, the 'cloth cap' and 'class warfare' had become redundant. Underpinned by Keynesian demand management, continued material improvement and social stability would prepare the way to socialism, according to the revisionists. It was the task of 'modernising' Labour to facilitate these developments. Although less damaging than the Australian labour movement's 'Great Split', divisions between Bevanites and Gaitskellites did prevent the Labour Party from presenting a united front at elections throughout the 1950s. This detracted from the positive picture of strong membership figures for both the unions and the Party and the dominant position of the BLP in many urban localities.[114]

By the time of the 1955 election the Labour Party's cause was adversely affected not only by disunity but also by the fact that the economic crisis of 1951 had given way to economic prosperity. As in Australia, the 'golden age' had arrived in Britain. It was similarly characterised by high growth rates, low unemployment, low inflation, a substantial improvement in living standards and mass consump-tion.[115] The Conservatives under their new leader, Anthony Eden (Churchill retired in April 1955), were quick to take credit for the economic recovery, boom and the accompanying increase in living standards, social stability and harmony. The *Daily Express* accurately reflected the new 'affluent' and 'apathetic' mood of the country just before the election in late May 1955. 'Too many people', declared the newspaper, 'are participating in these prosperous times. They are tasting the best food, wearing new clothes, buying TV sets' and 'furnishing their homes'.[116]

Yet the Conservatives left little to chance. In addition to claiming credit for improved living standards and promising 'more' in the future, they declared that Labour's 'plans' to turn the clock back to 'discredited' nationalisation, rationing and increased personal taxation would be a 'disaster', an invitation to 'bankruptcy'. They also drew attention to Labour disunity and, as in 1951, its 'outdated doctrines' of socialism and 'class hatred'. These 'plans' and charges were hotly dismissed by Labour's leaders. The Conservatives also saw the 1949 North Atlantic Treaty Organisation and the nuclear deterrent as 'vital' to the defence of 'freedom'.[117] They presented their party as being the best equipped to defend freedom and democracy. It was party of 'reconciliation', the 'national interest' and the 'friendship and united action of the English speaking peoples' of the Commonwealth and beyond. The Tories governed a 'small island, unconquered for nearly 1,000 years' in which its people 'live together in a neighbourly fashion without the bitter feuds and political passions which convulse many other countries'.[118]

It was within this favourable context, combined with Labour's 'dull and uninspiring' campaign revolving yet once again around 'consolidation', that the Conservatives won 344 seats as against Labour's 277. The former 'more than trebled' their majority. While Labour's support among men increased, 'there was a significant fall in its support among women'.[119]

The Conservative Party rallied strongly after the Suez fiasco of 1956, when British and French military forces had waged an unsuccessful war against Egypt over the administration of the Suez Canal and suffered a humiliating withdrawal. Under the charismatic leadership of Harold Macmillan, it continued to highlight economic prosperity and expressed a willingness to engage in 'real' and 'comprehensive' discussions about multilateral nuclear disarmament during the election of 1959. Increasing strike levels, the support given by some of its more prominent members to the Campaign for Nuclear Disarmament, formed in 1958, and the absence of anything really new and radical in its campaign, doomed Labour to defeat. The Conservatives once again increased their majority.[120] Only when the economic tide began to turn in the early 1960s, when Britain's systemic decline became a matter of major and enduring concern and when Labour was once again to offer salvation in the form of the creation of a new, progressive nation, would the political pendulum swing against the Conservatives.

Notes

1 See, for example, Macintyre, *Concise History*, p. 209; Bolton, *Oxford History*, ch. 3; Cain and Farrell, 'Menzies' War on the Communist Party', in Curthoys and Merritt (eds), *Australia's First Cold War*.
2 Bobbie Oliver, *Unity is Strength: A History of the Australian Labor Party and the Trades and Labor Council in Western Australia* (Perth: Australian Public Intellectual Network, 2003); Ross Fitzgerald and Harold Thornton, *Labor in Queensland: From the 1880s to 1988* (St Lucia: University of Queensland Press, 1989), ch. 4; Hagan and Turner, *History of the Labor Party of New South Wales*, Part Three; Robert Murray, *The Split: Australian Labor in the Fifties* (Melbourne: Cheshire, 1970); Bradom Ellem (ed.), *The Great Labour Movement Split in New South Wales: Inside Stories* (Sydney: Australian Society for the Study of Labour History Sydney Branch, 1998); Graham Freudenberg, *Cause for Power: The Official History of the New South Wales Branch of the Australian Labor Party* (Leichardt: Pluto Press in association with the NSW ALP, 1991), ch. 11.
3 Tom Sheridan, *Division of Labour: Industrial Relations in the Chifley Years 1945–9* (Melbourne: Oxford University Press, 1989), especially ch. 7, pp. 311–16.
4 James and Markey, 'Class and Labour', 26–7; Alastair Davidson, *The Communist Party of Australia: A Short History* (Stanford: Hoover Institute Press, 1969), pp. 141–2; Oliver, *Unity is Strength*, pp. 222–30; Hagan and Turner, *History of the Labor Party of New South Wales*, p. 163; Ashley Lavalle, 'Labor and Vietnam: A Reappraisal', *Labour History*, 90 (2006), 119–36.
5 Bolton, *Oxford History*, p. 43.
6 *Ibid.*, pp. 45–7.
7 Hancock, 'Rise of the Liberal Party', p. 144.
8 *Ibid.*; Macintyre, *Concise History*, 206; Martin, *Menzies: A Life*, ch. 5.
9 *Australian Worker*, 9, 30 November 1949; Crisp, *Chifley*, pp. 338–40, 353–4, 368–74; David Day, *Chifley: A Life* (Pymble, NSW: Harper Perennial, 2007).
10 Bolton, *Oxford History*, p. 73; Papers of Sir Robert Menzies (hereafter Menzies Papers), NLA, MS 4936, Series 30, Box 489, Folder 8, 'Election Material 1928–49'.
11 Hancock, 'Rise of the Liberal Party', p. 141.
12 *Ibid.*, p. 142.
13 Menzies Papers, Series 30, Box 490, Folder 8, '1949 Material; Federal Election 1951', Policy Speech of Rt. Hon. A.W. Fadden of the Australian Country Party at Boonah (Qld.) – Thursday, November 17 1949.
14 Bolton, *Oxford History*, p. 76; D.K. Rodgers Papers, NLA, MS 1536, Box 4, Folder, '1949 Election Correspondence etc.', Draft Article by Chifley for the *Melbourne Herald*, 28 November 1949; *Australian Worker*, 30 November, 7 December 1949; *Worker*, 19 September, 14 November, 5 December 1949.
15 Macintyre, *Concise History*, pp. 209–11; Deery and Redfern, 'No Lasting Peace?', 65.
16 Deery and Redfern, 'No Lasting Peace?', 65.
17 Menzies Papers, Series 30, Box 490, Folder 8, '1949 Material; Federal Election 1951', PM's Reading Copy for a Speech Delivered 3 April 1951, Canterbury, Victoria.
18 Davidson, *Communist Party of Australia*, p. 126; Deery and Redfern, 'No Lasting Peace?', 63.
19 See, for example, Redfern and Deery, 'No Lasting Peace?', 64–9; *Tribune*, 23, 27 July, 13, 17 August, 13, 17, 14, 17 December 1949, 13 May, 13, 19 October 1950, 8 February 1951 (for the Soviet Union as 'the Future: Peace and Progress Hand in Hand').

20 See, for example, *Australian Worker*, 24, 31 August, 7, 14 September 1949, 1 February 1950; *Worker*, 15 August, 14, 28 September, 19, 31 October, 14 November, 5 December 1949, 8 February 1950.
21 Deery and Redfern, 'No Lasting Peace?', 67; Murray, 'The Split', pp. 152–3.
22 Phillip Deery, 'Chifley, the Army and the 1949 Coal Strike', *Labour History*, 68 (1995), 90–1; *Australian Worker*, 7, 14, 28 September 1949; Crisp, 'Chifley', pp. 360–7.
23 Macintyre, *Concise History*, p. 205; Deery, 'Chifley, the Army', 80–1, 93; Crisp, *Chifley*, pp. 363–5; Sheridan, *Division of Labour*, ch. 12.
24 Menzies Papers, Series 14, Box 410, Folders on the Liberal Party, see especially Fadden and Page; *Worker*, 19 September, 14 November, 5 December 1949; *Sydney Morning Herald*, 20 October 1949.
25 See, for example, *Australian Worker*, 11 April 1951.
26 *Australian Worker*, 19 October 1949. See also the same newspaper for 7, 14 September 1949.
27 Menzies Papers, Series 20 Communist Party, Box 436, Folders 1–4, 7, Box 437, Folders 10–15.
28 Macintyre, *Concise History*, p. 215.
29 *Worker*, 9 January 1950.
30 *Worker*, 24 September, 1 October 1951; *Australian Worker*, 12 September, 17 October 1951; Menzies Papers, Series 30, Box 494, 'Election Material 1958', Folder 41, 'Election Speeches by Dr. Evatt 1954, 1955, 1958', pp. 20–2.
31 Cain and Farrell, 'Menzies' War', 123.
32 *Ibid.*, 124; Menzies Papers, Series 14, Box 418, Folder 66, 'Current Politics, 1950–51', issued by the Federal Secretariat of the Liberal Party of Australia, 23 May 1950.
33 Cain and Farrell, 'Menzies' War', 125; Macintyre, *Concise History*, pp. 214–15.
34 *Australian Worker*, 4, 11 April, 2 May 1951; *Worker*, 2, 9, 16, 30 April 1951; Menzies Papers, 'Election Speeches by Dr. Evatt', pp. 20–2.
35 Menzies Papers, Series 30, Box 489, '1951 Federal Election', Folders 1, 2; *Australian Worker*, 10 October 1951; Martin, *Menzies: A Life*, ch. 7.
36 Macintyre, *Concise History*, p. 215; Cain and Farrell, 'Menzies' War', 133; Nick Dyrenfurth, '"The Spirit of Sturdy Independence": Robert Menzies' Language of Citizenship, 1942–52', *Australian Journal of Politics and History*, 52:2 (2006), 202–3.
37 *Worker*, 10, 24, 31 May 1954; *Australian Worker*, 26 May 1954.
38 Murray, 'The Split', pp. 162–3; G.C. Bolton, 'Evatt, Herbert Vere', in John Ritchie (ed.), *Australian Dictionary of Biography*, vol. 14, *1940–1980* (Carlton: Melbourne University Press, 1996), p. 113; Martin, *Menzies: A Life*, chs 9, 10.
39 Murray, 'The Split', p. 163; Bolton 'Evatt', p. 113; Bolton, *Oxford History*, pp. 71–2; Macintyre, *Concise History*, pp. 215–16.
40 Hagan and Turner, *History of the Labor Party of New South Wales*, pp. 157–63; D.J. Murphy, 'The 1957 Split: "A Drop in the Ocean in Political History"', in D.J. Murphy, R.B. Joyce and Colin A. Hughes (eds), *Labor in Power: The Labor Party and Governments in Queensland 1915–57* (St Lucia: University of Queensland Press, 1980), pp. 488–94.
41 *Bulletin*, 17 February 1954; Ewan Morris, 'Forty Years On: Australia and the Queen, 1954', *Journal of Australian Studies*, 40 (1994), 1–13.
42 *Worker*, 8 February, 8, 15, 22 March, 10 May 1954; *Australian Worker*, 10 February 1954; Peter Spearritt, 'Royal Progress: The Queen and her Australian Subjects', *Australian Cultural History*, 5 (1986), 75–94; Bolton, *Concise History*, p. 140; Morris, 'Forty Years On'.
43 Morris, 'Forty Years On', 1; *Australian Worker*, 10 February 1954 (editorial).
44 Macintyre, *Concise History*, p. 216.
45 Robert Manne, *The Petrov Affair: Politics and Espionage* (Sydney: Pergamon Press, 1987).
46 *Worker*, 19, 26 April, 10, 17 May 1954.
47 *Worker*, 17, 24, 31 May 1954; *Australian Worker*, 19 May, 2 June 1954.

48 Murray, 'The Split', pp. 165–6.
49 Oliver, *Unity is Strength*, p. 214; Patmore, *Australian Labour*, p. 95.
50 Bolton, 'Evatt', pp. 113–14.
51 *Ibid.*, p. 114.
52 Murray, 'The Split', p. 177.
53 Manne, *Petrov Affair*, p. 263; Menzies Papers, Series 14, Liberal Party, Box 410.
54 *Worker*, 7, 21, 28 November, 12 December 1955; *Australian Worker*, 14 December 1955.
55 Manne, *Petrov Affair*, p. 264.
56 Murray, 'The Split', pp. 177–8; *Worker*, 19 December 1955.
57 *Australian Worker*, 14 December 1955.
58 Bolton, *Oxford History*, p. 148; Jim Hagan, *The History of the ACTU* (Melbourne: Longman Cheshire, 1981), p. 253.
59 In Queensland the Split assumed the form of a disastrous conflict between, on the one hand, the Australian Workers' Union, the traditional mainstay of the ALP, and, on the other hand, V.C. Gair, the long-standing ALP Premier of the state. Expelled from the ALP in 1957, Gair and his supporters set up their own Queensland Labor Party. The latter 'joined forces' with the DLP in 1962. The split ended the ALP's long-standing electoral dominance in Queensland. The party did not recover until the late 1980s. Mindful of the disastrous effects upon the New South Wales ALP of the 1930s split, the various factions within the NSW party managed to avoid a rupture in the mid 1950s and maintain party unity. The good relations existing between the ALP and the Catholic Church also helped matters. In overall terms, the Split was a complex phenomenon. It varied in character and intensity throughout the states and, as noted in the text, involved not only questions of communism and Catholicism, but also issues of labour-movement unity and autonomy and the external threat posed to them by the Catholic Social Studies movement. See Fitzgerald and Thornton, *Labor in Queensland*, ch. 4; Murphy, '1957 Split'; Hagan and Turner, *Labor Party of New South Wales*, pp. 157–63, 184–95; Ellem (ed.), *Great Labour Movement Split*; Murray, *Split*; Freudenberg, *Cause for Power*, ch. 11; Oliver, *Unity is Strength*, pp. 214, 219, 221, 230; Bolton, *Oxford History*, pp. 142–5; Love, 'Great Labor Split'.
60 Murray, 'The Split', p. 178; Scalmer, 'Crisis to Crisis', p. 97; Rawson, *Labor in Vain?*, pp. 119–20.
61 Bolton, *Oxford History*, p. 146; *Australian Worker*, 8, 22 November, 6, 20 December 1961; *Worker*, 20 November, 11, 25 December 1961.
62 *Australian Worker*, 26 November, 10 December 1958, 23 October, 6, 20 November, 4 December 1963; *Worker*, 28 October, 11 November, 9 December 1963.
63 *Australian Worker*, 18 December 1963; *Worker*, 9 December 1963. For the political roots of the ALP's internal modernisation see Terry Irving and Sean Scalmer, 'The Public Sphere and Party Change: Explaining the Modernisation of the Australian Labor Party in the 1960s', *Labour History Review*, 65:2 (2000), 227–46.
64 Hagan and Turner, *Labor Party of New South Wales*, pp. 144, 149, 167–71, 220–39.
65 Murphy, Joyce and Hughes (eds), *Labor in Power*, pp. xxi, 491.
66 Richard Davis, *Eighty Years Labor: The ALP in Tasmania 1903–1983* (Tasmania: Sassafras Books and the History Department, University of Tasmania, 1983), pp. 11–12, chs 2, 3, pp. 115–16.
67 Oliver, *Unity is Strength*, pp. 179–81, 251; Andrew Parkin, 'Dunstan Governments: A Political Synopsis', Allan Patience, 'Social Democracy in South Australia in the 1970s', in Andrew Parkin and Allan Patience (eds), *The Dunstan Decade: Social Democracy at the State Level* (Melbourne: Longman Cheshire, 1981); John Cain, *John Cain's Years: Power Parties and Politics* (Carlton: Melbourne University Press, 1995), ch. 1.
68 *Worker*, 28 January 1946, 11 December 1961, 28 October, 11 November, 9 December 1963, 17, 31 January 1966, 25 December 1972.
69 *Worker*, 30 January 1961.

70 In addition to the references in note 59 above, see Davies, *Eighty Years Labor*, pp. 50–3; Oliver, *Unity is Strength*, ch. 10; Cain, *John Cain's Years*, pp. 6–10.
71 Patmore, *Australian Labour*, pp. 95–6; Davidson, *Communist Party of Australia*, pp. 139–42, 183.
72 Menzies Papers, Series 30, Box 494, Folder 42, 'Newspaper Cuttings of Election Tours and Speeches, 1958', Folder 43, 'General Elections, 1958'.
73 *Australian Worker*, 8, 22 November 1961.
74 *Worker*, 28 October 1963, 9 December 1963.
75 Lavelle, 'Labor and Vietnam', 119–36; Bolton, *Oxford History*, p. 169.
76 *Worker*, 5 December 1966. See also *Worker*, 3, 31 January, 28 February 1966, *Australian Worker*, 30 November 1966 for 'pro-Communist' influence within the ALP.
77 Martin, 'Menzies'; Bolton, *Oxford History*, pp. 174–88.
78 Bolton, *Oxford History*, pp. 84–5.
79 Bolton, *Oxford History*, pp. 90–1.
80 Macintyre, *Concise History*, pp. 199, 207, 219.
81 *Ibid.*, pp. 207, 219–24; Bolton, *Oxford History*, p. 103.
82 Dyrenfurth, '"Spirit of Sturdy Independence"', pp. 222–3.
83 Scott, *Running on Empty*, pp. 49–51.
84 Sean Greenwood, *Britain and the Cold War 1945–1991* (Basingstoke: Macmillan, 2000); Phillip Deery, '"The Secret Battalion": Communism in Britain during the Cold War', *Contemporary British History*, 13:4 (1999), 1–28.
85 Morgan, *People's Peace*, pp. 52–4; correspondence from Sean Scalmer, 5 October 2009.
86 Harriet Jones, 'Introduction', in Harriet Jones and Michael Kandiah (eds), *The Myth of Consensus: New Views on British History 1945–64* (Basingstoke: Macmillan, 1996); Alan Campbell, Nina Fishman and John McIlroy, 'The Post-War Compromise: Mapping Industrial Politics', in Alan Campbell, Nina Fishman and John McIlroy (eds), *British Trade Unions and Industrial Politics*, vol. 1, *The Post-War Compromise 1945–64* (Aldershot: Ashgate, 1999), especially pp. 69–71.
87 Green, 'Conservative Party, State and Electorate'; David Lowe, 'Australia's Cold War: Britishness and English-Speaking Worlds Challenged Anew', in Phillip Buckner and R. Douglas Francis (eds), *Rediscovering the British World* (Calgary: University of Calgary Press, 2005), p. 361.
88 Saville, *Politics of Continuity*, ch. 2.
89 Deery and Redfern, 'No Lasting Peace?', 181; Deery, '"Secret Battalion"', p. 2; John Kelly, 'Social Democracy and Anti-Communism: Allan Flanders and British Industrial Relations in the Early Post-War Period', in Campbell, Fishman and McIlroy (eds), *Post-War Compromise*.
90 Deery and Redfern, 'No Lasting Peace?', 76–7; Clarke, *Hope and Glory*, pp. 235–7; Kenneth O. Morgan, *Labour in Power 1945–1951* (Oxford: Oxford University Press, 1985), pp. 261–2, 274–7.
91 Peter Weiler, *British Labour and the Cold War* (Stanford: Stanford University Press, 1988), ch. 7; Deery, '"Secret Battalion"', *passim*; Jim Phillips, 'The Postwar Political Consensus and Industrial Unrest in the Docks, 1945–55', *Twentieth Century British History*, 6:3 (1995), 302–19; Morgan, *People's Peace*, pp. 98–9.
92 Weiler, *British Labour and the Cold War*, pp. 276–84; Partha Sarathi Gupta, 'Imperialism and the Labour Government of 1945–51', in Jay Winter (ed.), *The Working Class in Modern British History: Essays in Honour of Henry Pelling* (Cambridge: Cambridge University Press, 1983), pp. 99–123; Anthony Carew, 'The Trades Union Congress in the International Labour Movement', in Campbell, Fishman and McIlroy (eds), *Post-War Compromise*; John Callaghan, *Labour Party and Foreign Policy*, ch. 6. This Cold War consensus, however, did not mean that Labour and Conservative approaches to de-colonisation were completely devoid of differences and conflicts. For a balanced discussion of this subject see Nicholas Owen, 'Decolonisation and Postwar Consensus', in Jones and Kandiah, *Myth of Consensus*.

93 Deery and Redfern, 'No Lasting Peace?', 77; Justin Davis Smith, *The Attlee and Churchill Administrations and Industrial Unrest 1945–55* (London: Pinter, 1990); Keith Middlemas, *Power, Competition and the State*, 3 vols. (Basingstoke: Macmillan, 1986, 1990, 1991).

94 Richard Stevens, 'Cold War Politics: Communism and Anti-Communism in the Trade Unions', in Campbell, Fishman and McIlroy (eds), *Post-War Consensus*.

95 Deery and Redfern, 'No Lasting Peace?', 78–9; Dan Keohane, 'Labour's International Policy: A Story of Conflict and Contention', in Brian Brivati and Richard Hefferman (eds), *The Labour Party: A Centenary History* (Basingstoke: Macmillan Press, 2000), pp. 372–4.

96 Deery and Redfern, 'No Lasting Peace?', p. 63; Stevens, 'Cold War Politics', pp. 168–70; Morgan, *Labour in Power*, pp. 294–6.

97 Deery and Redfern, 'No Lasting Peace?', 73–80.

98 Eric Hobsbawm, 'The British Communist Party', *Political Quarterly*, 25 (1954), 30–43; Morgan, *Bolshevism and British Left*; Weiler, *British Labour and the Cold War*, pp. 277–8.

99 Davidson, *Communist Party of Australia*, p. 183.

100 Thorpe, *History of the British Labour Party*, pp. 134–5; Clarke, *Hope and Glory*, pp. 239–40; 'Press Cuttings, General Election 1951', LP/ELEC/1951/2, LHASC, *Daily Express*, 26 October 1951, *The Times*, 26 October 1951; David E. Butler, *The British General Election of 1951* (London: Macmillan, 1952).

101 Fielding, Thompson and Tiratsoo, *England Arise!*, p. 209; *Worker*, 24 September, 29 October 1951; *Australian Worker*, 31 October, 7 November 1951.

102 Schenk, 'Austerity and Boom', p. 314.

103 'Press Cuttings, General Election 1951', *Manchester Guardian*, 27 October 1951, *Daily Express*, 10 October 1951; 'Press Cuttings, General Election 1955', *Daily Express*, 28 May 1955, *Observer*, 15 May 1955.

104 Bill Schwarz, 'The Tide of History: The Reconstruction of Conservatism, 1945–51', in Nick Tiratsoo (ed.), *The Attlee Years* (London: Pinter Publishers, 1991), p. 162.

105 Ina Zweiniger-Bargielowska, 'Consensus and Consumption: Rationing, Austerity and Controls after the War', in Jones and Kandiah (eds), *Myth of Consensus*, pp. 92–3; 'Press Cuttings, General Election 1951', *Manchester Guardian*, 17, 27 October 1951.

106 *Manchester Guardian*, 27 October 1951.

107 Bargielowska, 'Consensus and Consumption'; Brooke, 'Labour and Nation'; Martin Francis, 'Labour and Gender', in Tanner, Thane and Tiratsoo (eds), *Labour's First Century*.

108 Francis, 'Labour and Gender', p. 207.

109 *Ibid.*, pp. 207–10; Brett, *Australian Liberals*, pp. 34, 59–64, 119, 123, 127.

110 Clarke, *Hope and Glory*, pp. 239–40.

111 *Manchester Guardian*, 27 October 1951.

112 *The Times*, 25 October 1951.

113 *Ibid.*, 25 October 1951; Morgan, *People's Peace*, pp. 101–2.

114 Thorpe, *History of British Labour*, pp. 138–40; James and Markey, 'Class and Labour', 29.

115 Peter Howlett, 'The Golden Age, 1955–1973', in Johnson (ed.), *Twentieth Century Britain*.

116 'Press Cuttings, General Election 1955', *Daily Express*, 24 May 1955.

117 *Ibid.*, *Observer*, 15 May 1955, *Daily Express*, 24, 28 May 1955.

118 *Ibid.*, *Observer*, 15 May 1955.

119 Thorpe, *History of British Labour*, p. 141; David E. Butler, *The British General Election of 1955* (London: Macmillan, 1955).

120 Thorpe, *History of British Labour*, pp. 145–8; 'Press Cuttings, General Election 1959', *Daily Mail*, 2 October 1959, *Daily Telegraph*, 3 October 1959, *Daily Herald*, 1, 3 October 1959, *Daily Mirror*, 1 October 1959, *The Times*, 24, 29 September 1959.

CHAPTER NINE

Trans-national ties, electoral successes and bitter defeats

Trans-nationalism

For the Left, the 1960s was a decade of national and international protest and hope. It saw campaigns against the Vietnam War, nuclear weapons, racism, sexism, the destruction of the environment, the lack of 'real' democracy within society and continuing oppression and exploitation within the workplace and beyond. Students, 'hippies' and working-class people mounted 'counter-cultural' protests against traditional hierarchical structures and staid patterns of life. They wanted more freedom, equality, choice, democracy and opportunity in their work, in their personal lives, in leisure and in culture in general.

These protests took place in many countries around the world. Most impressive from a trans-national perspective were the ways in which protesting individuals and groups were aware of what was happening in faraway places and the ways in which ties, connections and exchanges of ideas and personnel developed for the first time or were renewed across national boundaries. For example, campaigners against Aboriginal exclusion and oppression in Australia looked to the Civil Rights movement in the United States, while the Aboriginal rights movement itself sought inspiration from decolonisation movements overseas, especially in Africa. Germaine Greer and Sheila Rowbotham were prominent among those women who pioneered and helped to spread the message of women's liberation around the globe. Black and white 'rank-and-file' struggles for 'workers' control' and improved conditions likewise transcended localities, regions and nations. Trans-national radicalism, as in the heady 'globalised' days of the late nineteenth and early twentieth centuries, was alive and well.[1]

Although often suspicious of, and in some instances hostile to, New Left, feminist, 'counter-cultural' and other forms of radical protest, the mid-century labour movements of Australia and Britain also continued to practise trans-nationalism. This was seen, for example, in the 'cross-fertilisation' of ideas and policies between the 1940s Labour governments in the two countries around the nature and process of post-war reconstruction, and the visits of Curtin, Chifley, Chifley's adviser, H.C. Coombs, and Evatt to Britain. In turn Bevin, Attlee, leading revisionist Anthony Crosland, future Labour Prime Minister James Callaghan and the British Communist leader, Harry Pollitt, were among the high-profile British labour leaders who visited Australia.[2] As noted in Chapter 8, Calwell and other ALPers partly sought inspiration for their 'modernisation' of both the ALP and Australian society from the 'modernising' social, scientific and technological 'revolution' of Harold Wilson in Britain.[3] Fabianism also spread from Britain to Australia. In the post-war years Fabian societies were established in all the Australian state capitals and Fabian philosophy became 'an expression of middle-class political mobilization in urban centres across the nation'. Australian Fabians sought, with limited results, to challenge the 'anti-intellectualism' of the ALP.[4] The revisionist ideas of Tony Crosland, Hugh Gaitskell and others also exerted some influence upon the ALP, especially in terms of the latter's future direction and its way out of the federal political wilderness during the late 1950s and the1960s. This influence, however, was very limited in terms of the ALP nationally. As also noted in Chapter 8, the main concerns of the largely 'traditional' ALP during these years rested with the restoration of party unity following the Split and the continuing, if increasingly limited, influence of communism within the party.[5]

Labour newspapers continued to carry frequent reports of labour movement personalities and developments 'overseas'. For example, Curtin's achievements, as noted earlier in Part IV, were hailed in the British press and among its labour leaders, while the BLP's victories in 1945 and 1950 were greeted with great enthusiasm in Australian labour circles. In late February 1974 Gough and Margaret Whitlam telegraphed Harold Wilson to congratulate him upon his election victory over Edward Heath. The Whitlams looked forward to 'the resumption of your great work for a better Britain and a brighter world'.[6]

Common trans-national bonds were also reflected in the continuing strength of the shared commitments of the Australian and British labour movements to the 'British' values and freedoms of democracy, constitutionalism, 'fair play', tolerance and opposition to 'tyranny', and the preservation of the Commonwealth as, in Arthur Calwell's words, 'a force for peace and a force for good'.[7] Evatt was prominent among the many labour leaders who echoed Arthur Henderson's, the TUC's and the ACTU's interwar appeals for 'complete unity' in the fight against totalitarianism, the sharing of relevant information and knowledge, and the welcome afforded to 'comrades and cousins' from abroad among 'all sections of the organised Labour Movement within the British Commonwealth of Nations' (Figure 4).[8] Following those held in 1925, 1928 and 1930, further Commonwealth Labour Conferences were organised in 1944, 1947 and 1957. These were designed further to promote these ideological, organisational and more informal, personal

Figure 4 Arthur Calwell, Australia's Minister for Immigration, welcoming British Migrants, ca. 1945–49

'bonds of unity', while the BLP sent 'a thousand copies' of Harold Laski's 1946 booklet, *The Secret Battalion: An Examination of the Communist Attitude to the Labour Party*, to the ALP.[9]

These continuing ties, however, were set within a post-war world in which there was 'a relative decline in formal internationalism within the social-democratic movement', and in which the British–Australian relationship, especially from the late 1950s onwards, became a 'more restricted and vestigial one'.[10] Between the 1960s and the revival of British interest in Australia's 'third way' politics in the 1980s there was, 'at key times', a 'lack of *comprehensive* contact between British Labour and the ALP'.[11] This was a reflection of the fact that, as argued by 'British world' scholars, the 1960s constituted the crucial decade in the collapse of the special tie between Australia and Britain and their shared British-ness, of what David Goldsworthy has termed Australians' 'higher identity as Britons' as being culturally and psychologically 'British' and heavily dependent upon the protection of the 'mother country'.[12]

This 'collapse' resulted largely from three developments. First, escalating economic problems not only 'severely undercut' Britain's hopes for 'a sustained or even an enhanced world role', but also contributed significantly to both the dissolution of the Empire during the 1960s and Britain's increasing concern with Europe and its markets as a key means of reversing its 'decline'. As highlighted by Stuart Ward, during the 1960s diminishing Australian 'goodwill' towards Britain was specifically related to the latter's moves to join the EEC, and its eventual entry in 1973. These were widely interpreted by Australians as a 'betrayal' on Britain's part. As Ward maintains, they 'fatally undermined the persisting assumptions about organic Anglo-Australian unity' and the overriding importance of British-ness among Australians.[13] The ALP responded with considerable 'regret' to Britain's proposed entry. While Britain had 'the right to please herself' [*sic*], the priority for Australians was to seriously consider 'the tremendous impact such a move would make on our trade and ultimately upon Commonwealth relations'. Despite Gaitskell's belief that Britain would not want to 'break' its links with 'Australia, New Zealand and Canada', Australia would have to be determined to 'study our own requirements as a nation, first and last'.[14]

Second, there was the growing importance attached by Australia to its friendship with the United States and the latter's key role in 'the defence of freedom' in the Asia-Pacific region. The United States increasingly replaced Britain as Australia's 'protector'.[15] Third, there were crucial changes in patterns of trade and immigration. By the early 1970s Japan had replaced Britain as Australia's best customer for her exports, while the end of 'White Australia' meant that many more immigrants from the Far East would henceforth be joining the growing number of mid-century arrivals from the countries of continental Europe and the Middle East, as well as the 'Ten Pound Poms'. By the early 1970s, 'The old British Commonwealth connection based on investment and migration was yielding to the compulsions of geography. Australia was becoming part of the Pacific economy.'[16]

Yet the decline of the special relationship between Australia and Britain and of Australians' 'Britishness' was, to quote David Goldsworthy, 'never a smooth, even or unilinear process'.[17] We must be careful not to pre-date or exaggerate the effects of the political and socio-economic changes noted above. For example, the extent and chronology of the 'Asianisation' and 'Americanisation' of Australia and of the 'Europeanisation' of Britain were uneven, limited and far from linear during the period under review. As noted in Chapter 8, the mid-century ALP was reluctant to become too close to and dependent upon the United States. A considerable part of the reason for this lay in the risks posed by America's unqualified and aggressive anti-communism to world peace, human survival and the fortunes of left-wing and other progressive political forces, including the ALP. As a counterweight to 'undue' US influence, the ALP supported important British and Australian attempts to build a closer empire defence relationship.

At the same time the links of family, kin and the commitment to common 'British' traditions and values persisted strongly among Australians and Britons beyond mid-century. They were reflected, for example, in the abiding popularity of the monarchy in Australia. As noted earlier, in 1954 the young Queen Elizabeth received a rapturous welcome from the multitudes of Australians who flocked to see her. In 1963 fewer Australians turned out to see the Queen, but her six-week visit was widely judged in the press and elsewhere to have been a resounding success. It was the shared verdict of Labour's Arthur Calwell and the conservative *Sydney Morning Herald* that the 'personal', 'intimate' and 'affectionate' ties between the Crown and Australia, 'founded not on practical advantage but on a sense of kinship and common family', constituted both 'the focus and . . . justification in the Queen as sovereign' and 'the really enduring' link between the two countries. This link, moreover, was becoming even more important in the face of, and would successfully 'survive', the immediate 'stresses and strains imposed by Britain's search for a new relationship with Europe'. It was reinforced, of course, by a 'broader', if perhaps 'less intense' but 'not less significant' sentiment for the Queen as the very popular Head of the Commonwealth.[18] As we will see in Part V, as late as 2000 the Queen's thirteenth tour of Australia – following, of course the failed referendum on the republic in 1999 – was widely hailed as a great success.[19]

The ALP and Australian politics in the 1970s

Gough Whitlam's recast ALP was in many ways the product of the new radical mood of the 1960s in its national, international and trans-national aspects. It was also the product of mounting frustration with the trade-union dominated 'traditionalism' of the party. The son of a senior public servant and himself a lawyer, Whitlam was 'a cultivated man of metropolitan background'.[20] Attuned to international develop-ments, he was confident of providing Australians with the 'progressive national reform' which he considered to be necessary after such a long period of Conservative domination of federal politics.[21] He was elected Labor leader in 1967 after 'a long struggle with the old guard led by Arthur Calwell'.[22]

Whitlam then set about modernising the party by discarding 'its socialist shibboleths, its preoccupation with trade union concerns and Cold War recriminations'.[23] He set out to 'de-escalate' the ALP's debilitating debate on Vietnam, while defending the right to peaceful demonstration, as seen most significantly on the occasion of the Vietnam Moratorium Campaign's massive anti-war rally in Melbourne in May 1970.[24] His visit to China in July 1971, 'scoffed' at by the Liberals, was a reflection of Whitlam's astute realisation that the Cold War was easing and that China wished to improve its relations with non-communist countries. (Communist China was admitted to the United Nations in October of the same year.) The aim was to widen Labor's remit in order to appeal not only to its traditional white trade union constituents, but also to women, to the more forward-looking sections of the middle class (partly achieved in the 1969 federal election) and to an increasingly 'multi-cultural' constituency. In sum, the 'mod-ernised' ALP would more accurately reflect the changing composition of Australian society.[25]

Mounting economic difficulties, internal coalition divisions, indus-trial conflict and McMahon's unpopular decision to step up the pros-ecution of those resisting national service at a time of phased withdrawal from Vietnam, formed the background to the 1972 federal election. Declaring 'It's Time', Whitlam seized his opportunity. Labor assumed federal office for the first time since 1949 on the back of an increase in its electoral support between 1966 and 1972 of 9.6 per cent.[26]

Once in office, the Whitlam government set about its task of 'the transformation of Australia'.[27] His Liberal predecessors had already laid some of the groundwork, especially Harold Holt and John Gorton in their progressive concerns with race, immigration and the arts. By the end of the 1960s the combined effects of an upsurge in Aboriginal protest and government initiatives had resulted in the Commonwealth having the power to legislate for Aborigines, to provide them with the right to vote, to welfare benefits and equal pay for pastoral work. Little success, however, attended Aboriginal land claims. In addition, during the 1950s and 1960s, and largely as a result of attempts to strengthen ties with non-communist elements in Asia, key aspects of the 'White Australia' policy were either dropped or eased. The former included the cornerstone dictation test, the latter, restrictions on the entry and qualifying period for citizenship of non-European migrants.[28]

Whitlam, nevertheless, undertook a reform programme of unprecedented scope and depth. In the areas of foreign policy and defence this included the formal ending of Australia's commitment in Vietnam, the abolition of conscription and the recognition of China. In terms of 'race relations' his government officially ended 'White Australia'. As embodied in the Racial Discrimination Act of 1975, 'racism was formally eliminated from domestic policy'. Whitlam abandoned the policy of assimilation towards Aboriginals, provided more support for their land rights and introduced medical and legal services under the auspices of the new Department of Aboriginal Affairs. These measures were part and parcel of an overarching commitment to the creation of an enriched society rooted in 'diversity' and 'multi-culturalism'. In the realm of gender, there was support for equal pay. In practice, women gained the 'full adult' minimum wage and 'more was promised' in terms of maternity leave, child-care centres, health centres and refuges. Whitlam's appointment of an adviser on women's issues also 'brought a new conjunction of feminism and social policy'. In addition, there was expanded support for health, education, the arts and media, urban and regional development. In these ways Whitlam 'extended the ambit of national government further than any peacetime leader before or since'.[29]

Whitlam's modernising and progressive drive, however, lost much of its impetus in 1974–75, especially in the area of economic policy. The ending of the post-war boom in 1973–74, the onset of a worldwide economic crisis characterised by 'stagflation' – high inflation combined with high unemployment and stagnant production – a 'wages explosion' and mounting industrial unrest in an attempt to keep pay abreast of prices, led to the widespread charge that he had 'wrecked the economy'. Whitlam's allegedly 'pro-Hanoi tilt', divisions within the government and the party, and proven instances of government economic incompetence and scandal – most notoriously and disastrously the ill-conceived and ill-fated 'loans affair' with a 'suspicious' Pakistani money trader – did the rest. The end was ignominious. In November

1975 the Empire, in the form of Governor-General Sir John Kerr and his Liberal supporters, 'struck back' against Whitlam's attempt to create a 'modern' and more independent-minded Australia. Kerr dismissed the Whitlam government on the grounds that it had lost the confidence of the parliament and 'commissioned the Liberal leader, Malcolm Fraser, as a caretaker prime minister to obtain supply and call an election'. The election was even more 'disastrous' for the ALP than that of 1966. In 1975 there was a 'uniform swing of 6.5 per cent against Labor' and a 'record majority' for the Liberal-Nationalists. The latter won 91 out of the 127 House of Representatives seats and 'commanded an absolute majority in the Senate'.[30]

Whitlam's bold but insufficiently considered experiment in progressive nationalism was defeated by a combination of bad economic luck on the international front, incompetence and a lack of sound judgement in economic management and a lack of common sense in terms of what was politically possible in a conservative society. Many conservative contemporaries highlighted 'the profligate', 'doctrinaire', 'amateurish' and 'bungling' approach of Labor's 'economic incompetents'. This judgement is too harsh in that it underestimates the adverse effects of the changing international economic climate on Australia and the extent of the difficulties facing the government in its attempt to tackle the new-found situation.[31] Yet, however admirable in intention and however much he remained convinced that he had done the right thing, Whitlam and his modernising colleagues were in all probability naive, insufficiently pragmatic and certainly economically overstretched and incompetent in their attempts to do so much so quickly.

Whitlam retired after the next federal election, in 1977, 'when his party suffered a no less ignominious defeat'.[32] The Liberal-National Party coalition, under the continued leadership of Malcolm Fraser, also won the election of 1980, albeit with its majority halved. Despite continuing economic problems and the government's 'flatness' and 'complacency', Fraser won a majority largely because of his 'responsible management of the economy'.[33]

The ALP, however, was not too despondent. It rebuilt from opposition, under Bill Hayden. On the very eve of the 1983 election Bob Hawke, president of the ACTU for eleven years, gained the leadership. As we will see in Part V, following his victory in 1983, Hawke began in earnest the process of 'modernisation' and the restoration of national unity.[34]

The BLP and British politics, 1964–79

Like Whitlam, Harold Wilson sought to end Labour's many years 'out in the cold' by establishing a 'new' and 'modern' nation. Like Whitlam,

Wilson was, in effect, renewing Labour's emphasis upon the idea of progressive nationalism, albeit in a different context and, to some extent, different form, in the manner of Curtin, Chifley and Attlee. Complete with his raincoat and pipe, his northern burr, well-publicised support for football – especially unfashionable Huddersfield Town Football Club – and his appeal to the pragmatic, 'down-to-earth' 'people' against 'amateurish' and 'out-of-date' Tory 'aristocrats', Wilson in many ways cut a very different figure to the cosmopolitan Whitlam. Yet the former was very bright, had the 'right' kind of 'meritocratic' educational experience – from grammar, rather than public, school to Oxford – was a very 'canny' politician and a skilled communicator well adept at handling the media. He may not have patronised the arts to the same extent as Whitlam, and his modernising drive was less cultural and more 'technocratic' in character, but it was still part of the same attempt to escape from the 'dead weight' of establishment 'tradition'.[35]

By early the 1960s Britain was experiencing growing economic problems. There was the recurrent problem of the 'stop-go' cycle, whereby imports increased, inflation rose, the balance of payments situation worsened and Conservative governments attempted to control credit and public sector wages and salaries. By 1964 Wilson, who had succeeded Gaitskell as party leader after the latter's untimely death in 1963 (he was only fifty-six), was also arguing that Britain was falling behind its international competitors and needed to 'modernise' in order to counteract the country's 'decline'.

Above all, there was a need for more centralised planning in relation to prices, incomes, investment, regional policy and the application of science and technology to industry in order to achieve long-term growth and stability, and so overcome the problem of 'stop-go'.[36] Wilson also placed great emphasis upon the creation of a more open and democratic society based upon equality of opportunity. This would be achieved by improved living standards, more educational opportunities and abidance by the 'professional ideal', whereby people progressed by means of their own abilities and talent rather than by the patronage of the out-of-date 'old boy' network.[37] Wilson delighted in mocking Sir Alec Douglas-Home, an aristocratic symbol of the 'old order', who succeeded Macmillan as Prime Minister upon the latter's resignation in 1963 (Macmillan had been rocked by the Profumo scandal and the French veto on British entry to the EEC).

As highlighted by Andrew Thorpe and Steven Fielding, much of the thinking of Wilson, a 'man of the left', in fact was in line with Gaitskellite 'revisionism'. Despite Wilson's stronger bias in favour of centralised planning, there was the same crucial emphasis upon economic growth, as opposed to extensive nationalisation, as the key to the creation of a future socialist society.[38] Yet by 1964 the changed context of these ideas – with economic boom and consensus giving way to mounting economic difficulties and Tory divisions – worked in Wilson's favour. He was quick to take full advantage of it.

The election revolved mainly around the question of economic management as the key to the achievement of a better future for all, a 'New Britain'.[39] Labour also stressed the need for greater British 'independence' in relation to both the United States and the EEC (Wilson supported Britain's 'conditional' entry). References to the 'thawing of the Cold War' and attacks on the Conservatives' nuclear weapons policy, however, were not accompanied by 'pledges to disarm'.[40]

Labour was extremely proud of its post-1945 role in 'transforming a white colonial Empire into a multi-racial Commonwealth'.[41] Yet the aftermath of the 1958 'race riots' in Nottingham and London and the electoral rise to prominence of racists such as Peter Griffiths and Enoch Powell saw Labour abandon its traditional commitment to an 'open door' policy, in favour of controls on Commonwealth immigration. As a sop to the liberal conscience, controls would be accompanied by Labour's anti-discriminatory Race Relations Acts of 1965 and 1968. In practice, these legislative measures were limited, lacked 'an effective cutting edge' and were 'overshadowed by the legislative turn to restriction'.[42]

While Britain and Australia were both moving towards the official outlawing of racial discrimination, this process, nevertheless, was more limited under the Wilson's government's legislative measures than under the more extensive and effective 'unravelling of the discriminatory apparatus' in 1960s and 1970s Australia. Whitlam's Racial Discrimination Act of 1975, widely outlawing a 'distinction, exclusion or preference based on race, colour, descent or ethnic origin' in the 'political, economic, social, cultural or any other field of public life', marked the culmination of a liberalising process which had first been evident in the 1940s and which had gathered great momentum from the 1950s onwards.[43]

The 1964 election resulted in a narrow win for Labour, with an overall majority of five. Despite the increasingly influential view in political and intellectual circles that mid-century affluence was stimulating the development of a more 'instrumental' or even 'bourgeois' working class, and signalling the 'triumph' of individualism over collectivism, the election saw Labour increase its vote among both manual and non-manual workers.[44] The *Guardian* attributed Wilson's victory to the fact that, in contrast to the stale Tories, he had offered a 'fresh approach', a 'creative programme' in terms of 'economic growth, efficiency, prosperity' and 'social justice'.[45]

In the wake of the 1964 election Labour put into place or strengthened the institutional machinery necessary to bring about the key aim of 'modernisation' under its National Plan. It was decisively returned to power at the March 1966 election in order to 'complete the job', while the Tories were seen as 'tired', 'discredited' and in need of 'modernization'.[46] It was largely as a result of Labour's victories in 1964 and 1966 that the ALP looked to Wilson's 'modernising' and institutionally 'strong' and 'healthy' party 'as a model' in order to revive its own desperate electoral fortunes and poor internal health and strength.[47]

Yet the domestic portents for the seemingly self-confident and ascendant BLP were not good. The deteriorating balance-of-payments position necessitated a 'strong dose of deflation'. When this was carried out in the 'July' measures of 1966, Labour's new creations, the Department of Economic Affairs and the National Plan were 'effectively dead'.[48] There occurred, moreover, escalating conflicts within the party resulting from Ian Smith's declaration of independence for 'white' Rhodesia in November 1965 and its adverse effect upon the unity and standing of the Commonwealth. Wilson's unconditional support for the Americans in Vietnam and the question of how most effectively to tackle the issue of 'racialism' at home also met with opposition from within and without the BLP.[49]

Between 1966 and 1970 Wilson's unrealistic goal of maintaining Britain's status as a Great Power imposed great strains on the country's finances. The government suffered a serious loss of face in 1967 when it was forced to devalue the pound. It also faced mounting industrial conflict and growing tensions with the unions over incomes policy. The struggle between the government and the TUC over the Prices and Incomes Bill in 1968 and Barbara Castle's proposals for legal restraints upon trade unions, as set out in her inaptly named White Paper, *In Place of Strife* (1969), inflicted serious damage on labour-movement unity. They also turned many of the unionised working class against the government. Labour's share of the working-class vote 'dropped 12.4 percentage points in the June 1970 election from that of March 1966'.[50] Lastly, although Labour was still widely expected to win the 1970 election, its cause also suffered from the headline news, two days before polling, that the country was running the largest trade deficit for just over a year. Edward Heath, the Tory leader, sounded warnings of the 'economic wrath to come' in the event of another Labour victory.[51]

As matters transpired, it was Heath who secured a shock victory in June 1970, on a swing of 4.7 per cent, 'the greatest since 1945'.[52] During the election campaign Heath, the 'radical marketeer', promised to legally control the unions, introduce a cooling-off period for industrial disputes 'endangering the national interest', reduce taxation and government spending, strengthen sterling, stop prices from rising and introduce more controls on immigration.[53] Although the *Guardian* maintained that Labour was in the process of delivering the promised 'growth and prosperity', 'social justice, regenerated regions and a sane foreign policy', the voters believed that improvements were not taking place quickly enough. Enoch Powell was attributed by the *Guardian* with having 'single-handedly' revived the fortunes of the Conservative Party in the West Midlands around the issues of race and immigration.[54] The influence of both Powell in the West Midlands and racism upon the general outcome of the election, however, were disputed.[55] Ironically, it was now the Conservative leader who received the plaudits for 'modernizing' and 'renewing' the fortunes of his party, while Labour was too 'smug' and 'complacent'.[56] In truth, Labour had failed sufficiently to deliver the brave new modern Britain promised in the 1960s and had alienated too many of its natural supporters as a result of its actions in 1968 and 1969.

The Heath government faced continuing economic problems in the form of rising unemployment and inflation. Under the terms of the Industrial Relations Act of 1971, sympathy strikes, the refusal of employers to recognise registered unions, breaches of legally binding contracts and the pre-entry closed shop became illegal. The unintended but predictable result was an escalation of industrial conflict in 1972 on a scale unknown since 1926. Faced with a national coal strike, the first since 1926, the government backed down. During the winter of 1972 and the spring of 1973 Heath abandoned his free-market stance in favour of a 'corporatist' attempt to control wages, prices, dividends and rents.[57]

The ending of the international 'golden age' in 1973–74 deepened the country's economic gloom. Britain, like Australia, experienced serious stagflation. But, as noted earlier, the economic problems of the former arguably were both more acute and chronic than those of the latter. Britain was widely perceived to have become the 'sick man' [*sic*] of Europe, characterised by a pervasive resistance to change, an outmoded social structure, low productivity, low investment, high inflation and technological backwardness. From the later 1960s through the decade of the 1970s it also experienced what was increasingly characterised internationally as the 'British disease' of escalating industrial and class conflict. The decade of the 1970s, indeed, was a time of systemic crisis not only for the economy, but also for British politics, class relations and society as a whole.[58]

Faced with the prospect of a second national miners' strike in two years, Heath called an election for 28 February 1974. This was dominated by the issue: 'Who Governs – The Government or a Trade Union?'

While appealing to Tory MPs to avoid 'union bashing' and while observing that the 'majority' of miners' leaders were 'moderate men who only wanted to get on with earning a living', the prime minister was determined to 'stand firm' against the 'dangerous militancy' in the unions, 'extremism and inflation'.[59] In response to a wage demand from the National Union of Mineworkers' (NUM) executive in November 1973, Heath had declared a state of emergency and introduced the three-day working week and other power-saving measures. In the considered opinion of the *Guardian*'s Peter Jenkins, Heath and the 'hawkish' majority in his cabinet were intent upon portraying themselves as defenders of 'the rule of reason, Parliament and Democracy' against the 'alternative', which 'ultimately can only be chaos and a totalitarian or Communist regime'.[60]

Leading figures in the Conservative Party resorted to a concerted attack on 'Reds under the Bed' in the press and on radio and television. Heath himself 'left little doubt that "Reds under the bed"', would be 'a major part of the campaign', according to the *Guardian*'s political correspondent, Ian Aitken;[61] Bernard Levin in *The Times* counselled the Tories to remain steadfast in their fight against the 'substantial and growing influence of the communists in the trade unions', in the face of 'the few accusations' directed against them of conducting a 'Red Scare'.[62] In the manner of Menzies, Conservative leaders condemned not only the 'extremist' and 'disloyal' minority of communists and other assorted 'Marxists', such as Mick McGahey, Lawrence Daly and Arthur Scargill, who had 'captured' the NUM and were intent upon industrial 'chaos', but also the mainstream labour movement, which had allegedly fallen under their control. While relevant labour and more general histories have drawn our attention to state surveillance, and press and Conservative attacks upon militant trade union leaders, both communist and Labour, this wider smearing of the labour movement, as a central feature of the election campaign, has been mainly overlooked or underplayed.[63]

The smearing of the BLP as extreme and 'unfit to govern', however, was fully documented in the contemporary press. For example, as reported in the *Guardian*, the Conservative Manifesto warned that 'Labour today faces the nation committed to a left-wing programme more dangerous and more extreme than ever before in its history'. Labour's 'moderates' had allegedly 'lost control', and 'the real power' had been 'taken over, for the first time ever, by the extreme Left-wing'. This had been made possible by the 'capture' of the BLP by 'a small group of power-hungry trade union leaders'.[64] According to Heath, Wilson 'dared not' associate himself with moves to postpone the strike until after the election because his 'title as leader of the Labour Party' depended upon the support of extremists who were 'hell bent upon a strike'.[65] *The Times* editorialised that the prime minister was right to confront the NUM, because of the 'definite political as well as industrial' motives of some of the union's leaders. McGahey, for example, was portrayed as being driven by 'class enmity', the 'overthrow' of 'the fundamental values of society' and the 'collapse' of the Tory government.[66] Heath attacked not only card-carrying communists on the NUM's national executive – they wished to 'use' the miners' wage battle for 'wider political objectives' – but all 'extremists', including members of the Labour Party who 'wanted to bring down this or any other Government' and subvert 'our whole democratic way of life'. He implored all 'moderates' within the labour movement and the country as a whole to cast their votes for the government.[67] Instead of Labour's 'narrow, jealous' and 'destructive' 'view of Britain today', the Conservatives offered 'moderation' and claimed to represent the 'whole country' rather than a 'greedy' and outdated class-based section of it.[68]

Responses to the smearing of Labour varied. Many Conservatives doubtless endorsed the view expressed by Lord Chalfont in the pages of *The Times* that the actions of members of the Communist Party, the International Socialists and other Marxists were 'attacking' 'our democratic system'.[69] Others disagreed. The liberal-minded *Guardian* believed that the Tories were pursuing 'Manifestly Wrong Policies' and that Mr Heath appeared to have 'extremists on the brain'.[70] Ian Aitken wrote a front-page article in the *Guardian* entitled 'Firm, Fair – and Straight for the Jugular', in which he expressed the view that the Conservative Party had launched 'the most blistering attack on Labour as the party of left-wing extremism since Churchill's famous "Gestapo" campaign in 1945 . . . Labour . . . it says, would wreck the economy and undermine Britain's free society'.[71] The Tory maverick, Enoch Powell, who had been dismissed by Heath from the Conservative shadow cabinet in 1968 for his 'rivers of blood' speech and who stood down as a parliamentary candidate and advised the electors to support Labour because of its opposition to entry into Europe, refused to join the Conservatives' witch-hunt. He ridiculed Heath by declaring that 'the Communists could only achieve the economic breakdown of the system by sending aeroplanes and rockets to scatter fivers over the countryside'. Powell, who would become Ulster Unionist MP for South Down after the October 1974 election, also insisted that the government should pay the miners' wage claim in full.[72]

Leading Labour politicians responded to Tory smears with a mixture of anger and contempt. As Pelling and Reid astutely observe, in the midst of the industrial crisis Harold Wilson 'was able once more to appear as the pragmatic reconciler bent upon industrial peace'.[73] Wilson was forthright in his views that the government's 'pitched battle' with the miners was 'never necessary', that the dispute could have been settled 'three months ago', 'without a strike' and that full blame lay with Heath. The latter had been 'ideological' and 'unfeeling' in actively seeking a showdown with the miners, wrong in his rejection of their pay claim (new evidence showed that Heath had acted upon inflated figures for miners' wages) and 'intransigent' in not accepting the proposal put forward by the miners' leader Joe Gormley, widely acknowledged to be a moderate, to defer the strike action. Furthermore, the government was 'using the miners as an excuse for a cut-and-run election' in which they were attempting to deflect the public's attention from their own economic 'incompetence'.[74]

Like Powell, Wilson ridiculed Heath's attempt to smear Labour. The Conservatives had achieved what 'Lenin, Stalin, Mao-Tse-Tung and Brezhnev together never achieved; they have made the British Communist Party look important'.[75] Healey was also 'shocked' by Heath's attempt to 'equate Labour voters and union members with Communist agents of a foreign power'. He criticised the prime minister for 'brainwashing' and expressed the belief that 'the British people will treat this reversion to McCarthyism with the contempt it deserves'.[76]

The smearing campaign did not enjoy the success desired by the Conservatives. According to a *Guardian* editorial entitled 'Mr Wilson Turns the Tables', the 'Reds under the beds' strategy had 'rebounded'. The 'Reds' had 'come out and voted pretty solidly' against Heath. These were 'not the Red extremists' with 'whose evil shadow he tried to frighten the electorate, but the great mass of left-inclined workers', especially in the industrial areas of the Midlands and the North.[77] The bitterly fought election had an inconclusive outcome. While the share of the vote for both Labour and the Conservatives fell sharply and the Liberals and the Scottish Nationalists made spectacular gains in terms of the votes cast in their favour, Labour received 301 seats to the Conservatives' 297. As a result of the decision of the Liberal Party leader, Jeremy Thorpe, to decline Heath's offer of a coalition government, Labour ended up in power without an overall majority. In response to this plainly unsatisfactory state of affairs, Wilson called another election for October 1974. In the meantime, his government quickly ended the miners' strike on terms favourable to the workers involved and repealed the Industrial Relations Act.[78]

The second election, almost as inconclusive as the first, brought Labour a majority of three. It was notable, once again, for Heath's attempt to tar Labour and for Labour denials of extremism and disloyalty to the national interest. Traditional Conservative anti-socialism was combined with an onslaught against the 'doctrinal outpourings' of Tony Benn, the 'Bogey-Man', the 'neo-Marxists' and the contemporary Labour Party. 'New Labour' had 'abandoned the social democracy of the past in favour of revolution by stealth', according to the Tories. It now wanted to rule over a country with 'no private education, no grammar schools, no private health service, no family business or family firms, no sector of industry which is not either State-owned or State-controlled'.[79] In the later stages of the campaign Heath called for the establishment, as in 'wartime', of a 'Government of national unity', of 'all the talents', to fight against the 'evils' of inflation, unemployment and extremism.[80] In response, Labour's representatives successfully associated Heath and his previous governments with economic mismanagement – they had 'brought Britain to the edge of ruin' – the 'ideological' breakdown of the tried and trusted method of industrial relations, unnecessary industrial conflict, social strife and economic suffering. The Labour Party, rather than the Conservative Party, was the true and loyal representative of the 'moderate' and 'pragmatic' national community and national unity.[81]

Between the end of 1974 and the election of May 1979 Wilson and (following Wilson's resignation in 1976) James Callaghan continued to tackle the country's political, economic and social problems. There were disappointments. Inflation and unemployment remained high, and in 1976 Denis Healey, the Chancellor of the Exchequer, was forced to introduce cuts as a condition of securing a government loan from the International Monetary Fund to prop up the value of sterling. Disappointments, however, were increasingly outweighed by successes, at least up to the winter of 1978. The referendum campaign on renegotiated Common Market terms went in the government's favour (despite strong opposition within the party and the country at large), nationalisation was extended and the 'Social Contract', a voluntary mechanism whereby the unions cooperated on wage restraint 'in return for action against prices and rents and social inequality', worked well. By the middle of 1977 two years of the social contract 'had not merely limited wage increases substantially but had also made inroads into inflation'. Moreover, the year 1978 was, on the whole, 'a year of economic recovery for Britain'.[82]

Yet disaster was soon to strike. The return to free collective bargaining, following the successes of the social contract, was not, as intended by the government, 'orderly'. The 'Winter of Discontent' of 1978–79 saw massive industrial and social-political conflict, and wage settlements 'go through the roof'. Prominent Labour politicians such as Callaghan and Healey, urging 'moderation' and 'restraint', maintained that wages increases for the most powerful bargaining groups were raising prices at the expense of the less-powerful and the nation as a whole. They were opposed by the large numbers within the party and the unions in favour of 'free collective bargaining'. Yet some on the Left were opposed to this form of militant labourism, as expressed in the demand for 'more', and believed that it would do great damage to the cause of socialism and Labour's electoral prospects. It would provide easy ammunition for those who believed that the labour movement had once again been taken over by 'selfish', anti-social 'extremists' and that the unions were 'holding the country to ransom'. The alternative, as articulated by Stuart Holland and other Labour left and Communist Party comrades, was to call for planning agreements, industrial democracy and public ownership of key firms in order to counteract the growing power of multinational companies in Britain.[83]

The May election saw the return of a Conservative government, headed by the 'Churchillian' anti-socialist Margaret Thatcher, the first woman in Britain's history to become prime minister. The Tories won 339 seats against Labour's 269 and captured 43.9 per cent of the vote, a 'decisive but not overwhelming' victory. On a swing of 5.2 per cent – 'the largest since 1945' – Labour lost support not only among skilled male workers, but 'in all sectors of the population' and, despite holding its own in most of northern England, Scotland and Wales, in 'most geographical areas'. There were serious losses for the Scottish and Welsh Nationalists and less serious losses for the Liberals.[84]

The election was a 'negative verdict' on Labour attempts successfully to tackle not only the 'Winter of Discontent' but also Britain's mounting socio-economic and political problems since the 1960s.[85] Like Whitlam, Wilson and (especially) Callaghan had been hit particularly hard by their failure to tackle the growing wage demands of workers in the face of worsening socio-economic conditions. In the general context of economic failure, Labour's 1979 election promises to introduce a wealth tax, extend the work of the supervisory National Enterprise Board and the scope of comprehensive education and improve housing and social welfare provision stood little chance of success.[86]

Contrary to the viewpoint that 'much' of the 'scaremongering' was 'carried on by the tabloid press or non-politicians',[87] the smearing of mainstream Labour was once again both an important and a much-neglected feature of a 1970s general election.

As the *Guardian* observed, Conservative speakers conducted 'what looked very like an orchestrated effort to play "the Red card" in the closing stages of the campaign'. This was a calculated response to Labour's early lead in the opinion polls.[88] In familiar vein Thatcher, along with major Conservative and Liberal figures such as Michael

Heseltine, William Whitelaw and Joe Grimond, vigorously attacked the 'anti-democratic' 'extremists' who had 'taken over' the Labour Party, the 'un-' and 'anti-British' nature of socialism and the 'excessive rights' and 'diminished responsibilities' of the trade unions. Although only a 'handful' of a few thousand were branded as 'destroyers' and 'fanatics', yet their influence in the labour movement was alleged to far outweigh their numbers. They 'lurked' behind James Callaghan and were 'determined' to 'transform' Britain into a 'Communist State'.[89] Whitelaw, a Tory 'moderate', predicted that Callaghan would soon be replaced by someone 'much more frightening and left-wing', while Tony Benn was once again targeted relentlessly as the 'extreme' socialist 'bogey-man'. Labour's leaders strongly refuted these charges of infiltration and extremism. But they were not helped by the fact that some Labour 'renegades', including Lord George Brown, joined in the smearing of the labour movement.[90]

The new prime minister, like Wilson and Callaghan, wanted to reverse the country's economic 'decline' and restore the country to 'health' and 'greatness'. However, whereas Wilson and Callaghan sought to achieve their goals mainly by regulatory, social-democratic means, Thatcher sought to meet her objectives by means of a free-market 'revolution'. The country would be 'saved' by means of trade union legislation and 'tough' but 'fair' policies on crime (to counter recent 'lawlessness'), defence (a revival of the rhetoric of the Cold War) and immigration (to prevent 'swamping'). The 'overbearing' power and spending of the state would be overcome by means of reduced taxation, by the active encouragement of individualism, independence and self-help, and the return of power to the 'moderate majority'. At this stage of her career, the Tory leader was interested far more in healing social wounds and bringing about 'peace', 'security', 'stability' and 'community' out of 'conflict', 'insecurity', 'chaos' and 'division', than in promoting the ideology of untrammelled individualism. Towards this end, the new prime minister sought reconciliation rather than conflict in industrial relations with the 'moderate majority' of trade unionists.[91]

In sum, Harold Wilson's collectivist vision of a 'New Britain' lay in tatters. In the context of the chronic and acute socio-economic and political crises of the late 1970s, and against the wider backcloth of 'decline', Thatcher and her colleagues had successfully tarred the BLP as extreme, doctrinaire, disloyal, sectional and unfit to represent the interests of the nation and the 'free world'. The future of the country now lay in the hands of a 'fundamentalist', anti-socialist free marketer.

As will be evident from the preceding narrative, economic issues exerted a major influence upon politics in 1970s Britain. But it will also be evident that politicians, their policies and their institutions were not passive reflections of pre-given economic 'facts'. Rather, these political agents played an active and important role in giving life, substance and social meaning to these 'facts', in putting their own interpretations and representations upon them and in trying to convince the electorate that their particular diagnoses and prescriptions were the best ones on offer. We have seen, moreover, that the interpretations and policies devised were couched not only in economic but also in political, social and cultural terms. For example, as noted by David Butler and Dennis Kavanagh, Thatcher's beliefs in reducing taxes and the role of the state and in restoring individualism and personal independence were as much moral as material in assumption and character.[92] We have observed that politicians' economic policies and prescriptions also often contained and conveyed to the public codes and messages about the issues of class and nation, of the free and un-free worlds, of sectional and national interests, and of what was pragmatic, responsible, moderate and loyal, as opposed to doctrinaire, irresponsible, extreme and disloyal. These policies were also frequently set within explicit or implicit racialised, gendered and classed boundaries.

They confirm one of the central theses of this study – that Labour politics and politics in general involved far more than 'bread and butter' issues. Yet, once again, the historiography of Labour politics in these years has for the most part concentrated too narrowly and literally upon the 'economic' within the restricting confines of the institution of the party. In the process, some of the important social, cultural, political and ideological significations and associations of these 'bread and butter' concerns and key relations between and among political parties and actors, such as the tarring of Labour, have been either ignored or understated.[93]

Conclusion

Part IV has investigated the mixed fortunes of Labour in Australia and Britain during the 'long mid-century' from the 1940s to the end of the 1970s. I have argued that Labour in both countries was most successful when, as during the 1940s and parts of the 1960s and 1970s in Britain and for most of the 1940s and the 'Whitlam years' in Australia, it combined 'modern', progressive economic, political and social policies, a vision of the 'new nation' and, at least in the 1940s and early 1950s, a 'new Commonwealth' with an appeal not only to its traditional and increasingly 'taken-for-granted' male working-class constituents but also to the wider 'radical people'. Labour electoral successes were also rooted in perceptions on the part of voters that it was economically competent and successful and that it was united. In contrast, Labour found itself 'out in the cold' for most of the period in Australia and for large parts of it in Britain when it was divided and when its political opponents appropriated the language and factors of economic success and improved living standards. While anti-socialism and the tarring of mainstream Labour as 'extreme' and disloyal to the nation and the Empire/Commonwealth were of fundamental and sustained importance to the successes of the Right at the federal level in Australia, they were of more variable and limited importance both at the state level there and in terms of the national political picture as a whole in Britain. These national differences stemmed largely from the contrasting geo-political situations of the two countries and, in key ways, their dissimilar political, social and cultural patterns and traditions of 'rule', of accommodation and conflict, inclusion and exclusion.

While the relevant labour historiography in both Australia and Britain for this period has been strong on domestic 'bread and butter' matters and the internal, institutional aspects of Labour politics, it has generally neglected the comparative and trans-national aspects. It has also, more so in the British than the Australian case, been far less attentive to the extra-economic and extra-institutional aspects of Labour politics and the important ways in which the fortunes of Labour were affected by its relations with other parties. This has led in Britain, for example, to either neglect or underestimation of the ways in which Labour's political opponents during the decade of the 1970s sought to tar it, with varying degrees of success, as extreme and disloyal. Lastly, we have observed that although ties and connections were maintained between the labour movements of the two countries, they became less intimate as Britain moved closer to Europe and Australia to the United States. As we will see in Part V, however, this state of affairs, began to change in the 1990s when, in response to the striking successes of Bob Hawke and Paul Keating at the polls, 'third way' Labour leaders in Britain looked partly to the 'Australian model' for inspiration in their battle against hegemonic Thatcherism.

Notes

1 For examples of the international and trans-national dimensions of 1960s radicalism see Sean Scalmer, *Dissent Events: Protest, the Media and the Political Gimmick in Australia* (Sydney: UNSW Press, 2002), ch. 1, pp. 50–5, 120–36; Bolton, *Oxford History* pp. 168–74, ch. 8; Ann Curthoys, *Freedom Ride: A Freedom Rider Remembers* (Crows Nest: Allen and Unwin, 2002); Nicola Pizzolato, 'Workers and Revolutionaries on the Shop Floor: The Breakdown of Industrial relations in the Automobile Plants of Detroit and Turin, 1947–1973' (PhD dissertation, University College London, 2003).

2 For Evatt and Curtin see, for example, *Labour Party Annual Report, 1942*; Middleton Papers, JSM/INT/ASA/3lii, JSM/INt/ASA/31. For Bevin see Alan Bullock, *The Life and Times of Ernest Bevin*, vol. 1, *Trade Union Leader 1881–1940* (London: Heinemann, 1969), pp. 617, 628–9. For Attlee see Middleton Papers, 'Labour Party International Department Delegation to Moscow and China, 1954', Box, 'Press Reports and Articles'; *Worker*, 6, 13 September 1954. For Pollitt see Communist Party Archives: Australia and New Zealand, 1960, CP/IND/POLL/04/11, 1 Folder, LHASC; *Tribune*, 20 April, 25 May, 22 June 1963. Pollitt died of a stroke at sea after visiting New Zealand and Australia. See *Tribune*, 6 July 1963 for a tribute to Pollitt. Scott, *Running on Empty*, pp. 27–32, 57, 65–71; Frank Bongiorno, 'Fabian Socialism and British Australia, 1890–1972', in Buckner and Francis, *Rediscovering the British World*, pp. 209–31.
3 *Australian Worker*, 18 December 1963; *Worker*, 9 December 1963; Scott, *Running on Empty*, p. 68.
4 Bongiorno, 'Fabian Socialism', pp. 217–19.
5 *Worker*, 5 December 1966; *Australian Worker*, 30 November 1966; Scott, *Running on Empty*, p. 62.
6 General Election Material, February 1974, 'Labour Party Information Department: News Releases', 27 February 1974', LHASC (uncatalogued). For pen pictures of British labour leaders see *Australian Worker*, 12, 19, 26 October 1949; *Worker*, 23 April 1951 for a tribute to Ernest Bevin, 'one of the greatest men to arise in twentieth-century politics'.
7 *Worker*, 4 March 1963.
8 For Henderson see *Worker*, 30 March 1927. For Evatt see *Labour Party Annual Report 1942*, pp. 97–8, Middleton Papers, JSM/INT/ASA/10, pp. 195–7. For the ACTU and the TUC see the material held in the ACTU file, N 21/63, 'England, New Zealand, Geneva 1937–1940', especially the correspondence between Walter Citrine of the TUC and C.A. Crofts of the ACTU, in the Noel Butlin Archives, ANU. I am grateful to Maggie Shapley, University Archivist, the Australian National University, for this reference. See also Scott, *Running on Empty*, p. 25.
9 Deery and Redfern, 'No Lasting Peace?', 66.
10 Correspondence from Stuart Macintyre, 4 October 2009.
11 Scott, *Running on Empty*, p. 7.
12 Wayne Reynolds, *Australia's Bid for the Atomic Bomb* (Carlton South: Melbourne University Press, 2000), pp. 3, 21–2, chs 2, 6; David Goldsworthy, *Losing the Blanket: Australia and the End of Britain's Empire* (Carlton South: Melbourne University Press, 2002), pp. 3–9, 174.
13 Ward, *Australia and the British Embrace*, p. 10; Goldsworthy, *Losing the Blanket*, p. 7; David Goldsworthy, 'Menzies, Britain and the Commonwealth: The Old Order Changeth', in Frank Cain (ed.), *Menzies in War and Peace* (St Leonard's, NSW: Allen and Unwin, 1997); Bongiorno, 'Fabian Socialism', p. 224; *Worker*, 2, 21 January 1963.
14 *Worker*, 21 January 1963; *Australian Worker*, 2 January 1963.
15 *Australian Worker*, 13 February 1963; Reynolds, *Australia's Bid*, ch. 9, pp. 173–83, 211–18; Goldsworthy, *Losing the Blanket*, pp. 175–7.
16 Bolton, *Oxford History*, p. 183.
17 Goldsworthy, *Losing the Blanket*, p. 2.
18 *Worker*, 4 March 1963; *Australian Worker*, 13 February 1963; *Sydney Morning Herald*, 18 February, 27 March 1963. See also *Age*, 18 February, 27, 28 March 1963 for a similarly upbeat account of the Queen's visit and reception. See Spearritt, 'Royal Progress', 233–7 for a more subdued account.
19 *Sydney Morning Herald*, 1, 3 April 2000. See also *Age*, 1 April 2000; *Sunday Age*, 2 April 2000.
20 Bolton, *Oxford History*, p. 174.
21 Brett, *Australian Liberals*, p. 145.
22 Macintyre, *Concise History*, p. 235.
23 *Ibid*.

24 Bolton, *Oxford History*, pp. 184–8.
25 Scott, *Fading Loyalties*, pp. 22–3.
26 Brett, *Australian Liberals*, p. 146; *Worker*, 10 January, 2 October, 13 November, 11, 25 December 1972; *Australian Worker*, 6 December 1972.
27 Robert Manne, 'The Whitlam Revolution', in Robert Manne (ed.), *The Australian Century: Political Struggle in the Building of a Nation* (Melbourne: Text Publishing, 1999), p. 188.
28 Macintyre, *Concise History*, pp. 234–5; Brett, *Australian Liberals*, pp. 146–7; Kirk, 'Traditionalists and Progressives', p. 57; Bolton, *Oxford History*, p. 175.
29 Macintyre, *Concise History*, pp. 236–8; Bolton, *Oxford History*, ch. 9; Manne, 'Whitlam Revolution', pp. 188–97; *Australian Worker*, 20 December 1972, 17 January 1973 (for Australian 'disenchantment', 'for a long time', with the Vietnam War); Hilary M. Carey, 'Australian Religious Culture from Federation to the new Pluralism', in Jayasuriya, Walker and Gothard, *Legacies of White Australia*, pp. 86–7.
30 Macintyre, *Concise History*, pp. 238–41; Bolton, *Oxford History*, pp. 231–43; *Sun-Herald*, 14 December 1975.
31 *Sydney Morning Herald*, 7, 13, 15 December 1975; Bolton, *Oxford History*, pp. 243–4.
32 Bolton, *Oxford History*, p. 243; *Sydney Morning Herald*, 10, 12 December 1977; *Sun-Herald*, 11 December 1977.
33 *Sydney Morning Herald*, 1, 5, 6, 13, 18, 20 October 1980; Bolton, *Oxford History*, ch. 10.
34 Macintyre, *Concise History*, ch. 9; Bolton, *Oxford History*, p. 270; Alan Ramsey, 'The Hayden Years: 1976–82', in Faulkner and Macintyre (eds), *True Believers*; Paul Kelly, *The End of Certainty: Power Politics and Business in Australia* (Crows Nest, NSW: Allen and Unwin, 2008), p. 19.
35 See the special issue of *Contemporary British History*, edited by Glen O'Hara and Helen Parr, 'The Wilson Governments 1964–70 Reconsidered', 20:3 (2006); Alastair J. Reid and Henry Pelling, *A Short History of the Labour Party* (Basingstoke: Macmillan, 11th edition, 1996), chs 8, 9.
36 Howlett, '"Golden Age"'.
37 *The Times*, 13 October 1964.
38 Thorpe, *History of the British Labour Party*, pp. 153–4; Steven Fielding, 'Rethinking Labour's 1964 Campaign', in the special issue of *Contemporary British History*, edited by Peter Barberis, 'The 1964 General Election – the "Not Quite But" and "But Only Just" Election', 21:3 (2007), 309–24; Jim Tomlinson, 'Labour and the Economy', in Tanner, Thane and Tiratsoo (eds), *Labour's First Century*, p. 61.
39 *Guardian*, 12 September 1964; David E. Butler and Anthony King, *The British General Election of 1964* (London: Macmillan, 1965).
40 *Guardian*, 6 October 1964; Thorpe, *History of the British Labour Party*, p. 155.
41 *Guardian*, 12 September 1964.
42 Kirk, 'Traditionalists and Progressives', 70.
43 Kirk, 'Traditionalists and Progressives', 64–71; Andrew Markus, 'Of Continuities and Discontinuities: Reflections on a Century of Australian Immigration Control', in Jayasuriya, Walker and Gothard, *Legacies of White Australia*, pp. 178–9.
44 Thorpe, *History of the British Labour Party*, p. 155.
45 *Guardian*, 17 October 1964. This newspaper had changed its name from the *Manchester Guardian* to the *Guardian* in August 1959.
46 *Guardian*, 8, 31 March, 1, 2 April 1966; *The Times*, 1, 2, 5 April 1966.
47 Scott, *Running on Empty*, pp. 68–9.
48 Tomlinson, 'Labour and the Economy', p. 62.
49 *Guardian*, 2, 7 March 1966; *The Times*, 22 March 1966; *Daily Telegraph*, 11 March 1966; *Daily Worker*, 26 March 1966. The *Guardian* claimed (1, 5 April 1966) that, unlike the election of 1964, race had not figured prominently in the 1966 contest.
50 Brooke, 'Labour and the "Nation"', p. 170.
51 *Guardian*, 16, 17, 18, 19 June 1970; *The Times*, 17, 18 June 1970.

52 Thorpe, *History of the British Labour Party*, p. 178; *The Times*, 20 June 1970.
53 *Guardian*, 20 June 1970.
54 *Guardian*, 17, 18, 19, 20 June 1970.
55 *The Times*, 28 May, 18, 20 (editorial; Professor Richard Rose), 30 June (Woodrow Wyatt, *Times Diary*) 1970; *Financial Times*, 15, 17, 19 June 1970.
56 *Guardian*, 20 June 1970; *The Times*, 19 June 1970.
57 Reid and Pelling, *Short History of the Labour Party*, pp. 144–6; Morgan, *People's Peace*, pp. 321–4.
58 Tara Martin, 'End of an Era? Class Politics, Memory and Britain's Winter of Discontent' (PhD dissertation, University of Manchester, 2008).
59 *Guardian*, 8 February, 2 March 1974; *The Times*, 8 February, 2 March 1974.
60 *Guardian*, 8 February 1974.
61 *Ibid.*
62 *The Times*, 8 February 1974.
63 It does, not, for example, figure either in the relevant histories of the Labour Party cited in this chapter or in the reminiscences of leading Labour politicians such as Denis Healey (*The Time of My Life*, London: Michael Joseph, 1989). For a partial exception to the general rule see David E. Butler and Dennis Kavanagh, *The British General Election of February 1974* (London: Macmillan, 1974), pp. 51, 73, 82, 173–4. While Butler and Kavanagh record the fact of smearing in the press, they underestimate its usage and importance among politicians. For reference to attacks on the 'militant minority' of trade union leaders, see Morgan, *War and Peace*, pp. 347, 349, 379; Thurlow, *Secret State*, pp. 333–9; Christopher M. Andrew, *The Defence of the Realm: The Authorized History of MI5* (London: Allen Lane, 2009).
64 Guardian, 11, 20 February 1974; *The Times*, 7 February (Ronald Butt), 8 February (editorial), 26 February (Bernard Levin) 1974.
65 *Guardian*, 11, 20 February 1974; *The Times* 9 February 1974.
66 *The Times*, 8, 9 February 1974.
67 *Guardian*, 4, 7, 8 February 1974; *The Times*, 9, 26 February 1974.
68 *Guardian*, 11 February 1974; *The Times*, 11 February 1974.
69 *The Times*, 11, 25, 28 February 1974.
70 *Guardian*, 11 February 1974.
71 *Ibid.*
72 *Guardian*, 4, 8 February 1974. The Conservative majority at Wolverhampton South West, the seat vacated by Powell in opposition to the government's EEC policy, fell from 14,467 to 6,901 in the February election. See *Guardian*, 1, 2 March 1974.
73 Reid and Pelling, *Short History Labour Party*, p. 146.
74 *Guardian*, 9, 22, 23 February 1974.
75 Butler and Kavanagh, *British General Election February 1974*, p. 82.
76 *Guardian*, 9 February 1974; *The Times*, 26 February 1974.
77 *Guardian*, 1 March 1974.
78 Reid and Pelling, *Short History of the Labour Party*, pp. 147–9.
79 *Guardian*, 2, 8 October 1974; David E. Butler and Dennis Kavanagh, *The British General Election of October 1974* (London: Macmillan, 1975), pp. 111, 173.
80 *Guardian*, 7 October 1974.
81 *Guardian*, 3, 1, 12 October 1974; General Election Material, February, October 1974, 'Labour Party Information Department: News Releases', 9, 10, 22 February, 22, 23 October 1974, Box, 'Manifestos: All Parties', LHASC (uncatalogued).
82 Reid and Pelling, *Short History of the Labour Party*, p. 157.
83 Scott, *Running on Empty*, pp. 73–4; Stuart Holland, *The Socialist Challenge* (London: Quartet, 1975); CSE London Working Group, *The Alternative Economic Strategy: A Labour Movement Response to the Economic Crisis* (London: Conference of Socialist Economists Books, 1980).
84 Andrew Thorpe, *History of the British Labour Party*, pp. 199–200; Reid and Pelling, *Short History of the Labour Party*, pp. 158–60; David Butler and Dennis Kavanagh, *The British General Election of 1979* (London: Macmillan, 1980); Andrew Gamble,

[233]

The Free Economy and the Strong State: The Politics of Thatcherism (Basingstoke: Macmillan, 1994), p. 105.

85 Andrew Thorpe, *History of the British Labour Party*, p. 200. For a similar view see *Guardian*, 8 May 1979.

86 Although some politically sophisticated contemporaries mistakenly believed that Britain's future lay more with 'pragmatic' than 'ideological' politics. See, for example, Peter Jenkins, 'No Brave New Worlds', *Guardian*, 1 May 1979.

87 David E. Butler and Dennis Kavanagh, *The British General Election of 1979* (London: Macmillan, 1980), p. 333.

88 *Guardian*, 1 May 1979.

89 *Daily Telegraph*, 25, 30 April 1979.

90 *Daily Telegraph*, 25, 30 April, 1 May 1979; *Guardian*, 26, 30 April, 1, 2, May 1979. Successful strike action prevented the publication of *The Times* during this period.

91 For Thatcher's policies see General Election material, 1979, 'Conservative Party Speeches', 'Conservative Central Office: News Service', LHASC (uncatalogued); *Daily Telegraph*, 30 April, 1, 2, 4 May 1979; *Guardian*, 20, 24, 26, 30 April, 1, 2, 3, 8 May 1979.

92 Butler and Kavanagh, *British General Election 1979*, p. 329.

93 Even those 'labour histories' concerned not only with economic, but also political and social explanations of Labour's electoral defeats have failed to consider the issue and significance of tarring and 'the politics of loyalism'. See, for example, Steven Fielding, *The Labour Party: 'Socialism' and Society since 1951* (Manchester: Manchester University Press, 1997), Introduction. The definitive works of Butler and Kavanagh on the 1974 and 1979 elections refer to, but underplay, the significance of smearing. See, for example, Butler and Kavanagh, *British General Election 1979*, p. 348.

PART V

Traditionalism, modernisation and revisionism

CHAPTER TEN

Successes and failures

The electoral record

The ALP and the BLP experienced mixed, fluctuating and sharply contrasting fortunes, both domestically and comparatively, between 1980 and 2010. For example, while Bob Hawke and Paul Keating achieved the unprecedented feat of securing the ALP five successive federal election victories between 1983 and 1996, John Howard's Liberal-dominated coalition government then ruled the federal roost for more than eleven years. There followed, of course, Kevin Rudd's landslide ALP victory in 2007. Yet Rudd's sudden fall from grace, in June 2010, left his successor, Julia Gillard, with the formidable task of reversing the ALP's steep fall in the polls. In August 2010, however, Gillard failed to secure an outright federal election victory.

The 1980s were also extremely successful years for Labor at the state level. Between 1982 and the early 1990s the ALP enjoyed virtually uninterrupted control in Victoria, South Australia and Western Australia, was in power in New South Wales from 1976 to 1988, and regained Queensland (albeit after being in the political wilderness from the Split onwards) and Tasmania in 1989. From the mid 1990s to the end of the decade Labor suffered defeats in most of the states, although it recaptured its former hegemony in New South Wales. The ALP, however, has dominated state governments during the first decade of the new millennium. On balance, the party has fared much better at the federal and state levels from the 1980s to the present than it did between the 1940s and the 1970s.[1]

In overall terms this has not been the case in Britain. As we observed in the last chapter, after occupying national office for most of the period from the mid 1960s to the late 1970s, the BLP was defeated in 1979. For almost two decades thereafter Britain experienced Conservative political rule, the messianic and radical 'market fundamentalist' Margaret Thatcher being succeeded by the more conventional, 'grey' figure of

John Major. As we will see below, during these 'wasteland' years Labour was racked by serious internal conflicts and a lack of strong leadership and common purpose. The party's 'rising stars', such as Tony Blair and Gordon Brown, looked to the successful examples of Bill Clinton's 'progressivism' in the United States and the Hawke–Keating pragmatic, 'third way' course in Australia in order to revive British Labour's fortunes.

In 1997, of course, the BLP did finally regain national office after effectively transforming and 're-branding' itself as New Labour. Intent upon avoiding the 'excesses' of both Thatcherite individualism and Labourite collectivist interventionism, New Labour set out to restore the party's political fortunes by creating a 'young', 'progressive' and 'modern' country along 'third way' lines. In this way the party would aim to realise Labour's 'traditional' values and goals under 'modern' conditions. For example, the 'traditional' policies and objectives of socio-economic regulation, fairness and justice would be combined with 'new' and 'modern' neo-liberal emphases upon an increased role for markets, individualism and competition.

It would become a matter of considerable political and academic debate as to whether elements of the 'new' outweighed those of the 'old' and 'traditional' in New Labour's practice. At this point it is sufficient simply to note the fact of this debate, that it had also taken place in relation to the Hawke–Keating 'experiment' in Australia and that I will pay attention during the course of Part V to the nature, the overall balance of elements of continuity and change and the similarities and differences in 'third way' thought and practice in Britain and Australia.

My immediate concern rests with the fact that just as Hawke and Keating achieved unprecedented electoral success, so did New Labour under Tony Blair. The latter won three successive general elections, in 1997, 2002 and 2005, an achievement unmatched by Labour in its previous history. In the wake of Blair's 1997 triumph, it was the turn of downbeat Australian ALPers, disheartened by the defeat of their party in 1996 and the growing hegemony of Howard's 'extreme', neo-liberal ideology, to visit Britain and to attempt to apply the 'lessons' of Blair's successes to their own party and country.[2]

The most recent British general election, of May 2010, however, has seen Gordon Brown, who succeeded Blair in 2007, defeated by the self-professed 'modern' and 'progressive' Conservative David Cameron. Cameron dismissed Brown's Labour Party as 'reactionary', as mired in 'the old ways of command and control'.[3]

The BLP's problems, while particularly acute in 2010, are by no means entirely new. For example, while 'early' and 'mid' New Labour enjoyed some success in local elections, it also encountered mid-term reverses. These 'consistently gave the government a share of the vote significantly below its poll ratings'.[4] Especially under Brown's leadership, moreover, a combination of factors underpinned the major decline in Labour's local standing, recruitment, appeal and electoral performance. These comprised the financial crisis and recession of 2008–9, the government's economic policy failings, 'some of the most personal attacks ever mounted' and cabinet resignations over Brown's 'governing style' and the scandals of MPs expenses and New Labour 'sleaze'.[5] In the European and county council elections 'meltdown' of June 2009 the Tories 'surged', the right-wing British National Party (BNP) won its first European seats and Labour received less than 16 per cent of the votes cast for the European parliament and 'lost control of its four remaining county councils'.[6] Defeats of this magnitude must be set within the context of the unravelling, over time, of New Labour's broad and initially successful 'catch-all' socio-political appeal, the haemorrhaging of its constituency base and the decline, despite some good results in the 2010 election, in its support in its traditional working-class heartlands of the North, Scotland and South Wales.[7]

Issues and explanations

Labour successes and failures at the polls between 1980 and 2010 have revolved around a set of issues made largely familiar to the reader in other chapters of this study. While these issues will be examined in detail in the course of Part V, it is important in this introductory chapter to outline them and to provide the reader with some brief examples.

First, economic concerns have dominated the political agenda in both countries during this latest phase of 'globalisation'. These concerns comprise the key issues of economic success and failure, competent economic management and the ability successfully to 'get the economic message across' to the electorate.

For example, 'old' Labour's inability during the Thatcher years to discard its reputation for economic extravagance, incompetence, adherence to outdated economic doctrines and being part of the reason, rather than the solution, for the country's economic decline, cost it dear. In contrast, the initial fiscal and monetary caution displayed by New Labour upon its assumption of office in 1997, combined with the boom years of the new millennium and the party's growing reputation for economic competence, underpinned the increasingly widespread beliefs that Gordon Brown was the most formidable Chancellor of the Exchequer in living memory, that he seemingly had a reasonable claim to have ended the historic cycle of boom and bust, and that in its 'new' form Labour had finally 'come of age' economically. Yet the recent financial crisis and recession have seen the reputations of both Brown and his party plummet. They have not only been held responsible by many for the crisis of a system of deregulated capitalism which they had so fervently championed, but have also been widely perceived in Britain as weak, indecisive, divided and largely ineffective in their responses.[8]

In Australia the Hawke–Keating economic 'experiment' was by no means an unqualified triumph. Yet we will see that Hawke and Keating were extremely successful in convincing the electorate that in their hands the ALP had become the party of 'superior economic management' and that, in contrast to the failures of the previous government of Malcolm Fraser, they would rally the nation around a programme of reforms in order to enable Australia to compete successfully in the 'new' world of 'globalisation'. Hawke, in particular, was especially persuasive in his argument that, although often painful in the short term, their economic reforms would be cushioned by improvements in job creation and the social wage, that they were the *sine qua non* of future prosperity and success and that (in the manner of Margaret Thatcher in Britain) that there was no viable alternative to them.

As indicated above, their electoral successes lasted from 1983 until 1996, although during the early to mid 1990s there were clear signs that many of the ALP's traditional supporters believed that Keating was becoming too extreme in his economic neo-liberalism and too 'politically correct'. Keating's nemesis, John Howard, offered moderate conservatism at the 1996 election and social stability in the face of the unending and often disruptive changes introduced by Labor.[9]

It was not until 2007 that Howard finally met his electoral downfall at the hands of the strongly Christian, clean-cut and moderate Kevin Rudd. Despite continuing economic prosperity, Rudd's criticism of Howard as having gone 'too far' in his economic neo-liberalism, as seen particularly in his attempt to replace the regulatory, needs-based traditional system of arbitration with the individualistic and divisive market-based scheme, Work Choices, found widespread support among the electorate. (It also raised the spectre of Bruce's unsuccessful proposal similarly to dismantle the Commonwealth system of arbitration during his 1929 federal contest with Scullin.)

Unlike Brown, Rudd was not tainted with support for deregulated capitalism. While endorsing 'open, competitive markets', he condemned unreservedly the 'greed' at the core of the 'extreme capitalism' or 'market fundamentalism' which had characterised the global economic system and economic orthodoxy since the 1980s. Rudd sought to restore a 'proper' balance between the 'flexibility' and 'rigour' of markets and the 'fairness' and 'fair go' traditionally characteristic of the Australian Commonwealth and its system of industrial relations. In addition, the 2008–9 recession was much milder and the recovery earlier and far more pronounced in Australia than in Britain. Rudd's unqualified 'orthodox Keynesian approach' to the crisis was far more successful in promoting recovery and renewed growth than Brown's vacillating approach between neo-liberal and regulatory policy prescriptions.[10]

Yet in June 2010 Rudd suddenly paid the ultimate political price – his effective removal from office by the power brokers within the ALP – for the widespread perception among voters that he, rather than the mining companies, constituted the real threat to the nation's jobs, investment and continuing economic prosperity.[11]

Second, notwithstanding their crucial importance, economic factors, once again, do not constitute the complete explanation of Labour's political successes and failures. As in the past, the extent to which Labour was able to appropriate the notion of the progressive, modern and inclusive nation had a strong bearing upon its political fortunes in both countries between 1980 and 2010. To be sure, apart from Britain in the 1980s, the 'Red' tarring of Labour as extreme and disloyal to the nation and the Empire/Commonwealth became far less widespread and significant than in the past. This resulted mainly from the end of the Cold War, the unambiguously pro-western stance of the 'modernised' ALP and New Labour and the diminished importance of Commonwealth ties. Yet the key importance of 'the national' in politics remained.

For example, the appeal to 'national reconciliation', 'national recovery' and 'national reconstruction' lay at the heart of Hawke's successful election campaign in 1983.[12] A key factor in Keating's victory against the 'Thatcherite' John Hewson in 1993 was that the latter was portrayed as 'un-Australian' in his adoption of 'free market dogmatism', too divisive and sectional and inattentive to the country's traditions of fairness, regulation and social reform. In contrast, Keating re-invented himself as the champion not only of 'a synthesis between market-orientated reforms and a revived version of the ALP social justice tradition', but also of progressive cultural nationalism.[13]

In turn, Keating, in 1996, and John Howard, in 2007, suffered from the fact that they were perceived to have become too sectional and insufficiently 'national' in their appeals to the electorate. Keating's neo-liberalism alienated much of the 'blue collar heartland', while Howard's appeal to Anglos, Celts and the rich, combined with a marked fall in his support among working- and lower-middle-class 'battlers', meant that his appeal at the 2007 election was too narrow and restrictive in character.[14]

At the same election a successful Kevin Rudd took great care to present himself as the 'true' representative of 'All Australians' committed to national reconciliation, harmony and progress. By mid 2010, however, Rudd had lost this position. His attempt to portray the largely foreign-owned mining companies and their opposition to the proposed 40 per cent tax on their 'super-profits' as 'greedy', 'unfair' and motivated largely by 'outside', 'self' and sectional interest rather than the welfare of the nation as a whole, failed to resonate with large sections of the population, especially in the mining states. In contrast, the extremely well-organised anti-government advertising campaign of the mining companies was hugely successful. The latter, as observed by Sean Scalmer, maintained that the tax 'made Australian projects uncompetitive, that mining had delivered Australian prosperity and that it would be put at risk by a punitive and impractical measure'. Although the companies presented largely economic arguments, some among the government's opponents resorted to the traditional anti-Labor smear that the government had adopted the 'old fashioned', 'outdated' and 'un-Australian' rhetoric of 'class warfare'.[15]

In 1980s Britain the failure of the Labour Party to develop a national appeal lay at the heart of its inability seriously to challenge the Tories at the polls. While Labour's support was concentrated in the North, Scotland and Wales and most of the big cities, with the notable exception of London, the Tories dominated England, especially from the Midlands southwards. Moreover, as Hobsbawm noted in the aftermath of the 1987 general election, Labour had lost 'majority support among the working class', with 'barely more than one skilled worker in three' voting Labour and 'six out of ten trade unionists' declining to support 'the party the unions had founded'. Perhaps most tellingly, in a manner reminiscent of the interwar years, 'almost half the Tory' vote in 1987 'came from workers'.[16] As we will see in more detail below, Thatcher and her colleagues were extremely successful in branding Labour as sectional, extreme, divided and unfit to rule. As seen especially in the Falklands War of 1982 and the 1984–85 miners' strike, the Tories were adept at capturing the national 'patriotic' ground.

It was hardly surprising that Neil Kinnock, John Smith and, especially, Tony Blair and his New Labour colleagues spent so much subsequent time and effort in attempting to recapture it. At the 1997 election New Labour successfully presented itself to the electorate, in contrast to the 'worn out', divided and 'sleazy' Conservatives, as a united, honest and 'new modern force for progress', as the builder of a 'young' and 'dynamic' country, ready to rise to the challenges of the 'new' era of 'globalisation' and as the most effective opponent of 'outdated establishment attitudes that hold us all back'.[17] In the run up to the 2010 election, however, it was the turn of the Tories and the Liberal Democrats successfully to portray New Labour as 'tired', 'reactionary', hopelessly divided and lacking a 'moral' vision, and themselves as the force best equipped the carry the nation forward.[18]

Labour's successful adoption of the 'national' rather than 'sectional' interest, with reference to the 'progressivism' of both New Labour and the Hawke, Keating and Rudd governments, marks an acceleration of the continuing retreat from or, more accurately, clear rejection of, the politics of 'class' and 'mass' in favour of an embrace of 'catch-all' issues and policies.[19] This is understandable in the context of de-industrialisation, the decline of heavy industry and its predominantly male manual workers. Labour 'progressives' in both countries carefully cultivated the image of their parties as representing the 'middle ground' of politics and the middle classes, or at least the more forward-looking of them, as well as their increasingly taken-for-granted, and somewhat neglected, traditional working-class supporters.

They also laid claim to the 'multi-cultural' interest and constituency. In the context of the invasions of Iraq and Afghanistan, the global 'war on terror', escalating Islamophobia and the attempted flight of war-torn refugees and other asylum seekers to 'the West', this claim has limited validity. Establishment commitments to multi-culturalism, toleration and openness have existed alongside their far less tolerant, more restrictive and often highly racialised insistence upon the crucial importance of 'assimilation' and the 'defence of national boundaries' against 'illegal' and 'extreme' would-be entrants.[20] As we will see below, the racialised politics of national 'solidarity', 'defence' and 'border security', complete with their constituent elements of inclusion and exclusion, good and evil, have been played, with varying results, by ALP and New Labour politicians, as well as their opponents, on several occasions since 1980.[21]

Third, questions of Labour unity and disunity, combined with the nature and quality of its leadership, have exerted a significant influence upon political outcomes. For example, extremely debilitating divisions, conflicts and splits within the early 1980s BLP, the formation of the Social Democratic Party (SDP) in 1981 and the weak leadership of Michael Foot contributed significantly to Labour's truly awful performance at the 1983 general election, when the party received its lowest share of the poll for sixty years, 28.3 per cent, and only 2.3 per cent more than the SDP-Liberal Alliance. The split in the progressive opposition, moreover, ensured that the Tories would retain power for the foreseeable future.[22]

The catastrophe of 1983 and Labour's continuing electoral failures in the 1980s and 1990s convinced Blair's 'early' New Labour of the need to develop strong and decisive leadership and the firm impression of internal party unity and common purpose in order to reverse Tory successes at the polls.[23] Blair's charismatic leadership and his skills as a communicator undoubtedly played an important part in the early and mid-term successes of New Labour. In contrast, growing internal dissatisfaction, divisions, and challenges to Prime Minister Gordon Brown's leadership have further added to New Labour's recent misfortunes and poor public standing.[24]

In Australia the easy-going and popular Bob Hawke brought much-needed healing powers and firm, but largely consensual, leadership to the ALP. The more abrasive Keating experienced a mixed response from both within the ALP and the wider electorate, while his successors, Kim Beazley and Mark Latham, failed to overturn Howard's ascendancy. By June 2010 Rudd's 'weak' shelving of the government's very moderate carbon emissions scheme and his 'bullying' at the hands of the mining companies, combined with his growing unpopularity and lack of an effective base or movement within the ALP, meant that he would 'have to go', whether willingly or unwillingly, in the interests of party unity, morale and wider support.[25]

Lastly, during this period the 'professionalisation' of both the ALP and the BLP proceeded apace. Mainly male university graduates and 'career' politicians increasingly dominated the leadership positions of both parties, especially beyond the local level. Partly as a response to the decline of the 'traditional' working class, these leaders were keen to appeal to the professional and other sections of the middle class. In terms of party policy, there was an increasing emphasis upon 'target setting' and other aspects of 'managerialism'.[26]

Having provided a summary of Labour's electoral record and identified key issues, areas of debate and explanation, I am now in a position to proceed to a more detailed investigation of Labour's fluctuating electoral fortunes. This is undertaken in the next two chapters. The first focuses upon Labour and anti-Labour politics between 1983 and 1997, while the second concentrates upon the past thirteen years.

Notes

1 James and Markey, 'Class and Labour', 25; Paul Kelly, *The End of Certainty* (Crows Nest: Allen and Unwin, 2008), p. 29; Australian Government and Politics Database, University of Western Australia, http://elections.uwa.edu.au; *Guardian*, 12 February 2010 (Julian Glover, 'The Abbott Portent'); *Sydney Morning Herald*, 23, 24 August 2010.
2 Pandazopoulos and Booth, *Blair Project*.
3 *Guardian*, 9 April, 7, 8 May 2010; *Observer*, 9 May 2010.
4 Alastair J. Reid and Henry Pelling, *A Short History of the Labour Party* (Basingstoke: Palgrave Macmillan, 12th edition, 2005), pp. 193–5; Charles Pattie, 'New Labour

and the Electorate', in Steve Ludlam and Martin J. Smith (eds), *New Labour in Government* (Basingstoke: Macmillan, 2001), pp. 32, 52–3.

5 See, for example, *Guardian*, 6 June 2009, 14, 26 January, 23 March 2010; *Observer*, 10 January 2010.

6 *Guardian*, 4, 8, 9, 13, 15 June 2009.

7 James and Markey, 'Class and Labour', p. 29; Pattie, 'New Labour and the Electorate', pp. 52–4.

8 *Guardian*, 1 January, 3 April 2009, 27 February, 3, 11 March, 9, 10 (Polly Toynbee), 16, 17, 19, 20 April 2010; *Observer*, 4 January 2009, 18 April 2010 (editorial, Andrew Rawnsley).

9 Kelly, 'Labor and Globalisation', p. 232; Kelly, *End of Certainty*, p. 19; Judith Brett, 'Relaxed and Comfortable: The Liberal Party's Australia', *Quarterly Essay*, 19 (2005), 1–79; Manne, *Left Right Left*, pp. 335–9.

10 Mungo MacCallum, 'Australian Story: Kevin Rudd and the Lucky Country', *Quarterly Essay*, 36 (2009), 13, 15–18; Robert Manne, 'Is Neo-Liberalism Finished?', *Quarterly Essay*, 36 (2009), 69.

11 *Sydney Morning Herald*, 27 April, 26, 28 May, 24, 25 June 2010.

12 Kelly, *End of Certainty*, pp. 19–26.

13 *Ibid.*, pp. ix, xii, xiv, xvii–xviii.

14 See the Geoff Pryor cartoon, 'Son of Labor. Paul Keating and the Australian Labor Party Lose the Blue Collar Heartland', in the National Library of Australia's digital pictures collection, http://nla.gov.au/nla.pic-vn3513725; Kelly, 'Labor and Globalisation', pp. 260–1; MacCallum, 'Australian Story', 30–1; O'Reilly, *New Progressive Dilemma*, pp. 16–18; *Sydney Morning Herald*, 26 (Judith Brett), 27 November 2007; *Sun Herald*, 18 November 2007; *Herald Sun*, 27 November 2007 (Geoffrey Blainey).

15 *Sydney Morning Herald*, 26 November 2007; Sean Scalmer, e-mail correspondence with the author, 5 July 2010.

16 Eric Hobsbawm, 'Out of the Wilderness', *Marxism Today* (October 1987), 12–19.

17 Blair, 'News Corp Speech', 17 July 1995.

18 *Guardian*, 26 January, 27 February, 6, 7, 9 April 2010 (David Cameron, 'Labour Are now the Reactionaries, We the Radicals – as this Promise Shows'); *Observer*, 3 January 2010.

19 Irving and Scalmer, 'Public Sphere and Party Change', 227; Kelly, 'Labor and Globalisation', p. 225.

20 *Guardian*, 18 May (Colley), 30 November (Sivanandan), 9 December ('Radical Muslims must integrate, says Blair') 2006; 25 September 2007 (Steve Bell cartoon, 'Browntongue hits Bournemouth'), 12 March 2008 ('Britishness').

21 See, for example, the harsh 'Pacific' and 'Indonesian' 'solutions' adopted by the Howard and Rudd governments to boat people seeking asylum in Australia in 2001 and 2009 respectively. Manne, 'Sending them Home', in his *Left, Right Left*, pp. 392–467; *Sydney Morning Herald*, 7–8, 16, 17–18 October, 12 November 2009; *Australian*, 15 October, 2 November 2009; *Canberra Times*, 28 October 2009.

22 Hobsbawm 'Out of the Wilderness', 12; Martin Pugh, *Speak for Britain! A New History of the Labour Party* (London: The Bodley Head, 2010), p. 373.

23 Dianne Hayter, *Fightback! Labour's Traditional Right in the 1970s and 1980s* (Manchester: Manchester University Press, 2005); *Guardian*, 4 March 2010 (Michael Foot: editorial, Michael White, obituary).

24 *Guardian*, 6 June 2009, 14 January 2010.

25 Kelly, 'Labor and Globalisation', pp. 227–30; Manne, *Left Right Left*, pp. 335–41, 354–6, 363–77; MacCallum, 'Australian Story', *Observer*, 25 November 2007, *Sydney Morning Herald*, 26, 27 November 2007, 16 April, 2008 (editorial), 25 June 2010.

26 Michael Thompson, *Labor without Class: The Gentrification of the ALP* (Annandale: Pluto Press, 1999); Scott, *Running on Empty*, ch. 3.

CHAPTER ELEVEN

From Hawke and Keating to the rise of New Labour, 1983–97

The international and national contexts

In order to chart and understand Labour and anti-Labour politics in these years we must first of all outline the international and national economic, political, social and cultural contexts in which they arose and which exerted a strong influence upon the political choices made. The international economic crisis of the later 1960s and 1970s constitutes the key point of departure.

As Robert Brenner has shown, between 1965 and 1973 the mid-century 'golden age' and its associated system of Keynesian demand management and regulation of the international economy foundered. This resulted from the fact that the advanced capitalist world faced mounting problems of falling profitability and, albeit with some time lags, 'severe reductions in the growth of output, of productivity, and of real wages, as well as sharply higher rates of unemployment and much more severe recessions'. These problems, and especially the acute and unusual one of stagflation (high prices combined with high unemployment), were exacerbated rather than caused by the oil price rise of 1973–74. According to Brenner, this international crisis of capitalist profitability, moreover, resulted from 'over-competition' and uneven development among national blocs of capital rather than from working-class and labour movement power and class struggle. In contrast to 'supply-side theorists' and politicians of the New Right, such as Thatcher and Reagan, Brenner saw working-class resistance to the crisis in the late 1960s and early to mid 1970s as 'more a consequence than a cause of the problems of profitability'.[1]

In response to the economic crisis, right-wing neo-liberal and neo-conservative ideas took strong and increasingly hegemonic international root. According to neo-liberals, the only effective solution to the crisis and the means of renewed capitalist advance lay not in the adoption of discredited regulatory Keynesianism, and even less in Soviet-style and social-democratic measures of 'command', but in the 'liberation' of market forces, in the 'liberal', deregulated capitalism of unrestrained, or barely restrained, competition, individualism, self-interest and choice.

As the 1980s progressed an increasing number of governments followed the leads offered by Margaret Thatcher and Ronald Reagan in their adoption of this free-market 'fundamentalism'. At the same time, some on the left, however, in Britain and elsewhere, offered a very different solution: more socialism in order to democratically control and subordinate to people's 'real' needs the power of capital. A particular target of the Left was the growing power of multi-national corporations. The latter, along with increasing international competition, the rapid movements of capital and commodities across national and international boundaries, the revolution in electronic technology and the increasing relaxation or dismantling of government and state controls upon financial institutions, business and movements of capital and labour, constituted key features of the 'new', 'globalised' world which was rapidly emerging out of the crisis.

Another prescription resided in the 'centre-left's' advocacy of 'new', 'third way' politics. These, as outlined by the sociologist Anthony Giddens in his famous book, *The Third Way: The Renewal of Social Democracy*, published in 1998, had two main aims. First, for 'progressives' to steer a new course between the 'market fundamentalism' of the New Right and 'outmoded' traditional labourist/socialist collectivism. Second, to select and combine those aspects of the broad traditions of labourism and liberalism relevant to the 'modern' world and to apply them *pragmatically* rather than *ideologically* in order to return Labour to power in a world increasingly dominated by the Right. The collapse of the Berlin Wall in 1989 and of international communism in general, and the declining fortunes of traditional social democracy, both confirmed this right-wing drift and gave added urgency and opportunity to the 'third way' 'project'.

During the 1970s and 1980s, moreover, it was becoming increasingly evident, both internationally and nationally, that economic restructuring was leading to the decline of the 'traditional', male-dominated industrial working class. A new 'class' was emerging. This was far more multi-racial and multi-cultural in character. It included far more women workers, especially in part-time work, and was geared far more to the service sector, both public and private, than to heavy industry. There was also growing international evidence that workers' allegiances to Labour and social-democratic parties were becoming less fixed and more contingent. As we will see below, some commentators and academic analysts related this loosening of class and Labour voting to the more fragmented, individualistic, consumerist and 'aspirational' nature of the new working class. Increasingly professionalised political parties, including Labour parties, sought successfully to address these new social and cultural as well as economic realities.

In addition to these common international issues, Labour in Australia and Britain also faced particular domestic challenges. The latter were characterised more by similarities than differences. For example, both the ALP of Hawke and New Labour under Blair were faced with the most pressing common political question of how to return Labour to power after very long periods of Tory and Liberal ascendancy. The Tories, of course, had been in power in Britain from 1979 to the election of 1997, while the Liberal-dominated Coalition had, with the exception of the Whitlam government, ruled in Australia from 1949 to 1983. In the later 1970s and early 1980s both Australia and Britain were characterised by increasing divisions and conflicts around living standards, wages and government failures in the fields of economic policy and management. As we saw in Part IV, industrial and class-based divisions and conflicts, however, were far more evident in Britain.

Lastly, both countries faced the common problem of how successfully to adapt to and become more successful in an increasingly, open, competitive and multi-cultural 'globalised' world. Australia, of course, had a protected economy and a predominantly 'white', at times siege-like, society and mentality. Its traditional dependence upon export markets for its wool, wheat, meat, energy and mineral wealth made it 'increasingly uncompetitive in a global economy dominated by advanced manufactures and service industries'.[2] In Britain, as observed in Part IV, the question of how to reverse the country's 'decline', both domestically and, more especially, in relation to the country's lack of international competitiveness, increasingly dominated the political scene from the mid 1960s onwards.

In examining Labour and anti-Labour responses and initiatives within these international and national contexts, I will first consider the case of the ALP's domination of federal politics between 1983 and 1996. I will then turn my attention to the BLP's experiences during the period of Conservative rule.

Australia under Hawke and Keating, 1983–96

Introduction

Hawke and Keating did not see themselves and their governments as pursuing a 'third way'. Rather, they saw themselves as pragmatically and successfully attempting to find solutions to Australia's pressing national and international problems. In so doing they sought to restore the ALP to its immediate post-war health and ensure that the Liberal-dominated opposition did not make a quick return to government. Yet, however professedly pragmatic, they made conscious, 'ideological' choices in terms of government policy and direction.

This section will demonstrate that, much like New Labour in Britain, they offered and practised a 'third way' combination of reconfigured regulatory labourism, reforming social liberalism and dominant economic neo-liberalism. In both national cases Labour sought to cushion the adverse effects of its 'liberation' of market forces by resort to regulation, where demonstrably necessary, and increased, but 'targetted', state spending, especially on social welfare. In stark contrast to New Labour, Hawke and Keating, however, attached central importance to the adoption of 'corporatist' and regulatory policies in relation to incomes, the social wage and, albeit in an increasingly qualified manner, workplace relations. As we will see below, Hawke's and Keating's agreement with the ACTU, in the form of the Accord, and their unqualified opposition to 'market fundamentalism' or 'Thatcherism', were crucial factors in the successful realisation of their goals. In contrast, Blair and Brown eschewed the 1970s 'corporatism' of the Social Contract in favour of voluntarism. They also distanced themselves from the traditionally special tie between the TUC and the Labour Party and were far more qualified in their attitudes towards Margaret Thatcher and 'Thatcherism'.

In sum, while we will see below that both the ALP under Hawke and Keating and New Labour shared a dominant policy commitment to economic neo-liberalism, this was tempered far more in Australia by continuing state intervention and regulation. In Blair's and Brown's Britain a much lighter regulatory and interventionist touch prevailed. We will also see that, notwithstanding the claim of non-ideological pragmatism, the 'governing practice' of Hawke and Keating, as argued by Chris Pierson and Frank Castles, is to be seen as a 'progenitor of third way thinking and as a specific source of new Labour policy development in a number of areas'.[3]

The political record

Hawke and Keating maintained in truly radical fashion that the only viable solution to the 'most severe' international and domestic economic crisis 'since the 1930s' lay in ditching much of the 'old-fashioned' Australian Settlement, rooted in the 'national-imperial' framework of protection, extensive federal and state regulation, the special tie with Britain and 'whiteness'. They argued in favour of 'opening up' the economy and the emerging multi-cultural society to meet the challenges of the new and highly uncertain international order in which the international financial markets increasingly dictated the agenda to national governments.[4]

Keating contended that Australia had to compete more effectively and efficiently in the increasingly 'globalised' world of intensified and extended market competition and establish itself as a credible major player, especially in the economically burgeoning Asia-Pacific region. This did not mean that Australia would turn against the West. Hawke, in fact, was a firm supporter of America's continuing anti-communism and the second Cold War of the 1980s. It did, however, signify that, without 'a reduction of costs and an improvement in trade performance', Australia was in danger of descending from a high-wage, easy-living 'paradise' into 'a third-rate economy . . . a banana republic'.[5]

The Fraser government's inability to tackle the immediate problems of a 'wages explosion', 'double digit inflation and unemployment', was the major factor in determining the outcome of the 1983 federal election.[6] The Liberals' attempt to resurrect the 'Whitlamite bogey' of 'socialist' financial irresponsibility and extravagance also fell flat on its face. In response to Liberal warnings that the voters would be better advised to 'stuff your money under a mattress than trust it to Labor', Hawke joked effectively about 'finding the money competing for space under the bed with the reds'.[7] In contrast to Liberal failure, Hawke, in the manner of his hero, Curtin, sent out a clear and positive message to the voters to 'trust me' to heal the divisions and conflicts of the Fraser years, to re-unite the country around the simultaneous fight against inflation and unemployment and to achieve economic recovery on the basis of a new economic policy.[8]

Labor won a landslide victory with a majority of twenty-five seats in the House of Representatives against a demoralised and divided Opposition. There was also a majority of Labor premiers in the states.[9] As the *Sydney Morning Herald* editorialised, Fraser's proven policy failures and switches, his lack of a 'plausible wages policy', his general 'negativity' and 'generalised scare-mongering' and the industrial 'confrontations' and 'conflicts' of his period in office suffered badly in comparison with the 'hope' offered 'openly', 'honestly' and 'charmingly' by Hawke, 'the apostle of consensus and reconciliation'.[10]

Hawke's successful strategy of promising to work harmoniously and productively with the unions and the employers to combat the twin evils of high inflation and unemployment constituted a key factor in both his election and post-election successes. Within a month of Labor's victory in 1983 union and business leaders sealed their agreement to the Accord, based upon wage restraint, a return to centralised wage fixation, job creation, the 'restoration of public medical insurance and other improvements in the social wage'.[11]

The importance of the adoption of the Accord, both domestically and from the comparative Australian–UK perspective, is hard to exaggerate. On the domestic front it promised to bring down inflation by means of wage moderation, while simultaneously increasing profits and providing much-needed jobs, all within the context of relative industrial peace and social harmony. In stark contrast, as we will see in more detail below, early and mid 1980s Britain were characterised by massive and bitter social, political and industrial divisions and conflict.

As noted in Part IV, the 1970s British equivalent of the Accord, the Social Contract, had failed after some early successes. British unions and employers, schooled in the tradition of free-market voluntarism in workplace relations as opposed to the state regulatory system of their Australian counterparts, for the most part did not welcome extensive state intervention, regulation and 'corporatist' solutions to their own and the country's economic problems. In addition, of course, Britain was now ruled by a prime minister, Margaret Thatcher, who blamed state intervention, collectivism and 'irresponsible trade-union power' for most of the country's ills and who sought to act decisively and ruthlessly to redress the balance in favour of individualism. Unlike the promising situation in Australia, the prospects for social harmony and industrial peace were virtually non-existent in Britain in 1983.

Hawke had learned important lessons from the failure of the Social Contract. Ralph Willis, who had worked as a research officer for the ACTU, visited Britain in 1978 as the ALP's shadow minister for economic affairs. Willis's purpose in Britain was to study the strengths and weaknesses of the Social Contract 'as part of his work in preparing "a credible anti-inflation policy" for the ALP opposition'. Willis concluded that, while correct in principle, the Social Contract had sought to impose too many constraints on the British unions and was too limited in scope, concentrating as it did mainly on wage restraint. In order to be accepted by the ACTU and to have a realistic chance of practical success, the Australian equivalent would have to encompass the 'social' wage, including jobs and social-welfare provision as well as wages. As Scott informs us, Willis's views, combined with the sobering experience of the early 1980s recession, paved the way for the emergence of the Accord and trade union support.[12]

Of utmost significance was the fact that the Accord worked successfully from the outset. During the 1983 election Hawke promised that 500,000 new jobs would be created in the first three years of his government. This target was reached 'five months before the deadline' as a result of the successful operation of the Accord, in defiance of 'most economic forecasters', according to Kelly. A total of one and a half million new jobs would be created before the end of the decade.

There was, moreover, 'no repetition of the wages explosions of 1974 and 1982 which had destroyed Whitlam and Fraser'.[13]

The huge size of the public deficit inherited from the Fraser government meant that Keating had to tread cautiously in his attempt to balance, on the one hand, fiscal expansion (to stimulate jobs and growth) and, on the other hand, cuts in spending and tax rises (to fight inflation). As a consequence, some of the ALP's expansionary election promises were put on the back burner. Keating, nevertheless, cut the prospective deficit of $8.4 billion by $1.8 billion in 1983. In 1983–84, furthermore, the government was lucky in that 'the drought broke, domestic demand lifted, the overseas economy picked up and corporate profits surged'. The 10 per cent levels of inflation and unemployment under Fraser were successfully reduced to 5 and below 8 per cent respectively in 1984–85. It was against this background that 'Hawke's prestige soared and the results dazzled the Labor Party'.[14]

Yet, while 1984 was Labor's 'golden year', the federal election in December did not bring about the 'smashing victory' widely predicted and expected. As Kelly notes, Labor's majority was reduced from twenty-five to sixteen seats and Hawke's image as an 'electoral messiah' was 'terminated'.[15] According to former party leader Bill Hayden, there was growing unease at the grassroots level that Hawke, for all his charisma, was too 'presidential' in style (the same criticism, of course, would be increasingly levelled at Blair in the 2000s) and that the government was becoming 'a party for bankers and big business'. In contrast, increasing numbers among the ALP's 'natural' constituents – adult male workers, their increasingly overstretched families and some among the newly asset-tested pensioners and taxed, lump-sum retirees – felt themselves as unfairly having to shoulder much of the economic burden.[16]

These criticisms were fuelled by the highly unsettling effects of the financial deregulation undertaken by the government in December 1983. In deciding to abandon the defence of the dollar and allow it to float, lift exchange controls, reduce controls on domestic banks and permit foreign banks to compete with domestic ones, Keating sought, in true neo-liberal or 'rational economic' fashion, to 'open up' the Australian economy to the 'bracing' wind of international competition in a way simply not countenanced in the regulatory past. Australia now possessed an 'unusual', probably unique, economic management model among contemporary countries, based upon a combination of the 'corporatist', regulatory Accord and deregulated financial markets.[17] As a result of deregulation the Australian economy began a roller-coaster ride, largely because it was henceforth highly dependent upon what Macintyre has termed 'the fickle judgement of internal currency traders'.[18]

There followed a 'rapid increase of overseas borrowing and a persistent trade deficit', 'sharp depreciations' in the currency, a 'sharp rise in the national debt', 'cuts in public spending, further wage restraint', plans to reduce tariffs and to 'relax' the regulation of wages. At the same time Labor pushed ahead with its economic restructuring. There was a share-market and investment boom, a 'credit explosion', involving many corporate crashes and bad practices as well as spectacular successes, heavy investment abroad by Australian corporations and the rapid emergence of a new type of high-risk, 'buccaneering' entrepreneurs who, like Alan Bond, Rupert Murdoch and Kerry Packer, were often 'mates' of Hawke and Keating.[19] These entrepreneurs, willing to 'chance their arms' financially, and at times illegally (Bond himself landed up in gaol while others 'fled overseas or escaped conviction'), were presented with a 'unique opportunity – lower wages, higher profits, easy money and world growth' – in which to make vast fortunes.[20]

By 1987, the year of the next federal election, the *Sydney Morning Herald*, pointing to the continuing 'enormity' of the economic problems facing the country, nevertheless continued to throw its support behind Hawke. This was because of his government's 'positive' record, its backing from the financial markets and its continuing determination to inflict immediate but necessary deflationary pain upon the country and remove industrial protection, subsidies and 'restrictive' work practices in order to achieve the ultimate goal of a more 'flexible' and prosperous modern economy. In contrast, the prospect of a Howard government, committed to tax cuts and 'breaking' rather than, as in the manner of the Accord, 'harnessing' the 'power of the unions', represented too much of 'a leap in the dark' and threatened discord and conflict in place of the prevailing national consensus and relative harmony.[21]

During the 1987 election campaign Hawke and Keating highlighted their record of 'certainty, stability, continuity' and their being 'best able to secure Australia's transition from a protected to an internationalised economy'. As Kelly observes, their election promises were 'modest'. Although they were still committed to job growth, the priority was to cut federal spending in order to tackle the current-account deficit and net foreign debt. In so doing the government would 'convince Australia's opinion-making elite in the media, business and banks that Labor had the courage to face the nation's economic problems'.[22]

They were also helped immensely by the ill-fated decision of the authoritarian and populist Nationalist premier of Queensland, Sir Joh Bjelke-Petersen, to run for prime minister. This decision, revoked at the last minute, created chaos and division in the ranks of the Opposition forces and prevented the Coalition's candidate, John Howard, from having sufficient time to mount a more effective challenge to the popular Hawke. Although there was a 1 per cent swing to the Coalition forces as compared with 1984, Labor 'increased its majority from 16 to 24 seats'.[23]

Yet, by the late 1980s the deregulated economic system had got out of control. The stock market crash of 1987 had already exposed the weak foundations of neo-liberal economic 'miracles' around the globe and those of many of the 'buccaneers' in Australia. Australia's consumption and investment boom of 1987–88 'overheated' the economy and forced the government to cool it down. In 1989 interest rates approached 20 per cent, many businesses and entrepreneurs came crashing down and the economy entered a serious recession. The 'great man', Keating, had mistakenly and catastrophically predicted a 'soft landing'.[24]

By the late 1980s the government's balance sheet was mixed. On the positive side were the undoubtedly important factors of electoral success, the Accord, job creation, improved productivity, an increased rate of workforce participation among women, restored public medical insurance and centralised wage bargaining, an easing of 'the plight of the poor' and significant material gains for those at the top of the social hierarchy.

Yet these were outweighed by many negative factors. The government's opening up of the economy and its abandonment of the ALP's traditional pursuit of equality in favour of enhanced equality of opportunity (a common 'third way' trait) had largely failed to deliver the promised goods. There was growing inequality and poverty (the latter concentrated especially among the old, sick and single mothers), lower growth than during the government-regulated post-war era, a 'persistent trade deficit and large external debt' and the failure of both the real earnings of the traditional male 'breadwinner' to rise and women's wages to increase as a percentage of those of men. In addition, it was now necessary for more members of families to undertake paid employment in order to 'make ends meet'. Increased pressure was placed on women to perform the 'double shift' of unpaid housework and often low-paid and part-time work outside the home. The government failed, moreover, to meet its loudly proclaimed goal of ending child poverty, while attitudes towards the unemployed hardened and the traditional virtues of 'mateship' and 'a fair go' were in danger of being swamped by the growth of individualism, competition, greed and selfishness. Yet none of this deterred the 'pugilistic' and self-important Keating from trumpeting the government's 'modernising' credentials and belittling much of Labor's past record.[25]

As the adverse effects of deregulation bit hard, so did criticisms of the Hawke–Keating 'experiment' mount within academia, the media, the churches and the Left. For example, in 1987 left-wing journalist and writer John Pilger described the probable re-election of Hawke as a 'political tragedy'. 'Australia', a 'nation of dynamism and decency, the most culturally diverse community in the world apart from Israel', was in the process of being 'hijacked by a new breed of politicians and their fast-money "mates"'. The latter included not only the terrible trinity of Bond, Murdoch and Packer, but also Sir Peter Abeles, head of the huge multi-national transport and shipping corporation Thomas National Transport (TNT), whose trucks had notoriously helped to 'break the siege of Wapping' in England in 1985 and so help Murdoch's News International to defeat the mass pickets and the print unions.

The 'two-man junta' of 'teddy boy' Hawke and Keating, his 'Very Important Mate', represented 'the real New Right', according to Pilger. While telling 'ordinary Australians' to make sacrifices in their own and the nation's interest, they brought about the conditions in which their corporate backers received tax reductions and accumulated vast fortunes. Their 'unrelenting monetarism' had resulted in massive increases in poverty, inequality, foreign debt and 'among the highest interest rates in the world'.[26]

Trade union leader and ALP Senate candidate, John Halfpenny, accused the federal government of handing the regulation of the Australian economy to the 'money market cowboys of New York, Tokyo and London', while the distinguished historian, Manning Clark, 'felt there was danger to Labor if it did not eventually return to the more traditional preoccupations of ... equality of opportunity, elimination of poverty and disarmament'.[27] In response, Hawke and the *Sydney Morning Herald* intoned that 'hard measures' were needed 'for hard times' and that there was no realistic alternative to Labor's tough but 'just' and 'successful' pragmatism.[28]

While their policies were sometimes criticised, Hawke and Keating nevertheless prevailed without too many alarms. Dissenting domestic voices were never loud or popular enough to constitute a significant threat to their hold upon both the ALP and the reins of government. The ALP did not experience anything approaching the high level of conflict between the left-, centre, and right-wing Labour groups which dominated and greatly debilitated the Labour Party in Britain during the first half of the 1980s. Moreover, while the Left was the driving force behind the British Labour Party's early 1980s ideological mixture of socialist planning and the defence of free collective bargaining, the 1980s Australian Left, both within and outside the ALP, simply did not gain a comparable level of power and influence. The tradition of 'free' collective bargaining, so dear to the hearts of Arthur Scargill and most other militant union leaders in Britain during this period and so fiercely defended by them, was very different from the mainstream Australian tradition of regulated and centralised wage fixation.

The crucial reason for Hawke's success and the weakness of the Left was that he successfully brought the mainstream trade union movement onto the side of government under the Accord. In contrast, as noted earlier, the Social Contract had failed in 1970s Britain and the 1980s governments of Margaret Thatcher were determined to challenge and 'cut down to size' the unions rather than collaborate with them in a corporatist manner.

The ACTU accepted Hawke's fundamental assumption and guiding principle that economic change and restructuring were absolutely vital to the development of a more competitive and prosperous economy and society. It also accepted the viewpoint that some immediate necessary pain would be overshadowed by much subsequent and longer-lasting pleasure, especially in terms of job creation, incomes and the social wage. The ALP's 'consensual' Labor strategy, a combination of traditional regulation and new economic rationalism, moreover, was seen as the only one acceptable to the labour movement and the majority of Australians. The alternative, the anti-Labor, anti-union and 'un-Australian' 'free-market dogma' of Thatcher, Reagan and their acolytes in Australia, was too dreadful to countenance. As a succession of trade-union and ALP national and state-based leaders declared consistently from 1983 onwards, their support for Labor's necessary structural changes was simultaneously totally at odds with the New Right's attempts to scapegoat the unions as being responsible for the economic crisis, 'reduce' or 'completely remove' their legal status, deregulate the labour market and the traditional system of workplace relations in the name of flexibility and fully to privatise the economy. While these labour leaders did sometimes criticise the neo-liberal aspects of government policy (for example, in the area of privatisation), there was a general and enduring consensus that its overall record was good.[29] For example, Edward Hodder, General Secretary of the AWU, declared in 1990 that, since 1983, Australian workers had benefited from increased jobs, 'stable wage increases', 'tax cuts', superannuation for the first time for 'many' and 'unprecedented industrial peace'. 'In short', he concluded, 'Australia has benefitted from the willingness of the trade union movement to discipline itself for the sake of our national well-being.'[30]

By the beginning of the 1990s, however, Keating's promise of a new 'golden age' still seemed very distant. There was the prospect of another world recession, while at home interest rates and the level of foreign debt were unacceptably high and unemployment would increase to over 10 per cent by 1992. The federal election of 1990 took place just before the advent of the economic crisis. The *Sydney Morning Herald* continued to support Hawke on the grounds that he was 'more likely' than his opponent, Andrew Peacock, 'to solve Australia's economic problems', largely by deflationary and deregulatory means and continued economic restructuring.[31] The ACTU once again praised the government's record on job creation and the social wage.[32] Yet there was growing concern in the ALP that, while people at the top and bottom of the social scale were better off, 'typical' (that is white male) wage earners and many of those 'in the middle' had not improved their real incomes under Labor. In the closest federal election since 1961 Labor achieved a narrow victory of nine seats in the midst of a 'divided, disillusioned nation'.[33]

Between 1991 and 1993 Australia suffered from a serious recession. Keating, who had overthrown Hawke as prime minister in December 1991, pursued a contradictory combination of neo-liberal and Keynesian policies, including increased government spending on infrastructure, capital works and jobs, as well as further privatisation and partial deregulation of the industrial relations system by means of decentralised 'enterprise bargaining' between individual companies and unions.[34] By the time of the March 1993 election low inflation and low interest rates coexisted with an unemployment figure standing at over 11 per cent. The Opposition, however, missed a golden opportunity to bring Keating to account. Rather than the election revolving centrally around the undoubted economic failures of the government, it centred upon the 'Thatcherite' policies of John Hewson, the opposition candidate.

Keating succeeded in portraying himself as a defender of both the Labor and Australian traditions of 'fairness' and 'social justice' against the 'extreme' and 'un-Australian' 'dogma' of Hewson. True to his New Right principles, Hewson proposed the introduction of a 15 per cent Goods and Services Tax (GST), 'further reduction of the public sector, speedier removal of tariff protection and labour market deregulation'.[35] As noted by Kelly, while Keating and Hewson were in broad agreement in terms of the overall free-market direction of the economy and while Keating himself had embraced the principle of a tax on consumption during the 1980s, they disagreed on 'the terms, conditions and pace at which the old order would be replaced'. Quick to detect the unpopularity of the proposed GST, Keating opportunistically and hypocritically attacked it as being regressive and ill timed. He also launched a broadside against Hewson's 'free-market purism' as being 'equivalent to the "jungle" of Reaganism and Thatcherism which other countries have just abandoned'.[36]

At the same time, sensing that the country was tired of unceasing economic change and disruption, Keating increasingly subordinated his economic neo-liberalism to his new, 'big picture' mission: the creation of an Australia characterised by economic efficiency, social solidarity and more active, responsible government, a 'new' Australia' of 'republicanism, Aboriginal reconciliation and an Asia-Pacific middle power status'. This two-pronged appeal – to 'true' Australian economics and 'true' national identity – was sufficient, despite the poor state of the economy, to give Keating victory with a majority of fifteen seats in the House of Representatives, an increase of six over 1990.[37]

Between 1993 and 1996 the economy appeared to have turned the corner. There were 'four years of low inflationary growth', although many wage earners continued to suffer from unemployment and uncertainty. Having won against the 'Thatcherite bogey' in 1993, Keating attempted to ride on the back of the economic recovery. Yet most of his time and energy went into promoting his new image as the architect of a 'new', more progressive and outward-looking nation. At the election of 1996, however, he suffered a crushing defeat – almost on the scale of Whitlam's 1975 loss – at the hands of the political veteran John Howard. In 1996, moreover, the Coalition won more working-class votes than Labor.[38]

Howard appealed successfully to the voters on four main counts. First, he played down his post-1996 emphasis upon the necessity of more extensive, rapid and 'pure' economic neo-liberalism, in favour of a more balanced policy mix. While advocating tax cuts, more encouragement for small businesses, less bureaucracy, improved productivity and a more deregulated labour market and industrial relations systems, he said that he would also seek to protect wages, adopt measures to alleviate the growing problem of youth unemployment, defend Medicare and protect the environment.[39] Second, realising that the country was tired of the chronic upheavals, divisions and insecurities of the Hawke–Keating era, Howard, in a way reminiscent of Hawke in 1983, sought to make the country more stable and united, more 'comfortable and relaxed' about the past.[40] Third, he would achieve his goals by abandoning the 'sectional' appeal of Keating during the 1990s – to the 'pampered', 'self-righteous', 'elitist' and 'noisy minority groups' of 'politically correct' 'feminists, environmentalists, the ethnic lobby, the Aboriginal industry and the intellectuals' – and rule in the interests of the nation as a whole, 'For all of us', according to the Liberal Party's 1996 campaign slogan.[41]

Howard's conservative Australia, moreover, would be a more 'balanced' combination of continuity and change, of respect for both tradition and progress, than Keating's 'new' and 'politically correct' model, which was seen as inexcusably dismissive of too much of the country's past. For example, while an independent country with a growing presence in Asia, Howard's Australia would not jettison its traditional ties to Britain, the British monarchy and its Anglo-Celtic past. While increasingly multi-cultural, it would reserve its right to place restrictions on immigration, especially from Asia, 'in the national interest'. And while continuing the commitment to 'reconciliation' with the Aboriginal people, it would both 'reserve the right' to make changes to Keating's Native Title Act (especially in relation to the competing claims of native title and pastoral leases) and more generally 'redirect the focus' from what it saw as Keating's 'more politically correct agenda' 'towards health, education, housing and employment'.[42] As at many times in the past, appeals to and contested notions of the nation thus played a major part in a federal election.

Fourth, there is no doubt that Howard's populist appeal to 'tradition' and 'the national', as against the 'special', 'politically correct' and 'elite' 'interest', combined with widespread disenchantment with the arrogance, intolerance and insensitivity of Keating, played a significant part in persuading a 'large group' of traditional working- and lower-middle-class Labor supporters to support the coalition. The new prime minister referred to them as 'Howard's battlers'.[43]

In the 1996 election some 'battlers' supported racist candidates. This was seen in the election of anti-multicultural racists in Queensland, Western Australia and elsewhere. These voters wrongly saw the Aboriginal people and 'coloured' immigrants as 'favoured', special-interest groups, 'privileged' legally and materially at their expense. The most notorious and successful racist, Pauline Hanson, won Oxley, 'the ALP's safest Queensland seat', as an Independent on the back of a 20 per cent swing of the vote. Hanson had been disendorsed by the Queensland Liberal Party, but, as Manne notes, the Howard government failed 'to respond at once to the Hanson threat – by reminding middle Australia unambiguously about how much we stood to lose if an anti-Asian breeze blew up in this country'.[44] In 1997 Hanson formed her own, initially very popular, One Nation Party. In these ways race and racism continued to constitute an important element in the late twentieth-century politics of Australian national identity.

As an endnote to this section, it is appropriate to observe that in the changed context of the mid 1990s the *Sydney Morning Herald* finally switched its allegiance from the Labor 'modernisers' to the Howard coalition dominated by economic liberals and social conservatives. The coalition represented another attempt to reconcile individual freedom and social cohesion, the personal, family, community and national interest. While Keating had been 'an imaginative leader', possessing 'a clear vision of Australia's place in the world', he had increasingly 'drifted' and 'lost his way' and 'commitment', according to the *Herald*. During the 1990s the needs and demands of the ACTU for labour market regulation and the preservation, however modified, of the traditional system of industrial relations had taken precedence over the continued necessity for more fundamental, market-driven change. It was now time, concluded the *Herald*, to give support to Howard, in the expectation that he would discard much of his 'moderate conservatism' of the election and press ahead with the more complete deregulation of the economy, including the crucial area of labour market deregulation. Above all, it was imperative that, under the Coalition government, decentralised enterprise awards would 'replace, not simply supplement, existing awards'.[45]

Labour under the Tories, 1980–97

In contrast to the protected and regulated Australia 'opened up' by Hawke and Keating, the Britain inherited by Thatcher rested its past economic glories upon nineteenth-century traditions of free trade, voluntarism, limited state intervention and regulation and the mainly unrestricted inward and outward flow of its 'white' and 'coloured' imperial subjects. Yet, as we have already seen, a combination of the global economic crisis and major internal problems meant that by the 1970s Britain had come to see itself, and was widely perceived by other countries, as the 'sick man of Europe'. From 1979 onwards the task of further 'opening up', 'modernising' and 'restoring the country to health' in a 'globalised' world fell to the Conservative monetarist and 'class warrior', Margaret Thatcher. Thatcher, like Howard, was a committed economic neo-liberal. At the same time, however, Thatcher, unlike Howard, combined aspects of socio-political conservatism with a large dose of social radicalism. While respecting selective British traditions, including the monarchy, individualism, enterprise and resolute anti-communism, Thatcher was determined to defeat all 'traditionalists', including those from the right and centre as well as the left, who stood in the way of her goal to modernise Britain. The latter was to be achieved not by 'economic recovery alone', but also, and more fundamentally, by 'changing' the 'national attitude of mind', by the creation of 'a new independence of spirit and zest for achievement'.[46] British society, culture and politics, as well as the economy, were to be thoroughly transformed and restored to 'greatness' by the widespread promotion and restoration of enterprise, individualism, independence and self-help, in the form of 'Victorian values', and the rejection of 'traditional' resistance to change, collectivism and dependence, the root causes of the country's 'sickness'.[47]

Unlike Hawke and Keating, Thatcher, as a 'market fundamentalist', was extremely hostile to the idea of developing any sort of agreement with the trade unions. The British prime minister was also far less concerned with the 'social' than Hawke and Keating. At times Thatcher indeed dismissed the very notion of society as meaningless, as being far too closely associated with socialism and collectivism. Instead, she saw Britain as being made up predominantly of self-interested individuals and families. In keeping with her anti-corporatism and individualism, Thatcher also sought drastically to reduce the size, interventionist scope and expenditure of the state and cut income tax. Yet, while opposed to the 'big' state, the prime minister insisted upon the necessity of a strong state. As Andrew Gamble has maintained, Thatcherism was a combination of the 'free economy' and the 'strong state'. The strong state would play a vital role, at some times conciliatory and at others coercive, not only in matters of defence, foreign policy, immigration and law and order (to repel external 'aggression', internal 'disorder' and resistance to the 'assimilation' of 'British values'), but also in the fight against 'extremism' and 'disloyalty'. In Thatcher's eyes, Labour's adoption of a left-wing programme at its 1980 annual conference in Blackpool fell into the latter category. At Blackpool Labour had 'unveiled' a 'sinister utopia', an 'Orwellian nightmare of the left'. Unless defeated, it could initiate another 'winter of discontent' and 'imperil' the future of 'this free nation'. The tarring of Labour and the imperative of constant 'patriotic' vigilance against its extreme and 'un-British' 'others', now in control of the party as well as important unions, had been returned to the political agenda.[48]

Both during and immediately after the election of May 1979 Thatcher, however, had proceeded with more circumspection. As Simon Jenkins has written, 'Thatcher had come to office in 1979 an unknown quantity. Her soft-focus femininity and Francis of Assisi quotations accompanied a bland manifesto mentioning neither monetarism nor privatisation. While emotionally on the right, Thatcher resisted hawks demanding an instant assault upon the unions'.[49] 'At first', observes Gamble', the government 'only picked quarrels' with the unions 'when it was sure of victory'. For example, while it backed the management during the national steel strike in 1980, defeated after four months, it retreated in the following year in the face of an overtime ban by the still powerful and feared miners.[50]

Yet the full force and determination of Thatcher's transforming mission became increasingly evident. Between the election and the Tory Party's Brighton conference of October 1980 the government took the first steps towards the reform of picketing law, the sale of council houses and the privatisation of British Aerospace and British

Telecom. It also abolished exchange controls and implemented a severe monetary squeeze, while increasing indirect and reducing direct taxation. By the time of the conference the signs were ominous. The country was in the throes of a deep recession characterised by an inflation peak of 21.9 per cent in May 1980, unemployment rising to over two million and 'from all sides' 'pleas to reflate the economy and soften an image hardening into stony-faced dogmatism'. Yet, as Thatcher famously declared at the conference, 'the lady' was not 'for turning'. Inflation, the number one enemy and the 'destroyer' of 'nations and societies', was to be defeated by an unfaltering commitment to 'monetary self-discipline'. Only by taking this tough action would the 'human tragedy' of unemployment be overcome, according to Thatcher. As Jenkins also wrote, 'the idea of an iron lady sure of the medicine the country needed and resolute in administering it became Thatcher's talisman'. There was to be no U-turn in the manner of Heath and his capitulation to the 'inflationary' wage claim of the miners in 1972.[51]

Thatcher briefly became 'the most unpopular prime minister since the war'. The inner-city riots of 1981 against unemployment, deprivation and racism, the violent nationalism and hunger strikes of members of the Irish Republican Army and considerable opposition to her policies in the country and on the part of the 'wets' within her cabinet, added to the Prime Minister's mounting problems. Yet the 'Iron Lady' refused to concede ground.

Between 1982 and the world recession at the end of the 1980s there occurred a remarkable change in the fortunes of Thatcher, her party and her government. Although the Conservatives received a modest 42.4 per cent of the vote in the general election of 1983 (1.5 per cent down on 1979), it was sufficient to achieve an overwhelming victory over Labour and a massive majority in the House of Commons (397 Conservative MPs against Labour's 209). Four years later the Conservatives also won easily, with an outcome not far short of that attained in 1983.[52]

This turnaround in the Conservatives' fortunes resulted partly from the fact that the world economy, including that of Britain, recovered strongly from 1982 onwards and paved the way for the development of the exhibitionist 'loads of money' culture characteristic of the more prosperous parts of England during the middle and later years of the decade. But, as highlighted by Gamble, it also owed much to the fact that the government 'emerged victorious from a series of major confrontations with its enemies'. These were the Falklands War, the miners' strike, the abolition of the Greater London Council (GLC) and the metropolitan counties and the conflicts with local authorities over rate capping and with the peace movement over the stationing of Cruise missiles in Britain.[53]

Of particular relevance to this study is the formidable strength and depth of patriotism, 'national euphoria', xenophobia ('Argie bashing') and pride in the country's past and present imperial record, displayed in Britain during the Falklands War, May to June 1982. Equally relevant and significant is the success with which Thatcher and the Tories exploited and benefited from these nationalistic and imperialist outpourings. There is a consensus among scholars and political commentators that the 'Falklands factor' was the 'single most important factor' in the election victory of 1983.[54] The Falklands conflict and the siting of Cruise missiles in Britain also illustrated the strength of the 'special tie' between Thatcher and President Reagan and the continued importance of defining the nation and the national interest in relation to an 'aggressive outsider', whether Argentina or the Soviet Union.

The eleven-month miners' strike of 1984–85 engendered deep, bitter and enduring divisions within the country. Thatcher's use of the full coercive and ideological forces of the state and the anti-union stance of much of the media were key factors in the defeat of the miners. The heavy toll taken by such a long dispute on the living standards and will to resist of the miners, their partners and their dependents, even with impressive help and support from sections of the public, combined with damaging differences and divisions among the miners' leaders and their regions, also played an important part. Once again at a time of domestic industrial crisis, there was also a strong Tory and establishment resort to the 'politics of loyalism'.

Thatcher and her supporters repeatedly accused the miners and their leaders of extreme and disloyal behaviour, of being the 'enemy within', as selfish, irresponsible and 'un-English' and 'un-British' in their support for the 'sectional' as opposed to the 'national' interest. Notwithstanding the strong rejection of these accusations by the miners and their counter-claims that the prime minister lacked loyalty and respect towards them, their hard-working families and their 'family values', their communities and their country, the establishment view largely prevailed.[55] Although there was an initial decline in the Conservatives' electoral fortunes in the wake of the strike, they soon recovered. From the perspective of the 1980s as a whole, moreover, the Conservatives, as in the interwar period, successfully harnessed loyalty to the nation to their own party-political cause. As noted by Tom Nairn, they saw the *real* England as 'irredeemably Tory'.[56]

The Conservatives lost seventeen seats at the 1987 election and Labour won twenty more than in the disaster of 1983. The former, however, comfortably won the election on the slogan, 'Britain is Great

Again. Don't Let Labour Wreck it'. Thatcher and her colleagues boasted that the country was enjoying the 'lowest inflation rate for twenty years', 'record' spending on the NHS, average take-home pay up '21% more than inflation', the 'fewest strikes for 50 years' and an end to violence on the picket line, as a result of the government's outlawing of secondary picketing. All this stood in stark contrast to the last Labour government, which had 'ended in the Winter of Discontent'. Thatcher appealed to many of those across the class structure who were prospering materially, the Liberal-Social Democrat Alliance failed miserably and Labour was unable to recover more than a third of its 1983 losses.[57] Most worryingly, despite its increasing moderation and 'modernisation' under Neil Kinnock, Labour continued to experience declining support among skilled workers, especially the 'newly affluent' home owners in the Midlands and the South. As political scientist Ivor Crewe observed, even though the Labour vote remained largely working class, the working class as a whole 'was no longer largely Labour'.[58]

Just fourteen months after the election Thatcher, in her position as Prime Minister, took part in the official bi-centennial celebrations in Australia. In the course of her speeches 'down under' Thatcher boasted that her governments had fundamentally changed Britain. They had effected a 'cure' to the 'British disease', as manifested in their successful attainment of a 'higher growth rate', 'wider ownership', 'lower taxes' and 'unparalleled prosperity'. Australian 'entrepreneurs' were praised for their contribution to Britain's 'transformation'. Furthermore, while increasingly concerning themselves with different geo-political spheres of interest, Britain and Australia were still deeply connected, as 'two strong, proud, independent' and 'successful' nations, by 'family and historic ties'. The abiding Commonwealth tie was accompanied by a shared commitment to 'western' traditions and values, to 'defend freedom and justice wherever they are threatened', to 'freedom' under the 'rule of law' and to parliamentary democracy. In response, Bob Hawke welcomed Thatcher and warmly endorsed her sentiments. Although the 1986 Australia Act marked the ending of most formal ties between the two countries, the 'informal ties of kinship and history' would 'never be severed'.[59]

Yet sharply escalating domestic problems meant that, as observed by Hobsbawm in October 1989, Thatcher and Thatcherism were increasingly in 'deep trouble' within her own country.[60] Mounting and unsustainable levels of personal credit and debt associated with the fragile economic boom of the later 1980s were exacerbated by Chancellor Nigel Lawson's tax-cutting and consumption-boosting 'give away' budget of 1988. Between 1989 and 1993 Britain was once again thrown into serious economic recession, and Tory boasts to have 'turned the economy round and reversed decline' were exposed as being without secure and lasting foundations.

In addition, there developed major divisions within and high-profile resignations from the Conservative Party around the issue of closer European union, while in the country at large there was serious opposition, including riots, to Thatcher's determination to press ahead with the introduction of the regressive and extremely unpopular community charge (poll tax).[61] A series of electoral reverses in 1989, 'collapse' in support for the Tories and a surge in support for Labour at the polls in 1990, and the unwillingness of Thatcher to change direction, sparked leadership challenges to the Prime Minister. In November 1990 a distraught Thatcher resigned and supported John Major as her successor.[62]

Despite Labour being well prepared and confident (indeed overly confident) of winning the next general election, in 1992, the warm-beer and cricket-loving Major, who wanted to rule over a 'nation at ease with itself', won unexpectedly with 43 per cent of the vote. The fact that blame for the continuing recession was attributed far more to Thatcher than to Major, combined with the government's proposed reduction in income tax, plans to scrap the poll tax and fears that the Tories would be replaced by 'something worse' – a Labour Party still too 'socialist' and not 'modern enough' – probably made an important contribution to the electoral outcome.[63]

Between 1992 and Blair's historic victory in 1997, however, Major's government was fatally undermined by chronic crises and disasters. Most significant in terms of these was 'Black Wednesday' in September 1992, when a speculative movement against the pound sterling forced its removal from the European Exchange Rate Mechanism and reopened divisions over Europe within the Conservative Party. The breakdown of the public services after 'many years of cuts', high unemployment and falling living standards and an 'unending series of scandals' concerning the 'sleazy' sexual, business and financial wrongdoings of leading Tories also contributed to the party's woes.

Notwithstanding the tragic death of John Smith, Kinnock's successor as party leader, in 1994, the Labour Party was increasingly in a very strong position to exploit fully the government's 'apparently terminal' slide in the opinion polls and in all elections.[64] Labour, under its new leader since 1994, Tony Blair, had done more than enough by the time of the 'cataclysmic' 1997 election to convince the electorate that it had successfully jettisoned its 'extremism' and sectionalism and that in its new, 'modern' and moderate form it would 'govern for the whole of the nation'.[65] As Murdoch's newspaper the *Sun* observed in 1997, it was now time to change political course and back Blair's 'change' and 'vision' agenda against the 'tired, divided and rudderless' Tory 'rabble'.[66]

Labour's landslide victory in 1997, of course, constituted a marked departure from its previously poor overall electoral record and performance during the era of Thatcher and Major. To be sure, Thatcher's unpopularity in 1980 had seen a significant improvement in Labour's ratings in the opinion polls. This, however, was a very short-lived development.

In contrast to the ALP, the BLP moved sharply to the left in the early 1980s in an attempt to reverse its electoral defeat, to develop a programme designed to successfully tackle the country's mounting economic and social problems and to accelerate the movement to socialism in the 'new era' of 'Thatcherism' and 'globalisation'. The leftward movement of the party and the growing influence of the unions in the election of the party leader, however, occasioned major internal divisions and splits.

Following Jim Callaghan's resignation in 1980, Michael Foot was elected leader by the parliamentary party, against Denis Healey. This was 'the first time since Lansbury that a man clearly identified with the left had been elected leader'. Although Foot, as Employment Secretary and Deputy Prime Minister, had staunchly defended the Social Contract and tried to keep the unions loyal to the Wilson and Callaghan governments during the 1970s, 'he was nevertheless still a unilateral disarmer and an opponent of the Common market'.[67] By 1981 a 'phalanx' of 'senior figures' on the right of the party had left, while in March of that year the pro-European and 'moderate' ex-Labour 'Gang of Four', Shirley Williams, Roy Jenkins, William Rodgers and David Owen, formed the Social Democratic Party. During the first six months of 1981 twenty-seven Labour MPs and one Conservative joined the new party. The Alliance, established by the SDP and the Liberals, 'soared in the polls' and won two by-elections. Later in 1981 left-winger Tony Benn was narrowly defeated by Healey for the post of deputy leader of the Labour Party. The problem of how best to deal with the 'pestilential' 'entryist' Trotskyite group, Militant, constituted a further source of internal Labour Party conflict.[68]

By the time of the June 1983 election Labour had adopted a left-wing platform of withdrawal from the EEC, the scrapping of nuclear weapons, the removal of US bases from Britain and a 'rapid expansion' of state spending to reduce unemployment and further democratic control and planning by means of more extensive nationalisation. In addition, there was widespread support within the party for the further extension of the 'municipal socialism' practised by the GLC, Sheffield City Council and other local authorities.[69]

From the *post hoc* 'triumphal' perspective of New Labour, 'old' Labour's 'outmoded' socialism of 1983, of course, was doomed to fail.[70] Yet a more historically contextualised reading suggests that matters at the time were far less straightforward and one dimensional. For example, while some within the ranks of the labour movement were extremely critical of the party's left-wing manifesto – the 'longest suicide note in history', according to Gerald Kaufman in the summer of 1983[71] – many others saw socialist policies as both an urgent neces-sity and a realistic alternative to the socio-economic 'disasters' brought about by 'extreme' and 'dogmatic' Thatcherite monetarism. Noel Thompson usefully reminds us that proponents of the rejuvenated socialist Alternative Economic Strategy constituted the dominant ideological group within early 1980s Labour.[72]

As noted earlier, the 1983 election, however, was an unmitigated disaster for Labour. The party's share of the poll was lower than at any time since 1922, its traditional manual working-class support had fallen dramatically (from a high point of 69 per cent in 1966 to around 42 per cent in 1983) and it had become a regional rather than a national political force.[73] As Labour's internal reports from members of the National Executive Committee (NEC), parliamentary candidates, leading trade unionists and regional representatives made clear, its manifesto and its policies in general were frequently condemned by the voters for their 'extremism'.[74]

Yet the reasons for Labour's failure went much wider and deeper than the question of policy alone. The formation and impressive early development of the SDP, combined with its very successful electoral alliance with the Liberals (the Alliance received 26 per cent of the poll as against Labour's 28.3 per cent and the Tories' 42.4 per cent at the 1983 election), meant that the majority of voters opposed to Thatcher's ruling minority were hopelessly divided. Although Labour secured 209 seats (a loss of 29) and the Alliance 23 (17 Liberal and 6 SDP), they were easily outnumbered in the new House of Commons by the Conservatives, with 397 MPs. In addition, the Labour Party had acquired 'a highly unfavourable public image'. Many voters saw Foot as a weak, 'shabby', indecisive and old-fashioned leader, simply unsuited and unable to manage the economy and run the country in the decisive manner of Thatcher, his party as disorganised and divided and Labour's election campaign as 'totally ramshackle' and outdated. In sum, Labour was widely perceived as being 'unfit to govern'.[75]

This was also Bob Hawke's view. Having secured his famous victory in Australia, Hawke visited Britain on the eve of the 1983 election. His impressions of the BLP were very unfavourable. Whereas the successful ALP was united, pragmatic and forward looking, the BLP was 'divided' and 'anachronistic'. From 1983 onwards those British Labour MPs who visited Australia were told by leading ALPers that they were 'still fighting old battles'. The imperative for the British party was to 'modernise', to become 'relevant' and adopt 'bold deregulatory reforms' of the kind introduced by Hawke and Keating in Australia.[76] The contextual irony, of course, was that these neo-liberal economic reforms were being introduced in Britain by socialist Labour's sworn enemy, the 'extremist' and 'dogmatic' Margaret Thatcher. Neither Hawke and his 'mates' in the ALP nor the visiting Labour MPs demonstrated, at least in public, an awareness, ironic or otherwise, of these politico-economic differences between the two countries. As Scott notes, British Labourites and socialists continued to view Hawke and the ALP as 'socialist' in outlook and practice![77] By the time the anti-socialist forces of New Labour achieved domination of the party the irony, of course, had largely disappeared. Much in the manner of Hawke, Keating *and* Thatcher, Blair was now leading the 'modernising' neo-liberal economic crusade for a 'New Britain'.

In returning to the 1980s, we may observe that by the time of the June 1987 British general election there had been a noticeable, but limited and uneven, improvement in Labour's overall fortunes. Even though Labour had no realistic chance of winning the election, it fought a much more efficient, organised and up-to-date campaign. It also advertised its backing by such prominent figures as the actress Julie Christie and the singer Billy Bragg. Neil Kinnock, who had succeeded Foot as leader following the latter's resignation in the wake of the 1983 disaster, moved to detach the 'soft' left of the party from its alliance with 'hard' Bennites, to expel Militant, to reassert leadership control over the party's affairs and institutions and return its policies to the 'political mainstream' in order to improve its appeal to the electorate. Kinnock, Healey and Roy Hattersley were strongly supported by the St Ermins Group of trade union leaders who sought to 'regain the NEC for the moderates, and to return the Labour Party to what they termed "sanity" and electability'. By 1987 these moves enjoyed varying degrees of success, but in overall terms the party had softened and modernised its image somewhat since 1983.[78]

During the election campaign Kinnock and his colleagues presented a strong 'moral challenge' to the 'divisive', 'uncaring', 'selfish' and 'unfair' policies of 'boss' Thatcher, as reflected especially in the proposed introduction of the poll tax. Labour promised to introduce a more caring, cooperative and democratic 'new era' by improving the 'quality of life', especially in relation to health, education, jobs and pensions, but found it difficult to develop a 'credible intellectual challenge'.[79] While Kinnock and his allies sought to 'wean the Party from the radicalism of the early 1980s', their acute awareness of the disastrous results of the internal divisions of the early 1980s, combined with the party's continuing commitments to left policies such as unilateralism and 'a significant extension of the public sector', meant that they had to proceed with caution. The Conservatives' attack on Labour's 'defenceless unilateralism' – as a policy for 'defeat, surrender, occupation' – was a crucial issue in the election. Labour's 'dubious economic credentials' and the views and actions of its 'loony left' were also seized upon by the Conservatives.[80]

As a result of the election, Labour's share of the vote increased by three points to 31.5 per cent and it gained twenty seats, including four held by black or Asian MPs. This left the party, however, trailing the Conservatives by 11 per cent and with 229 seats as opposed to the government's 375. The only consolation for Labour was that it increased the gap between itself and the Alliance, from 3 to almost 9 per cent. The Conservatives now enjoyed 'the second largest majority since 1945'. While Labour increased its share of the vote among trade unionists (a declining proportion of the electorate), its vote among manual workers as a whole 'barely rose', from 42 per cent to 43 per cent. It 'failed to improve its position significantly among non-manual workers', while among skilled workers 'only 36 per cent supported Labour, whereas 40 per cent voted Conservative'. The regional political divide between the Tory South and the Labour North hardened even further.[81]

Some two years after the election Hobsbawm gave a mixed assessment of the recent performance and future prospects of the two main parties. On the one hand, it was 'increasingly evident' that Thatcher's 'cause and policy' were in 'deep trouble'. On the other, and 'while the pendulum is swinging away from the Right, there is no sign of a genuine equivalent movement to the Left'. The 'most' that could be claimed for Labour was that 'it is no longer "unelectable", ie, that voters might now tolerate it as an alternative government'. Much depended upon whether Labour could 'take its chances', and whether Kinnock and his allies could 'inspire the people' by offering 'as positive a prospect of new times, of British renewal, of leadership into the future, as Thatcherism did in its own and different way'.[82] The key question for Hobsbawm, therefore, was whether Labour could recapture the progressive national interest and develop a truly national appeal.

Between 1987 and 1997 the Labour Party, under first Kinnock, then Smith and finally Blair, sought to respond positively to Hobsbawm's question by renewing and redoubling its efforts to make itself more modern, moderate, professional and appealing to individuals and groups across the social structure. As noted earlier, Labour met with unexpected defeat in the 1992 general election, held at a time of continuing recession. The party's slogans of 'Time for a Change' and 'Recovery and Renewal' and its pledges to abolish the poll tax, establish a Scottish parliament and 'save' the NHS failed to convince the electorate that it had sufficiently cast off its 'extremist' past and could be trusted to do a better job than the Conservatives on taxation and economic management. Kinnock's ill-advised 'victory' rallies proved to be premature and the party underestimated the doggedness, determination and survival instincts of John Major. As a result of the election, the Conservatives held 336 seats as against Labour's 271.[83] Thereupon Kinnock resigned, but the reforming momentum was maintained by Smith and accelerated by Blair. The latter, helped greatly by the suicidal tendencies of the Conservatives, swept triumphantly to office in 1997.

By then, and notwithstanding the fact that elements of pragmatism and continuity remained, the 'modernisation' process and the ideological break with 'old' Labour were well established. By the time of Blair's first government unilateralism in nuclear matters had given way to multilateralism, the socialist Clause IV to the vague promise of 'common endeavour', and nationalisation to privatisation and a 'partnership' between 'a thriving private sector and public enterprise'. Anti-business sentiment had been supplanted by the cultivation of support from Murdoch, industry and the City of London. As in Hawke's and Keating's Australia, Labour's traditional commitment to equality had given way, under Blair, to the pursuit of equality of opportunity. Under New Labour, militant trade unionism, the 'class warfare' of the 'Winter of Discontent' and the miners' strikes of the 1970s and 1984–85 became discredited aspects of the labour movement's past. New Labour highlighted the fact that it rejected totally these aspects, in favour of a harmonious system of 'partnership at work'. Keenly aware of its unpopularity among sections of the public, especially in 'middle England', Blair would afford the trade union movement no special treatment or influence. While opposed to her 'extremes', Blair and other New Labour leaders respected Thatcher for her attempt to legislate effectively against 'militant' and 'anti-social' trade unionism. Significantly, New Labour would retain much of the Tories' industrial relations legislation.[84] As seen above, in the different context of 1980s Australia Hawke had both cooperated with the unions and fundamentally opposed 'Thatcherism' in the interests of national unity and economic recovery.

'Young' New Labour sought inspiration for its 'project' not only from the progressivism of Clinton in the United States and the changing character of European social democracy,[85] but also from the 'successful' Hawke–Keating 'experiment'. Blair had positive memories of Australia from his childhood, when he lived in Adelaide from 1955 to 1958 and his father, Leo, lectured at Adelaide University.⁸⁶ In 1990 Kinnock sent Blair and Brown, then 'up-and-coming shadow ministers', to Australia. While there, Blair renewed his friendship with Geoff Gallop of the ALP and Peter Thomson, the radical cleric. It will be recalled from the Introduction to this book that, along with Kim Beazley (a member of Hawke's cabinet and a future leader of the ALP), Blair, Gallop and Thomson had met and become lasting friends while Blair was an undergraduate at Oxford from 1972 to 1975. In Australia Blair also 'struck up a particularly good rapport with Paul Keating'.⁸⁷

While the 1990 visit did not attract much press attention, Blair's two visits in 1995, especially on the occasion of his NewsCorp speech to Murdoch's executives in July of that year, attracted a 'blaze of publicity'. Blair was 'treated by much of the Australian press as the British Prime Minister-in-waiting'.⁸⁸ According to the 'Murdoch press', Blair's New Labour was the 'natural inheritor' of the 'radical' and 'populist' policies of Thatcher. The *Sydney Morning Herald* commended Blair, the 'first Labour leader to master the soundbite', upon a 'virtuoso performance' at the NewsCorp conference, and declared that 'unless Mr Blair does a Hugh Grant, there is nothing to stop him ousting Mr. Major at the next election'. The British electorate was 'fed up' with 'the complacency, sleaze, corruption and arrogance of the ruling Conservatives'.⁸⁹

The second visit during 1995, in December, saw Blair meet with Deputy Prime Minister, Beazley, and Prime Minister Keating, 'for the second time in less than a year', to 'discuss tactics'. Blair and his family spent Christmas at Peter Thomson's '158-acre farm in Victoria's high country'. Thomson subsequently moved to Britain, where he supported Blair 'up to and beyond' the election of 1997.⁹⁰

In 1995 and 1997 John Prescott, Blair's deputy in opposition and in government, also visited Australia and 'launched a campaign of mutual assistance between the two labour parties to secure the votes of expatriates in their respective national elections'. Denis MacShane, a BLP MP, wrote an article about the 'compelling model' of the ALP, while Peter Mandelson 'was impressed' by the ALP's 'very tough economic and taxation policies', and 'close but nonetheless disciplined . . . (and) carefully presented relationship with the trade unions'.⁹¹ Patricia Hewitt, the daughter of a high-ranking Australian public servant, Sir Lenox Hewitt, played a key role in facilitating and developing the Australian–New Labour connection. Hewitt worked as Kinnock's press secretary and played an important part in redrafting the party's policies in the 1990s. She became a 'privatising' health minister under Blair.⁹² New Labour's willingness and ability to 'learn lessons' from the successful ALP served it well at the 1997 general election. As a result of Blair's victory it was the turn of the ALP to 'look to' new Labour 'in its quest to regain government'.[93]

Notes

1 Robert Brenner, 'The Economics of Global Turbulence', *New Left Review*, 229 (1998), especially 94–138.
2 Macintyre, *Concise History*, p. 244.
3 Pierson and Castles, 'Australian Antecedents', 683. Interestingly there are no references to the Hawke-Keating 'experiment' in Giddens' *The Third Way* (Cambridge: Polity Press, 1998). For the view that the policies of Hawke and Keating represented 'the birth of Neo-Laborism' rather than 'emerging neoliberalism' see Joe Collins and Drew Cottle, 'Labor Neoliberals or Pragmatic Neo-Laborists? The Hawke and Keating Labor Governments in Office, 1983–96', *Labour History*, 98 (2010), 25–37. Collins and Cottle's argument pays insufficient attention to the *overall balance* of the policies of the Hawke and Keating governments. For 'early intimations of the Third Way' in the much-neglected New Zealand case see Melanie Nolan, 'Classic Third Way or Before its Time? The New Zealand Labour Party in Local and Transnational Context', *Labour History Review*, 75:1 (April 2010), 98–113.
4 O'Reilly, *Progressive Dilemma*, p. 14; Kelly, *End of Certainty*, pp. 1–16, 30. This section benefits immensely from Kelly's classic, if somewhat uncritical, study of the Hawke and Keating governments.
5 Macintyre, *Concise History*, pp. 248, 254–7.
6 Macintyre, *Concise History*, p. 246; Kelly, *End of Certainty*, pp. 50–3.
7 *Sydney Morning Herald*, 15 March 1993 (Sally Loane).
8 See Paul Kelly's incisive article, 'Hawke: a President Untied by Promises', *Sydney Morning Herald*, 4 March 1983; *Australian Worker*, 25 February 1983. By the 1980s the *Australian Worker* (incorporating the *Worker*) had precious little coverage of politics. The overwhelming focus now rested on the workplace affairs of the AWU and, to a much lesser extent, other unions. These developments, evident from the 1960s onwards, meant that the newspaper lost much of its pre-1960s importance as a key source of information and debate concerning the politics of labour.
9 Kelly, *End of Certainty*, p. 54; *Sydney Morning Herald*, 7 March 1983; *Age*, 7 March 1983; *Bulletin*, 15 March 1983.
10 *Sydney Morning Herald*, 4 March 1983.
11 Macintyre, *Concise History*, p. 247.
12 Scott, *Running on Empty*, pp. 230–2.
13 Kelly, *End of Certainty*, pp. 60–1, 64–8; Macintyre, *Concise History*, p. 247.
14 *Bulletin*, 15 March 1983; Kelly, *End of Certainty*, pp. 54, 60–1, 67–8, 7, 75.
15 Kelly, *End of Certainty*, p. 135; *Sydney Morning Herald*, 3 December 1984.
16 *Sydney Morning Herald*, 4, 5 December 1984; Kelly, *End of Certainty*, p. 141.
17 Kelly, *End of Certainty*, p. 77.
18 Macintyre, *Concise History*, p. 248.
19 For a devastating critique of the close relationship between the 'Silver Bodgie' (Teddy Boy) Hawke, the 'egocentric and pugnacious' Keating and their business and media 'mates', such as 'Rupert and Bondy', see John Pilger, *A Secret Country* (London: Vintage, 1992), p. 5, ch. 6.
20 Macintyre, *Concise History*, pp. 253–4; Kelly, *End of Certainty*, pp. 90–1; Pilger, *Secret Country*, pp. 288–94.
21 *Sydney Morning Herald*, 9 July 1987 (editorial, 'The Case for a Third Term'); *Age*, 13 July 1987 (editorial, 'Labor Triumph, Liberal Dilemma').
22 Kelly, *End of Certainty*, pp. 329–30, 342–3.
23 *Ibid.*, pp. 299–314, 355; *Bulletin*, 21 July 1987; *Age*, 13 July 1987.
24 Macintyre, *Concise History*, p. 250; Kelly, *End of Certainty*, chs 19, 26.

25 Graeme Duncan, *The Australian Labor Party: A Model for Others?* (London: Fabian Society, October 1989), p. 14; Macintyre, *Concise History*, pp. 250–4; O'Reilly, *New Progressive Dilemma*, pp. 47–9, 61.

26 See Pilger's articles in the *Sydney Morning Herald*, 9 July 1987 and the *Age*, 11 July 1987; Pilger, *Secret Country*, p. 259.

27 *Sydney Morning Herald*, 9, 13 July 1987.

28 *Sydney Morning Herald*, 13 July 1987.

29 See, for example, *Australian Worker*, 29 May 1987 (Mike Forshaw), 29 September 1987, 5 February 1990 (Bob Carr), 2 April 1990.

30 *Australian Worker*, 2 April 1990.

31 *Sydney Morning Herald*, 23 March 1990.

32 *Australian Worker*, 2 April 1990; *Sydney Morning Herald*, 21, 23 March 1990; *Bulletin*, 3 April 1990; *Age*, 26 March 1990; Duncan, *Australian Labor Party*, p. 14.

33 *Age*, 26 March 1990; *Sydney Morning Herald*, 26, 28 March 1990; Kelly, *Age of Certainty*, pp. 586–7.

34 O'Reilly, *Progressive Dilemma*, p. 47–9; Macintyre, *Concise History*, p. 258.

35 Macintyre, *Concise History*, p. 257; Kelly, *End of Certainty*, pp. xiv–xv; *Australian Worker*, 26 February 1993 ('Election Special').

36 Kelly, *End of Certainty*, pp. ix–xv, ch. 32; *Age*, 16 March 1993 (editorial).

37 Kelly, *End of Certainty*, pp. x, xii, xiv–xv, 679–80; Macintyre, *Concise History*, pp. 258–60; *Bulletin*, 23 March 1993.

38 Manne, *Left Right Left*, p. 335; Ramsey, 'Hayden Years', p. 127.

39 *Sydney Morning Herald*, 1, 4, 5 March 1996; *Bulletin*, 12 March 1996 for Howard's 'moderate conservatism' in 1996.

40 Brett, 'Relaxed and Comfortable'; Brett, *Australian Liberals*, pp. 184–5.

41 Macintyre, *Concise History*, p. 261; Brett, *Australian Liberals*, pp. 186–7.

42 Paul Kelly, *The March of Patriots: The Struggle for Modern Australia* (Carlton: Melbourne University Press, 2009). See Robert Manne's review of Kelly, 'The Insider', *The Monthly*, October 2009, 22–8; Manne, *Left Right Left*, p. 308; *Sydney Morning Herald*, 5 March 1996.

43 Brett, *Australian Liberals*, pp. 187–9; *Sydney Morning Herald*, 5 March 1996; Manne, *Left Right Left*, pp. 335–9.

44 Manne, *Left Right Left*, p. 347; *Sydney Morning Herald*, 5 March 1996.

45 *Sydney Morning Herald*, 1 March 1996 (editorial, 'A Government Loses its Way').

46 'Great Speeches of the 20th Century: The Lady's Not for Turning', Margaret Thatcher, October 10 1980 (London: The Guardian, 2007), pp. 7–8.

47 For Thatcher see, for example, Gamble, *Free Economy and Strong State*; Eric J. Evans, *Thatcher and Thatcherism* (London: Routledge, 1997); E.H.H. Green, *Thatcher* (London: Hodder and Arnold, 2006); Clarke, *Hope and Glory*, ch. 11; Bea Campbell, *Iron Ladies* (London, Virago, 1987); Bob Jessop et al., *Thatcherism* (Cambridge: Polity, 1988); Dennis Kavanagh, *Thatcherism and British Politics* (Oxford: Clarendon Press, 1987); Stuart Hall and Martin Jacques, *The Politics of Thatcherism* (London: Lawrence and Wishart, 1983); *Guardian*, 11 April 2009 (Germaine Greer, 'The Thatcher Years').

48 Gamble, *Free Economy and Strong State*, pp. 38–45, 63–8; *Great Speeches 20th Century, Thatcher*, pp. 16–17.

49 See Jenkins's Foreword to *Great Speeches 20th Century, Thatcher*.

50 Gamble, *Free Economy and Strong State*, pp. 112–13.

51 *Great Speeches 20th Century, Thatcher*, pp. 6, 13; *Guardian*, 11 October 1980 (Ian Aitken, Political editor); Gamble, *Free Economy and Strong State*, pp. 107–12.

52 Pugh, *Speak for Britain!*, pp. 372–3, 380–1; *Guardian*, 10, 13 June 1983, 10, 11, 12, 13, 15 June 1987.

53 Gamble, *Free Economy and Strong State*, p. 120.

54 Evans, *Thatcher*, pp. 24–5, 96–100; Gamble, *Free Economy and Strong State*, pp. 120–1; *Guardian*, 10 June 1983; Eric Hobsbawm, 'Falklands Fallout', Robert Gray, 'The Falklands Factor' and Tom Nairn, 'Britain's Living Legacy', in Hall and Jacques, *Politics of Thatcherism*, pp. 257–88.

55 Raphael Samuel, Barbara Bloomfield and Guy Boanas (eds), *The Enemy Within: Pit Villages and the Miners' Strike of 1984–5* (London: Routledge, 1986), pp. 3, 5, 25, 37, 39, 115, 161, 201; *Guardian*, 7 March 2009 (Arthur Scargill; editorial), 12 March 2009 (Seumas Milne).
56 Nairn, 'Britain's Living Legacy', p. 288; Eric Hobsbawm, 'Another Forward March Halted', *Marxism Today*, October 1989, 17, 19.
57 *Guardian*, 10, 11, 12, 13 June (editorial, 'The Gale of Certainties Blows On') 1987.
58 *Guardian*, 15 June 1987 (Ivor Crewe, 'A New Class of Politics').
59 *Britain and Australia, 'A Closer Relationship'. The Visit to Australia by the Prime Minister of the United Kingdom, the Rt. Hon. Margaret Thatcher, 1–6 August 1988* (Canberra, British High Commission, 1988).
60 Hobsbawm, 'Another Forward March Halted', 14–19.
61 Gamble, *Free Economy, Strong State*, pp. 130–6; Pugh, *Speak for Britain!*, p. 384.
62 Gamble, *Free Economy, Strong State*, pp. 136–8; Evans, *Thatcher*, ch. 10.
63 Reid and Pelling, *Short History of the Labour Party*, pp. 174–5; *Guardian*, 11 April 1992 (editorial, 'The Harsh Facts of Victory and Defeat').
64 Reid and Pelling, *Short History of the Labour Party*, pp. 177–8.
65 *Souvenir Mirror*, 3 May 1997 in 'General Election 1997: Election Results, Newspapers', 1 box, uncatalogued, LHASC; *Guardian*, 2 May 1997.
66 *Sun*, 18 March 1997, in 'General Election 1997: Election Results, Newspapers'. See also David Butler and Dennis Kavanagh, *The British General Election of 1997* (Basingstoke: Macmillan, 1997), ch. 1.
67 Reid and Pelling, *Short History of the Labour Party*, p. 156.
68 Pugh, *Speak for Britain!*, p. 363; Gamble, *Free Economy, Strong State*, pp. 117–18; Reid and Pelling, *Short History of the Labour Party*, pp. 156–60.
69 Pugh, *Speak for Britain!*, p. 372; Thompson, *Political Economy and Labour Party*, pp. 225–34; Reid and Pelling, *Short History of the Labour Party*, p. 161.
70 *Guardian*, 4 March 2010 (Seumas Milne).
71 For Kaufman see *Guardian*, 4 March 2010 (Michael White).
72 Thompson, *Political Economy and Labour Party*, pp. 226–34.
73 Pugh, *Speak for Britain!*, p. 373; Thorpe, *History of the British Labour Party*, pp. 211–13; Reid and Pelling, *Short History of the Labour Party*, pp. 161–2; Eric Shaw, *The Labour Party since 1979: Crisis and Transformation* (London: Routledge, 1994), pp. 26–8; *Guardian*, 13 June 1983 (Ivor Crewe).
74 'General Election, June 9th 1983', Books 1–3, uncatalogued bound volumes, LHASC.
75 *Ibid.*; *Guardian*, 4 March 2010 (Michael White, Seumas Milne, editorial).
76 Scott, *Running on Empty*, pp. 2–3.
77 Scott, *Running on empty*, p. 3.
78 Pugh, *Speak for Britain!*, pp. 380–1; Shaw, *Labour Party since 1979*, chs 2, 3; Hayter, *Fightback!*, p. ix, Introduction, ch. 10.
79 Pugh, *Speak for Britain!*, p. 380; '1987 Election. Labour Party Press Releases', uncatalogued material, LHASC.
80 Pugh, *Speak for Britain!*, p. 38; Shaw, *Labour Party since 1979*, pp. 76–9.
81 Pugh, *Speak for Britain!*, pp. 381–2; Thorpe, *History of the British Labour Party*, pp. 221–2; Reid and Pelling, *Short History of the Labour Party*, p. 169; *Guardian*, 12, 13, 15 June 1987.
82 Hobsbawm, 'Another Forward March Halted', 14, 19.
83 Pugh, *Speak for Britain!*, pp. 384–5; Reid and Pelling, *Short History of the Labour Party*, 174–5; Thorpe, *History of the British Labour Party*, pp. 222–7; Shaw, *Labour Party since 1979*, pp. 145–6; David Butler and Dennis Kavanagh, *The British General Election of 1992* (Basingstoke: Macmillan, 1992), ch. 12; *Guardian*, 9, 10, 11 April 1992; '1992 Election. Press Releases', especially 'Labour Party Briefings', uncatalogued material, LHASC.
84 Shaw, *Labour Party since 1979*, pp. 205–9; Reid and Pelling, *Short History of the Labour Party*, chs 12, 13; Blair, 'News Corp Speech'.

85 Giddens, *Third Way*, pp. viii–ix, 17–26.
86 Scott, *Running on Empty*, p. 1.
87 Scott, *Running on Empty*, p. 4; O'Reilly, *Progressive Dilemma*, pp. 13–14, 66–86.
88 Pierson and Castles, 'Australian Antecedents', pp. 693–4.
89 *Sydney Morning Herald*, 17, 18, 22, July 1995. Grant, the seemingly 'clean cut' and 'homely' British actor, had, in the words of the *Sun-Herald* (16 July 1995), been caught by the Hollywood police in a late night 'tryst with a Hollywood hooker'. Not everyone in Australia was 'seduced' by Blair's 'good looks' and 'ready smile' (*Sydney Morning Herald*, 17 July 1995). Writing in the *Sydney Morning Herald* (24 July 1995), political commentator, Jim McClelland, declared, 'There is something about the smiling new saviour, Tony Blair, that gives me the creeps.' 'High-sounding platitudes' of the kind offered by Blair at the NewsCorp gathering on Hayman Island were not enough. They were too 'post-modern' and paid too little attention to the 'nitty-gritty' of politics. In a similarly prescient observation, McClelland also condemned Blair's acceptance of the offer of a fully paid holiday from Murdoch.
90 *Age*, 27 December 1995; Andrew Mawson, 'The Rev Peter Thomson', *Guardian*, 26 January 2010 (obituary); *Sun-Herald*, 5 December 1995.
91 Scott, *Running on Empty*, pp. 4–5.
92 O'Reilly, *Progressive Dilemma*, p. 66; *Observer*, 10 January 2010; *Guardian*, 14 January 2010 (Seumas Milne).
93 Scott, *Running on Empty*, p. 5.

CHAPTER TWELVE

From Howard to Gillard, from Blair to Brown, 1997–2010

Howard to Gillard

The ALP's search for domestic success and for inspiration overseas from the triumphant Blairites proved, however, to be fruitless. Between his victory over Keating in 1996 and his defeat by Rudd in 2007, it was the coalition's John Howard who continuously ruled the federal political roost. Having won in 1996 on his programme of stability, moderation and an appeal to the nation 'as a whole', Howard and his coalition partners increasingly displayed their true colours of economic neo-liberalism and social conservatism.

For example, in its first two terms of office, from 1996 to 2001, the government undertook an ambitious programme of economic reform, including trade liberalisation, the partial sale of the important tele-communications and media company, Telstra, the introduction of a goods and services tax, cuts in income tax, public expenditure and government services, attacks on 'dole bludgers' (the 'work-shy') and support for private health insurance.[1] Howard also continued his vindictive attacks on the funding and standing of 'pampered' and 'politically correct' liberal and left 'elites' and their 'black-armband', 'guilt-ridden' view of Australian history in relation to the treatment of Aboriginal people, the Anglo-Celtic heritage and multi-culturalism.

Fears that the level of Asian immigration was too high, that multi-culturalism was spawning 'separateness' and 'conflict' at the expense of 'togetherness' and 'national solidarity' and that the 'wooing of Asia' was at the expense of the traditional tie with Britain had been prom-inently and controversially expressed by Australia's most famous historian, Professor Geoffrey Blainey, in 1984.[2] Whether consciously or not, Blainey's polemic in defence of 'old', white working-class Australia had given an air of respectability to the mounting racism which surfaced most dramatically and notoriously in Hanson's successful election campaign of 1996. What Robert Manne terms Howard's 'eloquent silence' following Hanson's maiden speech, combined with his 'general indifference to the cause of Aboriginal reconciliation', his opposition to the notion of Aboriginal 'custodianship' of the land and his 'hostility' to 'any genuine exploration of the idea of multiculturalism', 'encouraged a hostile populist wind to blow up over questions of Asian immigration, multiculturalism and Aboriginal reconciliation'.[3] Following the election of 1996, relations between, on the one hand, the Howard government and, on the other hand, Aboriginal leaders and ethnic communities, 'dramatically soured'.[4]

Howard continued to proclaim his attachments to Britain and the monarchy. These, of course, were highlighted during the referendum on the republic in November 1999, when majority support for an Australian head of state failed to carry the day in the face of insurmountable divisions among that majority concerning the form the republic should take.[5] Despite fears of 'serious protests' in the wake of the referendum and public hostility to the royal treatment of Princess Diana, the Queen's two-week visit to Australia in March 2000 passed off with 'few genuine incidents'. In fact it was widely hailed in the Australian press as 'one of the most successful charm offensives in Australian history'. Throughout the visit the Queen, as the continuing head of state, displayed a keen awareness of, and due respect for, the past, present and likely future wishes of the Australian people and, unlike Howard, the importance of Aboriginal reconciliation. Despite the fact, in the words of the *Sydney Morning Herald*, that 'few would now dispute ... that Australia has long since ceased to be British', many Australians, and particularly those with personal and familial connections, recognised the enduring importance of the 'tie of affection' with Britain and the British monarch. Large crowds, including 'vociferous', 'Anglo-Saxon, middle-class Australians', turned out to welcome Queen Elizabeth.[6]

While Howard continued to draw successfully on the economic neo-liberalism and the somewhat narrow, resentful and conservative 'populist' nationalism outlined above, his hold on power was by no means untroubled, especially before 2001. For example, in the election of 1998 there was a swing of almost 5 per cent to Labour. The ALP actually received a majority of the national two-party preferred vote, 51 per cent, and ended up being only eight seats short of a parliamentary majority, while the Coalition won 'with an unprecedented low number of votes, 49 per cent'.[7] The ALP's new leader, Kim Beazley, performed well during the election campaign and enhanced his reputation as a decent, engaging and tolerant man and politician, in contrast to the intolerance and mean-mindedness of Howard. The key and highly divisive issue of the election was Howard's intention to push ahead with the implementation of a GST. At the same time he cleverly 'sweetened the GST pill' by promising very generous tax cuts, especially to the middle classes, although this was against the distinctly unpromising backcloth of the impending global economic crisis. Unlike in 1996, One Nation was the biggest loser. As a result of the election it had no representatives in the House and just one in the Senate.[8]

Yet Labour's considerable improvement in 1998 was not maintained at the next federal election, of November 2001. This election took place against the background of the attacks on the World Trade Center in New York City and the Pentagon on 11 September, the resulting loss of 3,000 American lives, the launch of the 'war on terror', heightened concerns about border security and the hardening of the Howard government's attitudes and policies towards the 'boat people' from Iraq, Afghanistan and Iran seeking asylum in Australia.

In terms of the latter, three incidents were of particular importance. First, in August the *Tampa*, a Norwegian boat, was on hand to rescue 433 asylum seekers travelling to Australia. The *Tampa* was refused permission to enter Australia's territorial waters, and, fearing for the health of the refugees, the captain sailed towards Christmas Island. Australian troops then boarded the *Tampa* and transferred its mainly Afghan asylum seekers to an Australian naval vessel. A legal campaign was mounted in Australia to bring the asylum seekers into the country, but it failed. Second, in September a boat carrying asylum seekers sank and 353 were drowned. Third, in October Howard falsely claimed that Iraqi children had been thrown into the ocean from a sinking refugee boat. The clear implication was that the adults on board had selfishly and cruelly put their own safety and survival above that of the children. In fact no child had ended up in the water until the boat had sunk.[9]

There was a mixed antipodean response to these incidents. While New Zealand took in 150 of the *Tampa* asylum seekers, Australia set in place a system based upon 'the military repulsion of asylum seekers followed by their detention in offshore tropical detention centres until such time as their refugee status was determined'. As Manne observes, this system of 'mandatory detention, temporary protection and the Pacific solution' was 'incomparably the harshest in the Western world'.[10] It was deliberately insensitive and punitive. Its overriding objective was to deter all but the most desperate refugees from seeking asylum in Australia by making conditions in the detention centres extremely unpleasant. In practice it was highly racist, being directed against 'non whites' from the Middle East and Afghanistan. The existing detention centres, based mainly in remote desert areas within Australia, had already acquired a dreadful reputation – the 'most inhumane and destructive quasi-penal institutions in Australia's post-federation history', according to Manne – and between 1999 and 2002 they experienced riots, hunger strikes, 'mass breakouts' and much self-harm among the inmates.[11] Howard's 'Pacific solution' threatened to make the new centres, housing people who were often in poor mental and physical health as a result of their traumas 'at home', even more 'prison-like' than the existing ones. The Howard government, moreover, cynically sought to move the 'problem' offshore, well beyond the immediate gaze and concern of most Australians.

It is also important to note that these three incidents had taken place against a general backcloth of government- and media-generated 'scaremongering and disinformation' about asylum seekers from the later 1990s onwards. Refugees genuinely fleeing persecution, hunger and possible death in Iran, Iraq and Afghanistan were widely, falsely and cynically accused of being 'undeserving', 'scheming' and 'dishonest' and of wishing 'unfairly' to 'take advantage' of Australia's prosperity and social welfare system at the expense of Australians themselves. Some were suspected and accused of masquerading as genuine asylum seekers in order to import terrorism into Australia. Manne rightly concludes that the prospect of 'mass' immigration in these years 'excited the oldest Australian nightmare, of alien invasion from the north'.[12] By this time, however, the perceived 'invader' was to be not the communist but the Islamic fundamentalist.

It was against this background of nationalist, xenophobic and racist fear, frenzy and moral panic about the 'non-western', 'non-white' 'other', that the November election took place. Howard took full advantage of the situation. He highlighted his 'tough' but 'necessary' stance on asylum seekers and border security and vigorously supported the Americans' 'war on terror', both generally and against the Taliban government in Afghanistan. Afraid of losing votes by appearing to be 'too soft', and despite his initial refusal, Beazley had eventually come to support Howard's draconian asylum legislation in the wake of the *Tampa*. During the election campaign Labor also adopted a 'tough' position on asylum seekers and border controls and was 'largely silent' on multi-culturalism. This did not spare it from Howard's claim that the election of a Labor government would result in 'an escalation of illegal immigrants'.[13]

Interestingly, Howard was criticised for his 'brutalising' and 'heart-less' stance towards asylum seekers and his attempt to link the 'boat people' to terrorism not only by Paul Keating and Neville Wran, the former Labor Premier of New South Wales, but also by the past Liberal leaders, Malcolm Fraser (who had sympathised with and accepted the Vietnamese refugees of the 1970s) and John Hewson. The latter accused

Howard of cynically 'tapping', for personal and party ends, the 'latent racial prejudice in significant sections of the Australian community'.[14] Keating also claimed that the Howard government was 'falsely taking the credit' for the increasingly successful 'modern and open economy' created by himself and Hawke.[15] Howard responded by maintaining that the coalition was far better equipped than Labor to manage the economy during the global downturn, to curb the power of the unions and press further ahead with labour market deregulation.[16] During the campaign there was little mention of the issues of reconciliation and the republic.

The ALP needed a swing of 0.8 per cent to give it victory. It lost, however, as a result of the largest pro-government swing since 1966. Despite Beazley's attempt to give greater priority to economic issues, such as unemployment and the prospect of the GST being extended to cover fresh foodstuffs, working-class 'battlers' continued to abandon the ALP for the Coalition, while many of Hanson's One Nation supporters returned to the Coalition fold.[17] In truth, as observed by many commentators at the time, while economic questions figured in the election, they were greatly overshadowed by those of immigration, race, border controls, terrorism and the concern to protect national security and solidarity. It was the ability of Howard most successfully to exploit popular fears and prejudices on these questions and to expose Beazley's 'wavering' stance on asylum seekers that proved decisive at the election.[18]

Three years later the 'self-styled Lazarus', Howard, triumphed again and became Australia's second-longest serving prime minister. The October 2004 federal election took place against a booming economy and widespread prosperity. Labor had a new leader with an 'arresting personality', the young and inexperienced, but at times 'tactically brilliant', Mark Latham.[19] Indebted to British 'third way' thinking, Latham sought to combine the freedoms and rigour of the market economy with protection of the environment (for example, the 'locking up' of Tasmania's old-growth forests) and the establishment or re-establishment of a 'fair, generous, inclusive' Australia, especially in the fields of health, education and welfare. In contrast to Blair and his colleagues in Britain, however, Latham was very critical of George Bush and promised to withdraw Australia's troops from Iraq.[20]

Yet it was Howard's appeal to the electorate to continue to put their trust in him as a proven economic manager, as the defender of jobs (he 'wouldn't sacrifice working people's jobs for trees'), as the architect of a current growth rate of over 4 per cent, greatly improved living standards, low inflation, taxes and interest rates, a housing boom, and as the loyal and trusted ally of America, that won the day.

Bush congratulated his 'good friend', Howard, and Australia as a nation for being a 'great ally' in 'the war on terror', while Blair telephoned Howard to commend the Coalition's decision to support the invasion of Iraq.[21]

Latham had also been unable to solve the ALP's continuing conundrum of how successfully to combine to an appeal to, on the one hand, its traditional blue-collar workers and, on the other, the 'aspirational' upper-working and middle classes.[22] Labor lost seats in all the states and received its second-lowest share of the primary vote, 38.2 per cent, since 1931. Coalition control of the Senate followed and ended, after eight years, the ALP's ability to block controversial legislation there. This new state of affairs moved the *Sydney Morning Herald* to declare that Howard henceforth had the opportunity to 'stamp his free enterprise philosophy on Australia' with special reference to the 'overhaul' of industrial relations and the 'reduction of union power'.[23]

Between the elections of 2004 and 2007 Howard duly obliged. The electoral outcome, however, flatly contradicted his expectations. In 2007, on the back of a national swing of 5.6 per cent, the ALP under its new leader, Kevin Rudd, won eighty-three seats in the House of Representatives, a gain of twenty-three, against the Coalition's fifty-eight, a loss of twenty-nine. In addition, Howard lost his constituency seat of Bennelong. Rudd, who had replaced Beazley as leader as late as December 2006, had taken the ALP from what the *Bulletin* described as 'a position approaching despair a year ago' to 'a landslide victory'. The Liberals were now out of office not only federally but also in every state and territory.[24]

A combination of economic, social, political and cultural factors underpinned Rudd's stunning triumph and Howard's disastrous loss. By the time of the November 2007 election Howard, like Keating in the 1990s, was widely perceived to have become too extreme in his economic neo-liberalism, too enamoured of the rich and powerful and too insensitive to the plight of the 'battlers'. Howard was also seen as 'intolerant', 'mean-minded', outdated and 'reactionary' in his treatment of poor Australians and those outside the mainstream, such as Aboriginals and 'non-white' immigrants, particularly Muslims. The dominant response of his government to the Cronulla 'race riots' of December 2005 had been that Australia was not a racist country, that racism was not a factor in the riots, that no apology to the besieged Lebanese Muslim community in Cronulla was necessary and that the onus rested upon Lebanese and other immigrants to 'assimilate'. Some members of the 'host' society directly involved in the Cronulla disturbances described themselves as '100 per cent Aussie'.[25]

Of crucial importance to the outcome of the election was the fact that Howard's WorkChoices scheme proved to be hugely unpopular. Intended as a further 'liberalisation' of workplace relations, WorkChoices struck at the very collective and regulatory foundations of the traditional system of arbitration. It was widely criticised for increasing job insecurity and the power of employers and reducing wages, living standards and the role and influence of workers and their trade unions. Far from maximising individual choice, as promised, WorkChoices was seen to be a blatant, class-based and sectional attack upon the rights of 'the people' at work and the hallowed Australian tradition of 'a fair go'.

The 'un-Australian' reform of the workplace, moreover, was seen as being an integral part of Howard's wider commitment to an 'unfair' economic philosophy and policy. He had, observed his growing band of critics, promoted gross and growing material inequality and diminished equality of opportunity, deferred to 'parasitically' and 'obscenely' rich bankers and financiers and, in the midst of continuing national prosperity, greatly increased the fears of many on lower incomes that they would no longer be able to meet the high interest payments on their mortgages and 'make ends meet'. As a result, Howard lost the key support of the 'battlers', the group crucial to his election victories ever since 1996. Many of them now returned to their traditional Labor home. Howard was perceived by many as now ruling in the 'sectional', 'divisive', 'reactionary' and 'vindictive' rather than the 'national' and 'united' interest.[26]

In contrast, Labor's new 'Blairite' leader, Kevin Rudd, was determined to make a 'new' start and provide a 'fresh vision' for the country in the interests of 'fairness', progressive modernity and the needs of 'All Australians', including recent immigrants. The divisive and 'outmoded' class-based vindictiveness of WorkChoices and the greed and obscene extremes characteristic of deregulated capitalism would be replaced by 'fairness', 'flexibility' and 'consensus' within the workplace and a more 'traditional', civilised, cooperative, egalitarian, regulated and environmentally friendly socio-economic system. 'All Australians', including long-neglected and deprived Aboriginal communities, would be enabled by the state and encouraged to help themselves, both collectively and individually, to the benefits of a modern, civilised and prosperous life. Australian troops would be brought home from the 'unnecessary' and 'failed' war in Iraq, but the government would remain vigilant in terms of the threat of terrorism and the protection of Australia's borders. Aboriginal people would receive a long-overdue apology for their past suffering and oppression, an apology denied them by Howard. This was Rudd's 'vision' – a new, progressive, inclusive and multi-cultural 'agenda' designed successfully to meet 'the challenge of the future'.[27] Significantly, one of Rudd's advisers, and the drafter of his victory speech, was Alan Milburn, a 'Blairite' subsequently 'exiled from Brown's Labour party'.[28]

Up to Australia's spring of 2010 it appeared that Rudd would experience little difficulty in securing a second success at the forthcoming federal election. As noted earlier, unlike Gordon Brown, Rudd benefited greatly from the fact that he could not be identified with a discredited deregulated economy. We also observed that the Australian economy suffered far less from the financial crisis and the recession of 2008–9 than did its British counterpart. Partly as a result of Rudd's decisive and unqualified prime-pumping Keynesian actions and partly as a result of its booming mineral exports to China and India, the Australian economy also recovered far more quickly and markedly than did its British counterpart.[29] Rudd, moreover, was faced by a seriously divided opposition which in late 2009 rejected its moderate leader, Malcolm Turnbull, in favour of the more hard-line 'Howard-ite', Tony Abbott. The latter is widely regarded as a reactionary and increasingly out-of-touch climate change 'sceptic' or even 'denier'. He was a prominent figure in the coalition of forces that successfully rejected Rudd's legislation on emissions in 2009.[30]

Finally, while committed to multi-culturalism, Rudd was also careful to present himself as not being 'soft' and, he assumed, vulnerable at the polls on the questions of immigration, asylum seekers, border security and protection. Doubtless mindful of Howard's disgraceful, but very successful, exploitation of the *Tampa* and 'Children Overboard' affairs and 'fears of invasion' at the 2001 election, Rudd adopted the approach of detaining those asylum seekers bound for Australia by boat in Indonesian camps. Officially 'hardline on people smugglers and humane on asylum seekers' and in line with the letter of the United Nations Refugee Convention, Rudd's 'Indonesian solution', however, hardly reflected the spirit of the Convention and was all too reminiscent of Howard's harsh and unfeeling 'Pacific solution'.

The resulting widespread criticisms of the government's policy were expressed most vociferously by the trade unions during an increase in the 'traffic' of 'boat people' in October and November 2009. Unionists and others argued that conditions in the Indonesian camps would be worse than in the Australian-run centres and that the refugees, fleeing persecution, violence and probable death in Sri Lanka, Afghanistan and the Middle East, deserved more understanding, sympathy and humanitarian treatment from a Labor government. The government subsequently modified its 'Indonesian solution', without surrendering its reputation for 'toughness'.[31]

Yet by the end of June 2010 the political career of the man deemed in 2009 to be 'the most popular prime minister in Australian history' lay in tatters and the prospects of an ALP victory in the forthcoming federal election were placed in serious doubt.[32] As briefly noted earlier in this study, these sudden and dramatic developments resulted from two key factors. First, notwithstanding his oft-repeated pledge to successfully tackle climate change – 'the greatest moral challenge of our time' – in April 2010 Rudd shelved his very moderate and 'business friendly' carbon emissions scheme. The official reasons given for this action were that the measure would not get through the Senate and that, in the current climate of slow global progress on climate change, it was important to await the end of the Kyoto commitment period, at the end of 2012, when governments internationally would be required to make clear their commitments. There is also reason to believe that Rudd was alarmed by Abbott's strong and increasingly popular opposition to the scheme on the basis of 'no new taxes'. Significantly, Rudd did not even try to negotiate with the 'Greens' on the scheme. In any event, there was widespread criticism of Rudd's 'loss of nerve' and 'weakness' within the ALP and a significant growth in support for the Green Party, including many erstwhile ALP members and supporters.[33]

Second, having shelved his emissions scheme, Rudd then announced his plan to introduce a 40 per cent tax on the 'super-profits' of the mining companies. Appealing to the national interest, especially the country's 'fair' and moral regulatory traditions, Rudd argued that 'the minerals were owned by "Australians"', that the people should accordingly get a 'fair share', that 'the fruits of the mining boom should not be monopolised', especially by the mainly foreign-owned mining companies, and that the tax would be 'good' for the mining industry and promote its further expansion.[34] Yet, as noted earlier, the Rudd government proved to be no match for the extremely well-organised and very effective advertising campaign of these companies. The latter rejected charges of self-interest and wrapped themselves in the cloak of national well-being, especially of an economic kind. They portrayed themselves as having 'saved' the country from the worst effects of the recession and as key guarantors of Australia's continuing and future economic success. They claimed that the tax would cost jobs, lead to the delay or cancellation of new investment and projects and arouse serious concern in the international financial markets about the advisability of further investment in an 'anti-business' Australia.[35]

In the event, the companies won hands down. The tax was not popular among the voters, especially in the mining states, and the polls swung heavily against the ALP. By the end of June the power brokers within the ALP had become sufficiently alarmed to force Rudd's hand. Having declined to contest a leadership ballot, Rudd 'stepped down' and was replaced by his deputy, Julia Gillard, on 24 June. Within a week of becoming Australia's first woman prime minister, Welsh-born Gillard had negotiated a 'compromise' with the mining companies, further hardened the government's attitude towards asylum seekers (a 'big Australia' approach being rejected in favour of admitting 'the right kind of migrants'[36]), omitted Rudd from her cabinet (although not a future Labor government) and significantly revived Labor's standing in the polls. Alan Milburn once again joined the advisory team of a prospective ALP prime minister. Gillard's cautious and conservative approach, however, failed to bring outright victory in the August federal election.[37]

New Labour

By the mid 1990s John Major's Conservative government was, in the words of the *Sun*, 'tired, divided and rudderless'.[38] It had abjectly failed the test of competent economic management, was hopelessly divided over Europe (as was the Conservative Party at large) and was thoroughly discredited by extensively publicised examples of Conservative 'sleaze'. Promising a brand new, 'third way', government in the interests of all and the establishment of a 'young' and 'dynamic' country in which 'progressive' and 'modern' ideas would prevail, the 'youthful', 43-year-old Tony Blair and New Labour achieved an 'unprecedented result', a 'crushing triumph', at the 1997 election. In a 'dramatic' swing of over 10 per cent – the 'biggest since its legendary performance in 1945' – Labour was rewarded with 44 per cent of the vote and 418 seats, as against the Conservatives' 32 per cent and 165 seats and the Liberal Democrats' 17 per cent and 46 seats. The new government enjoyed a massive overall majority of 179 in the House of Commons.[39]

Labour's victory had been achieved not only on the back of the Tories' 'incompetence and corruption', but also on the ability of New Labour successfully to address its moderate and modernising message to 'Middle England'. It had convinced the middle classes of the South that it really had shed its 'extremist' past and that it offered them future prosperity and well-being. It had also restored its support among manual workers 'almost to the level of the 1960s'.[40] In the manner of 1945, Labour had thus once again become a 'national' party, capable of reaching out with its agenda for change 'into almost all geographical areas and almost all groups in the country'.[41]

Many people across the political and social spectra, including experienced and hard-bitten political observers and commentators, were variously impressed, exhilarated and excited by Blair's triumph and the future of the country. In the opinion of the *Guardian*, a 'Political Earthquake', a 'People's Victory', a 'Peaceful Revolution' had taken place. The Tories' defeat was 'cataclysmic' and the 'Thatcherite experiment' was 'over'.[42] Even though it still had 'reservations about some of New Labour's policies', Murdoch's *Sun* wanted to be seen to 'Give Change a Chance'. In backing Blair, the *Sun* saw itself as supporting a leader 'with vision, purpose and courage'. Blair was 'the breath of fresh air' needed by 'this great country', a man who had already 'transformed Labour into a free-market political force' and who would successfully face up to the 'global challenge'.[43]

The Times afforded a welcome to Labour's 'compassionate pragmatism', embracing 'free-market capitalism and rejecting socialism', while the *Mirror* enthused about the prospect of Blair's 'new Britain' 'standing tall in the world'.[44] Blair, himself, promised to 'represent' and 'govern for' the 'whole of this nation', to 'build a nation united with common purpose, shared values, with no-one shut out', to 'speak up for that decent hardworking majority of the British people' (a pledge reiterated by Gordon Brown in 2009 and 2010), to 'extend' educational opportunity, 'modernise' the welfare state and 'rebuild' the NHS, to establish a 'decent society' and to work with business to 'create that dynamic and enterprising economy we need'.[45] Finally, *Private Eye* put a sharp 'reality check' on Labour's triumphalism with its caption of a laughing John Major saying to the grinning Blair, 'I told you the Tories would win'.[46]

Once the election euphoria had subsided, the most pressing question, of course, was what New Labour, equipped with its untouchable majority, would seek to do and what it would actually achieve in its first term of office. The new government responded to this question by highlighting, much in the manner of MacDonald in the 1920s and Hawke and Keating in the 1980s, its 'fitness to govern', as demonstrated especially in its ability to manage the economy efficiently and its 'responsible' attitude towards public spending.

Tony Blair and his able and cautious Chancellor of the Exchequer, Gordon Brown, thus sought to demonstrate to the public, especially their recent and affluent converts from Conservatism in 'middle England', and the financial markets that Labour had unequivocally and fully cast off its traditional reputation for being the party of 'tax and spend' and 'boom and bust'. The immediate task was to achieve stable and sustainable economic growth 'through low inflation, low interest rates, low levels of government borrowing and prudent taxation'.[47] Towards this end the government generally abided by the previous Conservative government's tight spending limits, although

Brown did attempt to reduce poverty by reducing tax on the lower-paid, giving more help to the unemployed and establishing a minimum wage, as recommended by the independent Low Pay Commission. In overall terms, however, 'innovative social-democratic approaches to the economy and welfare' were overshadowed by what Reid and Pelling describe as the retention of 'Conservative methods in almost every other area of domestic policy, though supplemented with a new layer of central monitoring'. According to these historians, 'references to the "Third Way" soon became little more than rhetorical justifications for extending the role of the market'.[48]

The election of June 2001 gave New Labour what contemporaries generally described as another 'landslide', although this was not on the same scale as that of 1997 and a very high level of voter apathy took a considerable amount of shine off Blair's second polling triumph. (The turn-out, the lowest since 1918, was almost twelve points down on 1997.) The Tories under their new leader, the Oxbridge-educated but 'plain-speaking' Yorkshireman, William Hague, were 'routed' once again. Labour received 42 per cent of the vote and 412 seats to the Conservatives' 32 per cent and 166 seats and the Liberal Democrats, under the engaging Scot, Charles Kennedy, a very creditable 18 per cent and 52 seats.[49]

The buoyant state of the economy, Brown's 'consistent and prudent' economic management and his socio-economic policy improvements for children, single parents, the low-paid and pensioners, contributed significantly to Labour's victory.[50] The Tories concentrated mainly on their campaign to 'save the pound' by opposing Britain entry into the eurozone (Labour wanted to join, subject to certain economic conditions being met). Hague and his colleagues also sought to 'hit' asylum seekers 'hard' and cut taxes.[51] As Gary Younge wrote in the *Guardian*, the Conservatives' opposition to the single currency could potentially have had a 'broad, popular appeal'. They sabotaged their case, however, by appealing to 'petty minded patriots, nationalists and assorted bigots'. It was one thing to direct their 'foreigner bashing' against Britain's perceived enemies, as Thatcher had done successfully in the 1980s, but it was quite another to target it, as Thatcher and other right-wing Tories continued to do during the election campaign, against the country's allies in Europe. The *Financial Times* advised the Conservatives to abandon their 'inward looking' opposition to asylum seekers and their 'narrow nationalism' in order to 're-connect with the middle ground of British politics', the ground now occupied by Blair and his colleagues.[52]

Racism of another kind further disfigured both the election and Britain's reputation for toleration and fairness. During late May there occurred serious riots in Oldham, in which fights between 'white' and Asian youths were followed by a battle between around 500 local Asians and the police which lasted several hours. These were to be followed in the summer by similar 'race riots' in Burnley and Bradford. In the wake of the Oldham riots, long predicted in a declining centre of textile production and mounting ethnic tensions, the right-wing and openly racist British National Party (BNP) won its highest-ever number of votes in a parliamentary election, 6,552, in the constituency of Oldham West and Royton. Nick Griffin, the BNP's chair and its candidate, came third in a seat won by Labour's Michael Meacher, while in neighbouring Oldham East and Saddleworth the BNP's Michael Treacy came fourth, with 11.2 per cent of the vote. Much in the manner of Hanson's One Nation Party, the BNP exploited the incorrect fears of 'native whites' that 'coloureds' were benefiting materially from state and private provision at their expense.[53]

During the election campaign most of the national newspapers supported Labour, including, 'for the first time' in a general election, the *Daily Express*. While the Tories' campaign was generally portrayed in the press, including the *Daily Mail*, as being 'too narrow and negative', Labour, even as the *Mail*'s 'least worst option', was regarded as more positive and forward looking. There was general agreement, however, that continued support for Blair beyond 2001 was contingent upon his fulfilling his promises to improve and reform Britain's 'failing' schools, hospitals and transport system in order to 'transform' them into 'world class public services'.[54]

As matters transpired, Blair's total support for US President George W. Bush, the invasion of Iraq and the general 'war on terror', the feuding between Blair and Brown, fears that Iraq had made the Prime Minister an 'electoral liability' and questions of asylum and immigration dominated the political scene up to the next general election, of May 2005. They also meant that any serious and sustained attempt at public sector reform would have to be put on hold.

As a result of 2005 election, New Labour's share of the vote fell significantly as compared with 2001, from 42 per cent to 36 per cent, 'the lowest support ever for a single-party government'. Its number of seats also fell from 412 to 356, although it still commanded a 'comfortable', albeit much-reduced, overall majority of 66 and continued to make important inroads into the Tories' core middle-class vote. The Conservatives, with 32 per cent of the vote, made a net gain of thirty-three seats, while the Liberal Democrats, with 22.7 per cent and sixty-two seats, recorded their best vote since their formation in 1988. George Galloway, the expelled former Labour MP and a founding member of Respect, the socialist organisation, won impressively on an anti-war platform in Bethnal Green and Bow. The turn-out was once again very disappointing. Standing at 61.2 per cent, it was only slightly higher than the 'record low' of 2001. Perhaps the most important outcome of the election was that the two-party hold on politics had fractured. As Kavanagh and Butler conclude, Britain 'moved towards a three-party system to a greater extent than at any general election since 1945'.[55]

While Blair had undoubtedly received a bloody nose at the election, largely over the legality and morality of the invasion of Iraq, he had made a 'remarkable political comeback' from his unpopularity of 2004 and achieved an unprecedented third successive victory for Labour. There was no doubt that Labour's policy to give centre stage to its impressive record of economic stability and growth, the prosperous state of the country and its increasing levels of investment in the public services was highly successful, while the pro-war Tories did not benefit from the government's unpopularity over the war.[56]

The Conservatives, under their 'tough', right-wing leader, Michael Howard, enjoyed a clear advantage on questions of immigration and asylum. Fears of 'illegal entrants' and their 'swamping' effects upon Britain had figured prominently among Tory spokespersons and the press since the riots of 2001. Significantly, Lynton Crosby, who had run many successful campaigns on behalf of John Howard and the Coalition, including the anti-asylum-seeker 2001 election, was employed by the Conservatives for the 2005 British election. It was assumed that Crosby would bring his Australian experience successfully to bear on the highly charged issues of immigration and race in Britain. In the event, however, the issue of immigration 'did not match that of the economy' in the opinion polls and at the election.[57]

Moreover, following the riots of 2001, the terrorist attacks on US targets and a mounting refugee crisis stretching from Afghanistan to the Sangatte refugee centre in France, Blair and David Blunkett, his hard-line Home Secretary, took a leaf from John Howard's book. They attacked 'bleeding heart liberals' and advocated the introduction of 'tougher immigration controls' throughout Europe. They played their part in closing down Sangatte, located near the Channel Tunnel, in December 2002. Consideration was given to the use of warships to intercept 'people traffickers' in the Mediterranean. They relentlessly condemned those seeking to 'attack our way of life', including 'criminals' and other 'anti-social' elements within Britain's 'ethnic' communities who had taken part in the riots. Like Howard, they in fact adopted (whether intentionally or not) the western imperialist, racist and class-based position that predominantly 'non-white', non-western, poor Muslim asylum seekers and Muslim immigrants in Britain must 'assimilate' to 'core' 'national', white, middle-class values.

As in Howard's Australia, the issues of national identity and patriotism in Britain had thus once again become inseparable from race, origin, culture and religion. In New Labour's election manifesto of 2005 Blair himself stressed the importance of 'secure borders' and boasted that the number of asylum seekers had been 'cut by two thirds since 2002'.[58] As the *Guardian* had asked as early as May 2002, 'Whatever happened to the prime minister's pledge at the European summit in Finland in 1999 to provide a sanctuary for the persecuted?'[59]

Blair anticipated that a third term would provide the opportunity for his government to 'embed a new progressive consensus' and bring about an 'even stronger bond between economic progress and social justice'.[60] Yet by 2005 it had become very clear that Blair's 'opportunity' economy and society were far more market-based and unequal than social-democratic and egalitarian in character. Blair pressed ahead with his attempt to reform the public services by involving private sector companies and introducing more market-based competition, consumerism and 'choice'. Much in the manner of Hawke and Keating, his pro-business stance continued to attract much 'popular' criticism, as did his obvious preference for the company of, and admiration for, the rich and successful, irrespective of their politics.[61]

His close friendship with the right-wing Republican and fellow religious 'missionary', George Bush, similarly met with strong opposition among progressives and all those appalled by American atrocities in Iraq and their resorts to 'external rendition' and torture in Guantanamo Bay and elsewhere in the world. Lastly, in the wake of the appalling London bombings of July 2005, Blair pressed for 'draconian legal powers against terrorists' for which, in the opinion of the *Guardian*, a 'case has not yet been made' and which 'may cause as many problems as they solve'. In a highly charged response to the bombings the government insisted upon the essential one-ness of British identity and the overriding importance of assimilation, as opposed to the diversity, 'separateness' and integration of multi-culturalism.[62]

Blair's preference for a 'modernised' free-market market economy and a predominantly conservative social order, tempered by social-democratic reforms 'at the edges' and the rhetoric of enhanced equality of opportunity, should occasion little surprise. As Martin Pugh has observed, Blair was heavily influenced by his father, Leo, who emerged from a working-class socialist Glaswegian background to become a prominent Conservative barrister in post-World War Two Durham. Blair senior had his son privately educated and instilled in him the 'Conservative' virtues of self-help, hard work, free enterprise, competition and individual success. Blair junior's subsequent experience as an impressionable student at Oxford, largely uninterested in politics, was partly offset by his career as a barrister with a pro-Labour law firm in London and his relationship with Cherie Booth, a Labourite working for the same firm. The defeats of the 1980s saw Blair move from Labour left-winger, purportedly influenced by Marx, to New Labour 'moderniser'. Yet Blair remained a figure largely outside of and in key ways alien to the collective traditions of the labour movement. Whether, as Pugh claims, Labour was led for twelve years by a man 'whose views were basically those of a Conservative', remains a matter of debate.[63] Yet, of Blair's profoundly revisionist effect upon Labour there can be no doubt. To this day he remains unrepentant about Iraq, while his continuing 'fundamentalist' religious zeal and fondness for material wealth are self-evident.[64]

After a 'troubled' long-term relationship with his 'boss', Gordon Brown finally achieved the leadership of New Labour in June 2007. Unlike Blair, Brown was well versed in the regulatory and collective traditions of the labour movement. As such, he commanded respect, if not great affection, among many of its constituents. Yet he fully shared Blair's view that the party had to modify and change its traditional ways and means in the new era of 'globalisation'. As Chancellor of the Exchequer in Blair's governments, Brown indeed fully supported and further developed the 'enterprising' and 'dynamic' form of deregulated capitalism that Thatcher had been building. At the same time, however, much in the manner of Hawke, Brown had continued to highlight his enduring commitments to progressive, 'targeted' social welfare and educational reforms in order to further promote 'fairness' and 'opportunity' and to cushion the adverse effects of the 'liberated' market. As a result of his fiscal and other measures he undoubtedly eased the pressure on the poor, significantly reduced child poverty, increased the numbers of those moving from welfare to paid work and improved the quality of schools and access to higher education. In overall terms, however, Britain remained a deeply unequal and divided society. In ways strikingly reminiscent of Hawke and Keating, New Labour, spear-headed by the reforming activities of Brown, had, by the mid 1990s, effected limited and uneven socio-economic improvements, but had signally failed to meet its stated aims of making society more 'fair', 'just' and 'cohesive' in overall terms.[65]

Upon becoming leader Brown continued to attempt, largely unsuccessfully, to combine his commitments to 'the market' and 'fairness'. As Martin Kettle has recently argued, as Prime Minister, Brown enjoyed an 'initial aura of successful leadership' that was 'quickly lost' and then only 'partially regained'.[66]

He responded quickly and effectively to terrorist incidents in London and Glasgow, to floods and an outbreak of foot-and-mouth disease.

He also emphasised the key importance of 'Britishness', of 'British jobs for British workers', the imperative of 'assimilation' and the responsibilities of 'citizenship' in an insecure world.[67] His failure, however, to call a general election during the summer of 2007, when ascendant Labour, with a lead of eleven points, lost its nerve in the face of the Conservatives' promise to cut inheritance tax, led to the growing belief that the formerly formidable 'iron' Chancellor of the Exchequer had become the indecisive, vacillating Prime Minister.

The revolt against the government's proposed abolition of the 10p tax rate, poor by-election results and speculation about the quality of and possible challenges to the Prime Minister's leadership meant that Brown's reputation and standing dipped sharply between mid 2007 and the summer of 2008. Brown's leading role in the attempt to coordinate an effective international response, rooted in 'quantitative easing', to the financial crisis of 2008–9, restored some of his standing, especially in governing circles abroad. Yet this was not the case at home. The combined effects of the financial crisis and recession, the MPs' expenses scandal and Labour 'sleaze', further Labour resignations and challenges to Brown's leadership constituted major setbacks to his cause. His criticisms of the 'bankrupt ideology' of right-wing market 'fundamentalists' and his insistence upon the need to 'moralise' and regulate markets during the crisis-ridden period of 2009–10 came too late in the day to convince sufficient numbers of voters that he was no longer the champion of a predominantly deregulated, 'greedy' and 'uncaring' individualistic economy and society. He lost the May 2010 election and subsequently resigned as leader of the BLP.[68]

The election resulted in a hung parliament for the first time since 1974. The Conservatives won 36.5 per cent of the vote and 306 seats. These constituted gains of 5 per cent and ninety-seven seats on the 2005 election. Labour's share of the vote fell from 36 per cent in 2005 to 29 per cent in 2010, and it suffered a net loss of ninety-one seats. The Liberal Democrats' mid-April 'surge', when they stood on an estimated 28 or 29 per cent share of the vote, fell away badly in the last week before polling day. They ended up with fifty-seven seats, a loss of five seats on 2005, and 23 per cent of the vote, up 1 per cent on 2005. Meanwhile, the Green Party, in the person of its leader, Caroline Lucas, won its first seat in a British general election, Brighton Pavilion.[69]

New Labour's predominantly neo-liberal 'third way project', so bright, shiny and optimistic in 1997, had come to a sorry and bedraggled end. At the May election it experienced 'the greatest single loss of seats at any election since 1931', while its share of the vote was just 1 per cent above that received in the disastrous election of 1983 and 'its second worst share in the universal suffrage era'.[70]

The 'third way': continuity and change

I am now in a position briefly to evaluate the extent to which 'third way' politics in Britain and Australia from the 1980s to the present have been characterised more by change than by continuity. In short, did Labour continue, rework or break with its traditions and past practices in an attempt to 'modernise' itself and achieve success at the polls? As indicated early in Part V, this topic of debate has dominated much of the writing on Labour in Britain and Australia during this period.[71]

On the basis of the evidence presented above, I offer two arguments. First, in both countries Labour's pragmatic resort to elements drawn from labourist, social-liberal and neo-liberal traditions means that it is misleading, and therefore false, to present a picture of a simple, uniform, unqualified and linear movement from labourism to neo-liberalism. In this context we have seen, for example, that policies of state intervention, regulation, corporatism and economic neo-liberalism characterised the Hawke and Keating governments. Similarly, both Rudd and Brown sought to combine aspects of 'the free market' with those of social-democratic 'moral economy'.

Second, on balance, however, our selected 'third way' parties and governments have been characterised in practice more by change than by continuity. It has been the novelty, however complex, qualified, uneven and contingent in character, of their retreat from traditional, progressive labourism and liberalism and the adoption of a dominant and mainly conservative form of neo-liberalism that has mattered most. To be sure, this retreat has been more marked in the British than in the Australian case. Emphases upon state and government intervention, regulation, spending and agreements with the trade union movement figured far more prominently in the policies of Hawke, Keating and Rudd than in those of Blair and, albeit in a more qualified sense, Brown. And while all these 'third way' leaders differentiated themselves from 'market fundamentalists' like Thatcher and Hewson, this process, once again, was more pronounced in Australia. At times Blair found it hard to conceal his manifest admiration for the 'radicalism' of Thatcher.

Conservatism has been reflected in the fact that, in contrast to the albeit limited reforming credentials of traditional labourism, including Labour revisionists of the 1950s and 1960s, our 'third way' governments in both Australia and Britain have become more interested in defending and preserving, rather than significantly challenging, reforming and transforming, the prevailing form of capitalism. They have prized, above all else, their ability to manage capitalism more efficiently than their opponents, albeit with a 'social justice gloss'.[72] The language of 'modernisation' cannot conceal the fact that practitioners of the 'Third Way' have not only failed to tackle the structural causes of inequality, but have also left largely unchallenged and unreformed the dominant ideologies, structures and relations of power, control and authority in Australia and Britain.

Finally, in Britain at least, 'third way' politics seems to have run its course. This was confirmed in New Labour's recent election defeat. As Mehdi Hassan of the left-leaning *New Statesman* has concluded in relation to Britain, the 'Third Way' has 'turned out to be less a new route map than a neo-liberal dead end'.[73] As a result, all those on the British centre-left and left will seriously have to rethink the relationship between 'the market' and social justice, the public or social and the private spheres, individualism and collectivism and the role of the state and voluntarism.

Conclusion

Five main arguments have been presented in Part V. First, there is no doubt that in both countries economic matters dominated the political agenda. Second, in keeping with my findings throughout this study, economics, however, did not produce political outcomes in a simple, unmediated way. Rather, the issues of agency, representation, context, culture and socio-political factors also played a major role in shaping politics. For example, we have seen that the ability of Hawke and Keating, Blair and Brown successfully to appropriate the languages and practices of economic competence, success and prosperity at specific points in time and to discredit their opponents as lacking a viable alternative contributed significantly to their electoral victories.

Third, the question of the nation – the national interest and national identity – once again figured prominently in the politics of both countries. For example, while early 1980s Labour in Britain suffered very badly from its association with the 'sectional' and 'extreme' interest, early New Labour successfully recaptured the national, patriotic ground in the form of representing the 'whole' of the 'new', 'young' and 'dynamic' nation and its modernising, progressive present and future. New Labour's 'third way' economic and social policies were also cast as being in the progressive, national interest. At the same time the importance of the 'sectional' politics of class interest further paled before the overarching importance attached to the 'national' by Blair. The same conclusions apply to the successes of Bob Hawke and Kevin Rudd in Australia.

Fourth, questions of race have continued, whether implicitly or explicitly, significantly to inform Labour politics and political outcomes, especially since the events of 2001. For example, we have seen that while Blair, Brown and Rudd at various points in time embraced multi-culturalism, their notions of nation and citizenship have also been accompanied by racialised boundaries and limits, notions of conditional and unconditional inclusion and exclusion and of assimilation to 'core' national values and ways of life.

Fifth, while issues concerning the British Empire and Commonwealth saw a marked decline in terms of their formal influence upon the Labour politics of the period, nevertheless questions of support for the 'western alliance', for 'freedom and democracy' or coercive 'neo-imperialism' and 'orientalism', experienced a marked resurgence.

Notes

1 Macintyre, *Concise History*, pp. 261–2; *Sydney Morning Herald*, 1, 5 October 1998, 12 November 2001; *Age*, 5 October 1998.

2 Manne, 'The Blainey Affair', in *Left Right Left*, pp. 111–17.

3 Manne, *Left Right Left*, pp. 358–9; *Bulletin*, 16 November 1999 (Laurie Oakes, 'Hard Reign will be Falling on Howard').

4 *Sydney Morning Herald*, 5 October 1998 (Robert Manne).

5 The *Bulletin* (16 November, 1999) maintained that 'nationally almost 55%' were opposed to the republican model offered to the voters whereby the president would be appointed by two-thirds of both Houses of Parliament. Many of these opponents were 'discontented' and 'alienated urban and rural battlers' who had not been consulted on the 'elitist' model offered and who were in favour of a democratic system of election by 'the people'. See also *Age*, 6, 8 November 1999; *Sydney Morning Herald*, 8 November 1999 (editorial); Mark McKenna and Wayne Hudson (eds), *Australian Republicanism: A Reader* (Carlton: Melbourne University Press, 2003).

6 *Sydney Morning Herald*, 1, 3 April 2000; *Age*, 1, 2 April 2000.

7 Mike Steketee, 'Labor in Power', in Faulkner and Macintyre, *True Believers*, p. 157; *Australian*, 10 December 2004 (Michael Costello).

8 *Age*, 5 October 1998; *Sydney Morning Herald*, 1, 5 October (editorial, Manne) 1998; *Bulletin*, 13 October 1998.

9 Manne, *Left Right Left*, pp. 402–3, 433.

10 *Ibid.*, p. 403.

11 *Ibid.*, pp. 405–6.

12 *Ibid.*, p. 398.

13 *Sydney Morning Herald*, 8, 9, 12 November (Manne) 2001.

14 *Sydney Morning Herald*, 8 November 2001.

15 *Ibid.*, 8 November 2001.

16 *Ibid.*, 9 November 2001.

17 *Sydney Morning Herald*, 9, 12 November (Allard) 2001; *Bulletin*, 20 November 2001.

18 *Sydney Morning Herald*, 12 November (Manne) 2001; *Bulletin*, 13, 20 November 2001; *Age*, 11, 12 November 2001.

19 Manne, 'Mark Latham', in *Left Right Left*, pp. 363–5; *Australian*, 10 December 2004 (Costello).

20 Manne, 'Latham'; *Sydney Morning Herald*, 11 October 2004; *Age*, 11 October 2004.

21 *Sydney Morning Herald*, 8, 11 October 2004; *Bulletin*, 12 (Manne), 19 October 2004.

22 Manne, 'Latham'.

23 *Sydney Morning Herald*, 11 October 2004.
24 *Bulletin*, 4 December 2007; *Sydney Morning Herald*, 26 November 2007.
25 Tensions had been evident in Cronulla, in Sydney's south-west, well before 2005. The terrorist attacks of 11 September 2001, the subsequent declaration of 'the war on terror' and the sexual assaults carried out by Lebanese Muslim youths in Cronulla between 2000 and 2002 had resulted in the demonisation of Lebanese and other Arab Muslims as potential and 'sleeper' terrorists, as part of 'Bin Laden groups in our suburbs', and Lebanese-Australian young men in particular as displaying 'inherent criminality' and 'deviant masculinity'. The December 2005 riots were triggered by a fight on Cronulla beach between 'three off-duty surf-lifesavers and a group of four Lebanese-background young men'. The main riot took place a week later. It involved an attack by 5,000 mainly 'Anglo-Celtic' men on anyone they perceived to be 'Leb[anise] Muslim', 'of Middle Eastern appearance' or 'wog' on Cronulla beach. It was followed by 'revenge riots' against 'supposed Anglo-Australians' in Cronulla and the nearby beachside suburbs of Brighton and Maroubra. See Scott Poynting, '"Thugs" and "Grubs" at Cronulla: From Media Beat-ups to Beating up Migrants', in Scott Poynting and George Morgan (eds), *Outrageous: Moral Panics in Australia* (Hobart: ACYS Publishing, 2007), pp. 158–70; Scott Poynting, Greg Noble, Paul Tabar and Jock Collins, *Bin Laden in the Suburbs: Criminalising the Arab Other* (Sydney: The Sydney Institute of Criminology, 2004); Stuart, *What Goes Up: 2007 Election*, p. 59.
26 *Sydney Morning Herald*, 24, 26, 27 November 2007, 16 April 2008; *Age*, 21, 25, 27 November 2007; *Observer*, 25 November 2007; *Guardian*, 3 June 2007 (Will Hutton), 26 November 2007; Stuart, *What Goes Up: 2007 Election*, ch. 2; Tom Bramble, *Trade Unionism in Australia: A History from Flood to Ebb Tide* (Melbourne: Cambridge University Press, 2008), chs 7, 8.
27 *Sydney Morning Herald*, 26, 27 November 2007, 16 April 2008, *Age*, 21, 25, 27 November 2007; *Observer*, 25 November 2007; Stuart, *What Goes Up: 2007 Election*, pp. 120–2, 105; *Guardian*, 3 June 2007 (Hutton), 13 February 2008 (Barbara McMahon); Robert Manne (ed.), *Dear Mr. Rudd. Ideas for a Better Australia* (Melbourne: Black Inc. Agenda, 2008).
28 *Guardian*, 12 February 2010 (Julian Glover).
29 *Sydney Morning Herald*, 9 November 2009 (Ross Gittins, 'Keynes is Back in Favour').
30 *Guardian*, 12 February 2010 (Glover); *Weekend Australian*, 12–13 December 2009 (Dennis Shanahan).
31 *Sydney Morning Herald*, 16, 17–18, 29 October, 7–8, 12 November 2009; *Canberra Times*, 28 October 2009; *Australian*, 15 October, 2 November 2009.
32 *Guardian*, 25 June 2010 (editorial).
33 Scalmer, correspondence, 5 July 2010; *Sydney Morning Herald*, 27 April, 8 (Andrew Stevenson), 16 June (Phillip Toyne) 2010; *Age*, 26 May 2010 (Ross Gittins).
34 Scalmer, correspondence; *Sydney Morning Herald*, 12 May 2010.
35 Scalmer, correspondence; *Sydney Morning Herald*, 8 June (Phillip Coorey, Lenore Taylor) 2010; *Australian*, 5 June (Michael Stutchbury) 2010; *Canberra Times*, 28 May 2010 (Phillip Coorey); *Australian*, 15 June 2010 (Bryan Frith).
36 *Sydney Morning Herald*, 1 July 2010 (Elizabeth Farrelly); *Australian*, 26 June 2010.
37 *Sydney Morning Herald*, 25 (Damien Murphy), 28, 29 June, 1 July 2010; *Guardian*, 23 August (editorial), 24 August (George Monbiot) 2010.
38 *Sun*, 18 March 1997, in 'General Election 1997: Election Results, Newspapers', LHASC, uncatalogued.
39 David Butler and Dennis Kavanagh, *The British General Election of 1997* (Basingstoke: Macmillan, 1997); Reid and Pelling, *Short History of the Labour Party*, pp. 182–3; *Guardian*, 2, 3 May 1997.
40 Reid and Pelling, *Short History of the Labour Party*, p. 183.
41 *Guardian*, 3 May 1997.
42 *Ibid.*

43 *Sun*, 18 March, 2 May 1997, in 'General Election 1997'.
44 *The Times*, 2 May 1997, *Daily Mirror*, 3 May 1997, in 'General Election 1997'.
45 As reported in the *Daily Mirror*, 3 May 1997.
46 *Private Eye*, 2 May, 1997.
47 Reid and Pelling, *Short History of Labour Party*, p. 187.
48 *Ibid.*, pp. 185, 187–91.
49 David Butler and Dennis Kavanagh, *The British General Election of 2001* (Basingstoke: Palgrave, 2002); *Guardian*, 8 June 2001 (editorial).
50 Reid and Pelling, *Short History of the Labour Party*, p. 195; *The Times*, 8 June 2001, *Daily Telegraph*, 8 June 2001, *Sun*, 8 June 2001, *Daily Mirror*, 8 June 2001 in 'General Election 2001', LHASC, uncatalogued; 'General Election 2001: Tribune Web Page', LHASC, uncatalogued.
51 *Daily Express*, 8 June 2001 in 'General Election 2001'.
52 *Guardian*, 28 May 2001 (Gary Younge); *Financial Times*, 8 June 2001 in 'General Election 2001'.
53 *Daily Mail*, 8 June 2001, *Daily Mirror*, 28 May 2001, *Guardian*, 28 May 2001 in 'General Election 2001'; *Guardian*, 1 July 2002 (Faisal Bodi, 'Muslims got Cantle. What they needed was Scarman').
54 *The Times*, 8 June 2001, *Daily Mail*, 8 June 2001, *Daily Express*, 8 June 2001, *Daily Mirror*, 28 May, 8 June 2001, *Sun*, 8 June 2001, *Daily Telegraph*, 8 June 2001, *Guardian*, 8 June 2001 in 'General Election 2001'; Butler and Kavanagh, *British General Election 2001*, ch. 12.
55 Dennis Kavanagh and David Butler, *The British General Election of 2005* (Basingstoke: Palgrave Macmillan, 2005), ch. 12, Conclusion.
56 *Ibid.*, pp. 21, 82, 189–92, 196.
57 *Ibid.*, pp. 186, 190–1.
58 Reid and Pelling, *Short History of the Labour Party*, p. 200; *Guardian*, 22, 23, 24, 30, 31 May, 3 June, 6 September 2002; *Observer*, 26 May, 2, 9 June 2002; *Daily Mail*, 23 May 2002; *Britain Forward not Back*, Labour Party Manifesto, General Election 2005, p. 51.
59 *Guardian*, 24 May 2002.
60 *Britain Forward not Back*, p. 6.
61 Reid and Pelling, *Short History of the Labour Party*, pp. 196–7.
62 *Guardian*, 27 July 2005, 18 May 2006 (Linda Colley), 30 November 2006 (A. Sivanandan), 9 December 2006 (Will Woodward), 11 December 2006 (Letters and emails), 20 December 2006 (Joseph Harker), 30 January 2007; *Observer*, 31 July 2005 (Will Hutton, editorial).
63 Pugh, *Speak for Britain!*, pp. 387–94.
64 *Guardian*, 26, 29, 31 January 2010, 4 February 2010 (Seumas Milne).
65 *Guardian*, 1 January, 3 April 2009, 27 February, 3, 11 March, 10, 16, 17, 19, 20 April 2010; *Observer*, 4 January 2009, 18 April 2010; Reid and Pelling, *Short History Labour Party*, pp. 185–91; Kavanagh and Butler, *British General Election 2005*, pp. 189–96.
66 *Guardian*, 6 April 2010.
67 *Guardian*, 25 September 2007 (Steve Bell cartoon, 'Browntongue Hits Bournemouth'), 12 March 2008 (editorial).
68 *Observer*, 6 December 2009, 3, 10 January, 9 May 2010; *Guardian*, 1 October 2009 (Seumas Milne), 14 January (Seumas Milne), 27 February, 11 March ('Brown reaches out to 'mainstream mums' with warning over Tory spending cuts'), 12 March (Mehdi Hasan), 25 March (Seumas Milne), 6, 7, 8 May 2010.
69 *Observer*, 18 April, 9 May 2010; *Guardian*, 16, 17, 20, 23, 30 April, 1, 6, 7, 8 May 2010.
70 *Guardian*, 7, 8 (editorial, Julian Glover), 11 (editorial) May 2010; *Observer*, 9 May 2010.
71 See, for example, O'Reilly, *New Progressive Dilemma*; Scott, *Running on Empty*; Graham Maddox, *The Hawke Government and Labor Tradition* (Ringwood: Penguin, 1989); Thompson, *Labor Without Class*; Peter Beilharz, *Transforming Labor: Labour*

Tradition and the Labor Decade in Australia (Cambridge: Cambridge University Press, 1994); Collins and Cottle, 'Labor Neoliberals'; Duncan, *Australian Labor Party*; Bramble, *Trade Unionism in Australia*; Giddens, *Third Way*; Ludlam and Smith (eds), *New Labour in Government*; Steven Fielding, *The Labour Party: Continuity and Change in the Making of New Labour* (Basingstoke: Palgrave, 2003); Richard Toye, '"The Smallest Party in History"? New Labour in Historical Perspective', *Labour History Review*, 69:1 (2004), 83–104; Thompson, *Political Economy and the Labour Party*; Patmore and Coates, 'Labour Parties and the State in Australia and the UK'; Ashley Lavelle, 'The Ties that Unwind? Social Democratic Parties and Unions in Australia and Britain', *Labour History*, 98 (2010), 55–75.

72 Beilharz, *Transforming Labor*, p. 4.
73 *Guardian*, 12 March 2010.

CONCLUSION

The key argument presented in this book is that the neglected forces of nation, empire and race exerted a far more profound influence upon Labour politics in Britain and Australia between 1900 and 2010 than is suggested in the relevant literature. To be sure, this influence varied in time and place and was generally more pronounced in the Australian than the British case. This was mainly because the imprint of Britain, as the ruling imperial power and 'mother country', upon Australia and its labour movement was, on balance, more immediate, direct and marked than was that of Australia upon Britain. As a result, while the ALP constructed its attitudes and policies towards nation and empire in the determining context of British imperial 'presence', the BLP, as part of the ruling metropolis, tended to see its policies and outlook as determined far more by domestic influences, especially those of a 'bread and butter' kind, than by the 'external' factor of empire. While there also existed important, but variable, trans-national connections, ties and influences between the two Labour parties, British Labourites were also inclined to assume that these flowed far more from the imperial 'core' to the 'colonial periphery' than vice versa. This contrast in the experiences and outlooks of the BLP and the ALP within the circuits of empire left its mark upon the relevant national labour historiographies.

Yet we have seen that the situation was not static. As a result of the development of a more equal formal relationship under the emerging interwar Commonwealth and the shared commitment to the defence of democracy against tyranny during World War Two the ALP became far more unqualified in its predominantly positive attitudes towards Britain, the British Empire/Commonwealth and British-ness. In the post-war period of decolonisation and imperial decline further changes took place. Although affection towards Britain remained, and especially towards the British monarch as head of 'the British race', Australia's and the ALP's primary point of reference and geo-political focus changed considerably. As Britain turned more to Europe and Australia moved, albeit in a qualified way, closer to the United States, so did a shared sense of British identity, of British 'race patriotism', eventually collapse. Australians, including members of its labour movement, were henceforth far more concerned with the fortunes of their independent nation within the Asia-Pacific region than with the traditional primary loyalty to Britain. This important development, however,

[299]

took place somewhat unevenly rather than uniformly and over decades rather than at a stroke.

As mainly transplanted 'white' Anglo-Celts 'settled', at times very uneasily and hostilely, in a much older Aboriginal country and expressing chronic fears about close contact with and invasion by the 'inferior' 'coloured races' of the Asia-Pacific region, Australians, including members of the ALP, closely concerned themselves with questions of 'race' and 'white' national homogeneity up to the 1960s. In contrast, at least up to the post-World War Two period of greatly increased black and Asian immigration, British BLPers inhabited a very different geopolitical world. They tended to see Britain as a largely self-contained, naturally 'white' country, for the most part secure, relatively harmonious and for centuries free from invasion. Race seemed to be largely 'external' to their main concerns, as something far more 'out there' in the Empire rather than 'here', 'at home'. As a result, it did not impinge upon their daily concerns and consciousness to anything like the same extent as it did upon their early and mid twentieth-century Australian counterparts. Yet from mid-century onwards the increase in black and Asian immigration and the development of multi-culturalism in both countries, followed by the recent and current 'neo-imperialist' 'war on terror', the increase in asylum seekers and growing official concerns with border security and uniform assimilation, saw questions of race, citizenship and patriotism return to the mainstream political agendas of both countries and both Labour parties.

My argument has been developed in the course of the five parts comprising the book. While Part I is concerned mainly to set the scene, with reference to relevant debates, issues, explanations and developments, the other four parts are predominantly substantive in character. It is appropriate in the conclusion briefly to remind the reader of the contents and main threads of these substantive sections.

As demonstrated in Part II, questions of nation, empire and race were at the heart of the New Commonwealth, formed in 1901. The proposal for Federation, for the establishment of a more 'mature' and 'independent' nation within the British imperial system, had to receive the formal approval of the imperial powers in London. Once this had been received, late nineteenth-century Australian republican and anti-British feeling declined in extent and importance, although the mainstream labour movement continued to seek more autonomy and respect for its country within the imperial framework. At the same time notions of race and racial sovereignty also became foundational elements of the New Commonwealth. The Aboriginal people were largely excluded from the rights and responsibilities of citizenship, while the formal adoption of the 'White Australia' policy was designed to create an effective barrier against both Asian and Japanese 'invasion' from 'the north' and 'non-white' immigration in general.

The Australian labour movement, especially the precocious ALP, played a major role in shaping the characteristics and early development of the New Commonwealth. As such, questions of nation, empire and race were of central concern not only for the 'new' nation, but also for its labour movement. To be sure, the origins, rapid development and spectacular electoral successes of the ALP must, as emphasised in the literature, be sought partly in socio-economic, political and, I would add, cultural factors. I maintain, however, that 'nation' took precedence over 'class' in the remarkable rise of the pre-1916 ALP. The party sought, with great success, to represent not only the working class and the wider 'productive people', but all those committed to 'white' radical Australian nationalism, the 'enlightened' British Empire and the 'white' 'British race'.

In key ways, matters were very different in Britain. While the LRC and the BLP were, as demonstrated in the case of the South African War and 'Chinese labour', more concerned with the issues of nation, patriotism, empire and race than is suggested in most of the past and present literature, a combination of domestic socio-economic and political factors mattered most in their creation and development. Support is given to the perspective of 'traditionalists' that class-based concerns, albeit of a cultural and political as well socio-economic nature, were of major importance to the revival of independent labour politics in Britain. I simultaneously take on board the importance of the political factors, including political languages and representations, emphasised by the 'revisionists'.

Lacking the numerical and electoral strength and successes of its Australian counterpart, the BLP at this stage did not play a major part in the political life of Britain. It was simply not in a position to influence national debates about national and imperial identity and direction to anything like the same extent as the ALP. Similarly, the fact of Federation and the establishment of the New Commonwealth meant that, notwithstanding Britain's imperialist war in South Africa, these debates assumed far more immediacy and significance in Australia than in Britain. To be sure, in addition to the South African case, the British labour movement did concern itself with socio-economic and racial aspects of immigration to Britain. The absence of a substantial and long-established indigenous 'black' population in Britain, however, combined with the geopolitical differences between Britain and Australia noted above, meant that race was generally a less significant part of the young BLP's consciousness than that of the ALP.

As shown in Parts II and III, the period of World War One raised important concerns for both the ALP and the BLP in relation to pro- and anti-war sentiments, the introduction of military conscription for overseas service and allegiance to nation, empire and class. As highlighted in Part III, in the context of the fierce and divisive conflicts about conscription, the ALP's increasingly anti-war stance, the wartime and post-war upsurges in industrial militancy and political radicalism, the Russian Revolution of 1917 and the growth of communism as a global movement, the issues of extremism and loyalty to country and empire became of paramount political importance in Australia. Apart from Scullin's 1929–31 Labor administration, the Right ruled the federal political roost from 1917 up to 1941. Although Labor performed better at the state level, it failed both to reach its pre-war level of success and to match that of the interwar Right. I suggest that the increasingly conservative nature of Australian nationalism and the success with which the Right tarred the ALP with the brushes of 'Red extremism' and 'disloyalty' to the nation and the Empire constituted the main reason behind the political domination of the Right and the subordination of Labor. Yet I also maintain that the somewhat neglected factor of 'loyalism' constituted a necessary rather than a sufficient explanation of the Right's hegemony. As seen in the existing literature, the profound reversal of the ALP's pre-1916 political domination must also be attributed to the debilitating splits within the party in 1916 and 1931, Scullin's misfortune to win office when the economic growth of the 1920s was giving way to the Depression and the successful appeal of the Right not only to the wealthy, but to women and others across the class structure.

The interwar years in Britain saw Labour not only rise to a position of national importance, but also become the main alternative to the Tories. Labour achieved minority office in 1924 and 1929, but the interwar period as a whole was dominated by either Conservative or National governments. In sum, Labour's rise was real, but limited.

As demonstrated in the traditional and revisionist literature, Labour's rise owed much to its successful wartime record, including its avoidance of major splits, the establishment of a mass electorate, its firm class base and its ability to extend its appeal to sections of the wider 'people', including some women, its internal improvements in terms of organisation, finance and programme, and to Liberal disarray. On the negative side, as seen once again in the literature, Labour failed to deal successfully with unemployment and the Depression. It split in 1931, while the Tories successfully appealed to the middle classes and around half of the working classes over the issues of living standards, culture (Conservative 'respectability' versus Labour 'roughness') and the promotion of the national as opposed to the Labour/socialist 'class-based' and 'greedy' interest. I attempt to enrich the British literature by arguing that the much-neglected factor of 'loyalism', while less important than in Australia, did constitute part of the explanation for the electoral domination of the Right and the subordination of Labour in interwar Britain.

'Loyalism', mainly in its Cold War form, continued adversely to affect the fortunes of Labour between the 1940s and the end of the 1970s. As I show in Part IV, this was crucially the case in Australia, but less so in Britain. In Australia the ALP's spectacular federal successes of the 1940s gave way to the 'long' mid-century period of unbroken Liberal-Country Party federal rule from 1949 to 1972. While the Whitlam government was successful in breaking this rule in 1972, its defeat, in 1975, was followed by a further period of coalition rule up to 1983. In terms of the state level, the ALP performed much better at the polls up to the Split of 1955 than it had done during the interwar period. Yet between the mid 1950s and the end of the 1970s its state performance, while mixed, was mainly disappointing. In Britain, Labour also enjoyed an upsurge in its fortunes and a landmark election success during the 1940s. Thereafter the electoral picture was mixed. Conservative rule between 1951 and 1964 was followed by Labour successes between 1964 and 1970. The 1970s saw victories for both the Conservatives and Labour.

I explain Labour's poor overall electoral performance in Australia and its more mixed record in Britain in terms of a combination of 'traditional', 'revisionist', neglected and new factors. These include trends in living standards, economic management, internal party unity and disunity, progressive nationalism and loyalty to nation and Commonwealth. I maintain that Labour in both countries fared best at the polls when it successfully presented itself to the electorate as the champion of modernisation and economic competence and as the 'real representative' of not only its traditional working-class constitu-ents but also the wider 'progressive' people of the enlightened and forward-looking nation and Commonwealth. In contrast, it fared worst when it was divided and clearly seen to be incompetent, when it was once again successfully tarred by the Right as extreme and disloyal and when the Conservatives successfully took the credit for economic growth and improvements in living standards. In this Cold War era 'loyalty' was demanded, not only to the nation and the Commonwealth but also to the 'Free World'. The process of 'Red' tarring was most pronounced and successful in Australia, albeit far more so at the federal than the state level. It was generally less marked in Britain, but was employed, albeit unsuccessfully, by Churchill in 1945, and with more, although mixed, success by the Conservatives during the 1970s.

In presenting my arguments about 'loyalism' I attempt both to correct imbalances and neglect in the relevant national literature and to develop a new line of comparative investigation and explanation. I attribute differences in the force and success of the 'politics of loyalism' in Australia and Britain during this period to a plurality of factors. In terms of the key areas of political economy and geo-politics, while Britain's overriding priorities in this period rested with the maintenance of its great-power status in a period of increasing economic difficulties, Australia, as an 'exposed' 'white' power in the Asia-Pacific region, was obsessed with the 'advance of communism' and the 'threat of invasion' by 'coloured' communists from the North. In the eyes of Menzies, the ALP was both insufficiently alive to this threat and generally 'soft' on communism, externally and internally. Comparative difference also resulted from the more militant, pro-Soviet and influential position of the communists in the Australian labour movement of the later 1940s and early 1950s as compared with their British comrades, the more unequivocal anti-communism of the BLP as compared with the ALP, the far more influential role of Catholic anti-communists within the Australian labour movement, as seen especially in the disastrous Split of 1955, and the more consensual and accommodating nature of politics in Britain.

As shown in Part V, during the years from 1980 to 2009 the electoral and wider fortunes of the ALP and the BLP contrasted significantly. As against the striking successes of the Hawke and Keating governments between 1983 and 1996, the BLP failed to overturn the long period of Tory rule, from 1979 to 1996. Between 1996–97 and 2007 the fortunes of the two parties were reversed. The ascendancy of Blair's New Labour in Britain was paralleled by Howard's coalition domination of the Australian political scene. Between 2007 and 2009 Rudd's landslide victory and popularity contrasted markedly with the mounting problems of the Brown government and the British prime minister's growing unpopularity. During the first decade of the new millennium the ALP also dominated state governments. Lastly, alongside the BLP's defeat at the general election in May 2010 we must, however, set the ALP's disappointing performance in the August 2010 federal election.

I attribute Labour's successes and failures in both countries during this final period to a combination of well-established, less well-documented and new factors. These include questions and perceptions of economic competence and management, the declining influence of class, the ability successfully to define and command the 'national' as opposed to the 'sectional' interest, the racialised nature of representations of the nation and its 'defence' in a neo-imperialist world and the issues of party unity, disunity and leadership. In comparison with the interwar and Cold War years, the question of loyalism declined in significance, apart from the case of 1980s Britain. In both countries Labour was most successful at the polls when it was perceived to be economically competent and united and when it captured the languages of the 'progressive', 'modern' and (more) 'inclusive' nation.

Finally, this study has sought to make a contribution not only to the substantive issues and debates summarised above, but also to the further methodological development of the fields of imperial, comparative and trans-national history. Above all, it has attempted to make a case for the fuller integration of the neglected general factor of 'labour', and specifically Labour politics, into these fields. The success or otherwise of my attempt will be judged by readers and reviewers. My overriding hope is that the present study will inspire future scholars to build upon and extend its British and Australian imperial, comparative and trans-national foundations.

INDEX

Blair, Tony, UK prime minister 9,
32, 37, 39, 41, 238, 242, 243–4,
248, 265, 268, 270, 275n.89,
280, 285–91, 293, 294
Blatchford, Robert (1851–1943)
socialist 49, 83
Bloemfontein 83
Blunkett, David, Labour minister 289
boat people 278–9, 283
Bolshevism 98, 100, 111–12, 123,
136
Bolton, Geoffrey, historian 169
Bonar Law, Andrew (1858–1923)
Conservative prime minister
113, 118
Bond, Alan, businessman 253, 255
Bongiorno, Frank, historian 55
Boote, Henry (1865–1949) newspaper
editor, AWU 15, 73, 106, 125,
135, 139
Booth, Cherie 291
Booth, Simon, historian 80–1
Bow and Bromley 82
Bradford 288
Bragg, Billy, left-wing musician 268
Brenner, Robert, historian 246
Brighton 261, 292
Brisbane, Queensland 23, 98, 106;
riots 104–5
Brisbane Courier 105, 106
British Aerospace 261
British Labour Party (BLP)
Governments (1924) 34, 91, 113–15;
(1929–31) 35, 91, 118; (1945–51)
35, 39, 149, 160–7, 199–200;
(1964–70) 36, 39, 149, 220–1;
(1974–1979) 36, 226–7; (1997–
2010) 37, 39, 41, 238, 285–92
and Bolshevism 111–13; and
Catholics 21, 196; Cold War
loyalism 154, 156, 196;
Communism, opposition to
113–14, 121–2, 135, 196, 199–
201; Commonwealth 39, 151,
153, 198, 203, 220; conscription
47, 57, 97; disunity 204, 243,
244, 266; economic concerns

('bread and butter issues') 143,
151, 156, 164, 196, 198, 229–30;
economic policies 81, 91, 150,
286–7; economic problems 219,
221, 228, 239, 248; and Empire
81, 84, 139, 141, 142, 220;
established 33, 47–53, 63; and
Europe 152, 170, 196, 214, 217,
266, 287; immigration 151, 289;
and Imperialism 81–3, 134, 141;
Internationalism 120; 'Loony
Left' 269; loyalism 93, 110, 122,
124, 127, 162–3; membership
149; middle classes 61, 92, 165;
Militant expelled 268;
modernisation of party 204,
244, 270, 293; nationalisation
163, 166, 266; and Nationalism
122, 124, 139, 165, 241, 242,
294; New Labour 238–9, 242–3,
268, 270–1, 285–92; nuclear
weapons policy 197, 198, 266,
270; pacifism 85, 110;
patriotism 83, 134, 142, 163,
263; race 81, 84–5, 220, 287–8,
294–5; Red Scare smearing of
BLP 112–13, 114–16, 117, 120,
122–4, 204, 223–6, 227; Gestapo
smear 156, 161–2, 164, 224;
and Socialism 61–2, 99, 140,
155, 163–4, 167, 196, 266; and
South African War 82–3; and
trade unions 51, 59, 60–1, 67–9,
81, 92, 117, 121, 123, 149, 151,
196, 200, 221; and United States
288, 290; visits of BLP leaders
to Australia 8–9, 10, 17, 37,
211–12, 271–2; welfare state
163, 198, 286; women 51, 81,
92, 143, 151, 166, 203; working
class 71–2, 247
British Legion 98, 110
British National Party (BNP) 239, 288
Britishness 6, 7, 10–12, 75, 151, 188,
215, 292
British Telecom 261–2
Broken Hill, election 101

Commonwealth Bank 71, 77, 179
Commonwealth Labor Party 16
Commonwealth Labour Conferences 213
Commonwealth Nationality and Citizenship Act (1948) 174
Communist Party Dissolution Bill 186–7, 194–5
Communist Party of Australia (CPA) 36, 108–9, 121, 155, 178, 182–7, 189–90, 193
  banned 182; attempted ban 178, 180–2, 185–7; membership 182–3
Communist Party of Great Britain (CPGB) 113, 117, 121, 155, 164, 166, 197–201, 224
  membership 201; MPs banned 200
conscription 17, 21, 33, 47, 78, 121, 217, 302
Conservative Party (Britain)
  governments (1918–23) 111–12; (1924–29) 116; (1931–45) 35, 92, 118, 121, (1951–64) 150, 201–6; (1970–74) 221–6; (1979–97) 227–8, 260–5, 285; (2010) 292
  anti-socialist 103, 115, 118, 161, 225; Red Smears 112, 113, 114–16, 118, 120, 156–7, 161–2, 223–5, 227–8, 261, 303
constitutional crisis (1975) 217
consumerism 38, 166, 195, 203, 248, 290
Cook, Chris, historian 58
Coombs, H.C. (1906–1997) public servant 212
Co-operative Union 50
Country Party 107, 120, 168, 180
Crewe, Ivor, political scientist 264
cricket 23, 75
Cronulla race riots (2005) 281, 296n.25
Crosby, Lynton, political strategist 289
Crosland, Anthony (1918–1977) Labour politician 212

Crouch, Colonel R.A. (1868–1949) Labor politician 144
cruise missiles 263
Curtin, John (1885–1945) Labor prime minister 35, 120, 124, 126, 132n.85, 137–9, 149, 167–72, 212, 218, 250
Czechoslovakia 199

Daily Express 205, 288
Daily Herald 113, 199
Daily Mail 116, 288
Daily Standard 104
Daly, Lawrence (1924–2009) NUM leader 223
Darwin, Northern Territory 169, 189
Davidson, Alastair, historian 183
Davie, Michael, historian 11
Davis, W.J., trade unionist and LRC politician 68
Day, David, historian 14, 17
Deakin, Alfred (1856–1919) ALP prime minister 55, 56–8, 60, 69, 76
Deakin, Arthur (1890–1955) trade unionist 200
de-colonisation 209n.92, 211
Deery, Phillip, historian 183, 184
deflation 40, 119, 124, 221, 253
Democratic Labor Party (DLP) 36, 40, 178, 193, 208n.59
deregulation 252, 254
devaluation 221
Diana, Princess of Wales (1961–1997) 277
Diggers 97, 100, 101–2
Dock strike (1949) 197, 199
'dole bludgers' 276
Douglas-Home, Sir Alec (1903–95) Conservative prime minister 219
Dreadnoughts 76, 78

Easter Rising (1916) 97
Eden, Sir Anthony (1897–1977) Conservative prime minister 199, 204
Egypt 139, 205

New Left 211
New Liberalism 23
New Protection 60
New Right 246–7, 255–7
NewsCorp 271, 275n.89
New South Wales 17, 54, 76, 99,
    101, 120, 174, 191
  elections 33, 34, 36, 38, 109, 142,
    149, 150, 192, 237
New Statesman 294
New Zealand 8, 19, 23, 163, 214, 278
Niemeyer, Sir Otto (1883–1971)
    banker 124
Norfolk, England 142, 161
Nottingham 220
nuclear weapons 157, 196, 205,
    211, 270
  disarmament 205, 211, 266

O'Hara, Lawrence Joseph 102
Oldham, riots 288
One Nation Party 259, 280, 288
Orwell, George (1903–1950) author
    175n.26
Osborne Judgment (1909) 50, 68–9
Owen, David, SDP politician 266
Owen, Robert (1771–1858) socialist
    163
Oxley, Queensland 259

Packer, Kerry (1937–2005) media
    tycoon 253, 255
Paddington, Sydney 101
Pakistan 173, 203
Paterson, Fred (1897–1977)
    Communist MP 182
patriotism (Australia) 11, 105–6,
    143, 170, 188, 195
patriotism (Britain) 74, 81, 83, 93,
    103, 134, 140, 162, 263, 290, 293
  'race patriotism' 6, 74, 81, 170, 299
Peacock, Andrew, Liberal leader 257
Pearl Harbor 169
Pelling, Henry, historian 84, 164,
    224, 287
Perth, Western Australia 23
Petersham, Sydney 102

Petrov Affair (1954) 178, 189–90,
    195, 200
Petrov, Vladimir (1907–1991)
    diplomat 189, 190
Phillips, Marion (1881–1932) Labour
    MP 10
Phillips, Morgan (1902–1963) BLP
    General Secretary 171, 199
Pickering, Paul, historian 19
Pierson, Chris, historian 249
Pilger, John, journalist 255
Plymouth 50
politics of loyalism 93–6, 102,
    120–2, 194–5, 263
Pollitt, Harry (1890–1960) CPGB
    leader 212
poll tax 265, 268, 270
Powell, Enoch (1912–1998) maverick
    politician 220, 221, 224
Prescott, John, Labour politician 271
Price, Richard, historian 82
Prices and Incomes Bill (1968) 221
Prime Ministers' Conference (1944)
    171
Primrose League 103
Private Eye 286
privatisation 256, 261–2, 270
Profumo Scandal (1963) 219
protectionism 23, 55, 57–9, 84
Pugh, Martin, historian 290, 291

Queensland 36, 52, 54, 138, 142,
    157, 161, 174, 191, 193,
    208n.59, 259
  elections 32, 34, 54, 149, 150,
    192, 237, 259

Race Relations Acts (1965, 1968) 220
race riots (1919) 98, (1958) 220,
    (2001) 288, (2005) 281
Racial Discrimination Act (1975)
    217, 220
racialism 11, 26n.8, 39, 74, 84, 98,
    154, 211, 217, 220–1, 243, 259,
    276, 279–80, 281–2, 287–8,
    294–5
Rawson, Don, historian 74

Soviet Union 153, 197
Spain 168
Spence, William Guthrie (1846–1926)
    AWU trade unionist 62
Sri Lanka 203, 283
stagflation 217, 222, 246
Stalin, Josef 167, 191
Stop the War campaign 101
strikes 121, 135, 180
    coal strike (1949) 178, 183–4;
        (1973–4) 222, (1984–5) 242, 263,
        270; dock strike (1949) 184,
        197, 199–200; gas strike (1950)
        200; maritime strike (1890) 67;
        steel strike (1980) 261
Suez crisis 205
suffrage, female 17, 23, 70, 81; male
    55, 111
Sun 265, 285, 286
Sydney, NSW 23, 59, 101–2, 104–6
Sydney Labor Council 17, 101
Sydney Morning Herald 100, 104–5,
    109, 215, 250, 253, 255, 257,
    259, 271, 277, 281

Taff Vale decision (1901) 67–8
Tampa incident 278–9, 283
Tangney, Dorothy (1911–1985)
    senator 172
Tasmania 55, 142, 280; elections 34,
    36, 38, 149, 150, 192, 237
'Ten pound Poms' 215
terrorism 279–80, 282, 289, 291
Thatcher, Margaret, Conservative
    prime minister 9, 36–7, 150,
    227–8, 238, 240, 247, 251,
    256, 260–6, 268–9, 287, 293;
    Thatcherism 230, 249, 257,
    260–5, 266, 269
Theodore, 'Ted' (1884–1950)
    Queensland premier 105, 106,
    116, 124, 125
'Third Way' politics 3, 37, 41, 214,
    230, 238, 247–9, 254, 272n.3,
    280, 285, 292, 293–4
Thomas, J.H. (1874–1949) Labour
    minister 131n.74, 138, 140

Thomas National Transport (TNT)
    255
Thompson, Claude, socialist 53
Thompson, E.P., historian 5
Thompson, Noel, historian 267
Thompson, Peter, historian 164
Thomson, Peter, Anglican cleric 9,
    271
Thorpe, Andrew, historian 35, 49, 219
Thorpe, Jeremy, Liberal leader 225
Tillett, Ben (1860–1943) socialist 15
Times, The (London) 56, 59, 223,
    224, 286
Tiratsoo, Nick, historian 164
Tonypandy 17
totalitarianism 161–2, 194, 212
Trade Disputes Act (1906) 68, (1927)
    131n.78
trade unions
    Australia 8, 21, 34, 54–6, 59–62,
        69–70, 73, 98–9, 101–2, 109,
        121, 149, 153, 157, 178, 183,
        192–4, 215–16, 252, 255–6, 261,
        271, 282, 293; membership 37,
        60, 103, 149, 150
    Britain 48–52, 59–60, 67–9, 81–2,
        91, 97, 113, 124, 149, 151,
        196–7, 200, 221–3, 242, 268–9;
        membership 37, 50, 60, 117, 149
Trade Unions Act (1871) 68, (1913)
    68–9, (1973) 50
Trades Union Congress (TUC) 49,
    50, 123, 212, 249
transnationalism 12, 14, 211–14,
    299
Treacy, Michael, BNP candidate 288
'True Australianism' 63, 83, 134,
    136, 142, 177
Truman, Harry S. (1884–1972) USA
    president 163
Turnbull, Malcolm, Liberal leader
    283

unilateralism 266
United Australia Party (UAP) 33,
    40, 91, 93, 100, 120, 124–5, 135,
    137, 167–8, 172, 180

CPSIA information can be obtained at www.ICGtesting.com
Printed in the USA
BVOW09s1611300914

368922BV00003B/33/P